INDUSTRIAL RELATIONS OF DEVELOPING ECONOMY

INDUSTRIAL RELATIONS OF DEVELOPING ECONOMY

(WITH PARTICULAR REFERENCE TO INDIA)

DR. BISWANATH GHOSH
M.A. (Econ.), D.S.W., Ph.D., Dip. in French
Dean of Studies, I I M S Kolkata -64
Formerly Reader, Burdwan University

Himalaya Publishing House

MUMBAI ☐ DELHI ☐ BANGALORE ☐ NAGPUR ☐ HYDERABAD ☐ PUNE ☐ CHENNAI ☐ LUCKNOW ☐ AHMEDABAD

First Edition : 2001
Reprint : 2009

Published by : **Mrs. Meena Pandey**
for HIMALAYA PUBLISHING HOUSE,
"Ramdoot", Dr. Bhalerao Marg, Girgaon, Mumbai-400 004.
Phones : 23860170/23863863 Fax : 022-23877178
Email : himpub@vsnl.com
Website : www.himpub.com

Branch Offices

Delhi : "Pooja Apartments", 4-B, Murari Lal Street, Ansari Road, Darya Ganj, New Delhi-110 002
Phones : 23270392, 23278631 Reliance : 30180394/96
Fax : 011-23256286 Email : hphdel@vsnl.com

Nagpur : Kundanlal Chandak Industrial Estate, Ghat Road, Nagpur-440 018
Phone : 2721216, Telefax : 0712-2721215

Bangalore : No. 16/I (old 12/1), Ist floor, Next to Hotel Highland, Madhava Nagar, Race Course Road, Bangalore-560 001
Phones : 22281541, 22385461 Fax : 080-2286611

Hyderabad : No. 3-4-184, Linampally, Besides Raghavendra Swamy Matham, Kachiguda, Hyderabad-500027
Phone : 040-655501745, Fax : 040-27560041

Chennai : No. 2, Rama Krishna Street, North Usman Road, T-Nagar, Chennai-600 017
Phone : 28144004, 28144005 Mobile : 09380460419

Pune : No. 527, "Laksha Apartment", First Floor, Mehunpura, Shaniwarpeth, (Near Prabhat Theatre), Pune-411 030
Phone : 020-24496333, 24496323

Lucknow : C-43, Sector C, Ali Gunj, Lucknow - 226 024
Phone : 0522-4047594

Ahemdabad : 114, Shail, 1st Floor, Opp. Madhu Sudan House, C.G. Road, Navrang Pura, Ahemdabad-380 009
Mobile : 9327324149

Eranakulam : No. 39/104A, Lakshmi Apartment, Karikkamuri Cross Road Eranakulam, Cochin-622 011, Kerala
Phone : 0484-2378012, 2378016

Printed at : A to Z Printers, Daryaganj, New Delhi-110002

PREFACE

This book is a new and valuable addition in the field of Industrial Relations. I have felt there is scope for a new book in the field. From my experience as a teacher of this subject, I felt the dearth of good textbooks on Industrial Relations for our students. There are good American books but they are products of different social and legal environments and consequently do not fulfil the requirements of our students.

Like all management disciplines, IR as a functional management area has two aspects theory and practice. Foreign books do not serve the needs of our students so far as practice is concerned.

The present text is meant for students. It is comprehensive but concise, lucid and analytical.

The latest development in India's economic world is liberalisation and globalisation which may have far reaching consequences on I.R. The last chapter deals with that problem.

Since the legal foundation of IR in India is Industrial Disputes Act, 1947, it has been added in the Appendix.

I am simply surprised by the skill and speed with which Shri. K.N. Pandey has printed and published the book in such a short time. I take the opportunity to express my sincere gratitude to him.

September, 2001 **BISWANATH GHOSH**

CONTENTS

1. **INDUSTRIAL RELATIONS** 1 — 15
Industrial Relations — Objectives — Approach — Scope — Evolution — Plan Policies — Present Policies — State and Industrial Relations — Some International Practices — Practice of India — Practice at the Plant-level in India — Symptoms of Industrial Unrest and Treatment at a Glance.

2. **THEORIES OF INDUSTRIAL RELATIONS** 16 — 31
Unitary Theory — Understanding Industrial Relations — Conflict Theory — Social Action Theory. System Theory — Changing Roles of the Three Actors — Management — Workers Unions — The Government — Criticism — Marxist Theory.

3. **INDUSTRIAL UNREST : STRIKES AND LOCKOUTS AND THE MACHINERY FOR THE SETTLEMENT OF DISPUTES** 32 — 45
Types of Strikes — Machinery for the Settlement of Industrial Disputes — Conciliation — Arbitration — The Girl Approach — Adjudication — Preventive Measures — Joint Consultation — Code of Discipline — Grievance Procedure — Disciplinary Procedures.

4. **COLLECTIVE BARGAINING : LABOUR MANAGEMENT CONFLICT** 46 — 62
Introduction — Definition — Constituent Parts — Salient Features of Collective Bargaining — Functions of — Recommendations of the National Commission on Labour — Nature of — Forms of — Pre-requisites for Successful Collective Bargaining — Collective Bargaining V/s. Individual Bargaining — Three Concepts of Collective Bargaining — Strike and Collective Bargaining — Techniques of Collective Bargaining — Process of — Major Clauses — Advantages — Disadvantages Effects of.

5. **WORKERS' PARTICIPATION IN MANAGEMENT: LABOUR MANAGEMENT COOPERATION** 63 — 81
Introduction — Types of Participation — Forms — Methods — Levels of Participation — Features — Evolution — Rationale of Participation — Models of Worker's Participation — Objective — Experience in Other Countries — United Kingdom — Yugoslavia Trade Union Attitude — Government Attitude — Employer's Attitude — Indian Experience : Functions of Joint Management Councils — Stages of Participative Management — Evaluation.

6. **INDIAN INDUSTRIAL WORKER** 82 — 88
Identity — Aspirations and Attitudes — Attitude to Work — Attitude Towards Unions — Attitude to Outsiders — Attitude Towards Employer — Social Attitude.

7. **EMPLOYMENT OF WOMEN AND CHILDREN** 89 — 102
Employment of Women — Pattern of Woman Employment — Development Since 1947 — Training — Wages — Legislative Measures for Women Workers — Women and Trade Unions — Employment of Women — A Perspective — Employment of Children — Legislation Relating to Child Workers — Extent of Child Labour — Recommendations of the National Labour Commission.

8. **UNORGANISED LABOUR** 103 — 113
Assessment of Policies — Contract Labour/Construction Workers — Review of Trends — Employment — Wages and Working Conditions — Construction Workers — Agency — Recruitment Working Conditions — Wages — Casual Labour — Tribal Labour — Unprotected Labour.

9. **TRADE UNIONISM** 114 — 134
Introduction — Definition — Evolution — Development in India — Central Trade Union Organisations — Functions of Trade Unions — Methods of Trade Unions — Theory of Trade Unionism — Types of Unions — Recognition of Unions — Legal Framework for Trade Unions : The Trade Unions Act, 1926 — Limitations of Trade Unionism in India — Measures to Strengthen Trade Unions — White Collar and Managerial Trade Unions — Why White–Collar Worker's Unions? — Growth of White-Collar Unions and Present Position — Nature of Managerial Unionism — Why Managerial Unionism.

10. **WORKERS' EDUCATION PROGRAMME** 135 — 139
Introduction — Definition — Objectives of the Scheme.

11. **EMPLOYERS' ORGANISATIONS** 140 — 154
Origin and Growth — Industrial Associations — Aims and Objects of Federations — Role and Functions of the Employers' Organisations — Obligation to Constituents — Finances — Communications — Social Responsibilities — International Affiliations.

12. **DISCIPLINE, DOMESTIC ENQUIRY AND GRIEVANCE PROCEDURE** 155 — 176
Concept of Discipline — Importance — Objective of Discipline — Self-discipline — Negative Discipline — Approaches of Discipline — Step in Disciplinary Actions — Statement of Problems — Collection of Full Information on the Case — Types of Penalties — Choosing the Penalty — Applying Penalties — Follow-up of Disciplinary Action — Principles of Disciplinary Action — Announced Disciplinary Policy with Advance Warning — Consistency — Impersonality — Give Employee an Opportunity to Explain — Decide What Action to Take — Disciplinary Action as a Tool — New Concept of Discipline : The Hot-Stove Rules — Role of the Union — Statutory Law on Discipline — Acts of Indiscipline / Misconduct — Procedure for Domestic Enquiries — How to Frame A Proper Charge Sheet — Grievance Settlement — Basic Considerations — Steps in Handling Grievances — Principles of Handling Grievances.

13. **EMPLOYER–EMPLOYEE COMMUNICATION : MANAGER AS COMMUNICATOR** 117 — 188
Introduction — Definition and Nature — Effective Communication — Importance of Communication — Types of Communication — Media and Methods of Communication — House Magazine and Wall Newspaper — The Grape-Vine — Communication Failure — Barriers to Communication — Evaluation of Communication Media.

14. **LABOUR POLICY** 189 — 201
Attitude to Labour — Social Security — Industrial Relations — Wage and Social Security — A Critical Review of the Labour Policy.

15. **BONUS — LEGAL PROVISIONS** 202 — 209
Introduction — The Beginnings of Bonus in India — Bonus During and Immediately after the Second World War — Bonus as a matter of Right — Payment of Bonus — The Payment of Bonus Act, 1965.

16. **INDIA AND THE ILO** 210 — 215
Aims of the ILO — Structure — Declaration of Philadelphia — Principal Organs of the ILO — International Labour Conference — Governing Body — International Labour Office — Principal Activities — The International Labour Code — Technical Assistance — Educational Programme — India's Relationship with the ILO — Evaluation — Important ILO Conventions Ratified by India.

17. **LABOUR LEGISLATION** 216 — 231
Fundamental Principles of Labour Legislation — Social Justice — Social Welfare — National Economy — International Solidarity — Evolution of Labour Legislation — Defects — Factory and Establishment Legislation — Plantation Legislation — Mining Legislation — Transport Legislation — Wage Legislation — Social Security Legislation — Industrial Relations Legislation — Miscellaneous Legislation.

18. **FINDINGS AND RECOMMENDATIONS OF THE NATIONAL LABOUR COMMISSION, 1969** 232 — 243
Main Findings and Recommendations of the Commission — Indian Worker — Adoption to Change — Recruitment Agencies and Practices — Training, Induction and Promotion — Working Conditions — Social Security — Workmen's Compensation — Lay-off and Retrenchment — Integrated Social Security — Wage Policy — Minimum Wage — Incentives and Bonus — Rationalisation and Automation — Machinery for Wage Fixation — Workers Organisations — Employer's Organisations — Industrial Relations — Labour in Public Sector — Government Industrial Employees — Unorganised Labour — Contract Labour — Construction Workers — Casual Labour — Workers in shops and Commercial Establishments.

19. INDUSTRIAL RELATIONS IN THE CONTEXT OF GLOBALISATION 244 — 260
Changing Face of Trade Unions in a Liberalised Economy — Issues Related to Trade Unions — Towards a Conceptual Model — Internal Environmental Factors — Individual and Organisational Outcomes — Labour Flexibility and Industrial Relations.

Appendices

INDUSTRIAL DISPUTES ACT, 1947 261 — 364

I.	Preliminary	261
II.	Authorities Under this Act	282
IIA.	Notice of Change	285
IIB.	Reference of Certain Individual Disputes to Grievance Settlement Authorities	286
III.	Reference of Disputes to Boards, Courts, or Tribunals	287
IV.	Procedure, Powers and Duties of Authorities	293
V.	Strike and Lock-Outs	311
VA.	Lay-Off and Retrenchment	315
VB.	Special Provisions Relating to Lay-Off, Retrenchment and Closure in Certain Establishment	327
VC.	Unfair Labour Practices	334
VI.	Penalties	335
VII.	Miscellaneous	337

1

INDUSTRIAL RELATIONS

Industrial Relations

Industrial relations as being synonymous with employee relations may be defined as the relations between employers and employees in industry. According to Encyclopedia Britannica, the industrial relations include individual relations and joint consultation between employers and work people at the place of work, collective relations between employers and the organisations and the trade unions and the part played by the State in regulating these relations. Thus : *(i)* Industrial relations include individual relations in an industry; *(ii)* The collective relations between employers and labour (trade) unions and *(iii)* The role of the government in the regulation of these relationships *(iv)* Besides these there is the international aspects, particularly in terms of the influence exercised by certain international bodies like the ILO in shaping and developing the pattern of industrial relations in several countries. *(v)* In order that the term 'industrial relations' covers every sector of the labour force in all parts of the world, the International Institute of Labour Studies has defined it as 'social relations in production'.

Industrial relations is an art, the art of living together for the purposes of production. The emphasis is on the process of accommodation whereby the parties involved develop skills and methods of adjusting to and co-operating with each other.

The term 'industrial relations' or 'labour management relations' or employee relations is difficult to define precisely because it is too complex.

This is particularly so in a democratic society which allows freedom of action to the workers and their organisations and to the employers and their organisations and a series of laws are enacted to regulate their relations. In a totalitarian country trade unions are banned, as in Germany under Hitler or Italy under Moussolini. But even such a society has to enact laws to provide an acceptable relationship between the industrial employer and employees. In a Communist country where all persons employed are workers, industrial relations cannot result in any form of industrial action. But changes are taking place even in the so-called Communist countries; the upsurge of industrial workers in Poland and Yugoslavia are cases to point.

There is no uniform pattern of industrial relationship even in democratic societies. However, there are standards of industrial relationships which are contained in the Philadelphia Declaration of the ILO (1994) embodied in the series of Conventions and Recommendations evolved in the ILO conferences in which most of the democratic countries of the world participate. If a country ratifies a convention, its national laws have to conform to it. In fact, most of India's labour legislation after independence has been influenced by such conventions and recommendations.

There is no uniform pattern that can be prescribed for nations. The kind of industrial relations required to ensure harmony and co-operation will depend on a number of factors including the form of ownership of industry that prevails, the state of technology that is utilised, the state of techniques and relations of production in that society, the nature and character of the government, the views of the Government in relations to its own role, the instruments that the society has as its disposal to formulate public opinion, the socially — accepted concept of sanctions in the field of industrial relations and the socially accepted limitations on the use of action in the industrial field — whether it be by the employer or the employee.

Following Robert W. Cox enumeration of the patterns of relationship may be as follows :

(1) The peasant-lord system (in industrial employment it represents master servant relationship).

(2) The primitive market system.

(3) A small manufacture system (the beginning of industrial revolution where workers are getting slowly organised).

(4) The lifetime commitment system as in Japan where there is lifelong employment.

(5) A bipartite system of which collective bargaining is the main function as in USA and other democratic countries.

(6) A tripartite system in which the Government also plays an important role in labour management relations as in India.

Functions

Industrial relations system fulfills at least three major functions. *First*, it defines the relative rights and responsibilities of workers, managers and the state and establishes the power relationships between them. *Secondly*, it channels and controls the responses of workers and managers to the dislocation, frustrations and insecurities inherent in the industrial process. *Thirdly*, it establishes the net-work of rules — both substantiative and procedural which govern the workplace and work community. In short, the industrial relations system provides the structure and the machinery for the functional relationship between the managers and the managed in any industrial society.

There are three basic approaches to labour management negotiations — unilateral, bipartite and tripartite. In the unilateral approach, the employer alone decides the terms and conditions of employment for his workers. In the bipartite approach, the employer negotiates with his workers. This is collective bargaining. In the tripartite approach, a third party — the Government also participates in the negotiations.

Objectives of Industrial Relations

The objectives of industrial relations are as follows :

- To maintain and develop good employer-employee relations.
- To maintain industrial peace.
- To safeguard the interests of labour and management.
- To avoid as far as possible, industrial conflicts.
- To establish industrial democracy.
- To help the economic development of the country.
- To encourage collective bargaining as a means of self-regulation.
- To help maintain discipline amongst workers.
- To help Government in making laws.
- To help union and management to develop constructive attitudes to one another.

Approaches to Industrial Relations

Industrial relations which refer to the formal processes of consultation and negotiation are as old as industry and being inherent in industry, will always remain as a feature of industrial life. The participants in it are mainly three — the workers and their organisations, the employers and their associations and the agencies of the government. The participants should build up a stable, workable relationship among themselves and provide for the people a constant flow of consumption goods. The sectional groups in society sacrifice its broader interests to further their own ends and the conflict between the two assume the shape of industrial unrest. The agencies of Government which is the custodian of the interests of the community as a whole, play a significant role in shaping the pattern of relationships in the industrial setting. Industrial relations are collectively conducted between the workers and the employers through collective bargaining.

In the pre-industrial society, productive work was mostly organized on a small scale. Workmen frequently owned the simple instruments which they needed for their work. Hence, they either worked on their own or offered services to others with whom they would have direct and personal relations. With the advent of modern industrialisation, work organisations have undergone a basic transformation in terms of the scale of activity.

Modern industrial work has the following peculiarities :

(i) Industrial work is a group work. It brings together a large number of workers who work for the employer with whom they have scarcely any personal relationship. What is possible between them is a collective relationship. The other significant aspect of this feature is the relations among the workers themselves. Some leaders come up from among the workers and they wield considerable power.

(ii) It involves division of labour. A worker seldom makes a complete product. Work is fragmented and repetitive. The worker spends the best part of his life at the work place but his work does not interest him.

(iii) Industrial work is carried on under the control and direction of the employer. The workers do not own the instruments of production. They have only their services to offer to employers who own the instruments of production. As a result, workers have lost their freedom as independent producers.

(iv) Lastly, industrial work is wage work. Employers buy and workers sell their services. The buyer wants labour to be more productive and the sellers want it to be more rewarding.

Scope of Industrial Relations

From the definition and nature of industrial relations, it is not difficult to have an idea of the scope of industrial relations. Industrial relations refers to the continuing relationship that emerges out of the day-to-day association between labour and management. There are two important aspects of such relationship :

(i) Relations between individual workers and managers called personnel relations.

(ii) Collective relations between labour unions and management called labour relations or labour management relations. The patterns of labour-management relations is shaped by State interventions.

It also includes the study of —

- Industrial co-operation
- Industrial conflict
- Workers' organisations
- Employers' organisation
- Industrial Discipline
- Labour Legislation

Evolution of Industrial Relations

In India when the doctrine of *laissez-faire* prevailed, workers were at a great disadvantage as they contracted themselves with their employers. They were exploited — they received low wages and worked long hours in miserable physical conditions of work. The relationship between unequals inevitably resulted in the exploitation of the weak by the strong. This exploitation sowed the seeds of dissatisfaction and bred protest. Therefore, workers got together and formed trade unions; they built up their organisations to mobilise their own power. In the sphere of collective relationship trade unions emerged for the protection and furtherance of the workers' interests for the worker individually could not take up his own cause effectively with the employer.

As the industrial units grew large their ownership was increasingly divorced from management and a new managerial group was interposed between the owners/employers and the rank and file of workers.

The other important aspect of industrialisation is the formation of employers' associations to safeguard and promote the interest of their members through collective action.

The basic inequalities of the contracting parties in the employment relationship have called forth intervention by a third party, i.e., the Stage, in favour of the weaker section to ensure fair treatment to all concerned. The major instrument with the Government is legislation whereby norms to regulate the relationship between the two parties are specified and enhanced through the apparatus created for the purpose. The Government is prompted to influence the relationship between the employers/management and the workers and their trade unions, for it has the responsibility of satisfying the economic needs of the community. Therefore, the major influence in the field of industrial relations are the workers, the management and the Government. They play their roles, act and interact and evolve a process to regulate employment relationship.

Upto the late 20's of the 20th century, the employer-employee relationship in India was practically that of master and servant. The British Government followed a policy of *laissez-faire* and regarded the problem of industrial relations mainly from the point of view of law and order. Policy of the Government was to protect the social system from workers rather than to protect workers from the social system.

Workers were hired and fired as the principle of demand and supply governed industrial relations. The employer was in a commanding position and the conditions of employment and wages were very poor.

In the decades following the First World War, the mounting industrial unrest and political excitement within the country, the Soviet Revolution, the establishment of the ILO and the rise of the working class in Britain made the Government conscious of the danger and limitations of the prevailing policy.

After the First World War, the industrial relations concept assumed a new dimension in the sense that the workers now resorted to violence and employers to lockouts. There were numerous strikes and disturbances during 1928-29. As a result, the Government enacted the Trade Disputes Act 1929, to expediate the early settlement of industrial disputes. With the passing of the Trade Disputes Act in 1929, State intervention in the settlement of industrial disputes started. The Act vested the Government with powers which could be used whenever it considered fit to intervene in industrial disputes. It provided for only *ad-hoc* conciliation boards and courts of enquiry. The Amending Act of 1938 authorized the Central and Provincial Governments to appoint conciliation officers for mediating in or promoting the settlement of disputes. The Act, however, was not used extensively as the Government policy at that time continued to be one of *laissez-faire* and selecting intervention at the most.

The defects of the Trade Disputes Act 1926, were to a certain extent removed by the Industrial Disputes Legislation passed in Bombay in 1934 and 1938. The Bombay Trade Disputes (Conciliation) Act 1934, introduced for the first time a standing machinery to enable the state to promote industrial peace. A permanent cadre of conciliators were envisaged for settling matters which fell within their jurisdiction. The scope of the Act was limited to selected industries. The experience of the working of the Act led to the enactment of the Bombay Industrial Disputes Act, 1938. The Act provides for *(i)* compulsory recognition of unions by the employer, *(ii)* giving the right to workers to get their case represented either through a representative union or where no representative union in the industry existed, through elected representatives of workers or through the Government Labour Officer; *(iii)* the setting up of an Industrial Court with original as well as appellate jurisdiction, to which parties could go for arbitration in case conciliation fails and *(iv)* prohibitation of strike/lock-out under certain conditions.

During the Second World War the Government assumed emergency powers for the settlement of industrial disputes. In 1942, the Defence of

India Rules was promulgated to meet the exigencies created by the war. Rule 81A gave powers to the appropriate Governments to intervene in industrial disputes, appoint industrial tribunals and enforce the award of the tribunals on both sides. Under this Rule compulsory conciliation and adjudication were introduced.

After India attained independence, the Industrial Disputes Act was passed in 1947 which replaced the Trade Disputes Act of 1929. This Act not only provides for the establishment of permanent machinery for the settlement of industrial disputes but also makes these awards binding and legally enforceable. With subsequent amendments, the ID Act still continues to be the main instrument for Government's intervention in labour disputes.

Another development in the post-independence period was the setting up of the Indian Labour Conference, a tripartite body to look into industrial relations problems. It was set up with the objective of establishing cooperation between the trade unions, employers and the Government. It met once a year to discuss problems relating to industrial relations.

Industrial Disputes Act, 1947, continues to govern industrial relations on the legislative side. On the voluntary side, the Code of Discipline in Industry (1958) and the Industrial Truce Resolution (1962) continued to have their impact on industrial relations in the country. The conciliation machinery set up under the ID Act, 1947 continues to play its role in bringing the parties together and exploring ways for promoting amicable settlements.

The ID Act provides for settlement of industrial disputes through conciliation and adjudication. The Act empowers the appropriate Government to appoint conciliation officers and/or constitute Boards of Conciliation to mediate in and promote settlement of industrial disputes. It also empowers the appropriate Government to refer disputes for adjudication by an industrial tribunal. The Act makes a distinction between disputes arising in public utility services and those in other industries and provides for compulsory conciliation and adjudication to resolve the former. Besides, the appropriate Government could constitute a Court of Enquiry to enquire into matters relating to an industrial disputes. Restrictions are placed on strike/lockout in public utility services and during the pendency of conciliation and adjudication proceedings. The procedures and machinery provided under the ID Act have been modified from time to time in the light of the actual working of these provisions, the decisions of the judiciary and the influence of the bipartite and tripartite agreements.

In 1957 the emphasis of Government's attitude towards labour shifted from legal enactments to voluntary arrangements. In fact, the period between 1957 and 1965 can be regarded as an attempt to move away from legalism to voluntarism which had dominated industrial relations in India. As a result, the Code of Discipline was introduced in 1958. It enjoins on parties to refrain from taking unilateral action on industrial matters. But unfortunately, the Code has a limited success. As a result, the Government, has to rely on legislation to regulate labour-management relations.

Plan Policies :

The First Five Year Plan stressed the need for industrial peace for economic progress. While it wanted the state to arm itself with powers for intervention in labour disputes, the endeavour had to be to encourage mutual settlement, collective bargaining and voluntary arbitration to the utmost extent and thereby to reduce to the minimum, occasions for its intervention in industrial disputes and exercise of the special powers. Industrial relations must be so developed as to enable the worker to take a greater share in the working of the industry. The working of the Labour Appellate Tribunal came up for criticism in tripartite meetings and it was decided to abolish Labour Appellate Tribunal.

The Second Plan envisaged a marked shift in the industrial relations policy consequent on the acceptance of the socialist pattern of society as the goal of planning. It emphasized mutual negotiations as the effective mode of settling disputes. Among the other recommendations in the Plan were demarcation of functions between works committees and unions and increased association of labour with management. The Labour appellate Tribunal was abolished in 1956 and a three tier system of original tribunals - labour courts, industrial tribunals and national tribunals were brought into force.

The 15th Session of the Indian Labour Conference took note of these developments and the Second Plan recommendations had sought to evolve steps for their implementations. The Code of Discipline and Code of Conduct were drawn up and arrangements were made to educate workers.

The Third Plan did to suggest any major change in policy. It emphasised the economic and social aspects of industrial peace and elaborated the concept that workers and management were partners in a joint endeavour to achieve common ends. The voluntary arrangements agreed to in the Second Plan were strengthened by the Industrial Truce Resolution, 1962, adopted in the wake of the Chinese aggression. The ID Act was amended in 1965 with a view to give an individual worker the right to raise a dispute connected with his discharge, dismissal, retrenchment or termination of service, even if the cause of the individual worker was not espoused by any union or group of workmen. The Fourth Plan has made no reference to industrial relations policy and therefore the policy formulated during the previous plan period will continue.

The Sixth Plan stated tha. healthy industrial relations on which industrial harmony is founded, cannot be regarded as a matter of interest only to employers and workers but also of vital concern to the community as a whole. Further, in the ultimate analyses, the problem of industrial relations is essentially one of attitudes and approaches of the parties concerned. A spirit of cooperation stipulates that employers and workers recognise that while they are fully justified in safeguarding their respective rights and interests, they also bear in mind the larger interests of the community. This is the true significance of doctrine of industrial harmony in its three dimensional aspects.

The Industrial Disputes Act 1947 has been the main legislative frame-work which has provided the machinery and procedure for the settlement of disputes through mediation, conciliation, arbitration and adjudication. Steps were also taken in the past to provide a voluntary approach to industrial relations through Codes. A general feeling has developed that the existing arrangements have not proved effective in presenting disputes and promoting settlements. Since the submission of the report of the National Commission on Labour efforts have been made for evolving a new and comprehensive industrial relations legislation but these have not succeeded on account of the divergence of approaches among the trade union organisations on certain basic issues such as the machinery and procedure for settlement of disputes, the criteria and procedure for recognition of trade unions i.e., whether the representative character of trade unions should be determined through verification of paid membership of contending unions or through secret ballot; right to strike in essential industries including public utilities, role of government. in regulating industrial relations etc. While efforts must continue to minimize the areas of disagreement among the parties concerned and acceptable improvements in law and machinery effected, some of the changes in the existing laws on trade unions, industrial disputes and standing orders, which are generally considered essential for promoting industrial relations, need not be held over and should be carried out. These changes would help in streamlining the existing procedures and securing speedy justice to workers. The question of providing security of service to such categories of employees who are at present outside the ambit of labour laws also needs consideration.

It has been stressed that if the huge investments during the Five Year Plan are to yield the desired results, certain important measures cannot be delayed for long; e.g. the core sector including power, energy, coal, steel and transport needs to be insulated against uncertainties of the industrial relations situation to the maximum extent possible. If adequate consultative machinery and grievance procedures are evolved and made effective, strikes and lockouts can become redundant in these industries. In other areas also strikes and lockouts should be resorted to only in the last stage. Effective arrangements should also be made for the settlement of inter-union disputes and to discourage unfair practices and irresponsible conduct.

Present Policy to Industrial Relations

The Code of Discipline was evolved at the Indian Labour Conference in 1958 requiring employers and workers to utilise the existing machinery for the settlement of disputes. It was accepted by all the Central Organisations of employers/workers and several others. Under the Code of Discipline the implementing organisations assist in settling disputes pertaining to Central and State affairs. The Central Organisations of employers, workers and public sector undertakings excluding the All India Trade Union Congress in this context have set up committees for screening cases.

Screening procedure has been evolved to check prolonged litigation by the public sector undertakings in filing appeals in industrial dispute cases on which an award or a judgment has been given by an Industrial Tribunal or a Court. Under this procedure, only after obtaining the concurrence of the concerned administrative Ministry on the Law Ministry on the need for filing an appeal by the public sector undertakings on an award of judgement of the Labour Court/Tribunal etc., the case is referred to the Labour Ministry. In case the Labour Ministry and the concerned administrative Ministry do not agree, the matter is placed before the committee of economic secretaries.

The layoffs, retrenchments and closures are regulated under the provisions of the ID Act 1947. The Government has taken steps to further regulate layoffs, retrenchments and closures through the Industrial Disputes Amendment Act of 1982 and 1984. Accordingly under the act, any worker who has completed not less than one year of continuous service is entitled to a minimum amount of compensation for retrenchment/closure.

State and Industrial Relations

The concern of the state in labour matters emanates as much from its obligations to safeguard the interests of workers and employers as to ensure to the community the availability of their joint product/service at a reasonable price. The extent of its involvement in the process is determined by the level of social and economic advancement, while the mode of intervention gets patterned in conformity with the political system obtaining in the country and the social and cultural traditions of its people. The role of the State in regulating labour conditions will be different in a democratic set-up from that in a society which has a dictatorial government. In the former, the approach of the State will be consistent with what the will of people demands. The degree of State intervention is also determined by the stage of economic development. In a developed economy work stoppages to settle claims may not have as serious consequences as in a developing economy. Likewise, a free market economy may leave the parties to settle their relations through strikes and lockouts. But in other systems, varying degrees of State participation will be required in the building up of industrial relations. However, in all countries the State has assumed powers to regulate labour relations. In some, it has taken the forum of laying down bare rules for observance by employers and workers, in others, the rules cover a wider area of relationship and there is equally greater supervision over the enforcement of the rules.

Some International Practices

In the USA, the State has confined itself to enacting legislation for ensuring the workers' right to organise and bargain collectively and has constituted an independent authority to administer and interpret legal provisions and decide on complaints regarding unfair labour practices. Intervention of the State in industrial disputes is limited to actual work stoppages which could impair the national economy. But even within this area of State intervention, a wide latitude is given to the parties for settling their differences. The Government does not envisage direct interference in the process of collective bargaining.

Legislation has been introduced in the USA to cover a wide-range of aspects of industrial relations and although it would be an exaggeration to claim that industrial negotiations are solely the province of lawyers, legal profession comes close to dominating the scene. The National Labour Relations or Wagner Act of 1935 govern collective bargaining; the National Labour Relations Board can determine who shall have bargaining rights and issue over which they may bargain. The Labour Management Relations or Taft-Hartley Act of 1947, made collective agreements legally enforceable, introduced the concept of a 'cooling off period' (during which strike action has to be suspended), enabled a district court to issue an 80-day injunction against a strike or lockout which was causing a national emergency, regulated the internal affairs of trade unions and provided protection for workers who refused to join a union. The provisions in the Taft-Hartley Act concerning the internal affairs of trade unions were extended to the Landrum-Griffn Act of 1959.

In the UK, the industrial relations system has been marked by the primacy of free collective bargaining between the parties.

Many writers have argued that prior to the 1960s, UK has a 'voluntary' system of industrial relations. The adjective 'voluntary' means that the State plays no part whatsoever in industrial relations. If voluntary system of industrial relations means the absence of State intervention of any kind, the British system has never been voluntary. The State in Britain has always intervened on certain issues. For example, the State has intervened through the Factory Acts (1961), and associated legislation (such as the Mines Acts and the Offices, Shops and Railways Premises Act). These regulate working conditions by laying down rules for the notification of accidents and industrial diseases, the provision of proper ventilation, sanitation and maximum hours of work.

Another example of Government intervention in industrial relations in UK prior the 1960s can be seen in the field of wage regulation. The Trade Boards Act of 1909 set up trade boards for some trades where wages were so low and conditions of employment so poor that they had attracted universal condemnation. The boards were empowered to fix statutory minimum wage rates which were backed by an official inspectorate and the threat of legal penalties. Today the functions of trade boards are carried out by wage councils set up in 1945.

The assertion that UK had a voluntary system of industrial relations does not imply that the State has not taken an interest in or intervened in industrial relations in UK; rather it implies that the State has played a restricted role and has tried to keep industrial relations and trade unions away from the courts.

The role of the State in British industrial relations changed in the 1960s. *First*, the State intervened more decisively in the area of wages and salaries, a move crystallised in the notion of 'incomes policy'. *Second*, Governments attempt to introduce the law more centrally into collective bargaining, conciliation and arbitration. The Industrial Relations Act 1971 marks the high point of this policy.

The Australian system has had a long tradition of State regulation. The Government intervenes for the settlement of disputes. Collective bargaining in Australia is dominated by the law. Compulsory arbitration is not reserved for exceptional cases as in the USA, rather it is accepted as a normal part of industrial relations. So, collective bargaining, as it is understood in Europe, does not exist in Australia.

In Japan, the right to collective bargaining is guaranteed under the Constitution and the State has enacted legislation to promote collective bargaining. Direct state intervention is permissible in strikes which might jeopardise the national economy and public life. In other industrially advanced democratic systems, direct State intervention in industrial disputes is generally the exception rather than the rule.

In the former USSR, three important factors regulate the industrial relations system. *First*, the formation of a socialist society is characterised by the public ownership of the basic means of production. The building up of a workers' state makes the interests of labour and management non-antagonistic. *Second*, the operation of a centrally planned economy introduces its own constraints on labour and management. However, recently increasing powers are given to local trade unions and individual enterprises to take decisions on matters of employment, wages and productivity. *Lastly*, the influence of a single political party in running the government and in organising unions makes it necessary for the unions to perform a double role. They have to help in carrying out party policy and look after production interests and at the same time assume the traditional role of unions in furthering the interests of labour.

In the three developing countries in Asia — Mayanmar, Malaysia and Philippines, the concern of the State in industrial relations has been more marked. Besides laying down rules and procedures for the settlement of disputes, the State has provided arbitration machinery. In the last resort, Government has reserved to itself the right of making a reference to such machinery in cases where the public interest so demands or where a joint request is made by the parties.

Practice of India

State intervention in India has assumed a more direct form. The State has enacted procedural and also substantive laws to regulate industrial relations. In the distant past, State intervention in labour matters was for protecting the commercial interests of the British Rulers. Later, pressures from the public to guard the interests of workers in the face of difficulties created by the operation of the economic system prevailed. Since independence, State intervention in labour matters has been necessitated by larger need for the regulation of the economy with the focus on rapid overall growth. Apart from planned development, the requirements of the Welfare State envisaged in our constitution have been another important reason for State intervention.

Apart from the different roles played by the State, there are others which have a special significance in our context. The *first* is that of the State as an employer which has two aspects - direct employment of labour by the State and employment in industrial corporations constituted by the State. Handling of industrial relations in the case of its own employees, to whom all legislation framed from industry is applicable, falls in this category. This function of the State as an employer has been there over a very long period. To this was added another when, as a matter of policy, it was decided to operate a mixed economy wherein industries were to be run by both private entrepreneurs and the State. The policy statements show that as an employer the State binds itself to the rules which it frames for private employers. Where standards of good employment are disparate, the State seeks to set standards with a view to influencing the employers in the private sector. While this is the policy, in practice, it so happens that there is a fair amount of interaction between what the employers do for their employees in the two sectors. And this interaction is influenced by the new consciousness among the workers and ease of communication within the working class.

The *second* role which the State has to play in our context is the outcome of its Federal Constitution, and the fact that labour is a subject in the Concurrent list for the purpose of legislation. It has been a tradition in the country for long that the Central Government assumes the responsibility of enacting legislation on many aspects affecting labour, whereas the State Governments look after implementation, though they can legislate on their own also. In either case, a considerable measure of consultation has been the rule.

It is obvious, therefore, that the State cannot be a silent spectator in the development of healthy labour practices. It has to play a role which the parties to a dispute find acceptable.

Industrial relations in India have been shaped largely by principles and policies evolved through tripartite consultative machinery at the industry and national levels.

Tripartite bodies like the Indian Labour Conference/Standing Labour Committee/Industrial Committees were set up for setting union norms to guide industrial relations. Tripartite meetings provide a useful forum of communication between the parties represented on them. They help in narrowing down differences among the three groups in reaching consensus over matter of common interest, in providing a forum for communication among the parties and in sharing the responsibility of Government in maintaining industrial harmony.

Industrial Relations Practice at the Plant-level in India

There are five types of the prevailing patterns of industrial relations in India at the plant-level. These are :

- Regulative (Standing Orders)
- Consultative (Voluntary Jt. Consultation)
- Preventive (Works Committee/Joint Committee)
- Co-operative (Collective Bargaining Codes)
- Conflictive (ID Act)
- Participative (JMC)

By and large, the regulative and conflictive patterns in industrial relations seem to predominate at the plant-level in India. The positive patterns begin in consultation and culminate in participation via co-operation.

The regulative pattern marks the beginnings of industrial relations. It is characterised by the application and administration of the Industrial Employment (Standing Orders) Act and the enforcement of Standing Orders.

The consultative pattern will begin only if both management and employees believe in voluntary joint consultation and bilaterally practice it within the frame-work of their terms of jurisdiction.

There is a provision for the preventive pattern of industrial relations illustrated by statutory bodies such as Works Committee and Joint

Committee as machinery for the avoidance of problems of industrial relations. These are intended to prevent any industrial unrest and conflict and pave the way for the positive philosophy of co-operation in industrial relations reflected in collective bargaining.

Alternatively, the conflictive pattern is reflected in the working of the industrial disputes legislation as applicable to different industries in the country.

There is a long way to go from the regulative pattern to the participative pattern of industrial relations but this movement is essential for the progress of the country.

Symptoms of Industrial Unrest and Treatment at a Glance

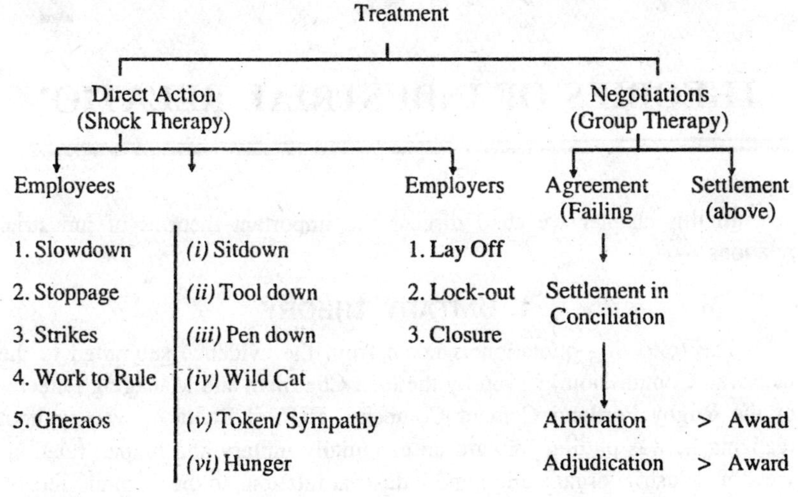

Fig. 1.1

❑ ❑ ❑

2

THEORIES OF INDUSTRIAL RELATIONS

In this chapter we shall discuss the important theories of industrial relations.

1. UNITARY THEORY

The following quotation is taken from the evidence submitted to the Donovan Commission in 1966 by the then Chairman and Managing Director of the Rugby Portland Cement Company, Halford Reddish, who without realizing it, was putting forward an essentially unitary and human relations view of industrial organization and industrial relations to the Commissioners:

(i) I am asked 'how good relations are achieved in a company which does not negotiate with trade unions.'

(ii) Our thinking proceeds as follows ....
Modern industrial organization is in effect a partnership between the labour of yesterday (which we call capital) and the labour of today (all of us who work for wages and salaries) ....

(iii) We deplore the use of the terms'industrial relations' and 'labour relations'. We prefer 'human relations', by which we mean a recognition of the essential human dignity of the individual ....

(iv) An employee, at whatever level, must be made to feel that he is not merely a number on a pay-roll but a recognized member of a team ....

(v) We reject the idea that amongst the employees of a company there are 'two sides' meaning the executive directors and managers on the one hand and the weekly-paid employees on the

other. Executive directors are just as much employees of the company as anyone else. We are all on the same side, members of the same team.

(vi) We recognize that the tone of any organization depends primarily on one man, on the executive head of it; on his philosophy, on his outlook, on the standards which he sets, on his example; in short, on his leadership.

(vii) Leadership is surely the key to good human relations - leadership at all levels. It must embrace, *inter alia* .... Maintenance of strict discipline, as firm as it is fair.... A conviction that loyalty must be a two-way traffic. I except every employee to be loyal to the company and to me as the temporary captain of the team: he has an equal right to expect loyalty from me... Communication - in the widest sense of the term.

The essence of the unitary theory of industrial relations, held by Halford Reddish and others, is that every work organization is an integrated and harmonious whole existing for a common purpose. They assume that each employee identifies with the aims of the enterprise and with its methods of operating. By this view, there is no conflict of interest between those supplying financial capital to the enterprise and their managerial representatives, and those contributing their labour and job skills. By definition the owners of capital and labour are joint partners to the common aims of efficient production, high profits and good pay in which everyone in the organization has a stake. It follows that there cannot be 'two sides' in industry. Indeed managers and managed alike are merely parts of the same 'team'. This team, however, is expected to be provided with strong leadership from the top to keep it working and to ensure commitment to the tasks to be done and to its managerial office holders.

This requires, on the part of management, at the minimum a paternalistic approach towards subordinate employees or, at the other extreme, a more authoritarian one, together with a suitable communication structure to keep employees informed of managerial and enterprise decisions. Conversely, employees are expected to remain loyal to the organization and to its management in difference to the common problems facing managers and subordinates alike. Thus, the unitary theory of industrial relations emerges from a belief that work enterprises, whether privately or publicly owned, are very much like a professional football team: 'Team spirit and undivided management authority co-exist to the benefit of all'. Work organizations, in short, are viewed as unitary in their structure and unitary in their purposes, and as having a single source of authority and a cohesive set of participants motivated by common goals. Consequently, industrial relations is assumed to be based on mutual co-operation and harmony of interest between management and managed within the enterprise.

One implication of unitarism is that factionalism within the enterprise, is seen as a pathological social condition.Subordinate employees are not expected to challenge managerial decisions or the right to manage, while trade unionism is viewed as an illegitimate intrusion into the unified and cooperative structure of the workplace. More than this, trade unionism competes almost malevolently with management for the loyalty and commitment of employees to their employer. In other words, unitary theory in its traditional or classical form denies the validity of conflict at work whether between management and employees, between management and unions, or even between the organization and its customers. The concepts of common purpose and harmony of interests further imply that apparent conflict is either *(a)* merely frictional, e.g. due to incompatible personalities or 'things going wrong', or *(b)* caused by faulty communication', e.g. misunderstanding' about aims or methods, or *(c)* the result of stupidity in the form of failure to grasp the communality of interest, or *(d)* the work of agitators inciting the supine majority who would otherwise be content.

Collective bargaining and trade unions are therefore perceived as being anti-social, anti-managerial mechanisms, since acceptance of two opposed and competing interest groups within the enterprise,in the persons of management and union representatives, only precipitates and crystallizes unnecessary and destructive industrial conflict between what are viewed as two non-competing, co-operative parties.

Understanding Industrial Relations

It soon becomes evident that the unitary theory of industrial relations is predominantly managerially oriented in its inception, in its emphasis and in its application. Indeed it is a theoretical perspective with which many managers and employers identify because it reassures them in their roles as organizational decision makers and legitmizes the acceptance of their authority by subordinate employees.

In summary, traditional unitary theory in its purest form stresses the harmonious nature of work enterprises and of industrial relations within them. To what extent it represents consistent and compatible view points amongst different status groups within particular organizations depends upon two main factors; *first*, the social structure of the organization; and *second*, whether the unitary value system is accepted by subordinate personnel within it. The latter is the linchpin around which unitary theory of industrial relations is accepted or rejected.

A variant of unitary theory, 'neo-unitary' theory, appears to have emerged in some organisations since the 1980s. It builds on existing unitary concepts but is more sophisticated in the ways it is articulated and applied within enterprises. Its main aim seems to be to integrate employees, as individuals, into the companies in which they work. Its orientation is distinctly market centered, managerialist and individualist. By gaining employee commitment to quality production, customer needs and job flexibility, employers embracing this frame of reference have expectations of employee loyalty, customer satisfaction and product security in increasingly competitive market conditions. Companies adopting a neo-unitary approach to managing people share a number of ways in which they do this; they try to create a sense of common purpose and shared corporate culture; they emphasize to all employees the primacy of customer service; they set explicit work target for employees; they invest heavily in training and management development; and they sometimes provide employment security for their workers.

The personnel management techniques used to facilitate employee commitment, quality output and worker flexibility include: performance-related pay; profit sharing; harmonization of terms and conditions; employee involvement; and a 'human resources' management function, rather than personnel management function. The emphasis of neo-unitary approaches to industrial relations — or what some of its protagonists describe as 'employee relations' — is that committed, motivated and well trained people are the key to corporate success.

2. CONFLICT THEORY

Conflict theory is based on two interrelated views of society and of industrial relations between employers and employees. The *first* is that although Western industrialized societies are still class based, they are essentially 'post-capitalist' in the sense that political and industrial conflict are increasingly institutionally separated within them and that industrial conflict has become less violent because its existence has been accepted and its manifestations have been socially regulated through agreed constitutional arrangements. The *second* view is that work organizations are microcosms of society. Since society comprises a variety of individuals and of social groups, each having their own social values and each pursuing their own self- interests and objectives, those controlling and managing work enterprises similarly have to accommodate the differing values and competing interests within them. It is only by doing this that private or public enterprises can function effectively. Industrial relations between employers and unions and between managers and trade unionists, are an expression of the conflict and the power relations between organized groups in society generally. As such, industrial conflict between managers and their subordinates has to be recognized as an endemic feature of work relationship and managed accordingly.

A major element in post-capitalist theories of contemporary society and industrial relations is the proposition that the nature of class conflict has substantially changed from that suggested by Marx in his nineteenth-century analysis. In Marxist theory class conflict is perceived as being synonymous with industrial conflict and political conflict. Under market capitalism, Marxists argue, the capitalists or the owners of the means of production are identical with the ruling class in industry and politics, while wage-earners, owning only their labour-resources, are relatively powerless in industrial relations and in politics. Capitalists are the social elite and the proletariat are the socially weak. What then, has changed according to post-capitalist analysis?

First, we now live in a more open and socially mobile society compared with the class-based social divisions associated with nineteenth-century and early twentieth-century capitalism. The widening of educational opportunity, the democratization of politics, and the growth of public sector industry have opened up recruitment to a whole range of sought-after roles in society, including those within industry, politics. education, the professions, arts and so on, which would have been inconceivable a hundred years ago. Moreover, the creation of the welfare state, mitigated the worst effects of social deprivation, economic inequality and abject poverty.

Second, the distribution of authority, property and social status in society is more widely diffused than in the past. The positions which individuals occupy in the authority structure of industry, do not necessarily correlate with their positions in the political structure or with their social standing in the community. The village postal worker can become the local councillor, the school teacher a Member of Parliament and the trade unionist a Justice of the Peace. Similarly, the union convener within the workplace might have potentially more industrial power than the senior management with which he negotiates. In other words, post-capitalists take the view that dominant and subordinate classes within industry need no longer necessarily correspond with the political or social divisions of society generally.

Above all these theorists believe, the institutionalization of conflict in industry not only has decreased in intensity but also has changed its form. Several changes seem to be of particular importance in this respect:

(1) the organization of conflicting interest groups itself;
(2) the establishment of 'parliamentary' negotiating bodies in which these groups meet;
(3) the institutions of mediation and arbitration;
(4) formal representations of labour within the individual enterprise; and

(5) tendencies towards and institutionalization of workers' participation in industrial management.

Thus, the emergence of trade unionism, employers' organizations and collective bargaining, together with union representation at enterprise and workplace level, now effectively regulate the inevitable social conflicts arising between management and subordinates at work. Even where these conflicts seem irresolvable, third party intervention, usually through state agencies providing conciliation and arbitration services, is now available to provide workable remedies. By this analysis, extending worker participation in managerial decision making, as happens in board level worker representation in countries like Denmark, the Netherlands and Germany, is seen as a logical progression in institutionalizing the power relations between managers and subordinates at work. Post-capitalist society is viewed as an open society in which political, economic and social power is increasingly dispersed and in which the regulation of industrial and political conflict are of necessity dissociated.

A second theoretical concept closely related to that of post-capitalism, and of central importance in the conflict theory of industrial relations, is 'pluralism'. According to Clegg one of its major propounders:

Pluralism emerged as a criticism of the political doctrine of sovereignty — that somewhere in an independent political system there must be a final authority whose decisions are definitive. Not so, said the pluralist. Within any political system there are groups with their own interests and beliefs, and the government itself depends on their consent and co-operation. There are no definitive decisions by finial authorities: only continuous compromises.

A plural society, is a relatively stable one but not static. It has to accommodate to different and divergent pressure groups to enable social and political changes to take place constitutionally. This is achieved through negotiation, concession and compromise between pressure groups, and between many of them and government.

It is from this analysis of political pluralism that industrial relations pluralism is derived. Just as society is perceived as comprising a number of interest groups held together in some sort of loose balance by the agency of the state, so work organizations are viewed as being held in balance by the agency of management. The pluralist concepts of political sovereignty and of managerial prerogative have much in common. Trade unions are viewed as the legitimate representatives of employee interests at work with the right to challenge the right to manage. There are also similarities between the processes of political concession and compromise, on the one hand, and of collective bargaining on the other. Above all, the pluralist argues, 'greater stability and adaptability is given to industrial relations by collective bargaining than by shackling and outlawing trade unions'. According to pluralist theory, the central features of industrial relations is the potential conflict existing between employer and employed and between management and managed within work enterprises. Unlike in unitary theory, however, trade unionism is accepted by pluralists as having both a representative function and an important part in regulating this conflict, rather than in causing it. Similarly, collective bargaining is recognized as being the institutional means by which conflict between employers and employees over the wage - work bargain, and its adaptation, is regularized and resolved. Industrial conflict, therefore, is accepted by pluralists not only as being inevitable but also as requiring containment within the social mechanisms of collective bargaining, conciliation and arbitration.

There is little doubt that the pluralist and post-capitalist analyses of industrial relations, with their emphasis on the twin virtues of collective bargaining and parliamentary democracy as separate but conflict-resolving and rule-making processes were the predominant academic orthodoxy in Britain during the 1960s and 1970s. Initially they were strongly associated with the thinking of a small group of University of Oxford academics. Their individual and collective views, had an important impact on the deliberations and findings of the Royal Commission, chaired by Lord Donovan between 1965 and 1968, and on its final report. The so-called 'Oxford' approach to industrial relations influenced not only public policy and a generation of scholars in the field but also industrial relations practitioners. During the 1980s and 1990s, however, neo-unitary theory enjoyed a partial renaissance amongst some managers and students of industrial relations, as shifts to the right in British politics, to market economics and the weakening of union bargaining power in segments of the labour market occurred.

Criticism of industrial relations pluralism also comes from other quarters. The latter believe, for instance, that those working within the pluralist framework implicitly accept the institutions, principles and assumptions of the social and political *status-quo* as unproblematic.

In doing so they add their professional status, personal prestige, and influential involvement in public policy making to the forces and influences which lead subordinate groups to continue seeing the *status-quo* as legitimate, inevitable, unchangeable, 'only to be expected', subject only to changes at the margin.

Others, such as Goldthorpe, have argued that the liberal pluralist approach to industrial relations is fundamentally conservative. Indeed the changes which it seeks to promote are ones designed to bring about the more effective integration of labour into the existing structure of economic and social relations, in industry and the wider society, rather than ones intended to produce any basic alteration in this structure.

Nevertheless, despite its critics and a renascent neo-unitarism, industrial conflict theory remain a major theoretical approach to industrial relations. Yet whilst collective bargaining fits easily into pluralist theory, consultation of joint problem solving does so to a lesser extent. For this reason it is useful to distinguish between 'hard' pluralism and collective bargaining, which are conflict centered, and 'soft' pluralism and joint consultation, which are problem centered.

3. SOCIAL ACTION THEORY

Social action theory in industrial relations emphasizes the individual responses of the social actors, such as managers, employees and union representatives, to given situations. It contrasts with systems theory which suggests that behaviour in an industrial relations system is explicable in terms of its structural features. Social action theory is preeminently associated with the studies of Max Weber. According to Weber, action is social 'by virtue of the subjective meaning attached to it by the acting individual... it takes account of the behaviour of others and is thereby oriented in its course'. He insists that in order for social actions to be explained theory must be interpreted in terms of their subjectively intended meanings, not their objectively valid ones. If only observable behaviour is examined, the significance and value which individual actors place upon their behaviour are likely to be misinterpreted.

Social action, then is behaviour having subjective meaning for individual actors, with social action theory focusing on understanding particular actions in industrial relations situations rather than on just observing explicit industrial relations behaviour. This contrasts with system theory which regards behaviour in industrial relations as reflecting the impersonal processes external to the system's social actors over which they have little or no control. In emphasizing that social action derives from the personal meanings which individual attach to their own and other people's actions, social action theorists are suggesting that social actors are constrained by the ways in which they construct their own social reality. 'On the one hand, it seems, Society makes man, on the other, Man makes society'. Individual actors, however, do not share the same value systems which 'means that individuals attach different meanings to their interaction'. Managers and union representatives, for example, do not come together because they have the same goals and values 'but because, their differing ends may be served by the same means'.

Figure below indicates the main influences affecting individual choice and social action in given situations.

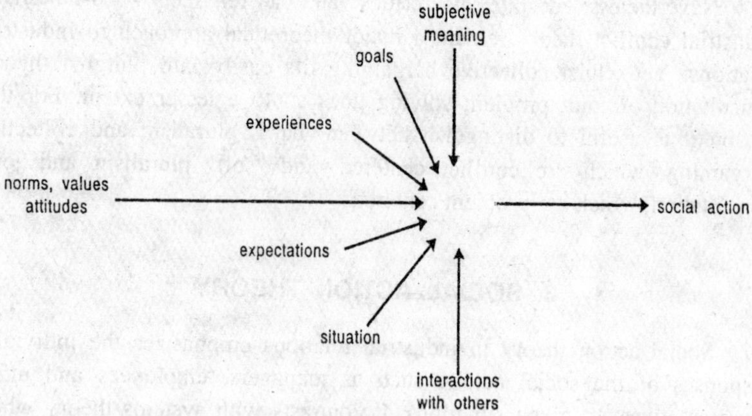

Fig. 2.1

The fundamental point is that social action emerges out of the meanings and circumstances attributed by individuals to particular social situations, thereby defining their social reality. Through interaction between actors, such as that between personnel managers and union officers, line managers and personnel specialists and union representatives and their members, individuals as well as having an element of choice in interpreting their own roles, and in acting out their intentions, also modify, change and transform social meanings for themselves and for others. The major difference between a social action approach in examining behaviour in industrial relations and a systems approach is this, action theory assumes an existing system where action occurs, but cannot explain the nature of the system, "while the systems approach is unable to explain satisfactorily why particular actors act as they do'. The first views the industrial relations system as a product of the actions of its parents, the other aims to explain the actions of its parts in terms of the nature of the system as a whole.

Social action theory also has its critics. Marxists argues, that those supporting the action frame of reference neglect the 'structural influences of which the actors themselves may be unconscious'. Whilst the consciousness of individual actors in the industrial relations system towards its politico-economic structures can be to some extent autonomous, it is limited in practice. This is because 'Definitions of reality are themselves socially generated and sustained, and the ability of men to achieve their goals is constrained by the objective characteristics of their situation'. Perhaps the most useful features of social action theory in industrial relations is the 'way in which it stresses that the individual retains at least some freedom of action and ability to influence events'. Although the structures of the industrial relations system may influence the actions of its actors, these in turn also influence the system as a whole including its outputs.

4. SYSTEM THEORY

System theory was first articulated by John Dunlop. Its purpose was to present a general theory of industrial relations and to provide tools of analysis to interpret and to gain understanding of the widest possible industrial relations facts and practice.

The systems theory views the industrial relations system as a sub-system of the wider society or the total social system. The wider society is seen as providing certain external influences and constraints but not as completely dominating industrial relations. An industrial relations system at any particular time is regarded as comprised of certain actors, certain context and ideology which binds the industrial relations system together and body of rules created to govern the actors at the place of work and work community. The creation of rules is the central aim of the industrial relations system and Dunlop isolates three groups of actors - workers, management and the government - who take part in the rule making process.

Thus $R = f(a, i, b)$

Where R = industrial relations system

a = actors,

i = ideology,

b = body of rules

In every country, workers, government and the management all interact to build up the country's industrial relations system. Each of these three actors has a role to play in the industrial relations drama. Generally in any economy there is also an ideology which is shared in common by the government, businessmen and workers. Such ideology may be defined in terms of democratic capitalism as in the USA, democratic socialism as in the UK, state capitalism as in Spain or state socialism as in the former USSR. In India, we have another economic system known as mixed economy. Mixed economy philosophy believes in the co-existence of both public and private sectors and there should be no conflicts of interest between the private and public sectors.

Democratic capitalism encourage collective bargaining supported by legislation and government intervention where necessary; democratic socialism also encourages collective bargaining but mainly as a voluntary process, the intervention by the government being rather rare. State capitalism does not allow full freedom in collective bargaining; trade unions are tolerated but not encouraged. State socialism assigns well defined roles to the trade unions, which work within the parameters of the overall political system. In a mixed economy, we have a mixture of all these approaches and there is a good deal of ambivalence.

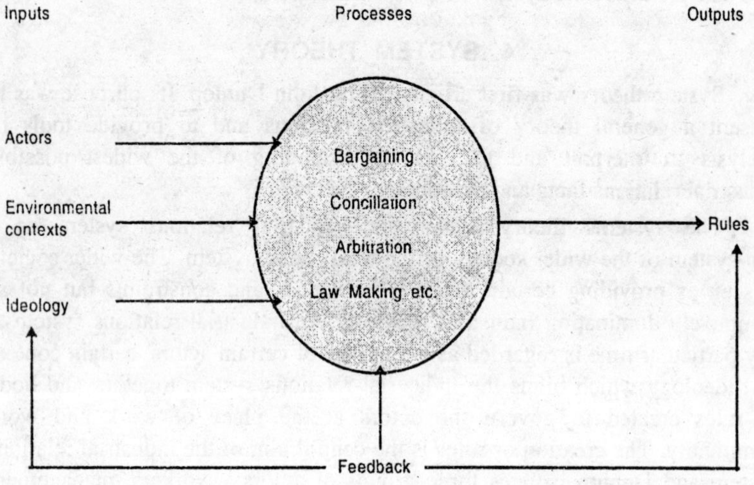

Fig. 2.2

As shows in the above figure there are three sets of independent variables in an industrial relations system; the actors, the context and the ideology of the system.

CHANGING ROLES OF THE THREE ACTORS

Management

The Exploitative Authoritarian System: This style of management was introduced in India by the colonial elite who set up modern industries during the nineteenth century. To this colonial elite labour was nothing more than a commodity. Labour was exploited ruthlessly, wages paid was barely subsistence, no job security and no welfare amenities.

Benevolent Authoritarianism: This style of management gave place to what may be called benevolent authoritarianism. The typical Indian business magnate finds this style of management congenial to his way of thinking. This style has survived until today and it believes in labour welfare. But this style does not concede to labour the adult's privileges of having a say in their own affairs.

Consultative Style: This is formally the prevailing management style in the public limited companies, in foreign concerns operating in India and in the public sector enterprises.

Participative Style: Under this style, labour is no longer a commodity or a child or an adult employee but is a friend and ally and even a partner in the joint endeavour to improve the productive efficiency of the enterprise. This style of management is not yet well developed in India.

Worker's Unions

The worker's unions assume the following roles in different socio-economic systems.

Sectional Bargainers: This is the most widely accepted role of the trade unions. They represent the interests of the workers and bargain with the management.

Class Bargainers: In some countries, e.g. France where national bargaining takes place covering all industrial occupations, trade unions or their federations play this role. In France, farmers have their own nation-wide union, so do the civil servants. The national bargaining takes place from time to time to determine the share of each class in the GNP. In India, we have now only the beginning of this process in respect of few industries, e.g. steel, jute, engineering etc.

Agent of the State: This is the role of the trade unions in socialist countries like the former USSR. Here the trade union is identified with the State apparatus and has well-defined role in ensuring the fulfilment of targets of production at the enterprise level. This type of identification with the State machinery is not to be found outside the socialist world.

Partners in Social Control: This type is exemplified in the system of co-determination of (West) Germany. Under this system, the representative of the workers sit on the boards of management and participate in all kinds of decision making. There is a beginning of this in India.

Enemy of the System: In all democratic countries there are unions which subscribe to the Marxist theory of class war. Trade unions are not merely a form of economicism but are designed to bring about a wholesale change in the existing economic system. Unions would encourage excessive consumption aspirations of workers (i.e., higher and higher wages) to bring about a state of labour unrest, contributing to the disintegration of the social order.

The Government

The third actor is the Government. The Government may assume any of the following roles.

Laissez-faire Philosophy: Under this system the Government follows a *laissez-faire* attitude to labour- management relations. The idea is to leave labour and management alone to settle a dispute. In a society where labour are economically weak and did not have a strong organisation of their own, meant that government was on the side of employers. During the 19th century governments almost everywhere followed this attitude but with the end of *laissez-faire* this attitude has become outdated.

Paternalism: Owing to the revolutionary ideas of men like Ruskin, Owen and others in UK and agitation by social reformers in UK and India, Government assumed a paternalistic attitude towards labour. A series of protective laws were enacted regulating working conditions, payment of wages and giving them certain benefits in case of industrial injuries.

Tripartism: Even before India attained independence tripartite form of consultation - consultation with employers, workers and the Government has started. After independence Government encouraged consultation with all interests before taking any policy decision.

Voluntarism: Voluntary arbitration is officially encouraged but has not taken root in india. The Government evolved a series of codes to regulate labour-management relations on a voluntary basis. As a result, came the Codes of Discipline, the Code of Conduct and the Code Efficiency and Welfare.

Interventionism: Along with tripartism and voluntarism, Government intervened in labour disputes through the process of conciliation and adjudication. Industrial strife leads to loss of production which the Government can hardly afford to ignore and so it came forward with its legislative machinery to prevent industrial disputes.

Since all the important variables of the industrial scene are integrated into the system, Dunlopian approach can explain the dynamics of industrial relations in India better than any alternative approach. One of the reasons for the confusion about the proper understanding of industrial relations is the failure to integrate knowledge of industrial scene with the overall perspective of Indian economy and policy. It is helpful in analyzing industrial conflict in the Indian context because it reminds the analyst of the whole range of factors that have to be considered in an attempt to explain strike or lockout. Some important variables like human motivations and attitudes which lie outside, should be brought within the scope of the systems of industrial relations to make the approach realistic, comprehensive and dynamic.

Criticism

Systems theory has its critics. On one hand, supporters of the systems approach have criticized its lack of analytical rigour and its static view of industrial relations. They have suggested that the model requires refinement and development.

On the other hand Marxist critics view systems theory as being too concerned with defending the political and economic *status-quo*. It provides a plausible explanation of reality in that it recognises conflicts which are visibly apparent yet it is as protective of the *status-quo* and as unquestioning about existing relationships, as the purely static unitary approach.

The major disadvantage of systems theory is that it is a static theory from which it is difficult to explain industrial relations change.

5. MARXIST THEORY

Marxist interpretations of industrial relations are not strictly theories of industrial relations *per se*. Marxism is rather a general theory of society and of social change with implication for the analysis of industrial relations within capitalist societies. In other words, Marxist analysis is essentially a method of social enquiry into the power relationships of society and a way of interpreting social reality. To understand the relevance of Marxist theory to industrial relations it is necessary to separate out those main features of general Marxist analysis which contribute to its special character as a means of interpreting relations between the capitalist and wage earning classes. Moreover, Marx himself wrote comparatively little about trade unionism and collective bargaining because neither of these institutions was firmly established in Britain when he was studying 19th century capitalise development. Thus, the application of Marxian theory as it relates to industrial relations derives indirectly from later Marxist scholars rather than directly from the works of Marx himself.

The starting point for the Marxian analysis of society is class conflict. Class conflict is synonymous with industrial conflict since the capitalist structure of industry and of wage-labour is closely connected with the pattern of class division in society. Thus, the conflict taking place in industrial relations between those who buy labour and those who sell it is seen as a permanent feature of capitalism, merely reflecting the power base of the bourgeoisie and the class relations of capitalist society generally.

Marxist model exemplifies the structuralist (technological, economic and political forces) explanation of industrial relations. Industrial relations occur within a dynamic conflict situation which is permanent and unalterable so long as the structure of society remains unchanged. The conflict situation is viewed as a product of the labour market in which on the one hand there are workers who have to sell labour power in order to subsist, while on the other hand there are buyers of labour who own the means of production and purchase labour power.

These two interests are irreconcilable. They are engaged in a perpetual conflict over the distribution of revenue. The two interests have a common purpose in increasing total revenue and so they have. But the conflict over distribution is in no sense lessened by this for the actual distribution of additional increments of revenue is determined by the power situation. Workers with no power may get nothing. There is no automatic distribution based on a sense of equity. Shares have to be fought for sometimes bitterly.

There are both short-term and long-term implications in the Marxist analysis of bourgeois society and of the class-based structure of capitalist industrial relations. The class struggle between labour and capital is regarded as being continuous, even where trade unions are absent. It takes place because capitalists and proletarians seek to maintain and to extend their relative positions in the economic power structure enabling "surplus value" to be distributed between them. Such conflict is seen to be unavoidable.

Trade union organisation in viewed as the inevitable consequence of the capitalist exploitation of wage labour. The vulnerability of employees as individuals invariably leads them to from collectivities or unions in order to protect their own class interests, although many Marxists do not believe that trade unions in themselves provide the basis for revolutionary action. Collective bargaining and militant trade unionism, however, cannot resolve the problems of industrial relations in capitalist society. They merely accommodate temporarily the contradictions inherent within the capitalist mode of production and social relations. Indeed the continuous relationship of conflict stems from a conflict of interests in industry and society which is closely linked with the operation of contradictory tendencies in the capitalist economic system.

More significantly, industrial relations become not ends in themselves but a means to an end, the furtherance of the class war between labour and capital, for by Marxist analysis, bourgeois society inevitably gives rise to political revolution by the proletariat. Out of this emerges a dictatorship of the proletariat, then socialism and ultimately the communism of the classless society. Trade unionism and industrial relations conflict are merely symptoms of the inherent class divisions within capitalism. They are a main element in the working class struggle against capitalist exploitation and in the eventual emergence of a socialist economy, followed by Utopian communism. It is out of trade union consciousness and industrial conflict that working class consciousness and political revolution can be precipitated. As such, these conflicts are instrumental in the formation of the proletariat into a class, overthrow of bourgeois supremacy, conquest of political power by the proletariat and in acting out the materialist conception of history. To Marxists, industrial relations are essentially politicised and part of the class struggle. They become overtly political when either class seeks to influence the state to intervene on its behalf. They become potentially revolutionary when working class organistions including trade unions, seek to abolish the power base of the bourgeois class within capitalism and to establish a socialist society.

The concept of alienation also played a crucial role in Marxian model on industrial conflict. Alienation arises from the fact that in the capitalist system labour is sold, it is bought by the capitalist and used to satisfy his need rather than those of the workers. Thus, the worker is estranged from the things he creates and thus, in turn violates the essential nature of man.

Alienation is most vividly seen in modern industrial labour. Two aspects are particularly crucial. The *first* is the division of labour which is seen by Marx as a means of promoting wealth for the capitalist but restricting even more closely the freedom of the worker. The *second* is the factory system of production which is looked upon as the most complete method of domination of the worker by the capitalist for he can control every activity of labour. However, it is crucial to appreciate that neither the division on labour nor the factory system were seen by Marx as important in their own right; they were only important because they represented the most developed form of treating workers as a commodity.

Alienation will not be overcome simply by increasing wages, while from some points of view this might be desirable, it will not result in freedom, but merely make the worker "a better paid slave". Similarly social reforms will not help to overcome alienation. Alienation will only be overcome with the overthrow of the capitalist system where labour stops being treated as a commodity.

❑ ❑ ❑

3

INDUSTRIAL UNREST: STRIKES AND LOCKOUTS AND THE MACHINERY FOR THE SETTLEMENT OF DISPUTES

Industrial peace is vital for national survival. We cannot afford loss of production, whether it is due to strikes or lockouts. But good industrial relations do not merely mean the absence of strikes and lockouts anymore than good health means the mere absence of disease.[1]

In a capitalist society industrial conflict is inevitable because conflicting interests predominate the industrial situations. Moreover, the present socio-economic system of unequal distribution of money and power creates social cleavages. The 'Have nots' struggle hard to gain power and consider the other party 'Haves' as holding it back from them, whereas the 'Haves', not only want to maintain *status quo* but also strive to increase power and construe the 'Have nots' as creating unnecessary bottleneck. This mutual mistrust and suspicion cause imbalance leading to industrial disputes.

Three general reasons leading to labour-management conflict may be mentioned. *First,* the demands and desires of both parties are always increasing but the means of satisfaction are limited. The demands of higher wages and more bonus by workers are never satiated as much as the desires for higher profits on the part of the employers. Higher wages means lower profits and *vice versa. Secondly*, labour is an unequal partner with capital in industry. In most of the countries industrial democracy has not been achieved and the principle of equal partnership is rarely given recognition in the individual matters in which he is vitally concerned. *Thirdly*, the maintenance and identification of the respective organisation encourage conflict. It is quite obvious that unions have to liquidate their organisations if they are in perfect harmony with the management. Thus, their very existence called for some sort of opposition, differentiation and strife. The same applies to management.

The specific causes of industrial disputes in India may be divided into two — economic and non-economic. An analysis of the history of industrial disputes in India shows economic causes have been responsible for most of the strikes in the country. In India labourers are poorly paid. The rise in price due to inflation has resulted in an increase in the cost of living. Wages have also risen to some extent by way of dearness but the rise in wages lags far behind the rise in the cost of living. Workers have to resort to strikes to get wages increased. Thus, the failure to evolve a need-based wage policy is the basic cause of industrial disputes. *Secondly*, what industrial workers want most is job security. Victimization and lack of job security have resulted in disputes. *Thirdly*, workers want fair wages and an opportunity for promotion. There is a growing feeling among workers that merit is not properly evaluated and that the jobs hold out very little chance for future advancement. This frustration breeds discontent amongst workers ultimately leading to industrial conflicts. *Fourthly*, there is a strong desire for democratic treatment on the part of labour. Workers want to be treated and respected as human beings. When he does not get proper treatment from the management naturally his feelings are injured which might disturb industrial peace. *Fifthly*, the introduction of schemes of rationalisation and automation are vehemently opposed by workers because it leads to unemployment. To prevent rationalisation, automation and VRS, sometimes the workers resort to strikes. *Sixthly*, one of the sources of friction between labour and management, as has ben pointed out by the Second Plan, is inadequate implementation and enforcement of awards and agreements. In some cases the awards have not been implemented even in the face of government's insistence on their implementation. *Lastly*, sometimes a prestige fight between labour and management results in the disturbance of industrial peace.

Industrial disputes manifest themselves in the shape of strikes on the part of workers, and lockouts on the part of employers. Lockout can be described as the antithesis of a strike. Just as a strike is a weapon available to the employees for enforcing their industrial demands, a lockout is a weapon available to the employers to persuade by a coercive process, the employees to see his point of view and accept his demands. In the struggle between labour and capital the weapon of strike is available to labour and is often used by it, so is the weapon of lockout available to the employer and can be used by him. Industrial peace is of vital importance because economic progress is bound up with it. If industrial peace is disturbed, production falls, costs of production rise and workers suffer hardship due to lack of incomes. The consumers suffer hardships since they have to pay high prices due to interruption in the supply of goods. The Government also suffers due to a fall of its revenue. As industrial unrest disturbs peace and benefits nobody, every endeavour should be taken to avoid disputes.

The right to strike and lockout is recognised in all democratic societies; reasonable restraint on the use of this right is also recognised. For safeguarding public interest, the resort to strike and lockout and in some cases, the duration of either are subject to rules and regulations, either voluntarily agreed to by the parties or statutorily imposed.

Under the Industrial Disputes Act, a distinction is made between a strike and lockout in public utilities and in other employments. A strike or lockout in the public utility service is illegal if it takes place (i) without giving to the employer a notice of strike within six weeks before striking; (ii) within 14 days of giving such notice; (iii) before the expiry of the date of strike specified in any strike notice and during the pendency of conciliation proceedings and 7 days after the conclusion of such proceedings. In industries in general, a strike or lockout is prohibited during the pendency of conciliation, arbitration or adjudication proceedings. Besides, the appropriate Government is empowered to issue an order prohibiting the continuance of any strike or lockout in respect of any dispute when a reference is made to a Court, Board or Tribunal.

TYPES OF STRIKES

(i) Primary strikes include sit-down, pen-down, tool down etc.
(ii) Secondary strikes.
(iii) Sympathetic strikes.
(iv) General strikes.
(v) Work to rule.
(vi) Wild cat strikes.

A strike may be defined as a concerted and temporary cessation of work by workers with a view to furthering or protecting their interests and rights in general and securing a fulfillment of their specific demands in particular.

Primary Strike: This is a typical form of strike. If affects the particular establishment where the workers are employed. Apart from cessation of work, it takes various other forms such as, pen down strike; 'tool down strike', 'sit-down strike', 'work to rule' etc. In these strikes workers peacefully enter the premises of the factory or the office, they generally sit down at their places of work. Clerical workers' refusal to do their work is known as pen down strike. Similarly, factory workers' refusal to work, with their tools is known as tool down strike'. Sit down strike' occurs when a group of employees interested in securing a certain objective in a particular business forcibly take possession of the premises of the owner and refuse to work. Sit-down or stay-in strike involves a tort of tresspass. Employees have a right to enter the employer's premises only for the purpose of their work.

Secondary Strike: A sympathetic strike is a secondary strike. This kind of strike is conducted out of sympathy for the cause of another group of workers who are on strike. Thus, the workers resorting to a sympathetic strike have no immediate grievance against their employer. The strikers hope to strengthen the morale of the workers for whom they are expressing their sympathy by going on a strike.

General Strike: A general strike is a simultaneous strike by a number of trade unions over a wide area. *'Bandhs'* are typical examples of such strikes. The objectives behind organising bandhs are political in nature. Whatever may be the purpose, bandhs often lead to widespread sufferings for general people. However, in some cases, workers employed in different industries in a city may call industrial strikes simultaneously without having any political objective. In contrast to general strikes, particular strikes are limited in scope and are confined to a single establishment.

Work-to-Rule/Go-slow: Under work-to rule, workers do not actually stop working rather than slowdown the pace of their work. Under work-to-rule the employees declare that they will perform their tasks strictly in accordance with the prescribed rules. In some industries, the nature of the business and the rules prescribed are such as to lead to a considerably slowing down of the pace of work if the rules are strictly followed. However, in actual practice many of the rules are often overlooked without causing any damage to the quality and quantity of work. Under such conditions if workers declare that they will work according to rules, they succeed in slowing down the pace of and reducing output without going on a formal strike. Such strikes are a common feature in post and telegraph department, banking and other Government offices. Employees resort to work-to-rule or go-slow for the fulfillment of their demands.

The legal interpretation is considered to be a serious type of misconduct and cannot be treated as a strike.

Gherao, Dharna, Hunger Strike and Picketing: Gherao involves confinement by workers of managerial personnel in their offices till their demands are fulfilled. At times persons under gherao are denied access to the toilet or kept starving for hours. This is the most brutal method of protest. A gherao is an offence, as it involves placing a person under physical constraint.

The movement of gherao started in West Bengal in 1967 and soon spread to Kerala and other parts of the country.

At one stage the movement in West Bengal became so widespread that many industries began to close and head offices of many companies shifted from Calcutta.

Ultimately, the question came up before the Calcutta High Court and the Court gave the judgment that Gherao was a cognizable offence punishable under IPC (Section 339 and 340) and offenders were liable to be arrested without warrant.

The National Commission on Labour pointed out that gheraos, apart from their adverse effects on industry and economy of the country, strike at the very root of trade unionism. Gheraos invariably tend to inflict physical duress on the person affected and endanger not only industrial harmony but also create problems of law and order. Gheraos cannot be treated as a form of industrial protest since they involve physical coercion rather than economic pressure. An amendment of the Industrial Disputes Act in 1982 included Gherao in the list of unfair labour practices on the part of workmen and their trade unions and prohibited it.

Dharna and Hunger-strike are not really strikes - they are forms of satyagraha. A dharna is a form of peaceful demonstration by a group of workers for getting their grievance redressed. They sit in front of the employer's residence or at the factory gate. A hunger strike is not a strike but a form of protest of workers to highlight their grievances.

Picketing is quite legitimate as a part of the striking process. But picketing is seldom peaceful. The employer's answer to any form of coercive picketing would be lockout.

Wild Cat Strike is a strike by a small group of workers without the backing of a union. Such workers may form an important section who are not willing to follow the union policy. Such strikes generally occur without any notice. Recognised unions dislike such strikes and disown them.

Conditions for the Success of Strikes: It is difficult to measure the success of strike for it involves both losses and gains. Gains achieved must be balanced against losses incurred. The success of strike depends on many factors. *First*, it depends upon the strength of unionism and the state of public opinion. The degree of unionism among the workers is determined by the nature of work they do and the extent of skills required for it. Thus, the miners of coal have greater unity than the young unskilled women in clothing or any other trade. If public opinion is in favour of strike action by union, the strike is bound to succeed.

Secondly, the success of strike also depends on the financial reserves of the union. Workers' union has to spend large sums of money for strike benefits to sustain strikes and publicity during the period of strikes. Larger the financial resources of the union, longer the period of strike and greater the possibility of success. Even if strike is lost the money spent in prolonging it is a good investment to show an employer how costly it is to resist the union programme.

The *third* factor on which the success of a strike depends is the phase of business cycle. In periods of industrial prosperity workers are more successful than employers while in periods of depression employers are more successful. For in periods of prosperity, the demand for labour is great and the employers will be more willing to concede to the demands of their workers and will be able to pass on additional costs in the form of additional prices, whereas in periods of depression, on the contrary, employers may be on the verge of closing their plants because of slackness is business and they cannot also pass on the additional costs.

MACHINERY FOR THE SETTLEMENT OF INDUSTRIAL DISPUTES

Where it is not possible for management and the union to resolve their conflict, a third party could be invited to intervene. A third party could perform any of the three roles i.e., conciliator, mediator and arbitrator. A conciliator acts as a facilitator when the main parties are trying to resolve the conflict. A mediator also acts as a facilitator but in addition puts forward recommendations. An arbitrator actually makes decisions to resolve the conflict.

The present machinery for the settlement of industrial disputes in India comprises *(i)* conciliation, *(ii)* arbitration and *(iii)* adjudication.

Conciliation

The aim of conciliation is to bring about a settlement in disputes through a third party intervention. The conciliation machinery can take note of a dispute or apprehend dispute either on its own or when approached by either party. It can either be voluntary or compulsory. Under the Industrial Disputed Act conciliation is compulsory in all disputes in public utility services and optional in other industrial establishments. With a view to expediting conciliation proceedings, time-limits have been prescribed — 14 days in the case of conciliation officers and 2 months in the case of a Board of conciliation. A settlement arrived at in the course of conciliation is binding for such period as may be agreed upon between the parties or for a period of 6 months and will continue to be binding until revoked by either party. The Act prohibits strikes and lockouts during the pendency of conciliation proceedings before a Board and seven days after the conclusion of such proceedings.

The performance of the conciliation machinery as indicated by statistics does not appear to be unsatisfactory. During the years 1959-'66, out of the total industrial disputes handled by the Central Industrial Relations Machinery each year, the percentage of settlement has varied between 57 and 83. The remaining disputes were settled mutually, referred to voluntary arbitration or arbitration under the I.D. Act or to adjudication.

The working of the conciliation machinery reveal certain defects such as the delays involved, the causal attitude of either party to procedure and lack of adequate background in the officer himself for understanding major issues.

The National Labour Commission pointed out that, to be more effective, the conciliation machinery should be part of the proposed Industrial Relations Commission. This will introduce important structural, functional and procedural changes in the working of the machinery as it exists today. The independent character of the Commission will inspire greater confidence in the conciliation officers. This will also, in due course, improve the attitude of the parties towards the working of the conciliation machinery.

Arbitration

Arbitration is provided by those countries which have provided for conciliation. This procedure is used after failure of conciliation. Arbitration is the means of securing a definite award on any controversial issue by referring it to a third party. Arbitration may be either compulsory or voluntary. Voluntary arbitration implies that the two parties, unable to settle their differences between themselves, agree to submit their cases to an arbitrator whose decision they agree to accept. Compulsory arbitration, on the other hand, implies that parties must submit their cases to an arbitrator and are bound to accept the award.

Voluntary arbitration as a method of settling industrial conflicts came into prominence with the advocacy by Mahatma Gandhi of its application to the settlement of disputes in the textile industry in Ahmedabad. The policies recommended in the Plans specifically mention voluntary arbitration. The I.D. Act was amended to make a provision for joint reference to industrial disputes to voluntary arbitration. The Indian Labour Conference in August, 1962 reiterated the need for a wider acceptance of voluntary arbitration. But, as against the emphasis in the Third Plan which considered that voluntary arbitration should be the normal practice in preference to recourse to adjudication, the cónference felt whenever conciliation fails arbitration will be next normal step except in cases where the employer feels that for some reason he would prefer adjudication.

To make voluntary arbitration more acceptable to the parties and to coordinate efforts for its promotion, Government has recently set up a National Arbitration Promotion Board (NAPB) with a tripartite composition. The Board will review the position, examine the factors inhibiting wider acceptance of this procedure and suggest measures to make it more popular.

The Girl Approach

Mr. V.V. Giri, who was formerly India's Labour Minister, subsequently, the President, pleaded for the settlement of industrial disputes not by compulsory arbitration, as at present, but by mutual negotiations and voluntary arbitration. This is known as 'Giri Policy' or 'Giri Approach'. If mutual negotiation fails to ensure any settlement of the disputes, the matter shall be referred to the conciliation officer. If the conciliation officers fail in their task, the disputing parties should voluntarily refer the dispute to the arbitration, the award of which is to be binding upon them. The reference to compulsory arbitration should be made during emergency and in case of public utility service. Mr. Giri also pleaded for the abolition of the Labour Appellate Tribunal on the ground that in the case of mutual settlement of disputes such institution would be unnecessary.

The Royal Commission on Labour was also against compulsory arbitration. It said that compulsory arbitration would defeat its own purpose. Instead of building peace it would create greater dissatisfaction among the workers.

Compulsory arbitration is not calculated to promote industrial peace for the following reasons :

First, compulsory arbitration is not conducive to permanent peace. Permanent peace can only be secured by mutual and voluntary agreements. So long as compulsory arbitration is present for the settlement of disputes, voluntary method cannot succeed. Mr. Giri has rightly said that unless compulsory adjudication is totally removed from the Statute Book — lock, stock and barrel — the parties, during the period of mutual negotiations, will not place all their cards on their table but will reserve the 'ace' one for the gain of compulsory adjudication. Moreover, compulsory arbitration encroaches on the workman's right to collective bargaining and deprives them of their important weapon — the strike — to redress their grievances. *Secondly*, the aware of tribunal may not be always to the entire satisfaction to the parties to the dispute. On the other hand, settlement of an industrial dispute brought about through collective bargaining is likely to be cordially accepted by both the parties. *Thirdly*, compulsory arbitration is criticized on the ground that the judges may not always be the right men to decide industrial disputes. Compulsory arbitration can only succeed if both the parties to the dispute have full confidence in the impartiality of the adjudicating body. *Fourthly*, compulsory arbitration retards the growth of trade unionism in the country and the habit of collective bargaining. It destroys the bond of unity and strength of the workers and prevents the growth of mutual understanding between employers and employees, which is essential for the maintenance of industrial peace. Compulsory arbitration is undemocratic and gives a rigidity to the economic system.

Our experience shows that compulsory arbitration has actually failed in India to bring about industrial peace. Since 1947, we have witnessed many industrial disputes which have not been settled by compulsory arbitration. Mr. Giri has rightly pointed out that compulsory arbitration stands as a policeman watching out for signs of discontent and at the slightest provocation takes the parties to the court for a dose of costly and not wholly satisfying justice.

Although the 'Giri Approach' is a step in the right direction, it should not be considered as a panacea for industrial peace. As labour is not well-organised in our country, the Government's right to interfere in industrial disputes cannot be questioned. A strike or lock-out is not a private affair. It affects the whole country. If the Government does not interfere, the life of the whole country may be paralysed. Thus, in certain cases, compulsory arbitration is needed in the country. But it may also be noted that compulsory arbitration is not the only method rather it is the last resort for the State.

Adjudication

Adjudication is only a form of compulsory arbitration and implies that the Government submits the case to an authority for adjudication and enforces its awards on the parties. The ultimate legal remedy for the settlement of an unresolved dispute is its reference to adjudication by the appropriate Government to constitute a labour court, industrial tribunal or national tribunal to adjudicate in a dispute.

It cannot be denied that during the last twenty years the adjudication machinery has exercised considerable influence on several aspects of conditions of work and labour management relations. Adjudication has been one of the instruments for improvement of wages and working conditions and for securing allowances for maintaining real wages, for standardisation of wages, bonus and introducing uniformity in benefits and amenities. It has also helped to avert many work stoppages by providing an acceptable alternative to direct action and to protect and promote the interests of the weaker sections of the working class, who were not well organised or were unable to bargain on an equal footing with the employer. As against these advantages, adjudication has many procedural defects. It is dilatory, expensive, and discriminatory. The fundamental objections are that the system of adjudication has failed to achieve industrial peace, that it has inhibited the growth of unions and has prevented voluntary settlement of industrial disputes and growth of collective bargaining.

The moot point is whether adjudication inhibits collective bargaining and is antithetical to it. The best justification for collective bargaining is that it is a system based on bi-partite agreements and as such superior to any arrangement involving third party intervention in the matters which essentially concern employers and workers. The system of adjudication, as it has been applicable in our country, did not exclude bi-partite agreements. The present trend favours the increasing adoption of collective bargaining to settle disputes and a gradual replacement of adjudication. There is a general preference for collective bargaining with a provision for arbitration in the event of failure of collective bargaining.

Preventive Measures

Certain measures have been suggested for the prevention of disputes and the promotion of good labour management relations. They may be grouped under *(i)* Joint Consultation, *(ii)* Code of Discipline. *(iii)* Grievance Procedure and *(iv)* Disciplinary Procedures.

(i) Joint Consultation: In India, Joint Consultation has assumed two forms — *(a)* Works Committees and *(b)* Joint Management Councils.

(a) Work Committees: Section 3(1)(2) of the I.D. Act provides for the setting up of a works committee consisting of representatives for management and employees, in every undertaking employing 100 or more workmen to promote measures for securing and preserving amity and good relations between the employers and workmen and to that end to comment upon matters of their common interest or concern and endeavour to compose any material difference of opinion in respect of such matters. The representatives of the workmen, whose number shall not be less than the number of the representatives of the employer, are to be chosen from among the workmen engaged in the establishment and in consultation with their registered trade union, if any. The Royal Commission on Labour suggested three ways to stabilize the industrial relationship. The *first* was to encourage the development of stable trade unions with access to those responsible for the management. The *second* was the appointment of labour officers in undertakings to look after the welfare of the workers. The *third* was the organisation of Works Committees in industrial establishment. The Commission insisted upon the importance of Works Committees as an internal machinery for the prevention and settlement of industrial disputes. The usefulness of Works Committees as a channel for joint consultation and the need for strengthening and promoting this institution was stressed in the labour policy statements in the successive plans. The encouragement given by the Government led to the setting of Works Committees in a number of undertakings; the pace of progress was, however, slow and uneven in different parts of the country. The number of works committees set up was 1,142 in 1951; it rose to 3,133 in 1965-66. But mere numbers do not count. The general feeling in the country is that the committees have not proved effective. The advisory nature of the recommendations, vagueness regarding their exact scope and functions, inter-union rivalries, union opposition and

reluctance of employers to utilize such media have rendered Works Committees ineffective.

The effectiveness of Works Committees will depend on the following factors : (1) a more responsive attitude on the part of management; (2) adequate support from unions; (3) proper appreciation of the scope and functions of the works committees; (4) whole-hearted implementation of the recommendations of the works committees and (5) proper coordination of the functions of the multiple bipartite institutions at the plant level now in vogue.

Joint Management Councils: The Joint Management Councils owe their origin in the Government's Industrial Policy Resolution, 1956. The main objectives in the establishment of JMCs were to promote cordial relations between management and workers, build up understanding and trust between them, effect substantial increase in productivity, secure better welfare and other facilities for workers and train them to understand and share the responsibilities of management. JMCs will thrive only in an atmosphere of mutual confidence and goodwill.

The essential features of the scheme for JMC are (1) the Council is entitled to be consulted on certain specified matters; (2) in some others, the management is expected to share information with the Council and (3) in a set of functions, administrative responsibilities have to be given to it. All matters such as wages, bonus and allowances which are subjects for collective bargaining were excluded from the scope of the JMC.

The Third Plan, in its approach to the problem of industrial relations, elaborated this policy of associating labour more and more with management and accepted the progressive extension of the scheme of the JMC's in all industrial undertakings found suitable for the purpose, so that, in due course of time, the scheme might become a normal feature of the industrial system.

There does not appear to be much support for the institution of JMCs in their present form. Even where the councils exist, they are ineffective and their functioning unsatisfactory in many cases. Reasons are not far to seek. Progressive employers who already have a system of consultation with their workers through a recognised union or works committees, find the JMC superfluous; managements are generally averse to having a multiplicity of joint bodies and so are union. In undertakings in which industrial relations are not cordial, JMCs cannot be expected to function satisfactorily.

In regard to the future of the JMCs, the National Labour Commission has accepted a cautious attitude. A JMC will be set up only when the system of union recognition becomes an accepted practice and both managements and unions gravitate towards greater co-operation.

(ii) Code of Discipline: The discipline to observe the rules of the game is an attitude of mind and requires, apart from legislative sanctions, persuasion on a moral plane. The socialist pattern of society requires that a worker's claim to improve his economic and social status be recognised. In their turn, workers too have to realize their responsibilities. Hard and efficient work on the one hand and avoidance of indiscipline on the other, will be needed for achieving the goal which the community desires to reach. In 1958, the Indian Labour Conference announced a Code of Discipline in industry laying down rights and obligations on all sides. The Code is intended to bind voluntarily employers and workers to settle their disputes through mutual negotiations and voluntary arbitration. The Code has been accepted since by all industries in the private sector, except the banking and the newspaper industries. The Code has also been accepted by all companies and corporations in the public sector except the Ports and Docks, Defence undertakings and Railways.

The Code enjoins on parties to refrain from taking unilateral action in connection with any industrial matter, to utilize the existing machinery for settlement of disputes and to abjure strikes and lockouts without notice and without exploring all avenues of settlement. It also discourages recourse to litigation and recommends that disputes not mutually settled should be resolved through voluntary arbitration. The employers are required to recognise the majority union in an establishment and set up a mutually agreed grievance procedure. The workers are not to resort to go-slow, coercion and intimidation. Unfair labour practices are to be given up, both by employers and workers. Both the employers and unions are required to take appropriate action against their members found indulging in action against the spirit of the Code.

The Code has had a limited success as also a limited use. The Code began acquiring rust and the parties were none too eager to take it off; they developed an attitude of indifference. As regards the future of the Code, the general feeling is in favour of giving a legal form to its important provisions regarding recognition of unions, grievance procedure, unfair labour practices and the like.

(iii) Grievance Procedure: Prompt redressal of individual grievance is essential for sustaining good labour-management relations. Absence of machinery for it leads to small grievances developing into collective disputes. Till the enactment of the Industrial Employment (Standing Orders) Act, 1946, the settlement of day-to-day grievances of workers did not receive much attention in our legislative framework. The Act has, however, limited applicability; it applies only to those establishments employing 100 or more workers and does not provide for bipartite discussion or for prompt redressal of grievances.

The model grievance procedure has successive time-bound steps, each leading to the next in case of lack of satisfaction. An aggrieved employee would first present his grievance to his immediate superior. In case the worker is di atisfied with the decision, he would go to the next higher authority. This is usually the departmental head. If the departmental head fails to give a decision within three days or if his decision is unsatisfactory, the aggrieved worker can seek relief through the 'Grievance Committee' consisting of nominees of management and workers. This Committee would communicate its recommendations to the manager within seven days of the grievance reaching it. The manager is expected to communicate his decision to the worker within three days. The worker would have a right to appeal to the higher authorities for revision of the mangers's decision. In case of failure to settle the grievance even at this stage, the union and management may refer it to the voluntary arbitration within a week of receipt of the management's final decision.

There is unanimity on the need for a statutory backing for the formulation of an effective grievance procedure which should be simple, flexible, less cumbrous and more or less on the lines of the present Model Grievance Procedure. Since delays cause frustration the settlement of an individual grievance should be prompt and quick in giving relief to the worker. It is a common saying that justice delayed is justice denied and this is certainly true in industry.

A grievance procedure whether formal or informal, statutory or voluntary, has to ensure that it gives a sense of *(i)* satisfaction to the individual worker, *(ii)* reasonable exercise of authority to the manager and *(iii)* participation to unions. The introduction of unions in the procedure is necessary, because ultimately the union will be answerable to members. It is also important that any procedure, to be effective, should be simple and have a provision for at least one appeal.

(iv) Disciplinary Procedures: The right to 'hire and fire' has been urged by employers as a remedy for improving industrial discipline. The right to hire belongs to them, but the other right has in recent years, been circumscribed. The employers contend that they should not be forced to take back a dismissed worker; they should have the option to pay compensation instead. On the other hand, workers have urged that in a labour-surplus economy, they should not be placed in a position where their right to work can be bought off by the employer through compensation. They also apprehend that the privilege claimed will be used by the employers to get rid of active union workers.

The Industrial Employment (Standing Orders) Act, 1946 and the Industrial Disputes Act, 1947 provide for *(i)* procedure to be followed in investigating cases which lead to disciplinary action and *(ii)* a substantive restraint which protects the union officials. It is only when punishment for an alleged misconduct leads to discharge or dismissal that difficulties arise.

Section 33 of the I.D. Act 1947, in regard to matters connected with disputes requires maintenance of *status quo* by the employer and restrains him from discharging or punishing a worker by dismissal or otherwise, during pendency of conciliation or adjudication proceedings in an industrial dispute, save with the permission of the authority holding such proceedings. In matters unconnected with the dispute, the employers' freedom to act is not curtailed, except that he is required to pay one month's wages to a workman before discharge or dismissal and seek the approval of his action by the concerned authority.

According to a recent Supreme Court ruling, the tribunal does not have jurisdiction to substitute its own judgement for that of management. However, the Industrial Disputes (Amendment) Bill, 1966, passed by the Rajya Sabha, provides that tribunals should have the power to set aside the order of discharge or dismissal and direct re-instatement of the workmen or give such other relief including milder punishment in lieu of discharge or dismissal as considered proper by it.

Disciplinary procedure for misconduct leading to discharge or dismissal cause dissatisfaction among workers in a country where employment opportunities are inadequate. Attempts by the State to regulate the procedures are considered by employers as undue interference in the exercise of their right to hire and fire. The present regulations in this regard do not find favour with the employers as a whole. The present law lays down specific procedures in regard to dismissal so as to ensure that there is no victimisation and that punishment is awarded on the basis of a full enquiry and established facts. It is suggested to change laws along the following lines: *(i)* standardisation of punishment for different types of misconduct, *(ii)* inclusion of a workers' representative in the domestic enquiry committee, *(iii)* having an arbitrator to give decision in a domestic enquiry, *(iv)* an adequate show-cause opportunity to workman, *(v)* presence of a union official to represent the case of a workman in the enquiry proceedings, and *(vi)* provision of a milder punishment in lieu of dismissal.

The Industrial Disputes (Amendment) Bill, 1966 as it stands, should be enacted without delay. According to it, Labour Court/Tribunal would be given appellate authority over the findings of a domestic enquiry. It gives to the aggrieved worker the right to appeal against the findings of the enquiry and empowers the Court to order reinstatement of a wrongfully dismissed or discharged workman or alter the content of the punishment in favour of the worker.

❑ ❑ ❑

4

COLLECTIVE BARGAINING: LABOUR MANAGEMENT CONFLICT

Introduction

Collective bargaining has been described as a civilized bipartite confrontation between the workers and management with a view to arriving at an agreement. This is most appropriate, for the object is not warfare but agreement. Collective bargaining institutionalizes industrial conflict just as election institutionalizes political conflict.

Definition

The ILO defines collective bargaining as: Collective bargaining may be defined as negotiations about working conditions and terms of employment between an employer, a group of employers, or one or more employers' organisations on the one hand and one or more representative workers' organisations on the other with a view to reaching agreement.

However the term collective bargaining is not a good coinage. It is opposed to individual bargaining and to that extent it has a relevance for the workers; but on the employers' side the bargaining may not often be collective in the sense that it may be bargaining between a single employer and his workmen. Again, on the workers' side where there are a number of unions, if the bargaining is with the recognised union, the process does not become collective. There is a further difficulty in India that the number of non-unionised members in a public enterprise may be larger than the number of unionised members. Yet the non-unionised workers cannot participate in the bargaining. Again it may be said that the word 'bargaining' which refers to a very common marketplace transaction between individual buyers and small time sellers is not an appropriate term to describe the process of negotiation that takes place between the worker's representatives and management to settle the terms and conditions of employment of labour.

The term collective bargaining as coined by Sydney and Beatrice Webb and given general currency in the United States by Samuel Gompers.

In unorganised trades the individual workman accepts or refuses the terms offered by the employer without communication with his fellow workman. For the sale of his labour he makes with the employer a strictly individual bargain. But if a group of workmen concert and send representatives to conduct the bargain on behalf of the whole body, the position is at once changed. Instead of the employer making a series of separate contracts with isolated individuals, he meets with a collective will and settles in a single agreement the principles upon which, for the time being, all workmen will be engaged.

There is much ignorance of people regarding the meaning of the term collective bargaining. Till now we have failed to give specific meaning to the term for many reasons. *First,* it has different meanings to different persons. *Second,* collective bargaining is dynamic, not static. It is relatively new. In terms of recognition, interpretation and extension, it is still in the process of growth. What is definitive today falls short of accurate description tomorrow. *Lastly,* specific meaning is also difficult because of the complexities implicit in the term. Collective bargaining is a function that partakes of the nature of psychology, debate, philosophy, human relations and dramatics. The proportions of each are not known, nor indeed are they fixed.

Constituent Parts

The term is a combination of two parts — collective and bargaining. Collective refers to group action as opposed to individual action. The voice of an individual worker in relation to the total working force is so insignificant that it counts for nothing. The employee has the right to leave and look for job elsewhere if he is unhappy with the present work situation. In individual capacity the employee does not hold the cards. The hazards of life make it necessary for every business to the organised in such a way that no individual is indispensable. Since he is not indispensable, the individual employee is unable to negotiate effectively on working conditions as an individual. The threat of discharge has him bound. 'Take it or leave it' is the ace of trumps in management's hands. Collective therefore means group action through representatives. On the management side, it means the management delegates at the bargaining table; on the side of workers, it means the union which may represent the local plant membership, the city-wide or region-wide or the entire national membership.

The term 'bargaining' is synonymous with haggle, dicker, chaffer or negotiate. It implies flexibility in place of fixed positions. The latter cannot be reconciled with bargaining. The implication is obvious: there is enough scope for a compromise or a mutual give and take before reaching any final settlement. The action in such a settling is fluid and mobile rather than adamant and inflexible. It will not be possible for the parties to stick to their respective guns. They have to be accommodating in their approach.

Collective bargaining is a procedure by which wages and conditions of employment of workers are regulated by agreements between the representatives of either party. It may be defined as an institutional process, the principal object of which is negotiation between company and union representatives in an attempt to reach an agreement on the terms and conditions of employment. Such negotiation normally culminates in the signing of a written instrument termed as collective labour agreement or union contract, which sets forth the terms and conditions of employment for a fixed period of time.

Collective bargaining is more than a procedure to regulate wages and employment conditions; it is more than a pay increase, an additional holiday or an improved pension plan or a grievance procedure. It is, of course, all of these and their importance can hardly be overestimated. But it is, in the fundamental sense, a process. It is a process which transforms pleading to negotiation. It is a process which permits employees' dignity as they participate in the formulation of their teams and conditions of employment. It is a process which enshrines the democratic ideal.

SALIENT FEATURES OF COLLECTIVE BARGAINING

Prof. Randle has mentioned the following features of collective bargaining.

1. It is a group action. The action is initiated through representatives of labour and management. When they sit together at the bargaining table to negotiate terms of employment, they represent certain groups.

2. It is flexible, fluid and mobile. Bargaining means haggling. It indicates a flexible position rather than a rigid attitude. It involves fluidity and ample scope for a compromise and a mutual give and take. Fixed position cannot be reconciled with bargaining. There is a constant movement and switching over to new positions during the course of bargaining.

3. It is a two-party process in the sense that it involves a number of steps. Both parties make proposals and counter-proposals. It is wrong to think that it is a charter of demands for one party only. It is a mutual give and take rather than 'take it or leave it.'

4. It is a continuous process. It provides a mechanism for continuous organized relationships between management and unions. Many people think that as soon as the negotiation of the contract is completed, the bargaining has come to an end. But this is not correct. The signing of an agreement is just the beginning. Collective bargaining goes on 365 days a year. The most important part of collective bargaining is that bargaining that goes on from day to day under the rules established by the labour agreement.

5. It is a bipartite process. The employers and the employees are the only parties involved in the bargaining process. There is no third party intervention.

6. It is dynamic. It is a relatively new concept; it is growing, expanding and changing; today it has no longer the form which it possessed yesterday. Its area has been extended, its coverage has been enlarged and its process has been altered. Previously it was emotional, turbulent and sentimental but now it is scientific, factual and systematic.

7. It is a series of checks and balances. It prescribes the rules and regulations under which the parties will operate. This is its legislative functions. The contract performs judicial function when it helps the parties in its interpretation and explanation. Its executive function lies in its enforcement as well as in provisions for discipline and grievance procedure. Its functions are closely similar to those found in democratic governments.

8. It is industrial democracy at work. Collective bargaining is industrial government through consent of the governed — the labourers. As in politics, we have greater faith in democracy than in dictatorship, so also in labour relations, we want to give an effective voice to a worker in his economic destiny. The principle of arbitrary unilateralism is giving way to self-government in industry. Basically it is democratic, joint-formulation of company policy on all matters that directly affect the worker in the plant. It is self-government in operation. It is the establishment of factory law based upon common consent.

9. It is a method for developing an industrial jurisprudence. Like the laws of the Government we have the laws of the plant. Around every plant develop different kinds of law, some emanating from the traditions unwritten or informal understandings; others composed of statutory law in the written contract, the arbitration award and other written documents. It is a method of introducing civil rights into industry, that is, of requiring that management be conducted by rules rather than arbitrary decision. Collective bargaining becomes a method of building up a system of industrial jurisprudence.

10. Collective bargaining is an art not a science. Every science has certain specific procedures and practice. It is not right to call it a science because all the attributes of collective bargaining are ever changing. It is an advanced form of human relations.

11. Collective bargaining is a 'win-win' process. Collective bargaining is not a competitive process i.e., labour and management do not compete while negotiating for the same object. It is essentially a complementary process i.e., each party needs something that the other party has, namely labour can make a greater productive effort and management has the capacity to pay for that effort and to organise and guide it for achieving the enterprise's objectives. A distinction is made between distributive bargaining and integrative bargaining. The former is a process of dividing up the cake which represents what has been produced by the joint efforts of labour and management. In this process if one party wins something, the other party will get a smaller size of it. So it is a 'Win-lose' relationship. But the better form of bargaining should be integrative i.e., a process where both the parties can win, each contributing something for the benefit of the other party. Such a process is integrative as it develops common objectives, a better understanding of each other's needs and capabilities, better respect for each other and greater commitment to the growth of the enterprise as a whole. Collective bargaining represents a win-win process.

Functions of the Collective Bargaining

The main functions of collective bargaining are:

(i) To fix the prices of labour services.

(ii) To establish a system of workers' rights in industry which may be termed as democratization of industrial relations systems.

(iii) To set up a machinery for the representation of employees in decisions affecting their individual and group interests.

Recommendations of the National Commission on Labour on Collective Bargaining

1. In the absence of arrangements for statutory recognition of unions except in some States and provisions which require employers and workers to bargain in good faith, it is no surprise that reaching of collective agreements has not made headway in our country. Nonetheless, the record of collective agreements has not been as unsatisfactory as it is popularly believed. Its extension to a wider area is certainly desirable.

2. There is a case for shift in emphasis and increasingly greater scope for and reliance on collective bargaining. Any sudden change replacing adjudication by a system of collective bargaining is neither called for nor is practicable. The process has to be gradual. A beginning has to be made in the move towards collective bargaining by declaring that it will acquire primacy in the procedure of settling industrial disputes.

3. Conditions have to be created to promote collective bargaining. The most important among them is statutory recognition of a representative union as the sole bargaining agent. The place which strike or lockout should

have in the overall scheme of industrial relations needs to be defined. Collective bargaining cannot exist without the right to strike/lockout.

Nature of Collective Bargaining

A distinct feature of the modern industrial era is collective bargaining. Collective bargaining is defined to cover the negotiation, administration, interpretation, application and enforcement of written agreements between employers and unions representing their employees setting forth joint understandings as to policies and procedures governing wages, rates of pay, hours of work and other conditions of employment. The process of collective bargaining is called bargaining because each side applies pressure on the other. Mere representation of views for consideration is not bargaining. The best known forms of pressures are threats of strikes and lockouts.

Collective bargaining is a process of voluntary agreement. Agreement comes when one or both of the parties would rather accept the other's terms than face the consequences. The term 'collective bargaining' was coined by Sidney and Beatrice Webb, the famous historians of the British Labour Movement in 1891. It is an extremely useful shorthand term for describing a continuous, dynamic, institutional process for solving problems arising directly out of employer-employee relationship.

The practice of collective bargaining has developed from the theory that the individual employee as such is an ineffective participant in the labour market. He has neither the knowledge nor the resources to take advantage of the best opportunities for disposing of his services. Under these circumstances if the worker acts in his individual capacity he is most likely to receive a lower level of compensation for his services. These limitations on the ability of an individual worker might be removed either through government interference or through collective bargaining. Government may fix up wages of an individual worker. Collective bargaining is a technique which seeks to determine the rates of pay without the arbitrary control of government. For this reason it is regarded as democratic means of achieving the compensation of human services. The practice of collective bargaining has developed mainly because individual workers have seen economic advantages to be gained in such co-operative marketing. It is through collective bargaining that workers improve their positions in the labour markets.

Collective bargaining represents a situation in which the essential conditions of employment are determined by a bargaining process undertaken by representatives of a group of workers on the one hand and of employers on the other. It is called 'collective' because employees pool their interests and bargain as a group and employers may also act as a group rather than as individuals. In collective bargaining, individual employees make the union their agent and accept the terms and conditions arranged by their representatives and employers recognise the union and its officers as the business representatives of their employees.

Prof. Slichter has rightly pointed out that collective bargaining does more than merely establish a few simple working conditions; it actually defines a broad area of civil rights in industry, by providing for both managerial and union action according to specified rules rather than arbitrary and capricious decisions. It sets up a system of 'industrial jurisprudence' in relationships between employers and employees. It thus provides an objective declaration of labour policy governing specified areas of employment relationships.

Collective bargaining is an institutional process of representations. The chief participants in collective bargaining do not act for themselves. They are representatives of their respective institutions. In collective bargaining the employer does not deal directly with his worker. He deals with an institution authorized to represent the workers for purposes of negotiating and administering the terms and conditions of employment. This representative nature of the organized union-management relationship applies to contract administration as well as to negotiation. Collective bargaining is a complex process because it involves psychology, economics, politics and poker.

Collective bargaining may occur at several levels. At the shop-floor level, it may take place between shop stewards and plant management and is called 'work place bargaining' or 'plant bargaining.' At the level of company it may take place between unions and management and has been designated as 'company bargaining'. At the level of an industry, it may take place between a union or federation of unions and an employers' association. This type of bargaining is called 'national bargaining.' In addition to 'formal bargaining,' there may be 'informal bargaining' exerting marked impact in organisational settings. Further the collective bargaining may be on *ad hoc* basis or permanent basis.

The conclusion of the collective bargaining is the collective agreement or 'labour contract.' It is the written statement of the terms and provisions arrived at by collective bargaining. It is either a mimeographed document or a small printed booklet.

From functional standpoint, collective bargaining may be regarded as an institutional process for *(i)* fixing the price of labour; *(ii)* establishing a system of industrial jurisprudence and *(iii)* providing machinery for representation of the individual and group interests of employees under the contract.

There are three kinds of collective agreements in India. *First*, there exists bipartite agreements arrived at in voluntary negotiation between the management and union. *Second*, there is collective bargaining arrangement legally designated as a 'settlement.' This type of bargaining is arrived at conciliation proceedings and is accordingly tripartite in character. *Thirdly,* there is an agreement called "consent awards." They are negotiated between the conflicting parties when a dispute is really proceeding or pending before an industrial court and thereafter included in the adjudicators' award.

Forms of Collective Bargaining

A distinction is drawn between 'conjunctive' and 'co-operative' bargaining by Chamberlain and Kuhun in their book, *Collective Bargaining.* Conjunctive bargaining deals with matters over which the aims of employers and labour diverge; essentially they are each pulling in a different direction. In the end the parties may recognise the need to compromise to enable the enterprise to continue in operation; however, the resolution of divergent interests through conjunctive bargaining provides a basis for operation of the enterprise and nothing more. The outcome of conjunctive bargaining will depend on the relative bargaining power of the parties concerned and coercion is the principal ingredient of conjunctive bargaining power.

The basis of co-operative bargaining is rather different; it is the fact that each party is dependent on the other and can achieve its objectives more effectively if it wins the support of the other. The aim of the bargain is not to persuade one party to give up something but to persuade both parties to take action so as to increase the total available. The parties approach conjunctive bargaining with the realization that the better the performance of each, the better the joint performance. Further each understands that the better the joint performance, the greater the advantage for both.

Walton and McKersie, in their book, *A Behavioral Theory of Labour Negotiations,* have drawn a distinction between 'distributive and integrative' bargaining. Distributive bargaining is similar to conjunctive bargaining; it refers to joint decisions for resolving conflicts of interests. Essentially it is a way of dividing limited resources. On the other hand, integrative bargaining is similar to co-operative bargaining; it refers to a joint problem-solving search process which results in benefits for both sides.

In Britain co-operative bargaining has ben discussed under the title productivity bargaining. The essence of productivity bargaining is that management and unions should reach an agreement about measures to be taken to increase production. The essence of productivity bargaining is an agreement on the appropriate level of wage increase and how any gains in productivity should be shared.

Productivity bargaining is the process whereby improvements in the pay and conditions of employees are negotiated in return for changes in work practices that aimed at improving the organisation's effectiveness.

Pre-requisites for Successful Collective Bargaining

Certain conditions must be satisfied for collective bargaining to be effective. These are as follows :

1. The parties must attain a sufficient degree of organisation. If the workers' organisation is weak, employers can say that it does not represent the workers and will refuse to negotiate with it. Unless the workers are able to form strong and stable unions, collective bargaining will not be successful.

2. Freedom of association. Freedom of association is essential for collective bargaining. Where there is no freedom of association, there can be no collective bargaining. Freedom of association implies workers as well as employers will have the right to form organisation of their own to protect their interests.

3. Mutual recognition. Collective bargaining cannot begin if the employers do not recognise the worker's organisation. The conflict of interests makes the two groups hostile to each other. They must recognise each other and realize that adjustment and understanding is essential for the achievement of organisational goals.

4. A favourable political climate. A favourable political climate is essential for successful collective bargaining. If the government encourages collective bargaining as the best method of regulating conditions of employment, it will be successful. Where the governments restrict trade union activities, there can be no collective bargaining.

5. Agreement must be observed by those to whom they apply. The worker's organisation must be strong enough to exercise its authority over its members. If the trade union has not power over its members, collective bargaining will not be effectively implemented.

6. Willingness to give and take. The difference between two parties can be adjusted by compromise so that agreement can be reached. Neither side should be too rigid on its demand. Their attitudes should be flexible and both sides should be ready to give up some of its demands. Unions should not rigidly insist upon unreasonable demands and should be ready to reduce its demands to come to an agreement.

7. Avoidance of unfair labour practices. Sometimes unfair labour practices are resorted to by both the employers and the trade unions. These will restrict the development of collective bargaining. Unfair labour practices should be avoided by both the sides and this will create an atmosphere of goodwill.

Collective Bargaining Vs. Individual Bargaining

Collective bargaining relate to group bargaining as opposed to individual bargaining about wages and conditions of work. Flanders has pointed out a number of differences between collective and individual bargaining. *First*, an individual bargain is about the buying or selling of a particular commodity whereas collective bargaining does not involve the buying or selling of anything; it is merely an agreement on the conditions under which buying or selling will take place. *Second*, an individual bargaining usually stipulates in detail the terms and conditions of trade, whereas in collective bargaining only the minimum terms and conditions are specified. *Thirdly*, individual bargaining is essentially a market activity (i.e. buying and selling) whereas collective bargaining is essentially a political activity (a strike or lockout is really a diplomatic use of power). *Fourthly*, because collective bargaining is a political rather than economic activity, different factors have to be taken into account, for examples, collective bargaining is frequently undertaken by professional negotiators who recognize the need to maintain relationship with the other side and therefore will not necessarily press their advantage to the full. *Lastly*, collective unlike individual bargaining is ,not restricted to a discussion of economic matters, but is concerned with other issues; it is concerned, for example, with workers' rights, the control of industry and so on.

Fox has discovered a number of errors in the above comparison of individual and collective bargaining. Flanders has argued individual bargain as the process by which the interests of buyers and sellers are finally adjusted in the act of exchange. The pitfall in this explanation is that it is assumed that bargaining always end in the act of exchange. In many instances this is not the case; instead the negotiations are broken off and no exchange is concluded. *Secondly*, Fox argues that there is a difference between the individual and the collective bargaining in that the latter, not the former, is a political process involving diplomatic use of power. Fox does not deny that collective bargaining involves the diplomatic use of power: his argument is that so does individual bargaining. *Thirdly*, Fox challenges Flander's assertion that the individual bargaining and the collective bargaining differ in that a refusal to conclude a contract is taken at face value in the former case, whereas in the latter case it is seen to be a bargaining ploy: the assumption behind a strike is not that the employees will seek a job elsewhere if the employer refuses to meet their demands but that sooner or later their present employer will be compelled to reinstate them.

THREE CONCEPTS OF COLLECTIVE BARGAINING

Prof. Neil Chamberlain, a noted Labour Economist, has made a three-fold classification of collective bargaining theories. Collective bargaining may be looked upon from three angles: *(i)* the Marketing Concept and the Agreement as a contract. The Marketing Concept views collective bargaining as a contract for the sale of labour. It is a market or an exchange relationship and is justified on the ground that it gives assurance of voice on the part of the organised workers in the matter of sale. The same objective rules which apply to the construction of all commercial contracts are invoked since the union-management relationship is concerned as a commercial one. *(ii)* The Government Concept and the Agreement as Law. The Government Concept views collective bargaining as a constitutional system in industry. It is a political relationship. The union shares sovereignty with management over the workers and as their representative, uses that power in their interests. The application of the agreement is governed by weighing of the relation of the provisions of the agreement to the needs and ethics of the particular case. *(iii)* The Industrial Relations Concept as Jointly Decided Directives. The industrial relations concept views collective bargaining as a system of industrial governance. It is a functional relationship. The union joins with company officials in reaching decisions on matters in which both have vital interests. When the terms of the agreement fail to provide the expected guidance to the parties, it is the joint objective, not the terms, which must control.

To some extent, these approaches represent stages of development of the bargaining process itself. Early negotiations were a matter of simple contracting for the terms of sale of labour. Developments of the later period led to the emergence of the governmental theory. The industrial relations approach can be traced to the Industrial Disputes Act of 1947 which established a legal basis for union participation in the management.

There are at least three different situations in which collective bargaining may take place, namely — (1) when the union is first recognised and negotiates for the first time; (2) when an old contract is about to expire or has expired or it is desired to amend it and (3) when it is necessary to adjust grievances or to resolve disagreements regarding the interpretation of a contract.

Strikes and Collective Bargaining

The right to strike is recognised in all democratic societies. Some of the important types of strikes are mentioned here. To begin with, there is economic strike which involves the use of the union's power over its members to secure economic advantages, e.g., wages, bonus, retirement benefits, sick leave etc. A general strike, on the other hand, is a strike in which all trade unions strike at the same time, thereby completely dislocating the economic life of a country. When a trade union which is not concerned in a dispute calls a strike in support of another union whose members are on strike it is known as sympathetic strike. An unofficial strike is one in which the employees of a particular firm go on strike without the support of their trade union. It is also known as outlaw strike. A flash strike (or wild-cat strike) is initiated by a group of workers in violation of a contract and without warning. A sit-down strike is one in which strikers do not leave their place of work but remain in the plant and in control of production facilities. A slow-down strike, also known as 'go-slow,' is not really a strike in the usual sense as workers do not cease work. Workers do not leave their work, they merely limit output while remaining on the job.

Since the right to strike is the ultimate weapon in collective bargaining, the two go together like love and marriage. Although the strike does not inevitably accompany bargaining, its availability as an instrument of pressure is an important condition of collective bargaining. Unions resort to it when all other techniques have failed. Management and union negotiators reach agreement on the terms proposed by one party are considered to be more advantageous by the other party than disagreement on those terms. Since a strike hurts management by stopping production and workers by cutting off their wages, neither party is apt to reject terms proposed by the other without serious considerations. According to the proposals of the other party usually involves a cost, but so does a strike which may be brought on by refusing to accede. The two costs must be balanced.

As long as strike threatens greater loss to at least one of the parties if it disagrees than if it agrees with the other's demands, there is reason for them to settle. Without such a threat they may continue to disagree indefinitely and never bargain seriously. The right of management to disagree to union terms in the face of strike threats is quite as important as the right of unions to use strikes to gain concessions. Thus, though collective bargaining need not always result in strikes, the possibility or threat of strikes is a necessary condition for collective bargaining. As a matter of fact, public policy has encouraged collective bargaining partly in the hope that the burden of strikes and their accompanying losses might be reduced.

Techniques of Collective Bargaining

Collective bargaining is a device of selling the services of union members in the best possible market and at the highest possible price. Although trade unions insist on preserving the free enterprise system and maintaining competitive controls in labour markets, many of the techniques used in collective bargaining introduce monopolistic factors into that process. Unions hope to develop and maintain a monopoly of available labour supplies. Since unions have initiated and advanced collective bargaining and since management has to offer little in the way of a positive programme of demands, unions have done more to shape bargaining techniques than have managements.

Standardisation is one such technique. It means the establishment of a uniform minimum price for each class of work. Unions insist on the point that bargaining can be effective only if workers in any one job are guaranteed a specified minimum wage per piece or per month. The second technique is restriction of membership. Unions seek to limit numbers of members in the union and to limit employment to unionists. Under open union practice, anyone who is acceptable to the employer is allowed to join the union. But under closed union practice, unions set such severe conditions for membership that very few can qualify. As a result, unions have limited the available labour supply in a given occupation to the present members of the union. Unions may restrict membership by setting initiation fees at a high level, or by imposing limitations based o sex, religion or nationality. The closed union practice is anti-social and an undemocratic device. Thirdly, attempts are made to ensure that only unionists get available work and that employers do not have a choice as to hire union members or non-members. To attain this end jurisdictional limitations are imposed. Jurisdictions may be either industrial or geographic. Under the system of industrial jurisdiction all work of a certain type are allocated to the members of a certain union and under the system of geographic jurisdiction a specific area is defined in which only the members of a specified local union may be used for such work. These limitations are imposed as a protection against the competition of other unionists either in different trades or in the same trade in other localities. Union power and control in the enforcement of jurisdictional limitations is frequently exerted through picketing. By putting pickets at the entrance of the offending establishment the union makes the public aware of the union's case. By providing pickets the union prevents the employer from carrying on his normal business activities. The major aim of the pickets is to prevent union members and others from working, thus controlling the supply of labour.

In all collective bargaining the unions seek recognition which means an agreement with the employer by which he recognises the union as the representative of the employees. There are many forms of recognition. The simplest form of recognition is that in which the union is recognised as the representative of union members only.

The absence of any recognition is open shop. Under the open shop no distinction is made between union members and those workers who are not members. No collective bargaining exists because the employer does not recognize any union as representative of employees. Under exclusive bargaining agent system management recognizes the union as agent for its members and further agrees that it will recognize no other union as the bargaining agent. In the preferential shop form of recondition the management will provide first chance for employment to union members. Under maintenance of membership form of recognition all employees who are members of the union must maintain their standing in the union and if they fail to maintain their standing in the union they are discharged. Under the union shop form of recognition, all employees must be members of the union. The management may employ non-unionists, but they must join the union when they become employees. Under the agency shop all employees in the bargaining unit must pay dues to the union recognised as the bargaining agent although they do not have to join that union. Under the Closed shop, only union members are employed. This form of recognition provides the greatest union control of labour supplies.

Sometimes unions seek to control or limit the output of their members with a view to putting pressure upon the management. Another collective bargaining device through which the union seeks to limit supplies of labour is the boycott. Unions refuse to work for the employers who do not come to terms with the union.

Collective Bargaining Process

The collective bargaining process provides a platform to establish a common set of concepts and attitudes for both the parties. Collective bargaining is a rule-making and goal-directed process. Yoder identifies two major phases of collective bargaining process — the negotiation phase and the contract administration phase. The negotiation phase involves the bargaining and establishment of contract terms while the contract administration relates to application and interpretation of these terms.

Negotiation is a process of advancing proposals, discussing and criticizing them, explaining and exploring their meaning and effects, seeking to secure their acceptance and making counter-proposals or modifications for similar evaluation. Negotiation may be positive or negative. In positive negotiation, the management tends to advance its own proposals while in the negative procedure it waits to see what the union will propose.

Contract administration relates to putting the signed agreement into effect. Union officials and the industrial relations officers should interpret the items to all participants in the organisation.

Collective bargaining forms a rational process where the parties are persuaded to change their original positions in the light of the facts and arguments given by the opposite group. Attempts are made to resolve differences of opinion by a thorough analysis and request for logical argument.

According to Dunlop and Healy, collective bargaining process involves three elements — bargaining demands, the deadline or threat of strike or lockout and changing positions and reaching agreement. Contract demands made by either group are usually initiated by several individuals including union members and heads of the departments. Frequently, conflicting issues are settled through a threat of strike or lockout at the last minute. It may be due to the fact that both the groups were far apart at the beginning of negotiations. The threat of strike or lockout compels each group to re-examine its offers of settlement. The deadline also tends to remove the element of bluff used in negotiations. Finally, the groups starting at divergent points should change their positions if they intend to reach an agreement. Changing position forms the heart of the collective bargaining process. At long last, the memorandum of agreement is reduced to contract language.

Major Clauses in Collective Agreements

The most frequently included subjects of collective agreement are given below.

Wage Clause: The wage clause is usually the most important and the most complicated clause in the agreement. The clause includes the basic wage policy and specific wage agreements. If piece rates are to be paid, the system to be followed, must be clearly indicated. An escalator clause, if it exists, will appear here.

Recognisation or Union Security Clause: The recognisation clause defines the status to be given to the union throughout the life of the agreement. It may provide for a closed shop, union shop or any other variant of the union security.

Hours of Work Clause: Many agreements include clauses dealing with working hours. Such clauses also deal with various shift arrangements, time off allowed for meal, provisions for over-time pay, provisions for holiday and related details.

Seniority Clause: Seniority clause indicates the system of seniority to be followed, the method of calculating seniority and the importance of seniority rights in the matter of promotion, selection of vacation periods, choice of shifts and other privileges.

Other Clauses: List of clauses mentioned above is not exhaustive. Many other subjects, e.g., grievance procedure, leaves of absence, welfare funds, shop rules, training of apprentices, disciplinary action, etc. may appear.

Advantages of Collective Bargaining

At the beginning unions were considered as necessary evils but in course of time a rationale for collective bargaining emerged which has been accepted by all. It is argued that collective bargaining is a good anti-cyclical measure. It is argued that the depression of the thirties was caused partly by the workers' inability to organise and bargain collectively and thus maintain their wage levels.

Secondly, collective bargaining has been considered an extension of democracy to the work-place. According to Sumner Slichter collective bargaining establishes a system of 'Industrial jurisprudence.' Industrial jurisprudence involves the function of collective bargaining as a method of introducting civil rights into industry.... of requiring that management be conducted by rule rather than by arbitrary decision. Rules made jointly by employers and workers are much better than those unilaterally imposed by employers on unions or by unions on employers. Moreover, this form of rule making is considered superior or Government imposed rules because it is more flexible. The people who experience the problems are in a better position than any one else to make the rules governing those problems.

Thirdly, the idea of participatory democracy has been accepted by many employers as a force for social stability. By participating in the formulation of working rules and joining political organisations, workers gain a stake in the system. For this reason many employers support efforts to extend the so-called 'free' labour movements to the developing countries. They feel that collective bargaining will buffer the spread of revolutionary in these countries. It is contended that revolutionaries do not make much progress in countries with advanced collective bargaining system.

Finally, collective bargaining is regarded as an equitable system because it equalizes power between workers and employers. Government helped employers gain power by permitting them to form corporate type of business activities. So, it is only equitable to protect workers in their right to organise and bargain collectively.

Disadvantages of Collective Bargaining

Collective bargaining generates many problems. *First*, there is the problem of strikes. The strike creates a dilemma for those who have accepted the institution of collective bargaining because it is difficult to have collective bargaining without the right to strike. At the same time strikes can inflict considerable damage on the public. Much attention has been given to the problem of how to maintain collective bargaining while preventing the damage that might be inflicted upon by the strikes. No effective solution has been found as yet.

The *second* limitation of collective bargaining is that since it is based on power and conflict it does the most for the people who need it least. The stronger workers in the labour market could protect their incomes because of their skills while the weakest workers in the workforce have very limited ability to form unions and hence unable to gain the benefits of collective bargaining.

Thirdly, collective bargaining does not contain sufficient safeguard for the public interest, which might be ignored by collusion between strong unions and employers to fix prices. In the USA where collective bargaining is a feature of industrial relations, it is claimed that it has impeded the economy's growth, imparted an upward drift to the general price level and periodically imperilled the nation's health and safety.

Effects of Collective Bargaining

What effect has collective bargaining had on the income of union members? Has collective bargaining enabled unions to obtain higher incomes for their members than would otherwise have been the case? If one looks at the overall share of the national income obtained by wage-earners then the evidence is less than clear. A number of authors have argued that over the century the proportion of national income allocated to wages has changed little. However, this does not necessarily lead to the conclusion that collective bargaining has had no effect. For example, it might be argued that without collective bargaining by unions the share of the national income devoted to wages would have dropped.

Collective bargaining is now widely accepted by the most industrialised nations. There are the following reasons for the acceptance of collective bargaining.

Firstly, collective bargaining is the means by which a 'normative system' is created for regulating industrial conflict and ensuring that it is kept within acceptable bounds. Collective bargaining does not prevent industrial conflict but it provides a forum for discussion and a means for systematic social change in the working code governing management-men relations.

Secondly, collective bargaining enables parties to a dispute to view the situation dispassionately than might otherwise be the case; it allows time to pause for thought and review the consequences of possible courses of action.

Thirdly, collective bargaining absorbs energy which would otherwise be more destructively directed. Thus, Harbison has argued that collective bargaining provides a 'drainage channel' for worker dissatisfaction.

Lastly, collective bargaining by providing a forum for meetings between management and unions, can help to facilitate improved relations and gradual change. It is argued that by collective bargaining the frozen fruits of industrial conflict are thawed. If the representatives of management and labour meet regularly for negotiations, gradual changes of social structure replace the tendency towards revolutionary explosions and civil war.

❑ ❑ ❑

5

WORKERS' PARTICIPATION IN MANAGEMENT : LABOUR MANAGEMENT COOPERATION

Introduction

The workers' participation in management is a mechanism through which workers have a say in the decision making process of an enterprise.

Preston and Post described three stages of managerial development which they refer to as the three managerial revolutions. The *first* managerial revolution was the appearance of management itself as a specialised function within 'hierarchical organisations'. The *second* revolution – professionalisation – was encouraged by the growth in industrial organisations and the complexity of managerial tasks. The *third* and contemporary revolution is participation'.

Industrial democracy means that workers and employers should feel that in their work they will be evaluated and respected as free persons of equal value within the framework of the rules and natural order and discipline that will always be needed in a well regulated industry. In an atmosphere of cooperation, mutual respect and tolerance, they should have the natural right to influence conditions and measures that affect them directly and the whole community inside the undertaking.

Democracy is essential to free human beings. They must have democracy in all aspects of their lives and above all in the place where they earn their livelihood. With the growth of industrial democracy, the pendulum has been swinging from management prerogatives to labour participation.

Participation means an act of taking part. It may be defined as taking part in a sharing of power and status between the managers and the workers. It also relates to a style of management enabling workers to participate in decision making process and exert some influence over the policy of the organisation. It forms a type of social co-operation between labour and capital and involves a change in attitudes.

Participation is not merely to protect and further one's interests but is also a system of checks and balances on both the groups which requires a great sense of responsibility and educated awareness to cope with the several aspects of the participative system.

In a factory there are two groups of people – managers and workers – with two different sets of functions to perform. Modern factory system has divorced managerial and operative functions. Workers' participation is an attempt to bridge the gap by authorising the workers to participate in managerial functions.

There is some confusion about the concept of workers' participation. In the informal sense, workers are participating in industry all the time. In most of the industrial enterprises workers can communicate with management through their unions. Suggestions schemes under which any worker can make any suggestions for the improvement of the working system have been installed in most of the industrial units in India. Some thinkers are of the view that collective bargaining itself is a form of workers' participation. According to Allan Flanders, collective bargaining is a process of power relationship. By this process organised labour penetrates into areas which are regarded traditionally as management functions.

TYPES OF PARTICIPATION

In the broadest possible sense worker participation means wider involvement and participation by a company's employees in the decision making process of that organisation. Several important points are implied in the concept. *First*, participation in decision-making is meant to include all employees : manual workers, middle-management and clerical staff and not simply the unskilled worker on the shop floor as is frequently assumed. *Second*, there is an important distinction between what Strauss and Rosenstein term immediate and distant participation. Immediate participation refers to workers' involvement in the day-to-day decision-making process of their work-group, be it on the shop-floor or among clerical workers in the office. This form of participation has manifested itself in the development of autonomous work groups, job enrichment schemes, work restructuring etc. – in this sense, worker participation in management is seen as a means of improving the quality of the worker's life on the job. Distant participation, on the other hand, refers to the process of including company employees at the top management level of the organisation, so that they may be involved in decision-making on long-term policy issues (e.g. investment, employment etc.).

The amount of participation depends upon its scope, degree and extent. The scope of participation refers to the range of managerial functions in which workers take part. By degree of participation is meant how far workers influence managerial decisions, on a scale extending from complete unilateral control by management at one end to complete unilateral control by workers at the other. Extent of participation is measured by the proportion of workers who take part, on the one hand and by how much they participate, on the other. For example, indirect participation through representatives involves less participation by individuals than could occur in direct participation.

Forms

Participation may assume two forms – ascending and descending. In ascending participation, workers may be given an opportunity to influence managerial decisions at higher levels through their elected representatives to worker's councils or the board of the enterprise. In descending participation, they may be given more power to plan and make decisions about their own work. They may participate through collective bargaining.

Methods

Participation may assume two different methods. *First*, participation may be individual. If a worker is employed in an undertaking he inevitably takes part in its operations. He can influence some of the decisions to be reached by making suggestions about them. However, workers' participation in decisions within undertakings usually refers to collective participation.

Workers' participation in management can be achieved by *(i)* information sharing, *(ii)* consultation, *(iii)* association, *(iv)* making workers share-holders and *(v)* joint decision-making. The first form does not allow employees to exercise any influence over managerial decision-making but it does give them the right to know about the affairs of industry in which they are employed. In the consultative form, participation entitles workers to be consulted by the management on certain matters before decisions are taken but the management has the right to accept or reject the advice. The *third* method of involvement of workers in industries is to make them shareholders in the company. This may be done by allotting shares to workers and inducing them to buy equity shares. The motive behind the scheme is that workers could take more interest in the company for which they are working. *Lastly*, the highest level of participation comes when the parties involved take decisions together and administer them jointly.

Levels of participation

Workers' participation is possible at all levels of management. Broadly speaking there are four levels of participation. At the initial level, participation is informative and associative which ensures that workers are able to receive information and offer their opinions on matters of general economic importance. At the next level, it is consultative participation which means that on matters affecting their welfare, the workers share their views with the management. At the next higher level, there is administrative participation which ensures that workers should have a greater share in the discharge of managerial functions. At the highest level there is participation in the decision-making process.

Features

1. Workers participation is now a global movement. A combination of social, cultural, political, economic and industrial pressures have created a world-wide demand for greater participation of workers in management.

2. The concept of participation is viewed by different people differently. There are people who think that workers' participation is the tool for solving most labour management relations problems. People use the term as a synonym for industrial democracy.

3. There are others who think it is a method for uprooting the present system of ownership and management of the economics.

4. Some persons are there who consider it as a tool of applied psychology to be used to counteract the dehumanisation of industrial work.

5. The idea of participation as an alternative to the capitalist pattern of management has emerged in response to *(a)* the threats from the emerging centres of countervailing power, particularly the organised labour, and *(b)* the demands of continuous production during the world wars when managers tried strategies to insure uninterrupted industrial activity.

6. Other factors which led to the growth for participation are the growth of public enterprises, experiments of industrial psychology (which proved that a person works better when he wants to work rather than when he is forced to work), development of scientific management which encouraged close cooperation between labour and management for increasing the productivity of the enterprise and the positive role of the ILO for a close collaboration between employers and employees.

Evolution

Workers' participation in management has a long history of evolution. It began as an ideological concept and emerged as concrete social reality mostly through political measures. From the beginning of industrial revolution social thinkers were concerned with the status of workers in the factory. It was argued that in order to prevent the exploitation of workers by the employers, the former should have as much power as the latter. In Europe, Compte and Owen advocated workers' participation in management with a view to securing social justice. Karl Marx and other extremists advocated unilateral control of the enterprise by the workers. But this is possible only under the socialist system. It was, however, realised that the complete control of industry by workers was neither feasible nor desirable in democracies. Therefore persons such as Webb and Cole thought that participation of workers in management would be sufficient to meet the needs of social justice.

The concept of workers' participation has its roots in the human relations movement in the domain of industrial and business organisations. There was acute social unrest in Western countries because labour was looked upon as a 'Commodity of Commerce'. This unrest finally impelled industrialists to recognise that labour is not a commodity to be sold off at an arbitrary price, he is not a cog in the machine but a human being. Having a capacity to grow and accept the responsibility of a citizen, a worker can participate in the affairs of the industry.

In the formal sense, the beginnings of the workers' participation may be traced to the Joint Committees set up in the UK, Works Committes in France, Works Councils in Germany and Collective Bargaining in USA during the First World War. Even in former Soviet Russia, a form of participation described as "socialist emulation" operated over a wide area.

In India the first attempts at participation were made in the early years of the 20th century. Some industrialists in Calcutta and Ahmedabad had formed Works Committee even before the First World War but these efforts made no progress.

Mahatma Gandhi was the most powerful spokesman of participation in the early years. His philosophy of trusteeship argued for participation. In his view workers and owners were equal partners in industry. He wanted the capitalists to be the trustees and not owners till workers assumed full control.

The first attempt at introducing participation through law was made soon after Independence. The Government took the initiative to popularise workers' participation in management. The major step in this direction was the enactment of the Industrial Disputes Act 1947 which requires the employer to constitute a Works Committee. Works Committee attempted to involve workers in a limited way to discuss work related issues. The main aim of these committees was to promote measures for securing and preserving amity and good relations between employers and workmen. The functions of Works Committee were not clearly defined. Participation was mainly limited to aspects of welfare management.

India is committed to establish a socialist pattern of society through the system of workers' participation in management which has been an important part in its labour policy since independence.

In 1958, Joint Management Councils were introduced. JMC's were entrusted with administrative responsibility for various matters relating to welfare, safety, vocational training, preparation of holiday lists etc. They were to be consulted in matters of change in work operation, amendment of formulation of standing orders, rationalization etc. to encourage smooth work operations and enhance productivity. JMCs did not receive much support from unions or managements.

It was alleged that JMCs and Works Committees appeared similar in scope and function and that multiplicity of bipartite consultative bodies served no purpose.

Subsequent to the nationalisation of banks, under the Nationalised Banks (Management and Miscellaneous Provisions Scheme 1970) the Government required all nationalised banks to appoint employee directors to their boards, on representing workmen and the other representing officers. The term of an employee director was to be three years. This was the first major attempt to place representatives of workmen on the boards of public sector corporations.

Rationale for Participation

Behavioural sciences contributed to the growth of workers' participation in management through their models, Prof. Kurt Lewin spoke of two different styles of leadership – authoritarian and democratic. The members belonging to the authoritarian group function in response to clear and specific orders from the leader. In the democratic group, the members together decide what they would do and how they would organise themselves. It is found, in the authoritarian group, the moment the leader turns his back, the productivity declines. In contrast, the presence of leader makes little difference in the democratic group. It is clear that members subjected to authoritarian leadership works only under supervision.

Overall satisfaction was also highest in the democratic group. These findings signify the importance of participative management. Hawthorne experiments also placed a high value on cooperation and partnership between employers and employees. This emphasis has been reinforced by the findings of the Michigan School.

The behavioural theories emphasise that participation increases satisfaction which in turn improves the output. Theory Y is consistent with participative management while Theory X aligns with more traditional autocratic style of managing people. In terms of motivation hygiene theory, participative management could provide employees with intrinsic motivation by increasing opportunities for growth, responsibility and involvement in the work itself.

Widespread alienation, dissatisfaction and lack of commitment in the work force, management theorists looked to the solution of these problems. Participation is assumed to increase morale, improve group cohesion and commitment to work. These behavioural theories contributed to the growth of participative management worldwide.

Peter Drucker has observed that traditional system of organisation based on the concept of authority and responsibility – a system of command – is no longer suited to the contemporary situation wherein highly educated people are entering workforce in larger members.

MODELS OF WORKERS' PARTICIPATION

1. Collective Bargaining Model : In theory collective bargaining represents a different form of participation. Collective bargaining provides to the management and the workers the right, through collective agreements, to lay down certain rules for the formulation and the termination of contract of employment as well as the conditions of service in an establishment. Collective bargaining has been used as an important method of influencing managerial decisions.

2. Works Councils Model : Works Councils are exclusive bodies of the employees. There may be one council for the entire organisation or a hierarchy of works councils from shop floor to the staff board. Members are elected by the employees of the respective sections. They have different functions in the management of an enterprise. Here is a basic assumption of a harmony of interests on key issues.

3. Joint Management Councils Model : These are joint bodies comprising the representatives of the management and employees. Their functions may range from decision making on some issues to merely advising the management as consultative bodies. In India JMCs are commonly used forms of workers' participation in management. Mostly their role is advisory and consultative, with decision making being left to the top management.

4. Workers' Self-Management Model : This model is characterized by a substantial degree of workers' participation on the main decision making bodies, completed with either a system of workers' ownership or the right to use the assets of the enterprise. A system of self-management in Yugoslavia is based on this concept.

OBJECTIVES

The objectives of worker participation in management may be broadly classified into four groups.

1. Ethical : In an ethical context, participation in decision-making is designed to promote individual development or fulfilment, in accordance with a conception of human rights and dignity to which the Universal Declaration of Human Rights (1948) gives the most widely publicised expression : "All human beings are born free and equal in dignity and rights. They are endowed with reason and conscience and should act towards one another in a spirit of brotherhood. Everyone is entitled to realisation of the economic, social and cultural rights indispensable for his dignity and the free development of his personality". This general proposition that all workers, as human beings, must be enabled to seek full development of their personality, has been elaborated in various doctrinal statements like national constitutions, programme of trade union movements and management statements. For example, the Advisory Committee set up by the Government of Jamaica defined worker participation as the extension of the individual's human rights at the work place and stressed that management styles should bring the worker recognition, treatment and attention as a human being rather than as a mere statistical unit of production. In support of this ethical approach it is pointed out that the workers who contribute to the production of goods and services – sometimes at the risk of their lives – are entitled to have their point of view taken into account as regards its operations.

The above humanitarian ideas are reinforced by the notions of equity and social justice now current in both the industrialised and the developing countries although such notions have often been neglected during the process of industrialisation and in proposed models of industrial organisation and management.

2. Socio-political : Socio-political objectives vary widely and are often presented under the label of 'industrial democracy'. Since in a democratic system workers have the same political rights as other citizens, it seems odd that they should not be entitled to a say, within the undertakings where they are employed, in decisions which directly concern them. A Swiss trade union writer states that political democracy is incompatible with the absence of democracy in economic life : a citizen cannot be regarded as sufficiently matured for political democracy and simultaneously denied democratic rights in economic life. Accordingly, those who wish to have the workers participate in decisions within undertakings and to strengthen political democracy by applying its principles in the economic field, have often declared their intention of changing the state of affairs described above Sometimes, the objective of making the workplace more democratic by way of worker participation in decisions at that level is part of a broader objective, namely to transform the whole economy. Industrial democracy is regarded as part of the general process of democratisation. In India the Second Five Year Plan which was directed to the establishment of a socialist society, stated that a socialist society was based not only on cash incentives but also on the idea of serving the community and its willingness to recognise such service; so individual workers must be induced to feel that in their own way they were helping to build a State directed towards progress. Consequently the introduction of industrial democracy was a prerequisite for the establishment of a socialist society. The Government of Jamaica states that the introduction of worker participation in a mixed economy can be called a logical development on the road to social equality, social justice and the total democratisation of power. Thus, in the social sense, workers' participation means the attainment of a measure of equality with the management group in functions where they have to work together and in the political sense, it means sharing in power in the decision-making process.

3. *Economic* : Economic objectives relate directly or indirectly to increasing the efficiency of the undertaking. By associating the workers with the decisions taken, it is hoped to improve the quality and quantity of output and the utilisation of labour, raw materials and equipment as well as the introduction of new techhiques. There is a growing awareness of the fact that the energy of those who actually do the work is not sufficiently used with a view to improving industrial organisation and methods. Through participation it is hoped to reduce the areas of conflict between labour and management to improve labour relations. Possible contributions to efficient use of human resources may come about for the following reasons :

- workers have ideas which can be useful;
- effective communications upwards are essential to sound decision-making at the top;
- workers may accept decisions better if they participate in them;
- workers may work harder if they share in decisions that affect them;
- workers may work more intelligently, if through participation in decision-making, they are better informed about the reasons for and the intention of decisions;
- workers' participation may foster more cooperative attitude amongst workers and management, thus raising efficiency by improving team work and reducing the loss of efficiency arising from industrial disputes;
- workers' participation may act as a spur to managerial efficiency.

4. *Psychological* : Workers' participation in management has a favourable impact on the behaviour of the workers. It instills a sense of belonging to the organisation in the minds of workers. It gives them self-respect. They feel dignified and behave in a responsible manner because now they are partners in decision-making process. These are also psychological objectives to be realised by the organisation.

EXPERIENCE IN OTHER COUNTRIES

United Kingdom

The beginning of workers' participation in management, in the formal sense, may be traced to the joint committees set up in the UK during the First World War. These joint committees were advisory in character and their functions included considerations and discussion of changes to be effected in methods of production, welfare, safety, training and personnel problems other than the problems of wages. In industries with strongly organised trade unions, the influence of these committees was less significant because collective bargaining was a more effective arrangement. However, committees play an important role in the unorganised sectors of the industry. In the recent years trade unionists are being appointed on the board of directors of nationalised industries.

In the USA, the workers' participation is not a popular movement. In the context of US industrial relations scenario, collective bargaining is the most effective way in which workers influence the decision-making process.

Even in former Soviet Russia, there was a developed form of workers' participation, described as 'socialist emulation' which operated in farms and factories.

Yugoslavia

Systems based on self-management represents the most far-reaching attempts at direct involvement of the workers in decision-making and management responsibilities. Self-management can be defined most simply as the management of undertakings by their workforce. This system is based on general legislation applicable to undertakings in the sector in which management – but no ownership-rights have been transferred to the workers. The right to participate is granted to the whole of the workforce, whether manual or non-manual workers; those who leave the undertaking do not retain any management rights. The workforce usually exercises its rights through an elected body often known as a 'workers' council' though in recent years some self-management systems have shown a trend to give a greater importance to workers' assembly or an assembly of workers' representatives. The competence of self-management bodies extends to all decisions taken in the undertaking. Self-management bodies have the right to dispose partly or wholly of the profits of the undertaking.

The Yugoslav system is certainly the best known example of self-management. Self-management was introduced in the country by a law of 1950. The Yugoslav self-management system was based on 'social ownership' as distinct from state ownership. The main self-management bodies at the workplace are the workers' assembly and the workers' council. In 'non-economic' establishments the latter body is simply called the council. In line with the aim of developing more direct participation of workers in self-management, "workers' assemblies" or general meetings, now have greater importance. They take the most important general policy decisions including the decision on the distribution of the net income of the production unit. The assembly may appoint committees but in most cases these committees have only a consultative role.

The number of members on the workers' council must be proportionate to the size of the workforce concerned. Its composition, powers and functions are laid down by internal by-laws and regulations. As regards day-to-day management, the workers' council has quite broad powers of supervision and even of decision and is responsible for seeing that the workers are properly informed.

The workers' council generally appoints an executive committee and often various specialised sub-committees to which it delegates consultative powers or powers of decision in clearly defined areas of competence. The assembly is not allowed to delegate its main powers of decision to the workers' council. It is the workers' council which elects the general manager and other top managers for renewable terms of four years. The council has the right to terminate their appointments.

One of the main reforms introduced from 1956 onwards in order to bring the self-management bodies closer to the individual worker consisted in decentralising management within the undertaking as much as possible by setting up workers' councils with the right to elect their own managers at the level of the workshop or department.

In one economic unit, a self-management structure exists at three levels: that of the unit taken as a whole; that of its different factories and that of its workshops or departments. The respective terms used at each of these levels are 'composite organisation of associated labour', 'organisation of associated labour' and 'basic organisation of associated labour'.

In a self-management system, the role of socio-political organisations such as the party and the trade unions has sometimes been questioned. In practice, this role is quite important. Yugoslavia does not have a plurality of political parties. Trade unions have the duty of facilitating the functioning of the self-management bodies. They have the right to arrange for the conclusion of self-management agreements. The Associated Labour Law of 1976 gives them extensive disciplinary powers, not only to conduct hearings before disciplinary committees at the workplace but also to initiate disciplinary proceedings in the interest of the personnel, against a worker whose unsatisfactory work or absenteeism is damaging the unit of which he is a part. Yugoslavia provides a good example of the dynamic character of participation in decision-making.

Trade Union Attitude

Most of the unions accept the concept of unilateral participation, because it anticipates trade union control over the economy on behalf of the working class. Trade unions do not accept joint management on the ground that it does not represent either a form of industrial democracy or participation in economic decision-making.

Under joint management system, management is free in making the economic policy of the enterprise. It has the need to listen to workers and to take union attitudes into account to minimize chances of employee non-co-operation in carrying out the decision made outside of the joint bodies. The union approach to the actual forms of workers' participation ranges from total rejection to conditional acceptance. Many trade unions ignore joint participation on the ground that it does not improve the essential position of workers in production and that it gives benefits only to employers. Trade unions which accept participation do so conditionally in the hope that such participation will be transformed into class struggle and not to some higher form of class co-operation.

The aim of joint management is to reduce industrial tensions and to entrust workers with the responsibility of improving production without taking part in the decisions on production.

Government Attitude

Relations between labour and management set the tone of social relationships in an industrial society. With the progress of industrialisation several attempts have been made by the government of India to democratize these relations and thus, extend democracy to the workplace. Industrial democracy has been conceived as an end in itself as well as a means to the better health and greater effectiveness of industrial organisations. The institutions of works committee and joint management council were some of the early steps taken by the country in its stride towards this goal.

Government's viewpoint in relation to workers' participation in management was first stated in the Industrial Policy Resolution. "In a socialist democracy, labour is a partner in the common task of development and should participate in it with enthusiasm. There should be joint consultation and workers and technicians should, wherever possible, be associated progressively in management. Enterprises in the public sector have to set an example in this respect". The Resolution further declares that, "for the peaceful evolution of the economic system on democratic basis it is essential that workers' participation in management should be accepted as a fundamental principle and an urgent need. In course of time management cadres should arise out of the working class itself. This will greatly help to promote social mobility which is an important ingredient of a socialist system".

The relevant references in the Five Year Plans show that Government's attitude towards workers' participation in management gradually took firm roots. The Second Plan sought to translate the spirit of this part of the Government's Resolution in the statement on labour policy. In doing so, it showed a measure of caution as much as it indicated the criteria against which the success of the experiment should be assessed. When the Second Plan was published the working of arrangements similar to the JMCs within the country was almost unknown. International experience which could be relied upon was also inadequate. For studying such experience as was available, a Study Team was sent to some European countries. The report of the team underlined a non-statutory approach and that too, on an experimental basis, to implement the recommendations in the Plan but warned against the dangers of copying from the more advanced industrial communities. The 15th Session of the ILO, in accepting this recommendation of the team, appointed a tripartite committee to work out details of the suggested experimental scheme. The present scheme of JMCs is based on the draft prepared by the two tripartite national seminars on the subject held in 1958 and 1960. The main objectives in the establishment of JMCs were to promote cordial relations between management and workers, build up understanding and trust between management and workers, effect substantial increase in productivity, secure better welfare and other facilities for workers and train them to understand and share the responsibilities of management. A requirement, which was considered basic to the establishment of the JMC, was emphasised in the first of these seminars (1958) in the following language : The seminar was convinced that Joint Councils will thrive only in an atmosphere of mutual confidence and goodwill. It took note of the gradual improvement in the attitude of employers and trade unions towards each other and felt that there was a need for continuous educative work both on the side of labour and management.

The Third Plan, in its approach to the problem of industrial relations, elaborated the policy of associating labour more and more with management and accepted the progressive extension of the scheme of JMC as a major programme.

The Third Plan stated that management cadres ought to arise out of the working class itself. The Draft Fourth Plan declares that joint management ought to be a main element in the structure of industrial relations. State enterprises were assigned a pioneering role because they can create among workers a sense of identification and personal involvement in the enterprise to which they belong. It was envisaged that the scheme should be developed gradually and voluntarily and should become an essential characteristic of the entire industrial relations system in the country.

Against these policy statements, considerable promotional effort was needed for the success of the scheme. This promotional effort has been as much the responsibility of governments, Central and State, as of the Central organisations of employers and workers. The Government of India, on its part, set up a tripartite committee on labour management co-operation to advise on all matters connected with the implementation of the scheme. A special cell was also set up in the Department of Labour and Employment. Most State Governments have designated special officers to promote the scheme. Although representatives of employers and workers supported the scheme at national conferences, they have shown inadequate interest in making their affiliates enthusiastic about it. Progressive employers who already have system of consultation with their workers through a recognised union or works committees, find the JMC in its present form superfluous; managements are generally averse to having a multiplicity of joint bodies and so are unions. In undertakings in which industrial relations are not cordial JMCs cannot be expected to function satisfactorily.

The Indian Labour Conference accepted the scheme of JMC in 1957 and assigned three roles to the proposed JMC – Consultative, Communicative and Administrative.

The consultative role includes general administration of Standing Orders, introduction of new production methods and reduction of operational costs. The communicative role includes receiving information, discussion and suggestion on general economic situation, production and sales, general running of the enterprise, annual balance sheet, profit and loss, long-term plan expansion, etc. The administrative role includes the administration of safety and welfare measures, operation of vocational schemes, preparation of list of leave and holidays, payment of rewards to workers for valuable suggestion, etc.

The essential features of the scheme for JMC are :

- the council is entitled to be consulted on certain specified matters,
- in some others, the management is expected to share information with the council and
- in a set of functions, administrative responsibilities have to be given to it.

Employers' Attitude

Employers' attitudes were best expressed at the seminar organised by the Council of Indian Employers in 1966. Employers think that workers expected more from the JMC than what this institution could give them. Some employers think that the JMCs should not be instituted in undeveloped cultural and social situations and they ought to grow later when Works Committees, Emergency Committees, Safety Committees and other committees have been well developed.

INDIAN EXPERIENCE : FUNCTIONS OF JOINT MANAGEMENT COUNCILS

The JMC should be consulted by the management on matters like – (i) retrenchment, (ii) rationalisation, and (iii) closure, reduction in or cessation of operations. The council would also have the right to receive information, to discuss and to give suggestions on –

- general economic situation of the concern;
- the state of the market, production and sale programmes;
- organisation and general running of the undertaking;
- circumstances affecting the economic position of the undertaking;
- methods of manufacture and work;
- the annual balance sheet and profit and loss statement and connected documents and explanation;
- long-term plan for expansion, re-employment, etc. and
- such other matters as may be agreed to.

The Council would be entrusted with administrative responsibility in respect of –

- administration of welfare measures;
- supervision of safety measures;
- operation of vocational training and apprenticeship schemes;
- preparation of schedules of working hours and breaks and of holidays;
- payments of rewards for valuable suggestions received from the employees; and
- and other matters.

All matters, e.g. wages, bonus, etc. which are subject for collective bargaining are excluded from the scope of the Council. In short, creation of new rights as between employers and workers should be outside the jurisdiction of the Joint Management Council. Individual grievances are also excluded from its scope.

In drawing up this list of functions it was made clear that if the parties to the JMC agreement so desired, the items in the list could be altered and transferred from one group to the other. In fact, much more was left to the parties to settle than is popularly recognized.

The JMCs represent higher form of workers' participation in management. They have been assigned higher social goals than those of the Works Committees. They aim at changing the social structure of enterprises from inside. More concretely, they lead private sector to fit into the framework of socialist order –the idea being that socialist order should be achieved by gradual and peaceful changes. The JMCs are perceived as an instrument as well as an agent of change. It was envisaged that they would become a more satisfactory form of participation than other committees in carrying out changes in the economic structure and industrial relations in enterprises. It was expected that they would bring about the desired transformation first in the public sector and then in the private sector. It was assumed that the existence of State ownership would encourage workers to participate in the labour management co-operation.

An undertaking must meet the following conditions before sitting up of a JMC –

- it must have 500 or more employees;
- it should have a fair record of industrial relations;
- it should have a strong and well-organised trade union;
- the employers, workers and trade unions should be ready to establish JMCs;
- private employers ought to be members of the leading employers' organisation; and
- the trade union should be affiliated to one of the central federations.

Although numerical progress was evident, JMCs did not become one of the main characteristics of the system of industrial relations in India, as was expected. The scheme did not cover more than 6% to 7% of the establishments employing 500 or more workers. This ratio is so small that one can say that the scheme is still in the pilot stage. The rate of implementation of the scheme was uneven in different sectors of the industry. It was implemented to a greater extent in coal mines than in the other sectors of the industry.

The following reasons account for the slow growth of JMCs. *First*, the approach of the management to the JMC continued to be paternalistic. Management is the initiator of the JMC. The existence of the JMC depends on the willingness of management to have it. In many cases, if management resisted the institution of JMC, then all interventions of governmental machinery fell through. It had unlimited arbitrariness. In many situations, one of the necessary preconditions, e.g., fair industrial relations, did not exist in the enterprise. Moreover, management had the exclusive right of dissolving or renewing the JMC.

Secondly, management continued to enjoy its autocratic and arbitrary power which were manifested in various ways. Management had discretionary powers to implement or delay the recommendations of the JMC. The scheme envisaged that some administrative responsibilities would be entrusted to the JMC. But, in may cases, managements were not willing to transfer these responsibilities. Moreover, the schedule of JMC meeting was prepared by management. Regular JMC meetings took place only in 40 per cent of the undertakings.

Thirdly, JMC was envisaged as a channel of communication between management and the mass of workers. It ought to communicate the management's opinion on production to workers and of the latter to the former on their technical, economic and social demands towards production. The management ought to give information on the technical and economic side of production to workers in order to develop their knowledge and attitudes on the company's general business. Such communication by the side of management did not exist or were slightly developed. In 75 per cent cases management did not give any information to workers. This task was not fulfilled because neither adequate communicative instruments nor the social climate for the exchange of opinion had been developed.

Lastly, although a worker is recognised as a partner of management in joint bodies, he is not an equal partner in reality. He cannot be so because he is subordinated to management by the entire system of responsibility, duty, control and obligation. In joint consultation if the workers criticized management, they do not get protection against the consequences of such action. Moreover, workers' and management's representatives have different social, economic, educational, cultural and political backgrounds and unequal social status. By all such elements, workers' representatives are in an inferior position. Due to these differences, worker-members do not have a similar chance to influence the decisions of their JMC. The influence of worker's representatives on management was further limited by the introduction of the principle of 'unanimous decision'.

Stages of Participative Management

There are three distinct stages in participative management in India – Works Committee, Joint Management Council and Worker-Director on the Board of Management. The Works Committee which owes its genesis to provisions contained in the Industrial Disputes Act, 1947 is to address itself only to welfare matters. The JMC seeks to translate the principles contained in the Industrial Policy Resolution. The scheme introduced in 1958 was envisaged as a voluntary measure aimed at giving the workers a sense of belonging to the undertaking. The scope of JMC is wider than that of Works Committee. Another point of difference between Works Committee and JMC is that the latter is to be entrusted with responsibilities of administering welfare measures, supervision of safety measures, operation of vocational training and apprenticeship schemes. At the present stage, participative management is identified with the JMC.

The participation of Worker-Director on the Board of Company in public sector is a recent innovation and still in the pilot stage. In pursuance of recommendations contained in the Administrative Reforms Commission's Report on Public Sector Undertakings, the government has recently drawn up certain guidelines. Necessary conditions have been laid down :

- There should be a duly recognised union/unions in operation in the company and the office-bearers are predominantly workers in the undertaking;
- The representatives sponsored by the recognised union for appointment as a Worker-Director is actually a worker employed in the undertaking;
- Relations in the undertakings as between the management and the recognised union have remained cordial with a tradition of mutual settlement of disputes.

The scheme envisages that the Worker-Director should continue to be a workman on the shop floor, subject to normal rules of discipline of the undertaking concerned. The Worker-Director would, however, be entitled to fees and allowances admissible to other part-time non-official Directors of the undertaking. He would initially hold office for 2 years and would cease to hold the position if he ceases to be a worker or if the union nominating him ceases to be recognised before the expiry of the full term of such Worker-Director.

The three distinct phases show that at the beginning the worker participation was limited in scope and advisory in role, in the second stage, it had certain administrative functions; and in the third stage, which is yet to be developed fully, the worker-director would be actively associated in the decision-making process of an enterprise.

Evaluation

Even though the number of bipartite committees in existence is quite impressive, it is generally felt that they have not realised the aims for which they were instituted. Although the ideal of joint management was advocated with the warmth of a slogan, no attempt was ever made to formulate the ways in which it can be brought about. Nobody seems to have any real interest in its success. It was not accepted seriously except as an empty slogan of industrial democracy designed to keep the labour in good humor. Prof. Zivan Tanic, an expert on the subject, went so far as to say that in the existing social, cultural and political conditions workers' participation in management is not likely to be successful in India. In March, 1972, a Seminar on 'Participative Management in Public Enterprises' was organised jointly by the Shri Ram Centre for Industrial Relations and the Indian Institute of Management, Calcutta, in collaboration with the Bureau of Public Enterprises, Government of India; it concludes that the working of the forms of participation in Indian industry like Works Committees and JMCs indicated that they have, by and large, failed.

No less a person than Mr. K. C. Reddy, former Union Minister for Commerce and Industry admitted in 1962 that the experiment had not proved a success. However, workers' participation was given its rightful place in the 20-point Economic programme (old) in order to foster greater trust and understanding between the workers and management to accelerate the pace of productivity.

We may suggest several psychological conditions for effective participation. *First*, the subordinate must be capable of becoming psychologically involved in the participational activities. *Secondly*, the subordinate must favour participational activities. *Thirdly*, the subordinate must see in it relevance to his personnel life. *Fourthly*, the subordinate must be capable of expressing himself to his own satisfaction about the things being considered.

In regard to the future of the JMCs, the National Labour Commission has accepted a cautious attitude. A JMC will be set up only when the system of union recognition becomes an accepted practice and both managements and unions gravitate towards greater cooperation.

❑ ❑ ❑

6

INDIAN INDUSTRIAL WORKER

According to the National Commission on Labour, a new industrial worker is emerging with distinct urban characteristics and social mobility. The social composition of labour is no longer restricted to certain castes and communities. Even, higher castes and young educated men and women are coming into industrial occupation. In the sophisticated employment like engineering, chemicals, machine tools the level of education of the workers is fairly high. There is a tendency for the younger people to leave family occupations, women workers are taking skilled work in modern factories. Industrial workers generally do not subscribe to any caste and communal prejudices. Socialisation at the work place tends to reduce caste prejudices. The white collar workers generally dislike outsiders to be their trade union leaders. These workers have high aspirations for growth and promotion than the older workers. He cannot be treated in the same manner as the bosses used to treat the first generation of industrial workers.

Identity

The industrial worker of today has acquired a dignity not known to his predecessor. He is no longer the unskilled coolie of the days gone by, engaged in an unending struggle to eke out his existence, neglected by society except for his labour and with very limited aspirations. He has a personality of his own. He shares the benefits, albeit meagre, which a welfare state with a vast population and inadequate resources can offer, and some more. He enjoys a measure of social security; he is secure in his employment once he enters it; he cannot be dismissed unjustly and has been given statutory protection against retrenchment and lay-off. In the days since independence, there has been a continuous rise in his money earnings. Several new amenities are a part of his working life both because of legislation and also because the conditions of the new industries require the provision of these facilities. Increase in money earnings has not been without struggles nor has it necessarily improved his standard of living.

With the changing industrial landscape of the country, growth of new industrial townships and dispersal of activity, a progress of industrial 'culturalisation' of working class has set in. New working class areas have come into being and old ones are expanding. In the new areas, adaptability to this culture naturally depends on the extent and strength of the workers' links with rural mores. Yet assimilation with a new way of life has not been necessarily slow.

The social composition of labour is undergoing a change. Labour is not restricted to certain castes and communities. Apart from the fact that caste and occupation have always interacted and the relation between the two has been elastic in our society, social mobility today accounts for the emergence of a mixed industrial work force. While in traditional industries this change is slow, one cannot escape noticing it in sophisticated employments such as engineering, metal trades, oil refining, and distribution, chemicals and petrochemicals, machine tools and machine building and synthetics and in many white collar occupations. The back-ground of the intermediate and lower cadres in the latter industries is overwhelmingly urban, their level of education is higher. They come from middle or lower middle classes comprising small shopkeepers, petty urban landlords, lower echelons of public service, school teachers and professional groups. They have a pronounced polyglot character.

The workers in the organised sector are generally unionized. As a result of unionisation the bargaining power of the workers are strong and as a result there are "high wage islands" in the organised sector of industry where workers draw much higher wage than the workers in the unorganised and rural sector.

The organised sector is generally located in urban areas or contributes to urbanisation of rural areas.

Compared to the organised sector, the unorganised sector is much larger. The unorganised sector is not affected by labour laws with the result that the working condition is often insanitary, and exploitative for the employees. The size of most establishments is very small and many of the establishments are proprietary concerns.

A ruthless exploitation of labour exists in those sectors where contract labour is employed as in construction industry.

One of the biggest difficulties in rapid industrialisation of the country is the absence of committed work force. This commitment is viewed as the commitment to industrial way of life. Most recent studies point out that the new industrial worker is more adjusted to his new work environment. We say that a committed industrial labour force has developed when workers no longer look on their industrial employment as temporary.

It has been stated by Myers and Kannappan that a committed industrial labour force has developed when workers no longer look on their industrial employment as temporary, when they understand and accept the requirement of working as a part of group in a factory or other industrial enterprise, and when they find in the industrial environment a more adequate fulfillment of personal satisfaction than they enjoyed in the village or rural society commitment in this sense also involves the 'structuring' of the labour force; and management, unions and government may each play a role in the development of a 'web of rules' which leads to a stable and committed industrial labour force.

Commitment refers to attachment and loyalty. Commitment is the relative strength of the individual's identification with and involvement in a particular organisation. It consists of three factors: *(i)* A strong desire to remain a member of the organisation; *(ii)* A strong belief in and acceptance of the values and goals of the organisation; *(iii)* A readiness to exert considerable effort on behalf of the organisation.

According to Clark Kerr India has workers of all stages of commitment.

1. There is first the uncommitted worker who is in industry but not yet of it, as seasonal worker and various types of contract workers. Such persons accept industrial employment only for a limited period, when he has no job on land. He gives up the job as soon as the temporary need is over.

2. The semi-committed worker is a man on the margin of two civilizations. He works more or less regularly in industry but maintains his connection with land. He looks at industrial employment as something permanent but at heart is a villager and maintains his contact with the village. The Bihari villagers in the jute mills of Calcutta or the Tamil workers in Kerala tea plantations belong to this category. These workers go back to the villages during the sowing and harvesting seasons. This type of labour contributes most to the high rate of absenteeism in a number of industries in India. As industrial, growth advances this worker who does not wish to lose his job, gradually loses his rural nexus.

3. There is the committed worker who has severed his connection with the land. He is fully urbanised and never expects to leave industrial employment. These workers accept slum life and addicted habits of drinking,

gambling, chewing and borrowing from money lenders and have the craze of the latest movies.

4. Lastly, there is the 'over-committed' worker who is committed not only to industrial life but to his particular occupation or his particular employer. Such a person is most reluctant to change his employer or to learn a new skill.

Gisbert has made a distinction between traditional industry workers and modern industry workers. Traditional industry workers are to be found mostly in jute and cotton industries while modern industry workers are found in engineering, chemicals, oil refineries, new steel plants etc.

The salient features of modern industry is that workers are generally younger, more literate, better educated and better paid than traditional industry workers. The modern industry workers are oriented towards cosmopolitanism and modernity while their counterparts in traditional industry are more rooted in kinship and sectionalism. The former represent the forces of progress, the latter those of tradition.

The psychological make up of industrial workers may be discussed under the following heads :

ASPIRATIONS AND ATTITUDES

A worker today is better aware that learning is essential for improved earning. He is keen about self-education at adult literacy centres and even more keen about the education of his children and their future. He wants them to enter more remunerative avenues which were denied to him because of requirements of skill. And this aspiration is not confined to the urban worker; it has travelled to rural areas but not to the too distant among them. It is a welcome sign that the worker, along with the rest of the community, is forward looking. Over the last twenty years the aspirations of workers have changed mainly because of the induction of a large number of young workers in the working force. Some of the workers' aspirations are the result of the social consciousness referred to earlier; others have arisen out of what they see around them. The role of political parties and trade unions in making workers conscious about their surrounding has been no less significant.

It is necessary to view the change in attitude in its different components : the worker's attitude to work; his attitude to the union and the issues connected with his organisation; his attitude to persons with whom he has to come in contact outside his work place; and also his attitude to his employer and the shop-floor superior.

Attitude to Work

It is a part of the worker's make-up that he does not generally mind the nature of work that falls to his lot. For instance, a worker in a tannery or in a sewer has to live with the obnoxious odours associated with the work; so has a worker in steel plant or a deep mine with the temperature to which he is subjected. A worker in the weaving shed gets used to the noise and humidity around him. He considers that it is in the nature of the job to put up with such inconvenience; he gets so conditioned to it that it is no serious inconvenience to him any longer. Inter-industry and inter-trade disadvantages in conditions of work, including wage rates, do not usually affect his attitudes. When, however, it comes to a question of conveniences outside the work-place, the worker is certainly anxious to work for a measure of equality.

Attitude towards Unions

As stated earlier, a worker today is more politically conscious than before, more articulate in his criticism of the existing order and more sensitive to his conditions and hardships. He has participated in political and constitutional processes of elections. Though it must be said to his credit that by and large he has not reacted violently to the passions of certain local communities based on language, region, caste and religion which have raised their ugly head in recent times in some regions, one need not infer that he has remained untouched by these cross-currents. Workers turn to the union for fulfillment of their aspirations. Their own participation in union activities may be marginal because of their pre-occupations, but they do not hesitate to avail of the services of their union when in need. When it comes to choosing the union to which they should belong, the consideration at the back of their mind is to support the one which can deliver the 'economic goods'. Thus, cases do occur where workers may differ from the union leader on political issues, but may still vote him to the union office, if they find that he is the right person to bargain with the employer.

Attitude to Outsiders

A worker is not too worried whether his leader is an 'outsider' or an 'insider' or what the definition of the terms should be. To him, a person who has the workers' cause at heart is as much an 'insider' as the operater who works on a neighbouring machine. The question is again who can deliver the goods. All he looks for in the leader, therefore, is sympathy for the cause and capacity to put across his grievances to the employer. He is prepared to pay for the services which the union is able to offer. It may be for a cause which is of direct economic interest to him or for welfare activities, but more for the former than the latter.

Attitude towards Employer

In considering this issue, we take note of the allegation made by some employers that the worker of today shows greater measures of defiance to his superiors. This new attitude has been attributed by some to the security that the worker has acquired through favourable legislation. We believe that in all such assessment, one is apt to ignore the general atmosphere that has developed in the country, particularly in its urban part and in the younger generation in the last few years. There is a certain degree of restiveness in the country which is a complex of many factors. It is more acutely felt by those who are at the growing point of change and who have been shaken out of the grooves rather than by those who have remained static. Such tensions will be more noticeable in a worker who has to carry out instructions than in a person who is self-employed. It is accepted that not all his worries are employer-based nor for that matter are the problems which the employer and his officers face all along the line necessarily worker-based. If the raw material is not of the proper standard and spare parts are defective and the supervisory staff helpless in the matter, irritations are caused and undiscipline can result. This is not to suggest, however, that this is also the major cause. There can, be certainly cases where one side or the other is directly responsible.

In understanding the significance of the attitudinal changes in workers to industrial relations, it is important to record the changes on the other side of the bargaining table also. Over the last twenty years, the handling of labour-management relations is getting increasingly professionalised, though this is not to suggest that such professional handling by itself is adequate. Thus, the institution of personnel managers and professionals, though necessary, is not sufficient for industrial harmony. Persons who are drafted for work in these capacities belong socially to the same group to which the union leaders belong. It is possible for the two to establish rapport. It has been the recent practice for them to discuss on a common platform issues which promote industrial harmony. While the views of the personnel managers publicly hold about labour are the employers' view, they seek and as expected to emphasise the workers' view-point within the management as an organisation. Their standing in the organisation will naturally depend upon the personality of the members constituting high level management, but by and large, it could be said that they have served as a good link between employers and workers though very often workers have expressed dissatisfaction about the manner in which they have functioned.

Disputes between employers and workers have been taking a legalistic orientation of late, mainly because of the emphasis on adjudication by industrial tribunals and courts. Added to this is the tendency of employers to go in appeal; recourse to appeals is not entirely unknown among unions either. Employers can engage lawyers and, to match them, unions have persons with legal acumen on their executive. As a result, both get legalistic in their approach. Sometimes litigious attitude on the part of employers and workers creates situations in which the employers gain because implementation of awards is postponed and lose because the disputed issues pending before courts unsettle workers and inhibit them from improving production.

Social Attitude

Basically, because the worker has not yet reached a standard which he considers satisfactory, his inclination would be primarily to struggle for his rights, though he need not be unmindful of any public cause. He does require in his own struggle the sympathies of others. His attitude towards the State is conditioned by the attitude of the State to his problems.

❑ ❑ ❑

7

EMPLOYMENT OF WOMEN AND CHILDREN

EMPLOYMENT OF WOMEN

Participation of women in economic activity is common in all countries, developed and developing. The extent of their participation depends upon factors too well-known to bear repetition. While in the developed countries, many of which are now characterised by full employment, the debate on the extent of employment of women is not keen, and in fact, there is room for more women in the working force, in countries which are marked by labour surpluses, the need for providing employment for women when many men are available for work raises questions which cannot admit of categorical answers. It is in these developing countries that incomes by and large are low and the family requires the assistance of an additional earner. Where social conventions do not weigh oppressively against bringing women into paid employment, family income can best be supplemented by a draft on the female population in the working-age group.

It is obvious that if a woman has to work, she will need more protection than man in her working environment in developing countries and in traditional occupations. Where more sophisticated equipment is used by the production process, compulsions for special protection will perhaps be less. The justification for protective legislation is thus recognised in all societies. The ILO has evolved several conventions to provide such protection. By their very nature, such measures of protection introduced restrictive influences on the demand for women labour. In labour shortage economics, the need for protection does not create difficulties because women are required for work and the employer is prepared to pay the price. Elsewhere, the relatively high cost of employing women can always be a reason for an employer to discriminate. This apart, institutional arrangements for training women have, by tradition, been slow to develop and vicious circle gets created against giving women their due share in work opportunities. But all this means a careful planning of requirements of manpower and preparing the labour force in advance for work which is likely to be created.

National Labour Commission have dealt with various aspects of protective legislation and have recommended that all such legislation is necessary for women workers. The Commission also emphasized that it requires to be implemented more effectively to give the satisfaction which women deserve on that score, irrespective of its cost to the employer. The commission propose to cover the question of discrimination only, whether it is in respect of employing women or in giving equal wage to them for work of equal value.

In our country the right of women to public employment is recognised under the Constitution. Articles 16(1) and 16(2) of the Constitution grant the right of equal opportunities in regard to employment to men and women without any distinction. The Directive Principle of State Policy which has a bearing on this issue is 39(a).

Pattern of Women Employment

Women workers constituted 59.4 millions or 31.5 per cent of the total workers in the country in 1961, according to the Census data. During the last 60 years, their proportion to the total working force has fluctuated between 23.30 per cent and 33.70 per cent. These fluctuations, in the main, are due to differences in the concept of 'worker' from Census to Census rather than to actual change in the extent of participation of women in economic activity. The bulk of women workers have all along been engaged in agriculture and allied activities. During the period for which Census data are available i.e., the years 1951 and 1961, the percentage of women in the total working force changed from 23.30 in 1951 to 27.96 in 1961. The increase is somewhat higher than in the case of men, but for reasons stated, the limitations of such comparisons have to be understood. This increase in women employment is mainly marked in the cultivator category, while in all others there has been a drop as compared to 1951. In the non-agricultural sector, the proportion of women in employment has shown a decline. The 1961 Census also reveals that in the non-agricultural sector women are employed in what is broadly called the 'services' group, which includes public service, education, medical and health, and the larger chunk of miscellaneous service categories.

Household and small-scale industries employed a large number of women than factories; in the former, women work more as helpers than as wage earners. Information regarding women employed as traditional artisans is however not available for the country as a whole. A recent survey of handicrafts and rural industry in Mysore State, however, brings out the pattern. As expected, the proportion of women in such skilled occupations will be higher in relatively less arduous tasks like mat making, pottery and manufacture of combs than in brass and copper ware and sculpture. A survey in a town in Uttar Pradesh also reveals the same features. Bidi industry, in the small scale group, is reported to be the most 'female intensive.'

In the organised industrial sector, during the 1950s, the increase in average daily employment of women in factories closely corresponded to the increase in total factory employment, though the proportion of women employment in individual industries was fluctuating. In recent years women employment in rice mills, cashew industries and tobacco curing has increased; it has registered a decline in other factory industries. This decline has been more marked in the textiles and basic metal industries. In both cotton and jute textiles, the decline of women employment is attributed mainly to technological changes rendering the jobs held by several women workers redundant. Fixation of minimum work load and standardisation of wages in the cotton textile industry necessitated retrenchment of women workers who were working mostly as reelers and winders where the work-load was found to be lower. Due to rationalisation, certain other departments were also closed, adversely affecting women workers. Rationalisation and mechanisation schemes in the jute industry eliminated some of the manual processes which at one time were the preserve of women workers. Certain occupations giving employment to women in the jute industry earlier were found to be hazardous and are therefore closed to women now by Rules framed under the Factories Act.

Women employment has also registered a decline in mines, particularly in coal mines. In the early days when work underground was not prohibited for women, tribal families migrated to coal fields and worked underground in family groups or in pairs, the man cutting the coal and the woman filling the tubs. Employment of women for work underground was completely banned in 1939 and the proportion of women thereafter dropped to about 1/10th of the total labour force as compared with 2/5th in 1919. The proportion is reported to have come down further to about 6.6 per cent in 1967. Besides prohibition of work underground, technological improvements also displaced women workers employed on certain unskilled occupations.

In plantations the change is not as drastic as in factories and mines. Employment of women in plantations has remained stable, the reason being the suitability of women for several operations in plantations; besides, the work is more akin to agriculture to which women have been accustomed since long. The other significant factor is the non-availability of local labour for a long time for work on the estates. To have better work commitment from migrants, it was convenient for the employer to bring them in family units. Also technological changes adversely affecting employment of women elsewhere have not taken place in plantations. The additional cost of protective legislation for women is offset in this industry by the suitability of women for work in plantations.

The spread of education, particularly in urban areas, has opened up more employment opportunities for women in non-manual, clerical, administrative and professional work. The largest expansion of opportunities has been in Government service. Besides increase in the scope of activities in this sector during the last three decades, the entry and prospects of promotion for women, it is said, are subject to the least impediments in this area of work. Openings for women are largely restricted in business firms to clerical and secretariat assistance and in professions to teaching and nursing. It is against this background that we examine the effect of Constitutional provisions.

Development Since 1947

Since Independence, the trend of employment of women is reported to be not encouraging, though in total employment there has been a rise and there is evidence to suggest that new avenues of employment are opening up for them. It is no consolation for a women who expects to take employment in what were once her traditional occupations to be told that she is not required for work, but many other women with special skills will be needed for employment elsewhere. What irks a woman in the present environment in India is that she will not be called for employment because of the change in processes which necessitates her replacement by a male hand; changes in the social climate which will prohibit her working at certain hours of the day; or worse still, because her employment would be uneconomic for her employer. One or the other of these has been stated as a reason for women's ouster from some of the important traditional and large scale employment openings. Traditionally the bulk of employment of women has been in agriculture, and this has continued. This is also true of cottage and small industries; but in both these sectors, there is a large measure of self employment in the sense that woman contributes to the industrial' chores of the family. Mainly because these avenues are still open to women and absorb a large majority of female working force, the total picture shows a rise in employment of women; but even this rise may not commensurate with the increase in the female labour force. In such matters, however, the opinion as reflected among the beneficiaries of the Constitutional safeguards will not go by the performance of the economy as a whole even if it were satisfactory. The demand will always be, and rightly so, to understand what women have achieved in securing employments which carry prestige such as employment in Government and in other organised industrial and commercial undertakings. In the former, judging from Governmental instructions and also from such statistics as are available, there will continue to be no discrimination, but in the larger sectors of employment, like employment in organised but non-governmental sectors, the proportion of women as stated earlier has fallen and continues to be inadequate. This situation has caused some anxiety to women and that is why the representatives of the All-India Women's Conference urged that the right of a woman to employment should in no way be considered subordinate or secondary to that of a man.

In view of the importance of the Constitutional directive, it would be necessary to probe further into the impediments in the way of employing women. Apart from those which fall within the realm of social and sociological factors, the economic reasons i.e., those which involve additional cost, fall in three groups: *(i)* training, *(ii)* wage rates, and *(iii)* special protection. We discuss these in that order.

Training

Our analysis of the pattern of employment of women has shown that the majority of women, have been employed on unskilled jobs or on such work where simpler and traditional skills are required. The low skill qualifications and equipment of women workers have, in particular, restricted their employability, more so in the wake of technological advance. Vocational guidance and training of girls have in fact long been neglected in the country, primarily because the girls were not considered to be 'bread winners' in the traditional family structure. The majority of girls are educated without any career planning for them; there is not much of education planning among boys either. In the lower income groups, girls are given education of training only when there are spare resources after allowing for the needs of education of male children, present or prospective. This apart, absence of vocational guidance and inadequate training facilities for girls has added to their difficulties.

The situation has slowly started changing since Independence. The compulsions of partition led to measures for helping widows and single women uprooted from their erstwhile homes. To enable them to make a living, centres for training women in sewing, embroidery, needle-work, spinning and weaving were opened. Some State Governments and private organisations also set up training centres for women. More recently, the Directorate General of Employment and Training has opened four Industrial Training Institutes exclusively for girls. A Central Training Institute has been set up to prepare instructors in crafts to be imparted to women.

Polytechnic for women have been opened in some cities; these train women in a large variety of industrial, commercial and secretarial occupations.

The adverse effects of technological changes and mechanisation on women's employment will be set right in the long run if facilities for acquiring new skills are provided for women workers. In fact, with technological advancement, women may find it less strenuous to work in factories. For a rational distribution of women labour in economic activity, it will be desirable to give preference to women for training in those trades and occupations for which they have special aptitudes. Vocational guidance programmes will serve a useful purpose in giving necessary information to women.

Wages

The Fair Wages Committee (1948) stated "where employment is on piece rate or where the work done by men and women is demonstrably identical, no differentiation should be made between men and women workers regarding the wages payable. Where, however, women are employed on work exclusively done by them or where they are admittedly less efficient than men, the fair wages of women workers should be calculated on the basis of a smaller standard family than in the case of man." Article 39(d) of the Constitution also suggests a move in the direction of equal pay for men and women for work of equal value. The progress in the implementation of this Directive Principle has been described in the words of the memorandum of the All India Women's Conference. The said memorandum has also made a reference to the progress in this direction even in the industrial sector. While stating fairly what had been achieved, there are poignant cases of different wage rates fixed for men and women for the same type of work, though such differences, as there were, could not be accounted for fully on the basis of the amount of work involved. Also, in the larger sectors where women are employed viz., agriculture and small industries, evidence shows that in fixing wage rates some State Governments have not been free from discrimination against women. By and large, therefore, we conclude that the position in this respect could have been more satisfactory. Our concern is all the greater, since those who suffer more, even among women as a group, are ignorant, unskilled and semi-skilled workers coming from communities which convention recognises as belonging to the lower social strata and for protecting whom Article 16 of the Constitution is presumably intended. In a way, women belonging to these communities are intended to be doubly protected *(a)* because they are the 'weaker section' and *(b)* because of the comparatively unfortunate communities to which they belong; and it is here that the protection is the least.

But even in this regard, we do not want to underrate what is being achieved. While generally conceding that the wages of women workers have been lower than those of men, the differences have tended to narrow down in recent years mainly for two reasons: *(i)* fixating of statutory minimum wages under the Minimum Wages Act and *(ii)* standardisation of wages for different jobs through the operation of the Industrial Relations Machinery.

LEGISLATIVE MEASURES FOR WOMEN WORKERS

The legislative provisions for protection and welfare of women workers are largely inspired by the ILO Conventions on *(i)* Maternity Protection, 1919; *(ii)* Night-work, 1919; *(iii)* Underground Work, 19935; *(iv)* Equal Remuneration, 1951; *(v)* Discrimination (Employment and Occupation), 1958. However, the actual wording of the enactments in India in which the protection is written draws heavily on the Indian experience. Maternity benefits are provided under the Employees' State Insurance Act, 1948 and the Maternity Benefit Act, 1961. The other legislative measures for women relate to certain restrictions on lifting of weight, employment in hazardous occupations, provision for separate toilet facilities, rest rooms, creches etc.

Legal provisions on engaging women during night and on underground work and hazardous occupations has obviously restricted women employment. The obligation put upon employers to pay equal wages for equal work and in addition bear the cost of providing certain extra benefits and facilities to women workers is also reported to have been responsible for the decline of women employment in factories and mines. We would like to mention at this stage the conclusions of a study conducted by the ILO (India Branch), which refutes the hypothesis of extra cost. This study which was largely based on published material, presented the problems and difficulties of women in paid employments in an attempt to discover practical solutions to enable women to play an increasingly full and effective part in national life and fulfill their responsibilities as home makers, wives, mothers and workers. A conclusion of the study was that the general impression that a decrease in the number of women employed in factories was due to statutory obligations or the compulsion to pay maternity benefits, was not borne by facts. The percentage of women employees in larger establishments employing 50 or more workers was higher than those in smaller ones. Benefit or no benefits where women were more useful, they continued to be employed. Plantations is an instance in point.

While there are the discriminatory practices which are reported to be in vogue, and in many cases the reports appear to be well founded, attention has been drawn to still another form of discrimination within the members of the 'fair sex' itself. To minimise the burden cast by maternity benefits, some employers recruit unmarried women only on condition that they will resign their posts on getting married. The clause which is discriminatory, unfair and unjust, has, on a petition, made by the affected women employees, been struck down by the Supreme Court.

The All-India Women's Conference has in its memorandum brought out an interesting point in connection with the discriminating practices. According to it, the majority of the occupations where women are employed are unskilled or semi-skilled. It is precisely in such unskilled and semi-skilled occupations that the non-wage costs associated with women's employment become uneconomical to the employer, since there are no compensating advantages in employing women on such jobs. Women, therefore, need to be absorbed more and more in skilled categories of work to make their employment more economic to the employer. If the current trends in the employment of women continue, the point sought to be made in the memorandum, will have been met.

Women and Trade Unions

Women workers did not, by and large, take to trade union membership in the early years. The reasons are not far to seek. Social factors disfavouring women working outside, greatly restrict their freedom to mix with fellow workmen. Their families expect them to return home after the day's work and keep aloof from such activities. Moreover, though a worker, a woman did not so far take to work outside her house as a way of life. This transitory interest in employment is a matter of the past. With social awakening and the newly acquired freedom, taste for economic independence, and therefore a stake in employment, women workers are becoming more alive to their interests and joining unions in larger numbers. The percentage of women union members is the highest in the plantations where, their employment has remained steady. Unionisation is also making progress in employments under the industrial categories: food, beverages, tobacco, textiles, mining and quarrying. It is noticeable that the extent of unionisation is positively correlated with the quantum of employment of women. Where women are employed in large numbers, they have naturally found it less inconvenient to join unions. We expect that unionisation among women will increase as more and more of them come out to take up paid work and social mores change to give them the necessary freedom for it.

Employment of Women — A Perspective

The outline of the perspective will be clearer if we first deal, more specifically with women's motivation for work and the social impediments that stand in the way. With a few exceptions in the higher strata of society, the majority of women take to work for economic reasons. A survey conducted under the auspices of the National Council of Women's Education in Delhi and Mumbai in 1962 showed that women work, if they are required to do so, because of economic compulsions of the family. About

70 per cent of the women who responded to the enquiry considered it necessary to work in order to supplement family earnings. This was a common consideration with all unmarried women who in some cases were reported to be supporting an old father or widowed mother or an unmarried brother or sister. The attitude of the guardian of these women was passive no longer; they encouraged their wards to seek work. In higher income groups, the motivating force behind seeking work was utilization of leisure, acquirement of vocational training and the desire to have one's own money. Another motivation reported by some respondents was that, in the view of their guardians, a working woman enhanced family prestige and got better prepared against unforeseen contingencies. the former indicates a change in social values as against the popular belief of the past against women employment for the very reasons of prestige.

The more important of the difficulties which come in the way of employment, however, are still-restricted mobility, inadequate training and housing facilities; the last concern more particularly for a single women. The guardians of women consider it unsafe to send their women wards away from their homes to take up work. Employment preferences of women workers continue to be for work locally available. Non-availability of housing facilities for a single woman acts as a major deterrent for many women who aspire for employments other than those available in their local areas, while transfer of location after marriage comes in the way of the stability of employment of married women.

In providing the perspective, we need not consider the rural context where women will take to work either paid or unpaid. We expect that in urban areas more and more women would be coming out of their homes to take up paid work because of the spread of education, development of means of communication, growing desire to live better and consequent liberalisation of traditional norms hitherto disfavouring women employment. Already, the waning joint family system is exposing the hitherto protected 'fair sex' to the vicissitudes of life. Earning female members are welcome to urban families and conditions are not likely to change in this regard in the foreseeable future; if at all, the welcome will be even more hearty. With an increasing number of girls going out for education, inhibitions regarding working with men are losing their hold. Improved household amenities and emphasis on smaller families will provide more leisure for being utilized in gainful occupations.

An important source of employment for women will be opened up with the enlarging of the welfare activities of the State consequent on the goals accepted for development. The social welfare institutions to be set up will offer employment openings for which women will be more suited. Another avenue too which women could look for will be in the institutions engaged in the development of social sciences and humanities. More of such institutions will be set up, since it has been widely recognised that the development of social sciences has lagged behind the advances made on the technological side. Social science institutes will require considerable assisting staff in using the new research techniques. Educated women will be suited for rendering assistance in collection and processing of information.

Our review of the employment pattern and job preferences of women is suggestive of coming changes in the occupational structure of women in the next two decades or so, particularly in the non-agricultural sector. Decline of women employment in factory and mining occupations requiring physical labour indicates not only a shrinking demand but also, to an extent, a tapering labour supply in these occupations in future. The latter is particularly borne out by the job preferences of women. The spread of education and training facilities will give further strength to such preferences. More and more women will be aspiring to become clerks, stenographers, secretaries, teachers and nurses. Expansion in business and governmental activities, will create more job opportunities of this nature.

As at present, in the industrial occupations, women will be looking for employments in skills which they have or will readily acquire. The technological changes and changes in production pattern have made it easy for women to acquire the limited skills necessary for a small fraction of a job which an operative is expected to handle. Women have made their place secure in chemical and pharmaceutical factories, in light engineering, and in factories which work for a variety of consumer goods. To the extent such industries develop, more of women will have employment openings, provided the basic training given to girls are so arranged as to fit into the perspective of development.

Skill generation and rational distribution of the women labour force as a part of social and economic planning, which would also reduce competition between men and women, are the widely recognised solutions to the problem of women's employment. With this orientation, it should be possible for an employer to follow a non-discriminatory policy in the employment of women. The additional cost, if any, will be accepted by employers on wider social consideration.

EMPLOYMENT OF CHILDREN

Employment of children has continued to be a problem since the early days of industrialisation. The Whitley Commission stated:

"...In many cities large numbers of young boys are employed for long hours and discipline is strict. Indeed there is reason to believe that corporal punishment and other disciplinary measures of are a reprehensible kind are sometimes resorted to in the case of smaller children. Workers as young as five years of age may be found in some of these places working without adequate meal intervals or weekly rest days, and 10 or 12 hours daily for sums as low as 2 annas in the case of those of tenderest years." It recommended legislation to fix the minimum age for employment at a higher level than that obtaining in many industries. In the following years the minimum age for employment of children was fixed at 12 years under the Factories Act and 15 years under the Mines Act.

The Labour Investigation Committee, 1946, however, found that the legislative measures relating to child employment met with little success in ameliorating conditions of work of child labour. It observed:

"The important fact that has emerged from the investigations is that in various industries, mainly smaller industries, the prohibition of employment of children is disregarded quite openly, and owing to the inadequacy of the inspection staff it has become difficult to enforce the relevant provisions of the law."

In the later years, the situation regarding child labour comparatively eased in factory industries; it persisted to give anxiety in the unorganised small industries. An enquiry conducted on the subject by the Labour Bureau, in the early fifties, came to the following conclusion:

"At present, therefore, in the factory industries child labour is not a serious problem. It is however doubtful if statistics compiled from the returns under the Factory Act tell the whole story regarding child labour. For, it is well within the experience of Factory Inspectors as well as other officers engaged on field enquiries that no sooner they make their appearance on the scene than quite a large number of children run away from the factory premises. These are often children below the minimum age for employment."

The Labour Bureau's study showed that in small industries and cottage industries such as match manufacture, cashewnut processing, bidi making, carpet weaving, employment of under age children, either uncertified or having false age certificates, continued. The actual hours of work were found to be in excess of the prescribed working hours under different enactments. In cottage industries, children were required to work as long as adult workers, except where home-work system was prevalent. The working conditions for children in the bidi and glass industries continues to remain deplorable. However, a redeeming feature reported by the study was that children were assigned comparatively light work wherever employed in plantations, factories, cottage and small-scale industries.

Legislation Relating to Child Workers

Our Constitution provides for protection of child workers. Article 24 lays down: 'No child below the age of 14 years shall be employed to work in any factory or mine or engaged in any other hazardous employment.' Articles 39(e) and 39(f) and Article 42 are also relevant in this connection.

The 'abuse' indicated in Article 39(e) and 'exploitation' in Article 39(f) could be wider, in their social content, than Article 42 which has specific relevance only to the working class. We have covered Article 39(e), in so far as wage employment of children is concerned, under working conditions. But this will have no relevance to cases where there is no wage paid employment and where a self-employed man uses his family, women and children, for gainful activity because of economic necessity. The real solution will emerge in this case only with a faster rate of economic growth and with social justice as an equally important aspect of growth. Article 39(f) is more relevant to women than children and its implications need not be discussed.

The important legislative provisions with a bearing on employment of children relate to minimum age of employment, working hours, health certification, employment on dangerous machines and the like. The minimum age for employment is fixed at 14 years under the Factories Act, 1948, 15 years under the Mines Act, 1952 and 12 years under the Plantations Labour Act, 1951. The Employment of Children Act, 1938 prohibits employment of children below 15 years in occupations connected with transport of passengers by railway and in work connected with handling of goods within the limits of any port. For employment in workshops connected with bidi making, carpet weaving, cement manufacture, cloth printing, dyeing and weaving, match manufacture, mica cutting, tanning etc., the Act lays down the minimum age of employment at 14 years. The Shops and Establishments Acts of various States prescribe different minimum age limits varying between 12 and 14 years. To ensure the physical fitness of children, the Factories Act, 1948 provides that children upto the age of 18 years will be employed on production of health certificate which will be valid for the year only. The Mines Act, 1952 provides that a child upto the age of 18 years can be employed, with such a certificate, as an adult worker for work below ground.

The Factories Act, 1948 prescribes for children and adolescents a working day of 4½ hours, with a spread-over of 5 hours. Young persons upto the age of 17 years are not allowed under the Act to work during night hours and on hazardous occupations. The Mines Act, 1952 lays down that adolescents will not be employed for more than 4½ hours in a day and prohibits their employment between 6 P.M. and 6 A.M., and on work below ground. The Plantation Labour Act, 1951 prescribes a 40- hour week for children and adolescents. In shops and establishments, the hours of work for children are fixed at 6 or 7 hours a day under the State laws on the subject.

Extent of Child Labour

Data regarding the extent of employment of child labour are inadequate. According to the Census of India 1961, there were 8 per cent workers below 15 years of age. Most of them were reported to be employed in agriculture and allied activities; the organised sectors of the economy accounted for only a small proportion. The first and second Agricultural and Labour Enquiries revealed that children below the age of 15 years formed 4.8 per cent of the agricultural labour force in 1950-51 and 7.7 per cent in 1956-57. In factories there has been a steep decline in the proportion of child labour from 0.48 per cent in 1948 to 0.25 per cent in 1952, 0.10 per cent in 1960, and 0.07 per cent in 1962. The number of adolescent workers also declined during this period. In plantations, which offered larger scope for employment of children, their proportion decreased steadily from 15.2 per cent in 1946-47 to 10.4 per cent in 1950-51.

The gradual reduction in the employment of child labour since Independence is due partly to the expansion of educational facilities by the State and also to relatively better enforcement of statutory provisions relating to child labour. Employment of child is almost non-existent in organised industries. It persists in varying degrees in the unorganised sector such as small plantations, restaurants and hotels, cotton spinning and weaving, carpet weaving, stone breaking, brick-kiln, handicrafts, and road building. Employment of child workers below the prescribed age is also reported to be continuing in far-off places and in rural areas where enforcement of statutory provisions is more difficult.

Quite often it is the feeling of sympathy rather than the desire to exploit which weighs with employers in employing child workers. Ironically enough, it is the same feeling which makes the inspecting officers to take a lenient view of breaches of the legal provision in this regard. This is, therefore, more of an economic problem. Under the excuse of preparing a boy for taking up productive employment as he reaches adulthood a small child is engaged to train his fingers in the required skills. Some employers told that unless the fingers were thus trained at a very early age, their adaptation later would be difficult.

There is prevalence of child labour in handloom and powerloom units. Usually a weaver has as his mate a child of the school going age. The education of the mate is no concern of the weaver nor of the person who engages the weaver. Children are not direct employees, but they help the weaver and collect whatever money they can get from him. In due course they learn the trade. If the education of a child is a casualty in the process, it is the poverty of the parents which is to be blamed. Brocade work is another intricate operation where child labour is quite common. Though the boys who were working there looked between 8-10 years of age or even younger, they were all above 14, the age at which adolescents were permitted to be engaged under the local rules. In several cases, the payment to the child was the responsibility of the adult worker whom the child helped. When the former himself gets a low age, he could be parting with but little of it for his helper. The whole arrangement appeared to be exploitative when seen in relation to the fact that such operations were carried on so near the factory premises. A similar arrangement prevails in carpet weaving, but in this case, the relative share of wages of the child worker is better. The low earnings of the artisan are compensated by the income of his mate, if the latter belongs to the same house. But this is at the cost of education of the junior operative. An artisan cannot afford to educate his wards though education is free. For him an uneducated child is an asset; desire to be educated becomes a double liability because of *(a)* loss of earnings if the child did not work and *(b)* expenditure on education howsoever small.

Recommendations of the National Labour Commission

The employment of children is indeed more of an economic problem than anything else. Nevertheless, the Commission consider denial of opportunity to children for their proper physical development and education to be an issue of a serious nature, keeping in view the larger interests of the society. While the economic difficulties are real, a way has to be found to give the child the necessary education in his more receptive years. This can be ensured by fixing the employment hours of children so as to enable them to attend to schooling. Where the number of children is adequate, the employers, with the assistance of the State Governments, should make arrangements to combine work with education.

❑ ❑ ❑

8

UNORGANISED LABOUR

We are going to discuss another group of workers, who cannot be identified by a definition, but could be described as those who have not been able to organise in pursuit of a common objective because of constraints such as *(a)* Casual nature of employment, *(b)* Ignorance and illiteracy, *(c)* Small size of establishments with low capital investment per person employed, *(d)* Scattered nature of establishments, and *(e)* Superior strength of the employer operating singly or in combination.

We do not propose to cover every sector of such employment, but take up categories where the number of workers is large and where information about them is available in some form. The categories naturally will be illustrative rather then exhaustive. These are: *(i)* Contract labour including construction workers; *(ii)* Casual labour; *(iii)* Tribal labour, and *(iv)* Other unprotected labour. There will be a certain measure of overlap between them. For instance, bidi and cigar establishment can fall under (iii), (v) and (vi); Contract labour will be found in (iii), and so will casual labour and so on. These categories will include workers who are protected by some labour legislation and others who are not. We expect that between them, the categories of workers dealt with will throw up a range of issues which will cover the rest of unorganised/unprotected labour as well.

The 1961 Census puts the total number of non-agricultural wage-earners at about twenty-four millions. If from this number the total number of workers employed in the organised sector, namely, registered factories, mines, plantations, government and quasi-government bodies, ports, insurance, banks etc., which number about fourteen millions is deducted, one gets a rough estimate of workers in the unorganised sector. Besides the ten million workers so arrived at, there are a large number of workers other than 'employees' in the cottage and household industries and handicrafts; according to the 1961 Census, the number of such workers is eleven millions, and these latter we cannot cover because of the absence of employer-employee relationship in them.

Assessment of Policies

Beyond a mention in the 1946 Policy Statement, Government have hitherto paid inadequate attention to these workers despite the fact that they constitute a fair proportion of those who produce goods and provide services. Even in the organised sector, a section of the total labour force has to be left out of the purview of legislation, because some establishments employ workers less than the minimum number prescribed in the law. In the absence of proper organisation, they are not able to establish their reasonable claims and secure proper working conditions. It is a common complaint that the benefits of labour legislation have not reached rural and unorganised labour. The Minimum Wages Act, 1948 was the first attempt at statutory regulation of wages, and to some extent, working conditions of labour employed in the sweated trades. Labour engaged in these employments, being unorganised, had weak bargaining power and had been deprived of reasonable wage and working conditions. Apart from the ineffectively implemented Minimum Wages Act, they do not have any other legislative protection. The Factories Act, 1948 and the Industrial Disputes Act, 1947, which contain specific and detailed provisions for items within their purview, were not designed to meet the conditions of and requirements in unorganised industries and employments. In taking cognisance of the plight of such labour, the Third Plan mentioned: "while considerable improvements had occurred in the living and working conditions of employees in large and organised industries, owing both to State activity and trade union action, a great deal of leeway remained to be made up in respect of the workers engaged in agriculture and unorganised industries and that their conditions should become a matter of special concern to government as well as to labour organisations." A reference was also made in the plan to the building and construction industry in which programmes of expansion called for greater attention to safety standards. The informal meeting of Labour Ministers in August, 1962 endorsed the Plan Statement and called for *(i)* Greater attention to be paid to the conditions of labour in unorganised industries which could not be governed by legislation effectively; *(ii)* Formulation of a separate code for laying down minimum service and working conditions for them; and *(iii)* Appointment of labour officers to assist in the proper enforcement of the code in (ii) above. In spite of this decision, no satisfactory machinery has been reported to have been set up for taking cognisance of labour disputes in several States.

Contract Labour/Construction Workers

'Contract Labour' can be distinguished from 'direct labour' in terms of employment relationship with the principal establishment and method of wage payment. Unlike direct labour which is borne on the pay or muster roll of the establishment and entitled to be paid wage directly, contract labour, by and large, is neither borne on pay-roll nor is paid directly. The establishment which farms out work to a contractor (s) does not owe any direct responsibility in regard to his/their labour. In several contracts the wage rates to be paid to labour are stipulated, but whether payment is made on that basis or not is hardly the concern of the contractor himself or of the person/organisation for whom the contractor works.

The advantages to the employer in employing contract labour are *(i)* production at lower cost; *(ii)* engaging labour without having to extend fringe benefits such as leave wages, Employees' State Insurance or Provident Fund contributions, and bonus; *(iii)* general reduction of the overhead costs and the administrative burden of maintaining an establishment; and *(iv)* the sheer 'economics' of farming out contracts for manufacture of certain components rather than investing capital and installing plants for their manufacture. Contract labour can broadly be divided into two set categories; those employed on job contracts, and others on labour contracts. Large establishments give out contracts of jobs or of particular operations, e.g., loading and unloading, to contractors on lump-sum payment. The contractor engages his own workers. The contractor can be an individual or an establishment or even a senior worker like a mistry or mukadam or a sirdar. The protection received by contract labour varies according to the situation.

Review of Trends

The Whitley Commission recommended the abolition of contract labour by implication. The Bombay Textile Labour Enquiry Committee stated that "if the management of the mills" did not "assume responsibility for such labour," there was "every likelihood of its being sweated and exploited by the contractor;" it also recommended abolition of the "contract system of engaging labour" as soon as possible and "that workers for every department in a mill should be recruited and paid directly by the management." The Bihar Labour Enquiry Committee condemn the practice of recruiting labour through contractors because they said: "the contractors ordinarily lack a sense of moral obligation towards labour which the employers or the managers are expected to have, and, therefore, do not often hesitate to exploit the helpless position of labour in their charge." The Rage

Committee (1946) found that the system of contract labour was very much in vogue.

As a result of these findings, the scope of the definition of "worker" in the Factories Act, 1948, the Mines Act, (1952) and the Plantations Labour Act, (1951), was enlarged to include contract labour. Contract labour in some sectors became entitled to the benefits of working conditions and hours of work admissible to the labour directly employed. The definition of the term "immediate employer" under the Employees' State Insurance Act, (1948) extended health insurance benefits to contract labour. All it means is that in providing working conditions as required under the statute, the strength of contract labour is to be taken into account. The Dock Workers' (Regulation of Employment Act), 1948 protected the employment, wages and welfare conditions of specified categories of contract labour employed at major docks. As a result of the recommendations of the Industrial Committee on Coal Mines, contract labour was abolished in railway collieries in 1948. The Central Public Works Department (CPWD) Rules for contractors became operative in 1948; job contracts were to be given only to contractors who were on the "Approved List" and who agreed to pay "fair wages" to workers and provide welfare services and housing of the specified standard. Non-compliance with those provisions would result in cancellation of contract. The "fair wage" is notified at the time of inviting tenders. A similar system was introduced by the railways for its contractors. The provisions of the Minimum Wages Act, (1948) applied to contract labour in scheduled employment. The Bombay Industrial Relations Act, (1946) and similar Acts in Madhya Pradesh and Uttar Pradesh cover labour contract. They are thus entitled in these states to bring up issues in dispute and enjoy protection and benefits as are available to directly employed workmen under the said Acts.

Incidentally, the benefits available to contract labour under these measures tend to vary from industry to industry, area to area, and even from one category of labour to another employed in the same industry and located in the same city. There are also differences in interpretation of the term 'contract labour;' inadequate procedures and poor implementation are other constraints. The Second Plan stressed the need for improvement in the working conditions of contract labour and pointed out that in the case of contract labour "the major problems related to regulations of their working conditions and ensuring them continuous employment." Surveys of selected industries were undertaken to ascertain the extent and nature of the problem in different industries. The problem also came up for discussion in the Indian Labour Conference and the Industrial Committee on Construction; the upshot of these was a general agreement on the need to abolish the system of contract labour wherever possible and to regulate it in other cases.

Employment

The practice of employing contract labour prevails in varying degrees in almost all industries and services; it is more prevalent in mining and in the construction industry. With the expansion of construction activity following substantial investment in the Plans, the size of contract labour has significantly expanded in the post-Independence period. While the data are for years that are somewhat remote, it is believed that the percentages obtaining currently may not have gone up because of the pressure that has been building up against engaging labour in this manner.

WAGES AND WORKING CONDITIONS

There is wide disparity in the wages and working conditions of direct labour and contract labour. Wage Boards constituted for different industries have recommended extention of uniform wage rates for both direct and contract labour. But in the absence of an effective implementation machinery, contract labour is generally paid wages below the rates prescribed for regular workers in the industry. Often they do not get any payment other than the basic remuneration.

Conditions of work are also far from satisfactory. Working hours are irregular and longer. The period for which payment is made varies from a day to six months. There is no security of employment, the job ends with the contract. If contract labour is employed on jobs within the premises of an establishment covered by the Factories Act 1948, they get weekly rest like direct worker. Leave with wages is not available to contract labour. In the matter of housing facilities, contract labour is not treated on par with direct labours. It is entitled to benefits under the ESI scheme but few establishments extent this facility. Similarly facilities under the amended Employees' Provident Fund Act, 1963 are not available to contract labour because they do not fulfil the qualifying conditions of regular employment of twelve months in the establishment. In some areas, where the practice of the contractor making advance payments to his labour obtains, contractors are reported to take advantage of the illiteracy and ignorance of workers and manipulate accounts so that at the end of the season the worker still owes to the contractor almost the same amount as initially advanced.

With a view to removing the disabilities of contract labour, a Bill for regulation and abolition of employment of contract labour was introduced in the Parliament in 1967. The Bill provides for *(i)* The registration of principal employers and licensing of contractors. *(ii)* The setting up of advisory boards of a tripartite character, *(iii)* The regulation of conditions of work, payment of minimum wages and other essential amenities relating to welfare and health of contract labour and *(iv)* A comprehensive definition of the terms 'work', 'principal employer' and 'workmen'.

Construction Workers

The building and construction industry covers a variety of works and operations. Its activities range from construction of dams and bridges, roads and tracks to factories and offices, schools, hospitals and ordinary residential buildings. Together with the workers required for maintaining 'construction.' this forms a major sector of employment. Most of these operations are seasonal, and at times involve fluctuations in the employment pattern largely due to climatic conditions. Building activity is at its peak during winter months, but is at a standstill in the rainy season. In minor construction projects, work is of short durations and workers are required to move from place to place where construction may be in progress. Big projects may employ workers at a stretch for many years; even so re-deployment of workers poses a problem. There has been rapid expansion in building and construction activity during the last fifty years. The workers were employed in major sectors of construction and maintenance. According to the estimates of the Planning Commission, construction industry added labour 2.3 million work opportunities during the Third Five Year Plan.

Agency

The Central and State Public Works Departments and Railways are major employers of contract labour; in the public sector, such agencies as the National Buildings Construction Corporation and the National Projects Construction Corporation also employ contract labour. There are in addition many building and construction agencies in private hands; some of them are well organised, but a large number operate on a small scale. Most of the construction works are actually executed by big and small contractors, the latter usually working as sub-contractors under a principal contractor. The Study Group on Construction Industry has pointed out that unregulated entry of persons in this industry, regardless of qualifications or resources, has been a major cause of chaotic labour condition and sub-standard or slipshod work. A classification and registration of building contractors may be a remedy against this malaise.

Recruitment

There is no agency specifically to regulate employment of unskilled workers. Technical and skilled workers are directly employed by Government and usually recruited through the employment exchanges. A contractor generally maintains a small nucleus of skilled workers for his operations and he deploys them at work sites. Most of the recruitment of labour, particularly of the unskilled type, is made through middlemen near about the place of work. The bulk of labour is employed through labour contractors. Government, whether it is Central or State, is the largest principal employer in the construction industry. It should be possible, by a suitable phasing of the programmes undertaken, to ensure a reasonably steady volume of work and employment. Simultaneously, to ensure greater security of employment, possibilities of introducing de-casualisation schemes of the type described earlier should be explored.

Working Conditions

Construction or maintenance of roads or buildings is one of the scheduled employments under the Minimum Wages Act. There is, however, no law to regulate service conditions, annual leave, safety provisions and social security benefits. The need for greater attention to safety conditions has been emphasized from time to time. In view of the casual and seasonal character of operations spread over large areas, it has not been possible so far to adopt safe working practices and facilitate adequate labour inspection. Many works are too small to provide for the services of a safety officer. Working and living conditions are also depressing in the absence of any specific legislation. Improvements cannot be enforced; and the enactment, though discussed from time to time in tripartite meetings, has not yet materialised. There should be no further delay in this matter. The absence of any regulatory and protective legislation applicable to the construction industry is responsible for several abuses, such as employment of child or female labour under conditions which are not permissible in factories and mines. Though the Central and State Governments prescribe certain standards in respect of wages and other amenities to be provided by contractors on Government contract, these are not usually observed. The enforcement machinery consisting of CPWD Labour Officers, or their counterparts in the respective States, is inadequate to look after a large number of contractors in their jurisdiction, and they cannot visit these establishments as frequently as they should. The failure to take prompt action to check and rectify irregularities, pointed out by them, encourages not only defaulting contractors but also makes law abiding elements among them negligent. To ensure that labour gets proper amenities, we recommend that the cost on them is accepted as a permissible item in the tender. And where there is already so, it should be the responsibility of the agency which supervises the work to see that the expenditure allowed is actually incurred and amenities provided. Mobile dwellings should be provided to labour at work-sites.

Wages

The system of wage payment in the industry is not uniform. Minimum wages have been fixed for certain categories: these vary from State to State and even from district to district within a State. A reason for this is multiciplicity of authorities. Some elementary protection is available in the form of a fair wage clause in the contract for Government works, but this is inadequate and is made more so because of the absence of any statutory enforcement machinery. Under CPWD Regulations for contract labour, which cover extensive work of building operations, fair wage is wage for time or piece-work notified at the time of inviting tenders. A worker is entitled to lodge a complaint against a contractor paying wages less than the minimum fixed. Under the provisions of Minimum Wages Act, 1948 and the Minimum Wages (Central) Rules, 1950, the contractor is bound to allow to the workers he employs one day's rest for six days of continuous work and pay wages at the same rates as for duty. In the event of any default, the Engineer-in charge can deduct the sum not paid to labour and pay the same to the persons entitled thereto, from any money due to the contractor by the engineer or SDO concerned. However, in the absence of any effective implementation machinery, these safeguards, quite often, have had only an academic value. The worker can complain only at the risk of losing his job. While recording the evidence at State headquarters, National Labour Communication made enquiries about the operation and enforcement of fair wage clause. In one State the senior officer of the Department had no knowledge of the inclusion of any such clause in the contract. Even where the officers had knowledge, instances of departmental or punitive action against defaulters were few and far between. The payment of wages is made on the basis of piece-rate to the head of a group of workers through the jamadar/petty contractor, and in such cases, the rate fixed includes the jamadar's commission or petty contractor's profits. This system of wage payment by contractors to sub-contractors on piece-rate basis and of payment by the latter to individual workers on daily rates is prone to abuse. There are complaints by workers about non-payment, short-payment, short-measurement of the work done and harsh deductions.

CASUAL LABOUR

The incidence of casual labour is determined by the nature of the task to be performed. In engineering industry, casual labour is employed to fill vacancies caused by absenteeism and temporary pressure of work. Employment of casual labour is a common feature in the Railways, the Public Works Departments, both Central and State, the State Electricity Corporations and employments in the private sector where the nature of work is similar.

Employment of casual labour in several categories of work is well recognised and not objected to. It is taken exception to mainly when such labour is continually employed for long periods to circumvent the provisions of law, which confer benefits to permanent workers through better working conditions, more amenities, and the like, and what is more, when used deliberately to restrict the scope for regular employment. Though de-casualisation has made some headway in State Government Departments, Railways and Ports and Docks and some industrial centres where several units of the same industry operate, there is still a large volume of casual labour which is engaged for varying lengths of time; not in all cases are they kept casual for bonafide reasons.

Though casual labour comes under the scope of some labour enactments relating to wages and regulation of hours of work and conditions of service, it is deprived of the advantages accruing from legislation which stipulates continuous employment for being eligible. Casual labour is thus denied annual leave with wages, maternity and sickness benefits because under the law a worker must complete a minimum period of work in an establishment as precondition for eligibility. Under the Factories Act, 1948 annual leave with wages is admissible only to workers who work for 240 days or more; under the Mines Act, 1951 to those who complete one calendar's service; under the Maternity Benefits Act, no woman is entitled to maternity benefit unless she actually works in particular establishment for a period of not less than 160 days (150 days under the Plantations Labour Act, 1951) in twelve months immediately preceding the date of expected delivery. The Employees' Provident Funds Act, 1952 is applicable only to workers who have put in 240 days of continuous service in one year. The sickness benefit under the Employees' State Insurance Act, 1948 is available to those who pay 13 weeks' contribution in a period of 26 weeks. All such stipulations are an invitation to an unenlightened employer to maintain a large complement of casual labour than is absolutely necessary. Many unions complained that employers arbitrarily terminated the services of casual workers to prevent them from completing the prescribed period of service and thus deprived them of the benefits. There are cases particularly in small establishments where within a week of termination of service, the same person is engaged afresh for the same job, making the employer's intention obvious.

In Central Government establishments and a few State Electricity Boards, however, interests of casual labour in the matter of payment of wages and other benefits such as weekly holidays, hours of work, night shift, payment of overtime, have been somewhat protected. In Railways, an employee after six months of service is entitled to the same wages and conditions of work as are admissible to regular but temporary employees; a casual worker is not to be deliberately discharged with a view to causing an artificial break in service, which will prevent him from becoming a temporary employee; but even with such instructions, the manner of their observance at times has caused irritation to workers. There are some complaints of discrimination in the matter of payment of wages to casual labour in the Railways. Departments of State Governments such as the Public Works Department, the Irrigation Department, Transport Corporations and State Electricity Boards mentioned that employment of casual labour was inevitable because of the very nature of their work. Several of them, however, accepted the need for reducing the complement of casual workers as also for providing some of the benefits available to regular workers to those who have to be continued in their casual capacity beyond a specified period.

Complete de-casualisation of labour is not a practicable proposition in the immediate future and entail a large measure of idleness and render the operations inconvenient and uneconomic, but in the long run it is a goal worth striving for. It should be possible to evolve and introduce some kind of de-casualisation scheme in stages in such sectors as construction industry in urban areas and departmental schemes in State Government Departments, such as the PWD, Irrigation, Transport and Electricity. A beginning should be made for better regulation of conditions of work of casual labour in all undertakings, public and private, through periodic review and consultations among representatives of employers, Government and workers.

Casual labour should be restricted to work which is truly of a casual nature and he should be employed only where regular workers cannot be employed. For this purpose, every enterprise should determine well in advance the strength of its labour force, both permanent and temporary, in consultation with representatives of labour. Wherever possible there should be a standing order which should, against the 'normal' strength of the enterprise concerned, fix the strength of casual labour. The prevailing practice of discontinuing employment of a casual worker for short periods and again re-employing him to debar him from enjoying the benefits of a permanent worker is pernicious. National Commission on Labour recommend that if employment is discontinued for a short period and the worker is re-employed, this short period should not be treated as a break in service. After a casual worker has completed a stipulated period of service, he should be allowed the same benefits which a permanent worker enjoys.

TRIBAL LABOUR

Tribal labour as an ethnic group is relatively cohesive and sensitive to changes which appear to its imagination to be almost revolutionary particularly as taking place in its homelands. Since Independence, large scale industries have been set up in the areas the peace which had not been disturbed over ages. The process of industrialisation has made a vital impact on the tribal economy and its social structure, which are disintegrating. The Study Group on Tribal Labour has observed that it will be a great loss for development if tribal people are not helped, given time to undergo this cultural mutation and to work out for themselves a synthesis of traditional and modern culture. Large industrial undertakings cannot exist as islands in tribal areas; these have to be integrated with the life of the tribal people at some points. There is thus the need for a basic change in employment policy towards tribal labour, which merely thought in terms of reservation of certain percentage of posts. New dimensions to this policy will be formulation of programmes for recruitment, training and promotion, all of which need to be reviewed and re-assessed from the point of view of actual benefits and effects they produce on tribal labour. Tribals have demanded certain privileges and rights and opportunities as 'sons of the soil', these demands cannot be brushed aside, because the tribals have lost their lands which have been acquired for development and have suffered on many counts to facilitate industrial undertakings to come up.

It is necessary for evolving a consistent and integrated policy towards involving members of backward communities in the industrial processes at work around them. Employment of tribal labour has improved of late, but mere reservation of posts will no longer help if steps are not taken to make them fit for the jobs, which are likely to be available. Steps should be taken to ensure that local tribal labour, especially the displaced labour, gets reasonable opportunities for recruitment to unskilled and semi-skilled jobs. It should be the duty of the management to arrange for training and education of these workers for skilled positions when employment opportunities are created or are available.

Employment exchanges in tribal areas should ensure that there is a longer time-lag between the arrival of the call-cards at the job-seeker's address and the date of interview. Simplification of registration and placement procedures in the employment exchanges should be undertaken, particularly in the case of tribal candidates who are illiterate or possess very low educational qualifications. The method of record-keeping should be overhauled. A liaison should be established between employment exchanges and voluntary organisations interested in tribal welfare to secure the help of the latter in spreading employment information and assisting job-seekers in filling in application forms.

UNPROTECTED LABOUR

Besides unorganised labour, there is a large element of unprotected labour, working in different parts of the country particularly in some of the larger towns and cities. Very little is known about it and much less has been done to ameliorate its conditions of work. The main difficulty in reaching relief to a worker in this category is the ill-defined arrangement he has with the employer or the person for whom he works on a specific job. The Maharashtra Government recently attempted to understand the position about these workers and to explore the possibility of reaching relief to it within the ambit of the existing labour legislation. On the basis of the findings of the committee specially appointed for the purpose, the Maharashtra Legislature has passed a Bill, The Maharashtra Mathadi, Hamal and other Manual Workers (Regulation of Employment and Welfare) Bill, 1968.

❑ ❑ ❑

9

TRADE UNIONISM

Introduction

'Time was when worker-employer relation was one of master and slave. Later it evolved as a relation of master and servant; after the industrial revolution it became one of employer and worker. Today the worker everywhere has developed a consciousness of his strength and aspires to be treated as a partner in industry. It is through the trade union that a worker exercises his strength'. Trade unions have become a major component of modern industrial relations system.

Trade union has been one of the first fruits of Industrial Revolution all over the world. So long as production was not in larger factories and was carried on by self-employed artisans with the help of apprentices, the disputes were settled by the rule of "give and take" and the problem never assumed serious proportion. Economy never experienced violent fluctuations as goods were sold in the local markets, retrenchment and closures were never a nightmare to the employees. But all this was completely changed by the industrial revolution. Personal ties between employer and employee got snapped and employee was treated more as a commodity than as a human being. In fact, he became a wage slave.

To meet the market situation employers economise labour cost by reducing the number of workers, cutting down wages and increasing workload. The workers realized the danger brought about by the changed situation. Revolt against this tyranny of the capitalistic system led the workers to the formation of unions.

Definition

The classic definition of a trade union has been offered by Sidney and Beatrice Webb in their monumental work, *History of Trade Unionism*. According to Webb, "a trade union is a continuous association of wage-earners for the purpose of maintaining or improving the conditions of their working lives". But now as the scope of activities of a trade union has increased, this definition is not considered adequate. Trade unions are no longer confined to wage-earners alone. Webbs' definition of trade union does not include the association of employers and of white collar employees which are generally regarded by English and Indian Law as trade unions. But in the popular sense of the term, the definition of trade union as given by Webb is still valid. The essence of trade union is found in the solidarity among workers as a security against the right to hire and fire of the employers.

This definition of a trade union is based on the assumption that under capitalism the functions of a trade union are based on three assumptions. The *first* assumption is the Doctrine of Demand and Supply. The workers know from their experience that individual bargaining will not safeguard their interests and so it is necessary to control the supply of labour on a national scale through organized union. The *second* assumption is the Doctrine of Living Wage according to which workers have the right to a minimum, sufficient to secure their efficiency as producers and citizens. The *third* assumption is the Doctrine of Vested Interests which means that the wages and other conditions of employment hitherto enjoyed by any section of workmen ought under no circumstances to be interfered with the worse.

We may add two other doctrines - the Doctrines of Partnership and Socialism - which are becoming powerful since the Second World War. There is an increasing recognition that workers are partners in industry and they should be associated with the affairs of management. As a result, joint consultative bodies have come into being. *Lastly*, socialism has become the ultimate objective of all trade unions. The trade unions aim at either abolishing capitalism or bringing a change in the capitalist order of the society.

The trade union has become a private government. The correct model of trade union has long been a puzzle. A union can be many things. It can be an agent of the state as in a totalitarian system, it can be an agent of the employer as under company unionism; it can be an agent of revolution under the radical control; it can be an agent of its class in a class society. But mostly, in modern capitalist society, it is the agent of its members. However, this does not settle how it will behave. It may follow an economic model and sometimes does, maximizing the income of its members. It may follow a political model and sometimes does, using the wage bargain as an instrument in conflict with another union or among union leaders. Mostly, however, it is a private government guided by bureaucratic leadership.

Trade unions are now considered a sub-system, which seeks to serve the specific sub-group's interest (i.e., workers) and also consider itself a part of the organisation. Therefore, there are trade unions of blue-collar workers, white collar employees and also employers.

Evolution

The growth of trade unionism is a response to the challenge thrown by the modern factory system. The development of modern industry from the eighteenth century onwards created conditions in which trade unions become necessary. In the age of individualism when the philosophy of *laissez-faire* held the sway, the wage-earners had to suffer great hardships and injustices. Trade unions were formed by workers for their own protection. Machine is said to be the major cause of the labour movement. It threatens the security of the individual worker who reacts in self-defence through a union to control the machine and ultimately intends to abolish wage slavery and establish workers' regime.

England in the second half of the 18th Century is the first home of trade unions. In UK the trade union movement started with the formation of friendly clubs of journeymen for social intercourse and mutual assistance in sickness and employment. These clubs also cooperated to resist wage-cuts, night work as overtime and forming unions in defence. In the USA trade union movement started with the craftsmen societies which were formed even before the factory system for the protection of native born skilled workers against the competition of immigrants. However, modern trade union movement started after 1850.

Initially formation and growth of trade unions met with a stiff resistance not only from employers but also from the Government in practically all industrially developed and developing countries. The workers had to struggle for years to get their right to form unions accepted by the employers and the State. The growing influence of trade unions made the Government and the employers apprehensive and so to curb their activities. Combination Act was passed in 1797 and 1800. These Acts forbade under severe penalty all combinations and concerted efforts to strikes, riots and machine wrecking. In 1824 the Government had to repeal that Act and trade unions ceased to be criminal conspiracies. It was in 1871 and 1875 unions were made lawful by enacting Trade Unions Act which protected their members and office bearers by making them immune from criminal and civil prosecution for peaceful picketing during strikes and lockouts. In USA also formation of unions was opposed bitterly by employers who in retaliation formed their own unions. The employers fought vigorously the unionisation of workers and at times these clashes resulted in violence, injuries and deaths. While in UK there was the notorious *Document*, in the USA there was what is popularly known as The *Yellow Dog Contract'* which the employer would compel a would-be recruit to sign pledging abstention from all trade union activities which practices continued in USA until 1935 when under Roosevelt Administration the new Industrial Relations Law, popularly known as the Wanger Act, set matters right.

Development in India

Trade union movement in India is of recent growth. It developed after the end of the First World War (1914-18) though labour unrest, agitation and strikes were not unknown before it. But labour before the First World War was lacking in combination, class consciousness and solidarity of interest.

First Period:1875 — Till the First World War: Industrial development of India on Western lines commenced from the middle of the 19th Century. It was at this stage of the industrial development of India that labour trouble began to emerge. But they were not upsurge of a landless proletariat. Whatever labour uprising took place in this period was only for the improvement of the working conditions in the factories. In India, as in other countries, trade unions grew out of the miseries created by industrial revolution. Although there were no unions in the real sense of the term, but sub-human employment conditions led to so many strikes during 1889-1900, organised by the workers themselves or under the guidance of some social workers. During this period labour leaders were only social reformers and they pleaded for human conditions of work from a humanitarian point of view. In 1875, a few social reformers under the leadership of Sorabjee Bangalee, started an agitation in Bombay to draw the attention of the Government to the miserable conditions of workers in factories, especially those of women and children and appeal to the authorities to introduce legislation for the amelioration of their working conditions. On the basis of the recommendations of the Bombay Factory Commission (1875) the first Factories Act was passed in 1881. But this Act was so inadequate that workers in Bombay protested against it. It was Mr. Lokhande who established in 1890 the Bombay Millhands Association, India's first labour organisation. The setting up of three factory commissions and enactment of the factories laws provided the necessary impetus for the formation of labour organisation. However, all these organisations were *ad hoc* bodies and could hardly be regarded as trade unions in the true sense. Besides, Lokhande, some other persons who organised early associations of workers, were Mr. P.C. Mazumder and Mr. Banerjee in Bengal, The Eosophical Society in Madras, Servants of India Society in Bombay and Brahmo Samajist Organisation in Calcutta, with the purpose of drawing public attention to the cause of labour.

Labour unrest again started at the time of the Swadeshi agitation which arose after the Partition of Bengal in 1905. The political unrest of the period provided a stimulus to labour uprising. Still it cannot be said that a labour movement in the true sense of the term had emerged in the country. The presence of labour leadership is essential for the development of labour movement. But the leadership was yet to develop from the rank of the working class.

Second Period:1918-29 : The end of the First World War witnessed the emergence of a labour movement in the country due to certain social, economic, political and international developments.

On the social side, an awakening had come amongst the masses. The Home Rule Movement which was going on at that time created a hope that after the war not only there will be a dawn of political advance but of a new status for the country. The false notion of the superiority of English race had gone. Masses began to look upon the Britishers as exploitators. On the political side, the passing of Rowlatt Act, the brutal massacre of Jallianwala Bagh, the starting of the Satyagraha by Mahatma Gandhi made the country prepared for a revolution. The Indian National Congress became a mass organisation and its leaders took upon themselves the responsibility of improving the lot of peasantry and industrial workers. On the economic side, the alarming rise of prices unaccompanied by a proportionate increase in wages made the condition of the industrial workers very sad and miserable. The economic distress created a ground amongst the workers to combine. On the international sphere an important factor which contributed to the development of trade union was the emergence of the International Labour Organisation. The success of proletariat revolution in Russia and the establishment of a workers' government over there influenced the labour movement of this country.

The year 1981 saw the formation of the first organised trade union-the Madras Labour Union by Mr. B.P. Wadia. Since then a large number of unions sprang up in almost all the industrial centres of the country. The All India Trade Union Congress, a Central Labour Organisation was formed by the Indian National Congress in 1920. Most of the unions existing at that time were affiliated to this central organisation. In 1922 the All India Railwaymen Federation was formed which was also affiliated to the AITUC. In 1921 an effort was made by Mr. N.M. Joshi to introduce in Indian legislature a Trade Union Act. However, his effort succeeded after five years in 1926 when Trade Union Act was passed legalising the right of workers to form unions and granting them immunity from civil and criminal prosecution for bonafide trade union activities. The Act continues to be the basic law governing trade unions in the country. This gave further boosting to the trade union movement in the country by providing that any seven persons can form their unions and get it registered under the Act.

Third Period:(1939 and onwards): In the '30s trade union movement received some setback due to economic recession but the outbreak of the Second World War and the formation of the populate Governments in the late 30s again quickened the pace of the growth of trade unions.

Trade unionism by 1939 had already become a consolidated labour force in the country. The war, however, provided a further impetus to its growth. The post-war period made the labour movement of the country a vigorous force. Socialism became the guiding philosophy of the movement. All the trade union organisations aim at bringing a change in the capitalist order of the societies but their methods and policies differ. While the All India Trade Union Congress believes in communism, the Indian National Trade Union Congress believes in the Gandhian philosophy of Socialism. While the former preaches revolution, the latter believes in the establishment of a socialist regime by peaceful means and non-violence.

The advent of independence, the new spirit of awakening, the changed outlook towards the unions both on the part of the Government and employers, the enactment of Industrial Disputes Act, 1947 and the desire of the political parties to help labour also contributed to the growth of trade unions in the country after independence.

Trade unionism has not only remained confined to industrial workers but has developed amongst the white-coloured class, the bank-employees, clerks, school and college teachers.

Present Position: Although no official latest figures are available regarding the number of unions and their membership, it appears that at present there may be more than 70,000 trade unions in the country and more than 70 federations. While the degree of unionism is fairly high in the organised industrial sector, it is negligible in the agricultural and unorgansied sectors where the bulk of the labour force (63%) is engaged and majority of workers live below the poverty line.

The tremendous growth in the number of unions does not reflect their real strength because the average union membership per union declined from 1026 in 1947 to 861 in 1987. As reported by the National Commission on Labour 73.2% of the unions had only a membership of below 300 and only 131 unions had only a membership of over 5000. Most of the unions are too small to be viable and have little following. The proportion of union membership to the total number of industrial membership is estimated at about 28%. The degree of unionisation also varies widely from industry to industry. The national trade union organisations have also associated themselves with world labour organsiations such as International Confederation of Free Trade Unions, a non-communist organisation and World Federation of Labour recognised by ILO and UNO.

CENTRAL TRADE UNION ORGANISATIONS

India is the only country in the world where there are as many as eleven central trade union organisations against one or two in the USA, UK, Japan and other developed countries. AITUC was the first such organisation set up in 1920 for representing India at the ILO annual conference. To free this organisation from the grip of communists another Central Organisation was formed by the Indian National Congress in 1947, known as the Indian National Trade Union Congress. In the same year with another split in AITUC the Socialist separated and formed Hind Mazdoor Sabha in 1948. In 1949 some of the radicals under the leadership of K.T. Shah and Mrinal Kanti Bose formed another central organisation with different ideology and political affiliation. Later on, some other central organisations were formed such as Bharatiya Mazdoor Sangh in 1955, Hindu Mazdoor Panchayat in 1965 and the Centre of Indian Trade Unions (1970) by the CPIM. In 1967 a central labour organisation shorn of any political ideology or control of any political party, known as National Front of Indian Trade Unions emerged under the leadership of S.P. Roy.

The Central Government recognises a central labour organisation for consultation and giving them representation on national and international forum if it has a membership of at least five lakh spread over four states and industries. So long Government has recognised only four organisations INTUC, AITUC, HMS and UTUC.

Functions of Trade Unions

The idea of forming a trade union is to secure collective strength for :

(i) Protecting and settling terms and conditions of employment of its members.

(ii) Negotiating and settling terms and conditions of employment and remuneration.

(iii) Improving the status and interest of workers in relation to work and living and

(iv) Promoting economic and social interest of its members.

From the above objectives of trade unions it is obvious that the primary functions of a trade union are to promote and protect the interests of its members. The union draws its strength from the support provided by its members. It has, therefore, to strive to secure better wages and improve their terms and conditions of employment and generally to advance their economic and social interest so as to achieve for them a rising standard of living.

The functions of trade unions may be discussed under the following heads, though there will be some overlapping.

1. Economic Functions: Originally the only function of trade unions was economic i.e. rescuing workers from exploitative employment and working conditions and use their collective strength to ensure workers adequate and fair wages, reasonable working hours, safe and healthy conditions at work, periodical rest and leave, some essential amenities at workplace like wholesome drinking water, first aid, washing and resting facilities. As a matter of fact, most of the early demands of the union which caused disputes resulting in strikes, were economic regarding wages, hours of working, safe and healthy working conditions and job security.

The unions started adding to the list of their demands such facilities as housing, medical aid, recreation, constitution of welfare funds and social security measures.

2. Social Functions: Besides the main economic functions, some unions have now started undertaking and organising welfare activities and providing variety of services to their members which may be grouped under the following heads:

- *(i)* Welfare activities provided to improve the quality of work life including organisation of mutual fund, cooperative societies for providing housing, credit, banking and medical facilities and training for women in various crafts to help them to supplement their family income.
- *(ii)* *Education:* Education of members in all aspects of their working life including improving their civic life, awareness in the environment around them, enhancement of their knowledge, their statutory and other rights and responsibilities, workers' participation scheme and procedure for redressing their grievances. Some central union organisations are also assisting the Government in implementing their workers' education scheme.
- *(iii)* Publication of periodicals, news letters or magazine for establishing communication with their members, making the latter aware of union policy and stand on certain principal issues and personnel matters concerning members such as births, marriages, promotion and achievements.
- *(iv)* *Research:* Of late, this is gaining importance and is intended mainly to provide updated information to union negotiators systematically collected and analyzed at the bargaining table. Such research is to be more practical than academic concerning problems relating to day-to-day affairs of the union and its activities and union and management relations. Some of the research activities are (a) collection and analysis of wage data including fringe benefits and other benefits and services through surveys of comparative practices, data on working conditions and

welfare activities; (b) preparation of background notes for court cases and also position papers for union officials; (c) collection and analysis of macrodata relating to the economy.

All the above mentioned activities and services are considered normal activities of unions in the Trade Unions Act, 1926, which stipulates the objectives on which general funds of the union can be spent.

*3. **Political Functions:*** For discharging the above functions unions have to operate not only on social, economic and civic fronts but also on political front. Unions have to influence Government policy decisions in the interest of workers. Legislative support which unions require for realizing some of their objectives and achievement of the long-term interests, taken them into the region of politics. Unions are not only to contribute in the formulation of policies but have also to see that policies are implemented. In several countries political process of the Government and participation in it have been attracting the interests of unions increasingly. Whether a union gets directly associated with a political party or has its own wing, should depend upon circumstances in each country. Considering that such political action association is legitimate, Trade Unions Act, 1926 permits the constitution of separate political fund to facilitate political action by a union.

The extent of unions' participation in the political process of the Government depends largely upon the stage of economic and social development. It ranges from the joint consultation at the plant/industry level to work on bodies like the Economic and Social Council in France, Planning Commission in Sweden or the Economic Council in Denmark. In a number of countries law specifies and activities that union may engage. In Sweden and Netherlands unions are made responsible for the implementation of the labour and social security legislation. Thus, while a union functions in the interest of its members, it should also accept community responsibilities. Consciousness of this wider responsibility will vary from country to country, depending upon the extent of wage employment. In a country like India where self-employment is sizeable, unions have to make special effort in understanding the interest of the total community. This aspect of the role of unions in a developing economy has been emphasized in our successive five year plans. It is in recognition of this fact that the very first planning Advisory Board constituted in 1950, had two labour representatives on it. Since then the labour representatives have been associated with Development Councils set up for individual industries and other tripartite bodies like the Indian Labour conference and Advisory Boards at the Central and State level in the formulation and implementation of labour programmes. This has enabled trade unions to perform their primary function for meeting the basic needs of their members.

(i) Securing for workers fair wages; *(ii)* Safeguarding security of tenure and improvement in service conditions; *(iii)* Enlargement of opportunities for

promotion and training; *(iv)* Improvement of working and living conditions; *(v)* Provision for educational, cultural and recreational facilities; *(vi)* Promotion of individual and collective welfare; *(vii)* Facilitation of technological advance by broadening the understanding of workers with their industry; *(viii)* Offering responsive cooperation in improving levels of production and productivity, discipline and high standard of quality.

Methods of Trade Unions

According to Webbs the objectives of trade unions are achieved through mutual insurance, collective bargaining and legal enactment.

1. Mutual Insurance: Mutual insurance involves the creation of a common fund to which every member should contribute. The fund is utilized for financing strikes, welfare activities and mutual benefit schemes.

From the very inception, trade unions have been spending a part of income for providing insurance and other welfare benefits for improving the conditions of their members, promoting the goodwill among them and maintaining solidarity within the organisation. The nature and extent of benefits provided has gradually expanded during the course of years. The effectiveness of the method is directly dependent on the income of trade unions. Where trade unions are rich, they are in a better position to provide insurance or other benefits to their members. The funds for mutual insurance come from membership subscriptions and donations.

The British trade unions have a strong tradition of adopting mutual insurance for the benefit of their members. In UK it was mainly the craft unions which provided mutual insurance.

The American trade unions have also a similar tradition of providing, out of their funds, benefits to meet the economic uncertainties to which their members are exposed.

The Indian trade unions have lagged far behind their counterparts in UK and USA so far as mutual insurance is concerned. Only a few trade unions in India have been able to develop certain welfare activities against the more common risks of life.

It was the early trade unions that developed mutual insurance for improving the lot of their members. At that stage, they were not on a position to develop the method of collective bargaining owing to the legal handicaps and hostile attitude of the employers. Once trade unions obtained legal recognition, they started giving more importance to collective bargaining. Collective bargaining has now become the most important method of securing the objectives of trade unions.

2. Collective Bargaining: As already mentioned collective bargaining has become the most important method used by trade unions for improving the conditions of their members. Collective bargaining involves concerted action on the part of the workers for improving terms and conditions of service.

The method of collective bargaining came to be emphasized after the trade unions secured recognition under law and became free from the criminal and civil disabilities which they had to suffer in their early stage. At that stage collective action on the part of workers for improving conditions of employment was illegal under the doctrine of restraint of trade. However, when the trade unions stood on legal footing, collective bargaining became the most important method of trade unions.

As a result of adoption of collective bargaining for the determination of terms and conditions of employment, trade unions were able to participate in the decision making process of an organisation. Collective bargaining has been fully discussed in a separate chapter.

3. Political Action/Legal Enactment: Legal enactment involves putting pressure on the Government for passing legislation for the realization of the objectives of trade unions.

Trade unions engage in political action for improving terms and conditions of employment. The main features of trade unions political action are — exerting pressure for protective or pro-labour legislations and setting up of labour parties or to develop allegiance to one political party or the other. Unlike mutual insurance and collective bargaining, which are designed to benefit only the trade union members or employees of a particular craft or industry, political action is intended to benefit the working class in general.

In the early days of the growth of union, when various legal disabilities prevented the trade unions from engaging in collective bargaining with their employers, there was a strong pressure for protective labour laws for regulating terms and conditions of employment. The series of protective labour laws that came to be adopted in UK during the 19th Century was essentially the outcome of the efforts of organised labour. Pressure for new labour legislations and improvement over the existing ones are still made by trade unions in many parts of the world.

In some countries, trade unions have also formed their independent labour parties or have come into relationship with other political parties of their choice. In UK, Trade Union Congress established Independent Labour Party. Similar labour parties have come into existence in many other countries. In India, trade unions have allegiance to one political party or the other. Thus, the INTUC has a close relationship with the Indian National Congress, BMS with the Bharitya Janata Party, AITUC with the Community Part of India and the HMS with the Socialist Party.

All over the world, trade unions are developing political wings and political links both for the purpose of securing reforms within the capitalist economic structure and for a fundamental reconstruction of the economic system by peaceful means, if possible and by violence, if necessary.

Theories of Trade Unionism

Theories of trade unions seek to answer the following four questions : *(i)* How to account for the emergence of labour organisations; *(ii)* How to explain the pattern of development of labour organisations. *(iii)* What are the ultimate goals of labour movement and *(iv)* Why do workers join labour organisations. Important theories of trade unionism are as follows :

1. Political Revolutionary Theory of Labour Movement of Marx: The theory is based on Adam Smith's theory of labour value. Its short-run purpose is to eliminate competition among labour and ultimate purpose is to overthrow capitalist businessmen.

To Karl Marx, the trade union was an "organising centre". Without organisation, workers compete with each other for available employment. Trade unions developed out of the attempts of the workers to do away with this competition for the purpose of obtaining at least such contractual conditions as would raise them about the status of bare slaves. The labour organisation provided the locus of the working class towards a change in the structure of society just as the mediaval municipalities were centre of organisation of the bourgeoisie, so the trade union for the proletariat. Thus, in addition to its original tasks, the trade union was to be the centre for organising the working class for its political emancipation.

2. The Webbs Theory of Industrial Democracy: Webb's book ***Industrial Democracy*** is the Bible of trade unionism. According to Webb, trade unionism is an extension of democracy from political sphere to industrial sphere.

To Webbs, the fundamental objective of a trade union is the deliberate regulation of the conditions of employment in such a way as to ward off the evil effects of industrial competition. The labour organisation utilizes the methods of mutual insurance, collective bargaining and legal enactment. According to Webbs, trade unionism is not merely an incident of the present phase of capitalist industry but has a permanent function to fulfil in the democratic state. The special function of the trade union is the democratic administration of industry. Webb's theory of trade unionism has not provided systematic answers to our first question.

According to Marx the ultimate objectives of trade unions are to overthrow capitalism, to capture the Government and to usher in a workers' State. Marx maintained an extreme view. On the other hand, Webbs considered trade unions as instruments to spread the ideals of democracy in the sphere of industry.

3. Tannenbaum's Theory of Man Vs. Machine: According to Frank Tannenbaum unionism is born of insecurity caused by machine and unionism overcome this inpecurity.

To Tannenbaum, labour movement is the result and machine is the major cause.. The machine threatens the security of the individual worker who reacts in self-defence through a union to attempt to control the machine. Tannenbaum sees the labour movement ultimately displacing the capitalistic system by the industrial democracy. His theory provides answer to three of the four questions posed above; he does not examine the pattern of growth of the labour movement.

4. Hoxie's Fundamental Classification of Unionism: Robert Hoxie classified unionism on the basis of their functions.

Hoxie classified four main varieties of unions - (a) Business unions are trade conscious rather than class conscious and protects the interests of various craftsmen. It accepts the existing economic system and demands only the right to bargain collectively to secure immediate objectives for its members. (b) Uplift unions are essentially idealistic in viewpoint. They may be trade, class or society conscious. It aspires to elevate the moral, intellectual and social life of the workers. (c) Revolutionary unions are radical in viewpoint and in action and eager to replace existing social order. It is class conscious rather than trade conscious. (d) Predatory unions are characterized by their ruthless pursuit of immediate ends. Its methods include collective bargaining, secret bribery and violence.

Hoxie provides an answer to the problem of the emergence of labour organisation in terms of "group psychology".

5. Perlman's Theory of the "Scarcity of Consciousness" of Manual Workers: Perlman wrote two books - *'A History of Trade Unionism in US' and 'A Theory of Labour Movement'*. He considered unionism as class struggle and considered it as communism of opportunity. He considered free competition as sin.

6. Simon's Theory of Monopolistic anti-Democratic Trade Unionism: He denounced trade unionism as monopoly founded on violence. He claimed monopoly power has no use save abuse.

7. Cole's Theory of Union Control of Industry: Cole's views are given in his book, *"World of Labour"*. His views are somewhere in between Webb and Marx. He agrees that unionism is class struggle and the ultimate is the control of industry by labour and not revolution as predicted by Marx.

Types of Unions

From the theories of Trade Unions it is clear that unions vary widely in their goals, their guidelines of policy, and strategy for attaining their objectives of policy. Broadly all the unions can be classified under the following heads :

(i) Revolutionary Unions : Such unions believe in the destruction of existing social and economic order and development of a new one. For attaining this objective they may propose a major shift in power and authority and use force for this purpose.

(ii) Reformist Unions : Such unions work and propose changes within the existing social and political framework of society.

(iii) Uplift Unions : They advocate extensive reforms well beyond the area of working conditions i.e., changes in the taxation system, elimination of property, abolition of death sentence and voting requirements'.

(iv) Business Unions : They depend on collective bargaining for attaining their objective and arriving at some collective agreement.

(v) Craft Unions : These unions cover members of single craft.

(vi) Industrial Unions : Industrial unions cover workers with a variety of skills employed in a single industry.

(vii) Affiliated and Non-affiliated Unions : Such unions may or may not be affiliated to central or national or inter-national unions.

Recognition of Unions

Collective bargaining will be possible only when the employer recognise trade unions as bargaining agent and agree to negotiate with it any matter affecting the interest of workers. A union may be strong and stable but unless it is recognized by the employer, it will hardly have any impact. Denial of recognition to a union is likely to make it militant and behave irresponsibly. Since there is no central law for compulsory recognition of unions, the employers are not bound to recognize any union and are free to recognize any union of their own choice.

In 1947 the Trade Unions Act was amended for making provision for compulsory recognition of unions. But the Act has not been enforced.

The Bombay Industrial Relations Act, 1946 is the first piece of State legislation which provides for statutory recognition of representative unions in the local area. This Act is applicable only to certain industries. In States other than Maharashtra and MP recognition of unions still remains a matter of discretion with employers.

The National Commission on Labour recommend that *(i)* It would be desirable to make recognition compulsory under a central law in all undertakings employing 100 or more workers or where capital invested is above a stipulated size; *(ii)* A trade union seeking recognition as bargaining agent from an individual employer should have a membership of at least 30% of workers in the establishment; *(iii)* The minimum membership should be 25% if recognition is sought for an industry in a local area; *(iv)* The minority union should be allowed only the right to represent cases of dismissal and discharge of their members before the Labour Court; *(v)* Industrial Commission should be appointed both by the State and Central Governments and one of the functions of such a commission is to verify the membership of the union for recognition by examining records of membership and subscriptions paid or if it considers necessary by holding election by secret ballot open to all employees. The Commission should define also the rights and privileges of both recognised and minority unions.

LEGAL FRAMEWORK FOR TRADE UNIONS - THE TRADE UNIONS ACT, 1926

Besides the Bombay Industrial Relations Act, 1946, and the Maharashtra Recognition of Trade Unions and Prevention of Unfair Practices Act, 1971, Trade Unions Act, 1926 is the only legal framework for the trade union movement in the country. It legalises the formation of trade unions by conceding to workmen their right of association and organising unions. It permits any seven persons to form their union and get it registered under the Act. Recognition of unions is optional and not compulsory. The National Commission of Labour recommended compulsory recognition of trade unions but still it has not been implemented. However, the latest amendment of the Industrial Disputes Act, 1947, makes registration compulsory, virtually by defining the term 'Trade Union' for the purpose of this Act, as a union registered under the Trade Unions Act, 1926. This disallows unregistered unions to represent workmen in conciliation, arbitration and adjudication of disputes under the Act. No worker would like to be the member of a union which is not qualified to handle his disputes under the I.D. Act.

Limitations of Trade Unionism in India

Indian Trade Union movement suffers from so many weaknesses as small size unions, poor finances, politicalisation and multiplicity of unions and outside leadership.

1. Small Unions and Poor Finances : The mushroom growth of unions has not accompanied by proportionate growth in the total membership. As a consequence, the total membership has been fragmented among too many unions adding to significant decline in the average membership per union. Average membership per union in 1987 was 861 against 1026 in 1947-48 and still less since 1987. With the small membership and low monthly membership subscription which is the main source of union fund (25 paise per month per member as prescribed under the Trade Unions Act, 1926), a union can hardly have sufficient money to have a whole time peon or a helper leaving aside pursuing any trade union activity. If a union is to grow, survive and meet the needs of its members for attaining its objectives, it needs money. Hence financial weakness is a major bottleneck in attaining a desirable degree of organisational effectiveness and viability. Lack of adequate finance and some wholetime workers, made the union an easy prey for the unscrupulous politicians who want to use unions as a ladder for climbing up in the hierarchy of political leadership and other outsiders who take to trade unionism as a profession for making money. Such persons get hold of the union and manage it and its finances more to serve their own interests than that of the workers.

2. Politicalisation and Multiplicity of Unions : Both politicalisation and multiplicity of trade unions are posing threat to industrial peace and harmony in India. Together with inter-union rivalry they frequently pose a serious managerial problem. Practically all through the history of trade unionism in the country, politics has played a significant part in its development. Some regard it as a by-product of political movement. Growth of four major political parties which have different ideologies and approaches in the distribution of power and role of labour in society. Affiliation of various trade union organisations to political parties has resulted in the multiplicity of trade unions in various industries as well as in the different units of industry, thereby reducing their bargaining power considerably and increase in inter-union rivalries.

Multiplicity of trade unions may also be due to the Trade Unions Act, 1926, permitting any seven persons forming a union, or due to unscrupulous employers encouraging and forming rival unions. At the national level there are as many as 11 central trade union organisations associated with different political parties and with approaches to labour problems. As these multiple unions owe allegiance to different political parties, there is bound to be inter-union rivalries among them making any collective bargaining and agreement difficult.

In a study of trade union movement in the West as compared with the movement in Asia, Africa and Latin America, E.M. Kassalow has referred to the fact that in ex-colonial developing economies there was a burst of trade union activities immediately after independence and political unionism was more common than economic unionism such as prevails in the developed countries in the West.

Multiple unionism may have some positive consequences such as encouragement of healthy competition, checking undemocratic practices by unions and developing an authoritarian structure with perpetuation of leadership and keeping the leadership alert and dynamic. But all these may be eclipsed by negative consequences when competition converts itself into unfair rivalries leading to inter-union warfare. Each union tries to counteract against the other.

3. Outside Leadership : Another distressing feature of trade union movement in India is the dominance of outside leadership which is a serious drawback to the trade union unity. No doubt, from the early stages the trade union movement has been built up by leaders committed to the well-being of the working class but seldom belonged to this class. They were either philanthropists or social reformers or politicians and their contribution was remarkable. This outside leadership still continues to guide the destiny of trade unions, but now most of the outsiders are no longer self-less dedicated social workers. They are either middleclass intellectuals or persons with low education taking up trade unionism as a profession. These outsiders generally occupy the key position of president or general secretary. The General Secretary who is usually the key full time official and who runs the union is generally an outsider. No doubt, the Trade Unions Act provides that at least 50% office bearers of a union should be from among the actual workers. But they are only secondary labour leaders who serve on the union executive as ordinary office bearers carrying little responsibility and it is the minority of outsiders holding dominant positions manage the activities of the union.

This continuance of the domination of outsiders is generally contributed to the illiteracy or low education of workers, hostility of employers towards unions and threats of victimisation of union members, lack of knowledge among workers of industrial practices in comparable organistions and complexities of union and management negotiations and the need for using the political influences of outsiders in formulation and implementation of labour policies of the Government.

Measures to Strengthen Trade Unions

The above mentioned weaknesses of unions are intensifying inter-union rivalries and reducing the bargaining power and their effectiveness in attaining their main objective of improving employment and working conditions of their members. For strengthening unions it is necessary that their weaknesses are minimized. The National Commission on Labour recommended following measures for removing the weaknesses of trade unions.

1. Trade Unions Act, 1926 should be amended to provide for (a) compulsory registration of unions; (b) reduction of percentage of outsider as union office-bearers (c) monthly subscription for union member may be increased form 25 paise to Re. 1/-; (d) the minimum number required for starting a new union should be raised to 10% of regular employees of a plant subject to a minimum of 7 and maximum of whichever lower; (e) the Registrar of trade unions should complete all preliminaries to registration within 30 days of the receipt of application; (f) the registration of union should be cancelled if the union fails to submit its annual return wilfully or otherwise, if its membership fell below the minimum prescribed for registration and the annual return submitted is defective in material particulars and if their defects are not rectified within the prescribed period. The cancellation should be subject to appeal to the Labour Court; (g) an enabling provision may be made to permit check-of system for collection of membership subscription on demand by a recognized union.

2. Formation of craft union should be discouraged. Craft unions operating in a unit/industry should amalgamate into an industrial union. Formation of centre-cum-industry and national industrial federation should be encouraged.

3. Steps should be taken to promote internal leadership and give it a more responsible role. The ex-employees should not be treated as outsiders.

4. Unity in trade union movement has to grow from within. Collective bargaining should be the main method of settlement of disputes. An independent authority for union recognition will hasten the process of inter-union rivalry. The latter is best left to the central organisation concerned to settle. If central organisation is unable to resolve the dispute, the Labour Court may step in at the request of either group or one motion by the appropriate Government.

5. Apart from paying attention to the basic responsibilities towards their members, unions should also take social responsibilities such as *(a)* Promotion of national integration; *(b)* Influencing the socio-economic policies of the community through active participation in the formulation of these policies and *(c)* Instilling in their members a sense of responsibilities towards industry and community.

WHITE COLLAR AND MANAGERIAL TRADE UNIONS

There was a time when unions and strikes were known only to workers in factories, mines, railways, docks etc. White-collar employees and professional people like doctors, engineers and lawyers, lecturers and senior executives thought it below their dignity to band themselves in unions, march the high streets and shout slogans. Today situation is different. Trade unions exist among most professionals, white collar employees, officers and managers and so do strikes and gheraos.

Highly paid employees in banks, in LIC and many other establishments are organised and so the Central Government and Semi-Government employers.

Why White-Collar Worker's Unions?

Seeing how unions of blue-collar workers had improved their service, employment and working conditions by bargaining collectively with their employers for better and regular payment of wages, bonus and other fringe benefits, and job and social security, white-collar workers also started uniting and organising themselves and forming their unions for fighting for better pay scales, more fringe benefits, internal promotion by collective bargaining, agitation and litigation. Other factors responsible for the growth of white-collar unionism are :

(i) Denial of both job security and social security to them by their exclusion from the purview of labour laws like Industrial Disputes Act, 1947, and laws relating to wages, bonus and social security against such social risks as sickness, maternity, premature death, permanent or temporary disabilities caused by accidents, old age and retirement.

(ii) Anomalies in pay caused by implementation of the recommendations of Wage Boards and Pay Commissions.

(iii) Nationalisation and consequent rationalisation of pay and perquisites.

(iv) Inconsistent and discriminatory promotion and salary policies which have been causing so many conflicts and disputes.

(v) Gradual narrowing of wages and salaries, differentials of blue and white-collar workers due to fast improvement in the wages and fringe benefits of the former on account of their union activities, and therefore causing feeling of deprivation among white-collar workers.

(vi) Inflation and soaring price resulting in erosion of pay and standard of living of white collar workers, and thus leading to demand for higher pay, dearness allowance and annual bonus and other fringe benefits. It is the union of the Government employees and public sector undertakings who had been excluded from the purview of the payment of Bonus Act, 1965, enabled them to receive now annual bonus worked out on the basis provided under this Act.

Growth of White-Collar Unions and Present Position

In India unionisation of white-collar workers began as early as 1897, when National Union of Railwaymen of India and Burma was formed. In 1905 Printers union was formed, and in 1907 Calcutta Postal Union started functioning. However, unionism among white-collar workers did not have significant growth before the Second World War. During this war banksmen formed their unions and their dispute was referred for adjudication. In the Post-World-War period rapid growth of industries and increasing number of banks and insurance companies, commercial offices, and also increase in the number of Government and semi-Government offices, accounted for tremendous increase in the number of white-collar workers.

Secretariat staff apart from railwaymen and postmen, are not allowed to form unions, since work in the Government is not an industry. That is why they call their organisation "association" and not union, which is generally registered under Registration of Societies Act, 1860 and not under the Trade Unions Act of 1926.

According to their conduct rules Government employees cannot go on strike. They cannot join an organisation in which non-Government employees participate. Also, they cannot have outsiders as office-bearers, nor can they work for any political fund. But in practice these restrictions have little meaning, as Government employees do go on strike and associate themselves with the unions of non-Government employees.

Salaried employees, known as white-collar employees, have been slow to form unions. This has also been the experience even in USA and Great Britain. But once they get over their initial coolness, they become as devoted to their unions or associations as manual workers.

Professional and technical workers start with professional organisations, which, in due course, undertake negotiation for better pay and condition of work and acquire the status of "near unions" which in due course tend to become more conventional unions.

Nature of Managerial Unionism

Hardly any organisation of managerial employees is a union. They are known as Officers' Associations registered either under the Societies Registration Act, 1860 or under the Trade Unions Act, 1926. The officers do not like their association to be equated with a trade union, though many of their organisations are registered under the Trade Unions Act, 1926. The purpose of managerial unions is not very much different from that of other trade unions for employees at different but lower levels in the hierarchy.

The officers eligible for membership of such associations are below the level of Director. They may be from the rank of trainees and upward upto the rank of Deputy General Manager, and in some cases even the General Manager. It is the junior and middle level managers who provide leadership of these associations.

In India, Managerial unionism is more in public sector than in private sector.

The emergence of Officers Associations in the public sector is relatively a new happening, whereas these associations have existed in the banking industry and insurance companies for a fairly long time.

Why Managerial Unionism

Feeling of *"relative deprivation"* has been an important reason for the officers/managers to organise themselves and form their associations for obtaining fair deal from their management. There has been a feeling that as compared to unionised cadre of workmen and lower staff they have been getting a raw deal. They complain about narrowing wage differentials generally.

Feeling of insecurity is another reason for the growth of officers unions. They do not have that enormous protection under the Industrial Disputes Act, 1947, which is enjoyed by the employees covered by this Act.

1. Growing Harassment of Managerial Staff by their Subordinates: The authority of the managers has been grossly eroded by the unionised workmen and staff. They are making it difficult for the managers to take work from them by being emboldened by the support from their union and protection they enjoy from labour legislation.

2. Neglect of Junior and Middle Level Managers in Bureaucratic Organisation : In such organisations junior and middle level managers feel lost. They find no ways of getting noticed by their top management who find hardly any time to provide necessary human touch. Decisions affecting them are taken unilaterally far from their working places - company's headquarters or Ministry. It is to make their presence felt and have some say in matters affecting them, that the managers/officers are organising and forming their associations.

3. Absence of Participative Forum : This has also encouraged the formation of Managers'/officers' associations. Managers at all levels do want to have effective say in the management of the organisation or the establishment where they work, as their survival and growth is closely linked with that of the organisation, and so they are very much interested to see how it works. In the absence of any forum set up by the management to involve them in its working, they are forming their association to utilize collective negotiations or bargaining as a participative forum for being associated with the management as closely as possible.

4. To be a Third Force between the Working Class and the Management : Being denied the protection of labour laws, and as well as of the privilege of a real manager, the junior and middle level managers have gone for the only option left to them, that is, the formation of the officers association. They would not like to be considered as part and parcel of either the working class or the management, but as a "third force" between these two groups.

❑ ❑ ❑

10

WORKERS' EDUCATION PROGRAMME

The Workers' Education Programme is sponsored by the ILO and is actively implemented both in developed and developing countries. In the developed countries like the USA and UK trade unions implement the programme. In India it is primarily Government sponsored.

Introduction

The value and necessity of education from the point of view of the individual as well as society cannot be overemphasized. Education is a value in itself, since it develops the personality and rationality of individuals. The assumption is that society recognising the innate value of rationality and learning, accords a high status to the educated. The second argument emphasizes the usefulness of educated persons to society at large. Their knowledge, by serving a social purpose, raises their status in society. From the point of view of the individual, education provides the necessary qualifications to fulfil certain economic, political and cultural functions and consequently improves his socio-economic status.

Education has come to be increasingly regarded ás a major instrument of social change. Education will bring about reduction of inequalities in society on the assumption that education leads to equalisation of status between individuals coming from hitherto unequal socio-economic strata of society. It is on this argument that the universal declaration of human rights included education as one of the basic rights of every human being.

Definition

The Encyclopaedia of Social Sciences defines workers' education thus :

Workers' education in contrast to other types of adult education seeks to help the worker to solve his problems not as an individual but as a member of his social class. It may aim to make him an effective member of his group by giving him a better understanding of his environment and by arousing his cultural interests. It may also aim to give him requisite special training for his office in his trade union or it may seek to inculcate in him a given body of social, political and economic doctrines.

Workers' education is generally differentiated from adult education as such although in India where the majority of the workers are illiterate, the workers' education programme does include efforts at imparting adult education.

The term "workers' education" has assumed different meanings in different countries due to historical reasons.

In a country like India where most of the workers are illiterate, the importance of workers' education cannot be overemphasized. Modern technology demands some degree of education from the workers. Secondly, the worker's awareness of his environment and of his responsibilities are a prerequisite to the development of an effective trade union movement.

It has been accepted all over the world that workers' education should be the responsibility of trade unions. In the USA, the unions alone undertake this work. In UK, the function is generally performed by both trade unions and voluntary social education bodies. Government and employers take no direct interest for this work. But in India workers' education has been almost entirely a Government responsibility.

In USA workers' education is considered as synonymous with training in trade union leadership. In UK, it covers trade unionism, general adult education and vocational education. In many countries of Western Europe, programmes of workers' education place a greater emphasis on education in citizenship than would be the case in UK. However, in developing world including India, the term workers' education is used in its wider connotation and it aims at making the worker a better operative, a better union member and a better citizen.

Economic development requires harnessing of all resources of the community to achieve the desired results. Capital is important but if the level of skill and knowledge of workers is not upto the mark, economic development would be retarded. Ignorance of workers is a strong barrier to the process of industrialization. Abilities and attitudes required to make modern technology productive are not available in the traditional agriculture-based occupations. Workers' education is an instrument in increasing worker potential for economic growth.

Industrial workers in most developing countries enjoy the advantage of having available to them the fruits of most modern and advanced technology. But they have to cope with the distance between primitive modes of work to which they are accustomed and the demands of complex technology with which they have to work. The lag between the available and the required competencies is wider and greater in India than in the West. Further, technology generates continuous change — new skills and occupations are constantly replacing the old. The modern society must have an educational system to cope with the situation.

Trade unions are generally regarded as the most powerful agency of workers' education. *First*, they are the chosen instruments of workers and as such it is their duty to improve the conditions of their members. *Second*, the acceptance of education by workers is likely to be more if the educators enjoy the confidence of workers and come from the workers' ranks. *Third*, all other agencies of workers' education, namely, the Government, employers and academic institutions do not reflect the needs, hopes and aspirations of workers to the extent that a trade union does. Consequently, they are not as suitable to run workers' education programmes as a union is.

In India trade unions also have been undertaking workers' education programme. Gandhiji included adult literacy in this constructive programme and asked all agencies to undertake that work. However, unions have not been able to do much due to paucity of funds.

The employers have not generally taken direct interest in workers' education.

The need for workers' education has been a subject of concern to many commissions and committees for several decades. The Royal Commission on Labour remarked that in India nearly the whole mass of industrial labour is illiterate, a state of affairs which is unknown in any other country of industrial importance.

Though this fact has been recognised since, no concrete steps were taken by Government to educate and enlighten the workers for a long time. This apathy continued for some years even after independence. It was only in the Second Plan that training of workers in trade union philosophy and methods found a place and was rightly considered a necessity if unions were to become self-reliant in respect of office-bearers. In view of the fact that most unions were not then equipped to undertake this responsibility, the Government had to take upon itself the task of running an educational programme under tripartite auspices. Accordingly, a scheme of workers' education was formulated by the Government of India in 1957 with the cooperation of Ford Foundation.

Objectives of the Scheme

The aims and objectives of the Workers' Education Scheme are :

(i) To develop leadership from rank and file and promote the growth of democratic process and tradition in trade union organization and administration.

(ii) To develop strong and more effective trade unions through better trained officials and more enlightened members.

(iii) To equip organised labour to take its place in a democratic society and to fulfil its social and economic responsibilities and

(iv) To promote among workers a greater understanding of the problems of their economic environment and their privileges and obligations as union members and citizens.

The Government of India appointed a semi-autonomous Board- the Central Board of Workers' Education to administer the workers' education scheme. It sets standards for teachers and programmes, arranges for the provision of necessary materials and aids and inspects and supervises all programmes conducted under its sponsorship. It also stimulates trade unions and educational institutions to undertake workers' education programme of the approved pattern and standard by making financial grants.

The Board operates a three tier programme for workers' education.

The *first* tier consists of Education Officers who are top level trainers employed in the service of the Board. The Education Officers are given an intensive training by the experts appointed by the Board. The Training Wing of the Board, known as the Indian Institute of Workers' Education, started functioning at Mumbai from 1970. It organizes regular training programmes and refresher courses for Education Officers, trade unionists and others. After the completion of their training, the Education Officers are posted to Regional Centres.

In the *second* tier, selected workers are trained by the Education Officers as worker-teachers at the Regional Centres in full-time training courses of three months' duration in batches of 25-30 each. This training is a continuous process at each Regional Centre which is expected to train between 75 and 100 worker-teacher trainees is made by a local committee attached to each Regional Centre. The trainees are sponsored by trade unions.

In the *third* tier, the worker-teachers on completion of training at the Regional Centre return to their respective factories and conduct programmes for the rank and file workers at the unit level classes,; generally, classes are held in the evening. All the necessary facilities are provided by the employer. The activity of the worker-teacher is supervised by the Education Officers.

In addition to these programmes, the Board conducts special short-term training programmes of 1 to 14 days' duration for white-collar workers, seminars, workshops, camps, etc.

Apart from the three-tier programmes, the Central Board organizes special programmes on productivity education and workers' participation in industry. This is done at the national, regional and field levels. The Board collaborates with the National Productivity Council in implementing the productivity programmes for workers and trade union leaders.

The syllabus for worker-teachers include trade unions, its objectives, organization, history and development, union-management relations, labour legislation and economics.

The Board gives grants-in-aids to trade unions and other institutions to encourage them to undertake workers' education programmes. The scheme contemplates that in due course of time the trade union movement should take over the primary responsibility for workers' education.

The Board finances its worker education programmes mainly through grants received from the Ministry of Labour and Employment.

The Central Board set up a Review Committee in 1964 which recommended making the scheme as mass movement involving trade unions, universities, State Governments as well as a periodic assessment of the Workers' Education Scheme.

❑ ❑ ❑

11

EMPLOYERS' ORGANISATIONS

Protection and promotion of the interest of members having identical interest — the prime motivation for the formation of any organisation — is as valid in the case of employers' organisations as it is in their counterpart. The intention is covering employers' organisations also under the Trade Unions Act, 1926 was to place both workers' unions and employers' organisations on par in matters of rights and responsibilities. The principle of giving equal representation to capital and labour on all consultative bodies like the Indian Labour Conference, Standing Labour Committee and Industrial Committees recognises this basic tenet in employer-employee relationship. In considering issues relating to employers' organisations, a basic distinction between them and workers' unions has to be kept in mind. While workers get together for joint action through a union, an employer is in many cases an organisation in himself and meets the union on equal terms. At the same time, employers find it convenient to organise themselves in furtherance of common objectives of evolving attitudes to labour or approaches to national policies, as also for standardisation of wages and other conditions of employment in an industry within a local area.

Origin and Growth

The origin, growth and development of employers' organisations have three distinct phases : *(i)* The period prior to 1930; *(ii)* The period between 1931 and 1946; and *(iii)* The post-Independence period. Each phase reveals its own structural and functional characteristics; in each the organisations had to undergo changes because of contemporary economic, social and political developments. These changes have been more rapid in some than in others. The periods referred to also coincided with important developments in the labour field, and these have had a great impact on the pattern and development of employers' organisation as also on their functioning.

Pre-1930 Period: This period was characterised mainly by the formation of associations of merchants in the form of chambers of commerce. During the latter half of the last century, industrial associations also came into being with the aim of protecting the commercial interest of their members and securing concessions from the Government Regional associations at important centres of industrial activity developed, but again with a different focus for action. The Bombay Millowners' Association, the Bengal Millowners' Association, the Ahmedabad Millowners' Association are instances in point. Because of the need for industrial development and promotion of indigenous entrepreneurship, society was kind to and proud of persons who were instrumental in setting up industrial establishments generally, and Indian employers particularly. Not until the First World War did the organisations consider it important to deal with labour problems; there used to be stray references about undue militancy shown by labour, but these also were rare. By and large, the attitude of the employers towards labour was one of indifference and, at times, of aggression. The task which the orginisations set for themselves was to defend their traditional rights through legislative bodies and social contacts. Individual members had autonomy in working their units and in dealing with labour as they liked. Notable exceptions were the Indian Jute Mills' Association (IJMA) and the Bombay Millowners' Association which, because of conditions created by the First World War, regulated the working hours of member mills and introduced a system of payment of standard remuneration to workers. The Ahmedabad Millowners followed, but somewhat later. Shortage of skills in those days made individual employers attract workers by better payment. The workers gained in the process, but this did not last long since the employers soon realised the disadvantage of such individual arrangements. In plantations and mines, for instance, the employers were cautions in not allowing 'poaching.'

It was during this period that unions started gaining ground. Simultaneously, the movement for the liberation of the country also gathered momentum. The Indian National Congress was trying to synthesise the interests of workers and employers by bringing them politically under one fold. The limited success achieved by it in the process was confined to some industrial centres, because a fair section of employers was outside the pale of such political influence. The combined effect of factors like the setting up of the ILO, the enactment of the Trade Unions Act, 1926, and the Trade Disputes Act, 1929, was the realisation on the part of individual employers of the need for greater coordination of their collective interests.

A Period 1931-46: Organising chambers of commerce and industrial associations for dealing with a variety of problems connected with industry was the rule prior to 1930. Some of these chambers dealt with labour matters too. The All-India Organisation of Industrial Employers (AIOIE) and the Employers' Federation of India (EFI) came into existence in 1933 to comprehend and deal with problems of industrial labour in a concerted manner. The All-India Manufacturers' Organisation (AIMO) followed in 1941. The setting up of these organisations was again, as in the case of workers' unions, in response to the need then felt for representation on international conferences and legislative bodies. For a long time since 1920, the Government of India used to nominate delegates/members to represent employers' interests at such forums from amongst members of chambers of commerce but the employers soon realised that the chambers of commerce could not effectively look after their interests in labour matters. Each of the three organisations referred to above had a different sponsorship. The AIOE consisted mainly of indigenous entrepreneurs and had links with the Federation of Indian Chambers of Commerce and Industry. The FEI of those days had predominant membership of British Industrial interests. The AIMO was sponsored by comparatively small sized establishments to look after their interests. The Government of India Act, 1935 made provision for representation of employers and labour in legislative bodies through special constituencies. The constituents of the AIOE and FEI thus got an opportunity to be represented in the Central and Provincial Legislatures. Labour legislation in the thirties in some Provinces made it necessary for local employers' organisations to expand their services to members in the labour field. The creation of the Labour Department in the Central Government and the constitution of tripartite bodies like the Indian Labour Conference and the Standing Labour Committee during the years of the Second World War helped develop further these activities within the local associations and federations.

Post-Independence period: The period since Independence witnessed the growth of planning, expansion of industrial activity, extension of the democratic apparatus, passing of several labour laws and growing trade union movement, all of which acted as a spur for the strengthening and expansion of employers' organisations. Experience of working together convinced employers of the advantage of united action. Employers' organisations grew in strength mainly to meet the requirements of individual employers for advice on labour matters. In some cases, they built up their strength to match that of organised labour; in others, it was the other way round. At present, employers' organisations are organised at three levels : *(a)* employers operating through their local organisations or otherwise; *(b)* industrial associations which cut across State boundaries; and *(c)* federations which comprise representatives both of industries and centres. Of the three, the local organisations which operate mainly through the chambers of commerce cover all industries in an area; their activities in the labour field are comparatively less extensive. It is the arrangements in the latter two which require a more detailed discussion.

Industrial Associations

The industrial association is the general pattern of organisation of employers in India. These associations are formed at the area/regional level as also at the all-India level. Regional/industrial associations are generally affiliated to the central industrial organisation at the apex. Individual employers are also admitted to the apex. The main reason for the development of associations, industry-wise, is the common nature of problems confronting each industry. The setting up of wage boards on an industry-wise basis, industrial committees at the Central and State levels, and development of collective bargaining at the industry level in certain regions, have helped their growth. Jute, cotton textiles, engineering, tea, sugar, cement, paper and chemicals are important industries which have associations at the all-India level with branches in areas/States. In turn, most of these associations are affiliated to national federations. Development of these associations was gradual. They have been instrumental in providing specialised labour advisory services and developing training facilities for management personnel in the last ten years.

Existence of more than one industrial association in a particular industry is a problem which has at times hindered the progress of collective bargaining on an industry-wise basis. Difficulties of multiplicity have, to a certain extent, been overcome in coal mining and plantations where joint committees have been formed to ensure a uniform approach by employers in dealing with industrial relations problems concerning the entire industry and in making representations to the Government. We are of the opinion that this is a healthy development; multiplicity of employers' organisations within an industry is not conductive to collective bargaining. Wherever, at present, there is more than one organisation of employers dealing with an industry, National Labour/Commission suggest that these should be amalgamated into a single organisation and the first step in this direction would be the constitution of Joint Committees to deal with the problems of the industry as a whole or to negotiate on behalf of the industry at that level.

The Commission is aware of the limitations of the managements in the public sector to join industry-wise organisations primarily meant for employers in the private sector. The reluctance of some undertakings to fall in line with the private sector may have some justification, but as employers there is an identity of interest between the public sector and the private sector. The Government of India had already permitted public sector units to join the respective industrial associations. There is reason to believe that this is being done. It expected that, in due course, public undertakings will be able to play a role in the counsels of the industry to which they belong and through them in the wider forums available to private employers. There is an equally strong case for cooperatives to join the respective industrial associations.

Labour Commissions' recommendations supporting the growth of industry-wise unions and their recognition will acquire greater strength if parallel arrangements are made on the side of managements. As stated in the Second Plan : "in the interests of industry-wise bargaining in an area, provision should be made for the certification of employers' associations as representatives of industry in an area. Any agreement entered into by such associations would then be binding on all members of the associations, as well as on non-members. The implementation of this recommendation is long overdue. Arrangements should be made through the Industrial Relations Commission for certification of employers' organisations at the industry/area level for purposes of collective bargaining.

At the national level, apart from the AIOE and the EFI which have had representation on consultative bodies in labour matters, the AIMO has also been given a seat almost since Independence. The AIMO is an omnibus multipurpose body which represents the voice of small and medium-sized employers, but its membership is not restricted to them. Unlike the AIOE and EFI, the AIMO combines in itself both the trade and labour interests of its members. Membership of these organisations is open to individual firms or joint stock companies engaged in any industry and to any association/chamber of commerce representing an industry/industries in the country. Between them the three federations cover almost all employers; some employers/associations are members of more than one national federation. It is true that the spheres of influence of these organisations vary from area to area and from industry to industry, but their functions are not exclusive; indeed, they have a mutuality of interest. This explains the reason for a firm or an association joining more than one federation.

All the three federations have special committees to deal with specific problems. Besides, they operate through their regional committees and maintain close links with the respective chambers of commerce as well. In many cases, the labour departments attached to a chamber of commerce and to a federation are common to both. For example, the representatives of firms and associations connected with the Bengal Chamber of Commerce and Industry in the Eastern region and who are also members of the EFI, have formed the Eastern Regional Committee which is the same as the Industrial Affairs Committee of the Chamber. These members of the Eastern Regional Committee serve on the Executive Committee of the Employers' Federation of India. The Labour Department of the Chamber acts as the Secretariat of the Eastern Regional Committee. The position in regard to

Regional Committees in other parts of the country is not any different. Since the headquarters of the EFI is located in Mumbai, its Western Regional Committee is serviced in part by the main secretariat of the EFI. Arrangements in the case of AIOE are somewhat similar. The regional committees serve as a vital link between the Federation and the chambers as also its affiliated industrial associations. The AIMO activities centre round the functioning of 20 special committees, one of which is for industrial relations. It membership is spread throughout India and has nine State Boards, four Regional Boards and seven District Councils.

Aims and Objects of Federations

(a) Employers' Federation of India: The principal objects for which the EFI has been established are embodied in its Constitution. These are :

(i) "To promote and protect the legitimate interests of employers engaged in industry, trade and commerce;

(ii) To maintain harmonious relations between management and labour and to initiate and support all well considered schemes that would increase productivity and at the same time give labour a fair share of the increased return;

(iii) To collect and disseminate information affecting employers and to advise members on their employer/employee relations and other ancillary problems."

These objects lie within the field of what may broadly be termed 'industrial relations.' Although consideration of braod economic problems is not altogether excluded, the EFI does not generally comment on commercial questions of customs, taxation and the like which lie in the sphere of the Associated Chambers of Commerce and Industry.

(b) The All India Organisation of Employers: The objects of the AIOE are *inter alia* :

(i) "To take all steps which may be necessary for promoting, supporting or opposing legislative and other measures affecting or likely to affect directly or indirectly, industries in general, or particular industries;

(ii) To nominate delegates and advisers, etc., to represent the employers of India at the International Labour Conference, United Nations Organisation, International Chamber of Commerce and other conferences and committees affecting the interests of trade, commerce and industries, whether as employers or otherwise;

(iii) To promote and support all well-considered schemes for the general uplift of labour and to take all possible steps to establish harmonious relations between capital and labour."

(c) The All India Manufacturers' Organisation : The objectives of the AIMO are :

(i) "To help bring about the rapid industrialisation of the country through sound and progressive economic policies;

(ii) To help in increasing the aggregate wealth of India;

(iii) To raise the standard of living of the people of India by utilizing the fullest possible extent all the available national resources and talent in the country; and

(iv) To play a positive role in relieving the pressure of population on land."

The industrial relations functions of the AIMO are similar in material particulars to those of the EFI and AIOE.

All these federations function through their regional offices which have, over the years, developed departments well equipped to deal with labour matters. The two federations, AIOE and EFI, operated severally in securing representation on consultative bodies, but jointly in their approach to problems connected with labour. Such a joint front was for a long time on an informal basis. With the coming together of these two main bodies in the Council of Indian Employers (CIE) in 1956, it is this Council which has now taken on the functions of choosing delegates to represent Indian employers in international conferences/committees. It is this Council which is a member of the International Organisation of Employers at Brussels in place of the AIOE and the EFI which were earlier affiliated separately. The period since Independence is thus particularly important because of the joint approach by employers to labour problems, informally in the first half and somewhat more formally in the second. Building up of adequate specialised advisory services in labour matters and training of management and personnel officers at various levels have been the result of this joint approach, although a beginning in this direction had been made earlier by individual industrial associations.

Apart from these important activities, the two main Federations took special steps to organise the movement for scientific management. The All India Management Association which has been active in the last ten years and which is supported by local associations is now an active force in the counsels of management. The two management institutes set up about ten years back and the departments for the study of management set up in some universities and the training courses they organise have to some extent helped in meeting the shortage of trained management cadres.

Multiplicity of organisations at the national level has not been a problem with employers' organisations. Unified representation of employers' interest at tripartite forums has, for all practical purposes, been effectively secured by the main employers' organisations coming together under the

CIE. But the AIMO is outside the CIE. It will be desirable that the CIE brings this organisation also within its fold. It is easier for the employers' organisations to come closer, because there are no special ideological differences to divide them. The CIE can continue to provide the coordination. Determination of representation on important national organisations should rest with the apex body. Taking into account the nature of agenda to be discussed at any meeting, the reconstituted CIE will be in a better position to nominate persons competent to partake in the deliberations. Some organisations at the industry level and the Employers' Federation of India at the national level, originally registered under the Companies Act, are now registered under the Trade Unions Act, 1926, while many are still outside its purview. One can realise the psychological difficulties in employers' associations registering under the Act, which though designed for both employers and workers, has a special appeal to workers' organisations. If such barriers are considered insurmountable, separate arrangements for registration will be appropriate. In any case, registration of employers' organisations should be made compulsory.

Role and Functions of the Employers' Organisations

The main role and functions of an employers' organisation is to protect and promote the interest of its members. The membership of employers' organisations is basically composed of corporations/employers who have certain purely economic ends to pursue. All enterprises have to survive the test of economic viability. For a proper appraisal of the role and functions of an organisation, this aspect cannot be brushed aside. Naturally, its activities are designed and directed in such a manner that their members stand to gain. Also the organisations have to work on a broader plane; labour problems are only a part of their overall responsibilities. Economic, commercial and fiscal matters and policies are equally or even more important for them. Services rendered by the organisations in representing their members' views on Government's policies, rules and regulations and in giving advice to members on the interpretation and extent of applicability of agreements arrived at various bipartite and tripartite bodies and on Acts and Regulations which come into force constitute their main functions. Labour departments/advisory services, which has come in vogue in many employers' organisations to advise and assist members have been the direct consequence of the recognition of these functions.

Employer's organisations find it necessary to have legislative support for realisation of their objectives. The pursuit of their activities leads to their involvement in politics or to their developing lobbies without directly aligning themselves with any political party. There is evidence on record to show that individual employers, and not the employers' organisations, have used these avenues to the extent necessary, although providing finances to political parties or sponsoring candidates are not unknown to the organisations or industrial associations, national or local. Political activity by employers' associations may be as inimical to peace in industry as that by workers' associations, particularly when we are envisaging employers' organisations to include both public and private sector units. This should be eschewed. It is thus that they will be able to establish rapport between the two sectors and work exclusively to the interest of industry rather than to the sectional interests of one or the other form of ownership.

The pursuit of economic gains by employers' organisations does not mean that they should not recognise social responsibilities. With planned economic development and increasing democratisation of the institutional framework of society, there is active consultation by the State with all organisations, including those of employers, for formulation, *inter alia*, of economic, educational, social and labour policies. Employers' organisations are, therefore, expected to take a stand consistent with the social and economic objectives of the community/country as a whole and be active in promoting policies and measures that are not contrary to the general interest of the community. Along with their gains, they should keep in view the needs of the developing economy, the requirements of planned growth, importance of maintenance of peace in industry and the desirability of an equitable distribution of the national wealth. There can, however, be differences as in the case of trade unions, as to priority between the interests of the community and the interests of their members. Since these conflicting interests require to be harmonised, it would be appropriate to deal with the role and functions of the employers' organisations by studying them specifically in relation to their obligations to their constituents on matters which impinge directly on labour.

Obligation to Constituents

The functions of national organisations on the labour side are somewhat limited. In the industrial relations system, as it exists today, the powers and responsibilities are largely concentrated in the associations operating at the industry/area level or in the individual employers. While in Sweden and Italy the national federations are negotiating bodies as well, in India they neither participate in any negotiation with unions nor do they deal with the industrial relations problems of their constituents. Barring exceptions, instances in which all-India organisations have espoused the cause of an individual employer/company are few.

The main obligations that are being discharged at present by national organisations in the labour field are to formulate policies for the guidance of delegations to international conferences and tripartite meetings and advisory bodies. Organising broad-based discussions on certain aspects of labour problems and occasional training courses and seminars have also been recently acquired functions. As such, the activities of the national organisations are almost exclusively directed to dealing with and influencing policy at the national and international levels, ascertaining and representing the view of their constituents, and ensuring that the decisions adopted are properly understood and implemented by the constituents. Collection of data to aid and support their stand and dissemination of information to members and the public are important aspects of their activities. In these tasks, regional committees set up by them are the main functionaries. These committees have in their turn constituted screening committees in some centres to examine proposals made by their constituents for filing appeals against the decisions of tribunals and labour courts. This is one of the obligations imposed on them by the Code of Discipline. While the labour commission take note of the setting up of these committees, it would like to record that there is dissatisfaction both among unions and Governments about the manner of working of these committees.

Industry-wise associations occupy a key position in the industrial relations system, as they are better placed to appreciate the problems of the industry concerned and provide guidance to their constituents. The local/regional industrial associations are in a still better position to do this. Because of the ease with which they can contact their members and reach unions and *vice versa*, the role of these associations in industrial relations has been quite significant. The philosophy behind providing such machinery, supplementary to that which takes care of influencing Government policies in other matters, is that the function of these associations is as much to safeguard and promote the long-term benefits of the industry as to look to the short-term interests of individual employers. In undertaking these obligations effectively, the industrial associations have built up their own hierarchy. The central industrial organisations primarily undertake the function of representation at various bipartite or tripartite bodies at the industry level.

In the Eastern and Western regions, particularly in industries such as jute, tea, coal, engineering and cotton, the industrial association have played an effective role in sponsoring standard practices and in giving guidance to members on all matters governing industrial relations. Direct negotiations between industrial associations and trade unions have not made head-way, because collective bargaining at the industry level or on a national plane has not yet developed.

There are instances, however, where an area/industry-wise understanding has been reached between an industrial association and the trade unions in the meetings of the industrial committee or even in conciliation. Industrial associations particularly those at the local/area level, maintain informal contacts with trade union organisations. Labour departments of such associations have resolved disputes between workers and managements of their constituents units.

To complete this part of the account, it would be useful to record the work done by some individual industry/central organisations, since it has lessons for the future. Apart from the conventional role that the IJMA has been performing, its contribution in training management personnel and in organising extensive training for junior supervisory staff has been noteworthy. The IJMA started its labour department in 1939 to study labour relations within the industry and encourage a uniform approach to the solution of the industry's labour problems. One of the main promotional activities of the Indian Engineering Association, the Engineering Association of India and the Indian Mining Association is to provide expert labour advisory services to their constituents. The U.P. branch of the Indian Sugar Mills Association has got a separate labour department fully equipped with technical staff; the services of the staff are extended to the constituent units. The UPASI, the Indian Tea Association and the Indian Tea Planters' Association have developed on somewhat similar lines. In the Western region, the Bombay Millowners' Association and the Ahmedabad Millowner's Association have built up certain traditions of industry-wise negotiations. Their role in collection and dissemination of statistical information relating to trade, commerce and labour has been commendable. For this purpose, they have gradually built up a full-fledged research and labour advisory service. These organisations have also been instrumental in the development of training institutions for Managers and Personnel/Welfare Officers.

In certain areas a tradition of industry/area-wise negotiations has evolved, and in some undertakings run by enlightened employers, collective bargaining has taken root. We have recognised elsewhere the important role which collective bargaining and arbitration can play in promoting industrial harmony, and in this context, the role of employers' organisations is clear. They should also encourage collective bargaining and should also encourage voluntary arbitration and wean away reluctant employers from recourse to third party intervention. This can be achieved only when individual employers change their attitude. Labour Commission's recommendation for legislative support for union recognition requires, in addition, an educative effort on the part of organisations among their members. It requires that employers' organisations should strengthen themselves by way of provision of adequate research facilities and equipping themselves with data for understanding the problems of the concerned industries. It is only thus that they can assist and advise companies in matters of negotiations.

Because of complexities introduced in dealing with industrial relations in the context of technological change, technicalties involved in interpretation of labour legislation and also sound understanding of industrial case law and practices developed in enlightened case law and practices developed in enlightened concerns, managerial functions have acquired new dimensions. The old pattern of employer-manager functions combined in one person is yielding place to a specialized managerial and personnel system.

Some employers' associations have not only been inducting personnel management consciousness among their affiliates, but have also built up their own cadres to assist managements in dealing with personnel problems. However, taking an overall view, there are no regular and scientific arrangements for training of supervisors and middle management personnel in the art of handling labour. This aspect of training should receive due attention from the employers' organisations. It is difficult for smaller units to have the full-time services of personnel officers; nor is it necessary for them to do so in view of their small size. This is a field where associations can assist them by making available their own officers and rendering guidance in matters of personnel policies.

From the view point of labour management relations, employers' association should accept the following functions:

(i) undertake promotion of collective bargaining at various levels;

(ii) encourage observance and implementation by its members of bipartite and tripartite agreements in real spirit and form;

(iii) expedite implementation of wage awards by members without undue delay and reservations;

(iv) work towards elimination of unfair labour practices by employers;

(v) encourage adoption by members of personnel policies conducive to productivity and industrial peace;

(vi) promote rationalisation of management or organisation to improve productivity;

(vii) arrange employers' education *(a)* in the concept of labour partnership in industry, *(b)* for ensuring identity of interests of labour and management and *(c)* for promoting harmony between the goals of industry and the community; and

(viii) work towards the collective welfare of its members through training, research and communication in the field of labour-management relations.

Commission on Labours do not propose statutory provisions to compel employers' associations to undertake the above functions, but hope that these functions would voluntarily be adopted and discharged by them.

Finances

Employers' organisation rely heavily on subscription from members. They have two rates of subscription — one for individual members and the other for associations. EFI collects subscriptions from ordinary members at the rate of Rs. 50/- per 100 workers employed subject to a minimum of Rs. 1,000/- and maximum of Rs. 12,000/- annually. Membership subscription from associate members is Rs. 170/- per vote, each vote representing 1,000 to 2,000 employees covered. AIOE has fixed Rs. 750/-

per year for individual members and Rs. 1,000/- for subscriptions. AIMO charges Rs. 100/- annually from individual members; district associations, company members, State associations, and chambers of commerce have to pay an annual subscription of Rs. 150/-.

Communications

For the efficient and effective functioning of employers' organisations, an essential requirement is the existence of active communication, from the association to its constituents and *vice versa.* It is through such communication that the association can represent the view of its members and facilitate implementation of the commitments it makes. As at present, the procedure seems to be to exchange views through annual and special meetings, occasional discussions and through seminars devoted to specific subjects, in all of which the constituents are expected to participate. Federations also issue instructions, circulars, research papers, annual directions and directives, where necessary to their constituents. Even with these arrangements, difficulties have arisen when the constituents are fairly dispersed. Some employers have pointed out that there is scope for improvement in the arrangements for exchange of views between the central organisations and their constituents on a continuing basis. Commission on Labour heard statements from industry/local organisations that the central organisations have sometimes made commitments at the tripartite committees on issues of vital economic consequence without adequate prior deliberations. Such grievance could be exaggerated. With the best of intentions, it will be difficult for apex organisations to satisfy all members, each having its own peculiar problems. Communication between an employers' organisation and organisations of workers to discuss common problems is rarer still. This does not mean that problems do not exist, rather there is reluctance on the part of both to get together.

The inadequacy of the present system of communication is perhaps reflected in non-implementation and non-acceptance of obligations under certain agreements accepted by the organisations. In the midst of this general complaint, it is worth mentioning that some employers' organisations like the IJMA, the Indian Sugar Mills Association, the Bombay Millowners' Association, the Ahmedabad Millowners' Association and the United Planters' Association of Southern India (UPASI) have worked out arrangements which give adequate satisfaction to their respective constituents in this regard. Apart from the conviction that they have about the usefulness of constant and continuing exchange of views, easy accessibility to members is the main reason for the success achieved by these associations.

It is alleged that the system of voting and representation adopted by the Central Federations tends to favour the bigger industrialists and employers, and this has created difficulties in proper and effective representation of medium-sized units which form the backbone of the country's industrial structure. Inadequate consultation with such units is reported to be the cause of ineffective implementation of their obligations by employers. It is found that such grievances are more psychological than real. It does not mean that if prior consultation had taken place, the obligations could have been less onerous on employers. Difficulties in implementing tripartite conclusions/decisions have sometimes arisen at the establishment/plant level because of difference or due to the special circumstances prevailing at the unit level. In the implementation of agreements, persuasion is the only instrument which the employers' organisations can adopt. It is obvious that in such matters other sanctions cannot work. The causes for non-implementation of agreements are many and varied; ineffective and inadequate communication is only one of them. What has been said about national organisations is equally valid in case of industry/area-wise associations. Employers' organisations should build up their internal consultation system in such a manner that all matters, which have far-reaching impact on members, are scrutinised by the constituents prior to any decisions that might be taken at the national level.

Social Responsibilities

The role played by the employers in the country's development needs no elaboration. Consistent with their interests, they have contributed to the national progress. However, the community gets directly concerned with employers' organisations only when it fails to get goods of approved quality at reasonable prices. Service and courtesy to customers are really an indication of good employer practices. Employers' organisations should see that their members do not exploit the community through combines, trusts or monopoly operations. These observations have a special relevance in the context of other developments in the economy. The surpluses that are generated in an industry are a social product; their distribution has to be according to the contribution made by labour and capital, keeping in view that the community has an equal claim on the increases in production and productivity.

Employers' organisations have a stake in the success of the national plans for economic development. In this context, important aspects of social responsibilities of employers are in the following fields :

(i) *Promotion of national integration* : Employers' organisations can help to achieve national integration by paying due regard to the sentiments of the local people where a project is located. But this has to be within the overall national interest;

(ii) Eliciting responsive cooperation from the unions in improving levels of production and productivity.

(iii) *Maintaining high standards of quality and competitive prices in the inter-national market :* Difficulties of foreign exchange are well known; these have hit employers in their expansion plans. What is suggested, therefore, falls within employers' enlightened self-interest;

(iv) *Helping civic authorities and seeking their cooperation in matters connected with improvement of the area in which the establishment is located :* Where an establishment is set up in an already settled town, this function acquires a special significance. By the very setting up of a unit, particularly if the size is large, civic amenities get taxed. It is true that the employer in turn is taxed on that score, but the duty of the employer should not end there. He has to see that by establishing his unit he does not make the life of persons in the area more difficult. The advantages that accrue through an industrial development are looked upon by the people as a matter of right; not so the inconveniences;

(v) *Bridging the gap in regional disparities in the economic development of the country :* This is indeed a Governmental function, but the employers' organisations can certainly help; and generally,

(vi) Pursuing of policies that are conducive to the development of industry and the economy and to the fulfillment of priorities of planned development from time to time.

International Affiliations

The International Organisation of Employers (IOE) was established in 1920 to reinforce, at the international level, the activities of the larger national employers' organisations aimed at preserving and developing an economic and social system based on free private enterprise. One of the important tasks of the IOE is to assist employers' delegations at the tripartite meetings of the ILO. A member of the general secretariat of the IOE has acted as secretary to the employers' group at almost every ILO meeting held since the ILO was established. The IOE also helps its member organisations to exchange mutual experience and facilitates the study of common problems and keeps them informed of labour and social problems the world over. The members of the IOE belonging to our country have often pleaded the cause of developing nations and emphasized the need for channelising the investible resources of the institutions affiliated to IOE into countries starving for want of capital. The contacts in the IOE have helped members from our country in reaching collaboration arrangements which have been in vogue in India, particularly since Independence.

❑ ❑ ❑

12

DISCIPLINE, DOMESTIC ENQUIRY AND GRIEVANCE PROCEDURE

CONCEPT OF DISCIPLINE

Discipline is an important aspect of man management. Personnel management is far more important when people are being fired rather than hired. Employee indiscipline is both the cause and effect of the state of industrial relations. Other indications of indiscipline in a plant may be the high rates of absenteeism, labour turnover, accidents and sickness, multiple unresolved grievances, low and faulty turnout, increasing wastage, low motivation and morale of work force and greater number of interruptions and conflicts.

In the wider sense, discipline means orderliness — the opposite of confusion. In the military circle, the term discipline is synonymous with regimentation. In the industrial context, it does not mean strict and technical observance of rigid rules and regulations. It simply means working and behaving in a normal and orderly way, as any reasonable person expects an employee to do. It is as much a basic necessity for the people working in a plant as in other segments of society.

Importance

Importance of discipline in industry can hardly be overemphasized. Orderly behaviour is essential for achieving the organisation's objective. Without discipline no enterprise would prosper. If discipline is necessary even in a family which is a compact, homogeneous unit, how can an industrial organisation with heterogeneous people, work smoothly without discipline? What the management has to do when the employee is at fault, is to take disciplinary action. Discipline should be directed against an act and not against the person. Discipline is said to be good when employees follow willingly the rules of their supervisors and the various rules of the company. Discipline is said to be bad when employees either follow rules and regulations unwillingly or actually disobey them. Poor discipline suggests the need of correction. The fundamental reason for taking disciplinary action is to correct situations that are unfavourable to the company. 'Basically discipline is a form of training. When disciplinary problems arise, it may be as much management's fault as the workers.' Many disciplinary problems grow out of management's failure to inform employees what is expected of them.'

The word 'discipline' has unpleasant associations with punishment but with the addition of the "just cause" concept involving a limitation on the employer's right to discipline and discharge, the word been extended to embrace a system of training and education of both the employee and his supervisor, designed to achieve orderly conduct.

The keystone of just cause is the principle of 'corrective' or "progressive discipline" that is, the misconduct must be handled under a system of warnings and graduated penalties which gives the employee time to reflect upon his errors and mend his ways before the final act of discharge, when efforts at correction have failed.

Objectives of Discipline

Discipline is essential for the smooth running of an organisation, for the maintenance of industrial peace which is the very foundation of industrial democracy. Without discipline, no enterprise would prosper.

The aim of discipline is to obtain a willing acceptance of rules and regulations of an organisation so that organisational goals may be attained.

As a system of orderly conduct, modern industrial discipline has many benefits for the employer and the employee alike. It enhances efficiency and reduces costs. Absenteeism and employee turnover are minimized. Equipment is given better care and scrap losses decline. The employees gain a sense of security and safety. They work without fear of unfair penalty for misconduct which they could not reasonably be expected to prevent. Their self-respect and respect for the company is preserved.

Two different attitudes towards discipline are in action today — the autocratic and democratic. Autocratic type of discipline is enforced by constant supervision by the superior and threats of punishment. The trouble with this type of discipline is that it does not take into account the desires of those commanded, it appeals only to the fear motive and not to other positive motives and also requires constant supervision.

The new method of discipline is defined as an orderly conduct of affairs by members of an organisation who adhere to its necessary regulations even if they desire a harmonious cooperation with the ends of the group and willing recognition that to do their own wishes must be brought to reasonable union with the requirements of group in action.

The statement that "discipline is what the leaders make it" is the observation of Fayol on managerial responsibility for discipline. A manager who shirks this responsibility is failing in his duty to manage. In many cases indiscipline stems from the managerial faults and lapses. Even where indiscipline results from the faulty attitudes and behaviour of subordinates, the responsibility lies with the manager because of his power of influencing and controlling of eliminating their attitudes. The Government of India has prescribed model Standing Orders to cover disciplinary procedures.

Self-discipline

The best discipline is self-discipline. Generally, if workers feel that the rules by which they are governed are reasonable, they will willingly observe them. Rules are respected not for fear of punishment but for their reasonableness and legitimacy. With the development of the human-relations approach in industry, increasing attention is being given to employees as individuals. The human-relations approach lay emphasis on developing sanctions from within, in contradistinction to the traditional viewpoint which believes in controlling the worker from outside. According to the new approach a sense of responsibility is inculcated amongst the employees by means of increased participation, delegation and job enlargement.

Discipline is required only when all other measures have failed. Management should ideally try to establish what has been called "positive discipline." an atmosphere in which subordinates willingly abide by rules which they consider fair. In such an atmosphere the group may well exert social pressure on wrong-doers and reduce the need for 'negative' (i.e., punitive) discipline.

Since disciplinary action involves penalties and since dealing out penalties has dangerous implications, management must fully know when, why, how and to whom the disciplinary action should be taken. Only then this action will gain its purpose with a minimum loss of employee goodwill. Even when the conduct of an employee deserves punishment he accepts it with some amount of ill-feeling. However, to forgo punishment when it is due is to invite trouble and to inflict punishment when it is not due is doubly dangerous.

Most people prefer an orderly atmosphere in which to work, if management does not deal effectively with those who violate rules, the disrespect for order will spread to the employees who would otherwise prefer to comply.

Disciplinary action in most companies is taken by line-executives. Personnel people are not the "axe men." Occasionally the personnel department is made responsible for taking final action on such serious penalties as discharge of workers. In any case, the personnel department has heavy responsibility to aid all executives in taking disciplinary action.

Negative Discipline

Traditionally supervisors have thought of discipline in a negative sense, i.e., only as punishment. Many executives still see discipline primarily as a means to enforce external demands for responsible behaviour. They do not place any reliance on spontaneous self-discipline. Instead they expect orderly behaviour to depend primarily on fear of penalties. Thus, they exercise discipline as punishment partly as deterrent and partly as a retributive justice. However, the idea of discipline is to supplement and strengthen self-discipline within each individual and within the work group. Any act of clear disobedience shall be considered ground for disciplinary action. The type of correction depends upon the cause of poor discipline. If the attitude is unfavourable because the company is at fault, the action to be taken involves the removal of the cause and convincing the employee of the desire of the company to be fair. As already said, when the unfavourable attitude of the worker is due to his fault, the action to be taken is known as "disciplinary action." Now the question is how severe should the penalty be? Many companies have provided what is called 'progressive' or corrective discipline which calls for increasingly severe penalties each time a man is disciplined.

Disciplinary action has two major aspects — the employee is at fault because of some failing of his own and some form of penalty is to be? applied. In handling disciplinary cases the two major aspects — the steps to be taken and the principles to be followed in each step — should be carefully observed.

Approaches to Discipline

Management can make five possible approaches to any act of indiscipline —

(i) Judicial Approach: Under this approach the nature of offence in a particular situation is determined by carefully weighing the evidence and taking all the steps prescribed for disciplinary procedure. The law of natural justice is followed, i.e., the offender is given an opportunity to defend himself, cite mitigating factors and to plead for clemency. This is a fair process but it is time-consuming and leads to delays. In India we are more accustomed to this approach than to any other. This approach is best exemplified by domestic enquiry.

(ii) Human Relations Approach: Under this approach the offender is treated as a human being. If he has violated the rules, the human relations approach would ask the question, why did he violate the rule? For example, sleeping during the night-shift might be due to the fatigue caused by factors over which the man has no control, e.g. illness in the family. In such a case an attempt should be made to help the worker to get over such a personal difficulty or to change the shift of duty or to shift him to a job which he can conveniently handle rather than take an extreme view and punish him severely.

(iii) Human Resources Approach: Under this approach every employee is looked upon as a resource to the employer and that the human resource is the most important factor of production. This resource has to be trained, motivated and brought up to the level of efficiency required by the organisation. Indiscipline on the part of workers due to *(a)* failure of the training and motivating system and *(b)* the individual's own failure to measure upto the requirements of conduct prescribed as the prevailing norm in the organisation. In the latter case, it is violation of the prevailing norm. The disciplinary authority has to look into two objectives of the disciplinary process: *(a)* Is the violation so serious as to jeopardise the functioning of the organization, if the offender is allowed to continue? *(b)* Can the offender be reformed by disciplinary action? In this context extreme form of penalty like discharge or dismissal will be rarely resorted to as the offending human resource will have to be trained and motivated to work within the requirements of the organisation's norm of behaviour. This approach would naturally attach a good deal of importance to discipline being more a matter of self-control or self-discipline than a matter of external control.

(iv) Group Discipline Approach: If the organization has well-established norms of conduct it should try to involve groups of employees in the process of discipline. If the management succeeds in making the group accept the organization's norms as their norms by virtue of such involvement, then the main function of discipline will be a delegated function than a management task. The group as a whole can control an individual worker who is its member much more effectively than the management can through penalties.

(v) Leadership Approach: Every manager has to develop a leadership quality as he has to guide, control, train, develop and lead a group of men and act as a leader whatever may be his position in the organisational hierarchy. He can administer discipline among the men whose work is under his direct supervision much more than even the top management can. He has a day-to-day relationship with his men and the worker listens to him. Again they would listen to him all the more if his own behaviour is disciplined.

STEPS IN DISCIPLINARY ACTIONS

Disciplinary action involves the following steps. 1. Statement of disciplinary problems; 2. Collection of full information on the case; 3. Types of penalties; 4. Choosing among the alternative penalties; 5. Application of the penalty; and 6. Follow up of the case.

Statement of Problems

This most important step in the whole process of disciplinary action is to make sure about the problem that demands discipline. Five points must be answered in arriving at a statement of a disciplinary problem: *(i)* Determining the nature of the violation. The executive should very carefully proceed so that the chance of falsely including a case under disciplinary action is eliminated. Right from the start, a wise executive must not mis-interpret circumstances. If an employee is falsely accused the executive has to face unfortunate consequences of his foolish action. *(ii)* Stating the violence. When the executive is sure that a violation has occurred, he should state objectively the character of violation. The specific rule, regulation, or order that was broken must be determined. *(iii)* Determining the circumstances. A violation may be execusable or not, depends upon the circumstances. Any extenuating or accentuating circumstances should be considered. *(iv)* Individuals involved. In case of violation the executive must ascertain which individual or individuals were involved in a violation. If a single individual has broken a rule he should alone be taken to task but if other people are involved in the case, they should also be punished. *(v)* Nature of Repetitions. Lastly, it is significant to state when or how often the alleged violations occurred. The frequency of violations determines its seriousness. An employee who has been absent without excuse several times in a month, deserves a more serious reprimand than one who has been absent but once. The above mentioned steps will reduce the dangers of false accusations.

Collection of Full Information on the Case

Gathering facts is essentially supplementary to the preceding step as well as others to follow. When an employee breaks a rule or fails to meet established standards of work or of conduct, the executive cannot afford to ignore such unsatisfactory conduct. But instead of taking hasty action, he should make a thorough investigation into the case. The supervisor has to make sure if there are any extenuating circumstances, such as ill-health, family troubles, etc. In the process of fact gathering, the executive should not confuse opinions with facts. If opinions are mistaken for facts, it is easy to reach wrong conclusions.

Types of Penalties

The sequence of penalties are as follows: *(a)* Oral Warning; *(b)* Written Warning; *(c)* Disciplinary Lay-off and Suspension (temporary removal from service); *(d)* Demotion in Rank; *(e)* Withholding of Increments; *(f)* Fines; *(g)* Adverse Remark in Service Book; *(h)* Dismissal (removal from service for misconduct with a stigma) and *(i)* Discharge (removal from service without any stigma).

When a man breaks a rule or fails to maintain standard, an oral warning that repetition may eventually call for discipline is in order. At this stage disciplinary action remains unofficial because it does not become a matter of written record. The aim of oral warning is to help the employee correct his behaviour by telling him that his undesirable conduct cannot be tolerated.

Written warnings are the first formal stage of corrective discipline. If an employee does not respond to oral or unofficial warning, then a formal written warning containing a statement of the offence is called for. In an unionised concern such an official document should be issued in the presence of the supervisor. Written warnings are often prepared in four copies — one for the personnel department, one for the supervisor, one for the foreman and one for disciplined employees.

Disciplinary lay-off or suspension are next in severity. Disciplinary lay-off may be for several days or weeks. Many companies skip over this stage of discipline because it is too cumbersome to replace an employee for a few weeks. To whom written warnings fail, lay-off involving a loss of income, may be a shock that serves to bring them back to their sense of responsibility. Since suspension is a form of lay-off it should not be used unless the offence calls for at least a lay-off.

Demotion in rank or down-grading is a preliminary step to discharge. The usefulness of demotion as a disciplinary measure is questioned as it suffers from a number of disadvantages. Losing pay over a period of time is a long form of constant humiliation as compared with the sharp slap of a lay-off. Again, if a company is to retain a man in any capacity, it makes more sense to use his highest skill. Moreover, demoted employee will be constantly dissatisfied and that his dissatisfaction may spread to co-workers affecting adversely morale, productivity and discipline of the work force. Withholding of increments as a form of punishment is seldom used these days.

There is a provision for fines for certain acts of omission and commission as per Section 8 of the Payment of Wages Act, 1936. Fines can be imposed only for certain acts of omission and commission specified in notices approved by the competent authority. The total amount of fine which may be imposed in any wage-period on any employed person is not to exceed an amount equal to half an anna in the rupee (i.e. 3 paise) of the wages payable to him in respect of that wage period. No fine shall be imposed on any employed person who is under the age of 15 years. All fines shall be recorded in a prescribed register and credited to Fines Fund and the said fund is to be utilized only for such purposes beneficial to the workers as are approved by the competent authority.

All major cases of indiscipline/misconduct are recorded in the service book which serves as an index of evaluation when promotion or some other employee benefits are given. When lay-off is inevitable, those with adverse remarks are to be penalised first.

Discharge remains the ultimate penalty. It is generally referred to as "industrial capital punishment." It is such a drastic form of action that it should be reserved only for the most serious offenses or for people who will respond to no lesser penalty. For the employee, discharge is a serious setback. It makes difficult for him to secure a new job if the prospective employer comes to know that he was discharged by his employer. Since it reduces his chances of earning a livelihood, it may affect his mental equilibrium. For the organisation also discharge involves serious waste and losses. They represent time and money spent in hiring, training and supervising an employee who now leaves the firm. Considerations of such costs as well as pressure from unions have greatly reduced the number of discharge as compared with earlier times. The only plus factor in discharge is that it is clearcut, forceful and final action.

However, sometimes discharge for "just cause" is necessary. It is such a serious step that correct procedure for management is important. The executive should be able to prove that he followed "due process." The dismissal notice should state and explain all charges against the employee. Adherence to "just cause" requires that management should be in a position to establish the employee's guilt, thereby justifying disciplinary action.

Choosing the Penalty

After a case calling for disciplinary action has been properly examined and alternative penalties considered, the particular penalty to be applied should be chosen. This should be done fairly and fearlessly. To overpenalise the employee is unfair but leniency may encourage more and more violations. Every effort should be made to prevent the occurrence of disobedience, but if drastic action is necessary, it should be taken without hesitation. Infractions of rules that go without penalty encourage the rule-breaker to continue on his way. In the choice of a penalty, it should be remembered that it will serve as a precedent if a similar case has never been handled. Employees will compare current decisions with what has gone before.

Applying Penalties

The next step is the application of the penalty. It involves a positive attitude on the part of management. If the disciplinary action is a simple reprimand, the executive should calmly dispose of the matter. When drastic action is called for, a serious attitude should be taken. Reprimands and penalties are always unpleasant to handle, hence the quicker and more impersonally the matter is handled, the better. Penalties are most effective when the punishment is closely associated in the mind of the wrong-doer with the act that brings it. If the penalty is delayed, the employee may have forgotten the wrong doings and think that the company is picking on him.

Follow-up of Disciplinary Action

The ultimate aim of disciplinary action is to help develop good discipline. Its aim is to make sure that employees do not willingly break rules or disobey orders. The disciplinary action cannot repair the damage done. Hence, disciplinary action must be evaluated in terms of its effectiveness after it has been applied. Disciplinary action has been effective so long as there is no recurrence of bad discipline. It is wise practice to check the performance and attitude of employees who have been subject to disciplinary action.

PRINCIPLES OF DISCIPLINARY ACTION

In taking disciplinary action, it is wise to follow certain principles and to assume certain attitudes towards employees in general.

Announced Disciplinary Policy with Advance Warning

Management should consistently follow an announced disciplinary policy. An executive is in an unassailable position if the record shows that his action was based on established facts, that he has made a genuine effort to help the wrongdoer, given ample advance warning and finally put a hardened offender on notice that his unsatisfactory behaviour would no longer be tolerated.

The employee, in turn, is responsible for the timely and proper exercise of his right to protest against any disciplinary action that is unjustified. However, he must do so in an orderly and peaceful manner. Any resort to direct action is in itself a recognised ground for discharge.

Discipline is regarded as fair by workers if it is accepted without resentment. And unexpected discipline is universally considered unfair. This means that (i) there must be advance warning that a given offence will lead to discipline and (ii) there must be advance warning of the amount of discipline that will be imposed for a given offence.

Consistency

If two men commit the same offence and one man is more severely disciplined than the other, naturally there will be cries of favouritism. Supervisors lose the respect of his subordinates if they impose discipline in a whimsical and inconsistent manner. Consistent discipline is fair and is far more likely to be accepted by the workers involved.

Impersonality

It is very difficult to impose discipline without causing the person disciplined to feel resentful and aggressive. But the supervisor can minimize the danger by imposing discipline in as impersonal a way as possible. 'Discipline is most effective and has least negative effect on individuals, if the individual feels that his behaviour at the particular moment is the only thing being criticized and not his total personality.

Once the supervisor has decided what discipline is appropriate, he should impose it quietly and impersonally. After disciplining a subordinate the supervisor must not tend to avoid him or to alter his attitude towards him. Shifts in attitude are dangerous for they generate corresponding changes in the subordinate's attitude and ultimately the whole relationship may be destroyed. The supervisor should make him feel that bygones are bygones and that the act was punished, not the man. It is essential to believe that employees can be trusted even though they occasionally break rules. After all, even the best workers make mistakes of omission and commission.

Give Employee an Opportunity to Explain.

Disciplinary action should not be taken without giving the employee an opportunity to explain his actions. This is an important part of the supervisor's investigation. If he gives an explanation it should be investigated to find out whether what he says is true.

Decide What Action to Take

The supervisor must know the principles of "Corrective Discipline." It means the purpose of discipline is to correct improper conduct. It should not be punitive in nature; it should not be used solely for the purpose of punishment. Discharge is disciplinary action which is not corrective in nature. So discharge should be resorted to only when previous efforts to bring about correction have failed. The application of the principle of Corrective Discipline consists of an initial reprimand or short disciplinary lay-off depending upon the nature of the offence. If this action does not bring about correction, a more stringent penalty should be given. If this action does not still impress him sufficiently, a still more severe penalty is given, as a final warning. If the employee continues to engage in misconduct, then discharge is the right remedy.

The disciplinary action must not be too severe but it must be severe enough to constitute a reasonable attempt to bring about correction. In deciding what disciplinary action to take, the employee's prior misconduct record should be checked. The employee's length of service as well as the period of time which has elapsed since the employee's last disciplinary action is also an important factor. Lastly, disciplinary action must be recorded. This will give an idea of happenings to any manager who might need it.

Disciplinary Action as a Tool

An executive must consider disciplinary action as a tool and not as a weapon of supervision. He should see reprimands and penalties in the same light as brakes on a car. They "slow down" employees when needed, they act as a preventive but they cannot cure an accident. Therefore, when a penalty is applied, it should be in the manner of using a tool and not as a threatening gesture.

Executives must be convinced that disciplinary action is needful and effective. Disciplinary action is a tool that must be used for the company's benefits. Executives should not shrink from taking disciplinary action when it is needed. They must feel that penalties assigned in a given case were not only justified but also beneficial to employees. At the moment an employee may dislike to be penalised but it may be good for him in the long run. It is a general rule that nobody should be penalised publicly.

In taking disciplinary action it is essential to remember that disciplinary action has its after-effects. This comes about in two ways — *(i)* a given penalty does or does not serve to change the employee's attitude towards company rules; *(ii)* a given penalty in a given case is considered as a precedent. In the future when similar wrongdoers are to be disciplined, the penalty should not be changed.

NEW CONCEPT OF DISCIPLINE: THE HOT-STOVE RULES

Inflicting discipline puts the supervisor in an anomalous position. He expects his subordinates to continue to help him even when discipline is painful. The question, "can he impose discipline without generating resentment?" Douglas McGregor thinks that it can be done by what he called the "hot-stove rule." This rule draws an analogy between touching a hot-stove and undergoing discipline. When you touch a hot-stove your discipline is immediate, with warning, consistent and impersonal.

Let us look at these four characteristics as applied to discipline. When Mr. X burns his hand he is angry with himself. Sometimes he is angry with the stove too, but not for long. He learns his lesson quickly because:

- the burn is immediate
- he had warning

- the discipline is consistent and anyone who touches the stove is burnt
- the discipline is impersonal — a person is burnt not because of who he is but because he touched the stove.

The person is disciplined not because he is bad but because he has committed a particular act. The discipline is directed against the act, not against the person. There will still be resentment against the source of the discipline, but the more automatic the discipline becomes, the more the resentment is reduced.

ROLE OF THE UNION

Discipline is properly a management function in which the union does not take part. The union's true role here is that of a protagonist in protecting its members against unjust management action. Unions rarely object to discipline provided it is applied consistently and provided the rules are clearly publicised and considered reasonable. Management should not expect the union to discipline members who violate the rules. When the union does impose discipline, it is abandoning its traditional role as worker's defender and management is failing to assume its responsibilities.

Most unions contracts require *(a)* that the company may discipline employees only for "just cause;" *(b)* and that any employee who feels he has been unjustly disciplined may appeal to higher management through the grievance procedure and if management's answer is unsatisfactory, to arbitration. The arbitrator makes the final decision on whether the discipline was for just cause.

STATUTORY LAW ON DISCIPLINE

Under the Industrial Employment (Standing Orders) Act, 1946, every industrial establishment, employing 100 or more workmen (50 in West Bengal) is required to define with sufficient precision the conditions of employment including the rules of discipline and procedure for punishment for indiscipline.

Acts of Indiscipline/Misconduct

Every act of indiscipline is called a misconduct. Under the model Standing Orders suspension upto 4 days and dismissal for various acts of indiscipline have been provided for. These acts of indiscipline include the following:

disobedience and insubordination

theft, fraud, dishonesty in connection with employer's business or property

wilful damage/loss of employer's goods

taking or giving any bribes/illegal gratification

habitual absence/unauthorized absence for more than 10 days

habitual late attendance

habitual breach of any law applicable to the establishment

riotous or disorderly behaviour during working hours at the establishment or any act subversive of discipline

habitual negligence or neglect of work

frequent repetition of any act of omission, for which fine may be imposed and

striking work or inciting others to strike in contravention of any law.

Under the model standing orders prescribed under the rules made by the West Bengal Government the following misconduct have been added.

Drunkenness, intoxication, engaging in trade within the establishment, disclosing secrets, habitual breach of rules for maintenance of any department, allowing unauthorized person to operate machines, unauthorized collection of funds, smoking where prohibited, holding meetings without authority, convention for offence involving moral turpitude, refusal to accept charge-sheet, sleeping while on duty, participation in illegal strike or wilful go-slow tactics, gambling within premises and money-lending or borrowing within the premises.

PROCEDURE FOR DOMESTIC ENQUIRIES

Domestic enquiry is the expression used in industrial employment while departmental enquiry is the expression used in Government employment. Both imply an enquiry into an allegation of misconduct against an employee of the organisation. It embodies judicial approach to discipline. All such enquiries are guided by two principles of natural justice (1) No man shall be the judge in his own case and (2) Hear the other side. The *first* principle precludes the appointment of a person for conducting the enquiry who himself is interested in the outcome. The *second* principle places upon the authorities the obligation of affording every opportunity to the offender to defend himself.

The procedure for domestic or departmental enquiry by an employer into the misconduct of his own workman is as follows:

Charge-sheet: If a *prima facie* case has been established and the offence is quite serious, a charge-sheet may be prepared on the basis of the allegations made. It should be in writing detailing the allegations of misconduct. It should also indicate the time within which the workmen charge-sheeted should submit his explanation. The charge made in the charge-sheet must be clear and precise. A proforma of charge-sheet is given here.

Suspension: Where, in the interest of discipline, the shutting out of the charge-sheeted workman is necessary, the employee should be suspended. He is to get wages for the period of suspension if so provided in the standing order.

Service of Charge-sheet: If the workman is present, it should be handed over to him in the presence of witness after explaining the content of the charge-sheet in a language known to him. If the delinquent workman is absent or refuses to accept the charge-sheet, it should be sent to his last address under registered post with acknowledgement due. If he refuses to accept it or if it comes back undelivered otherwise, the charge-sheet has to be published in a local newspaper with wide circulation.

Explanation: The explanation given by the worker within the given time has to be considered.

Notice of Enquiry: If the explanation is found unsatisfactory, a notice giving the time, place and date of the enquiry together with the name of the enquiry officer has to be served on the worker. The enquiry officer must not be one who has issued the charge-sheet because it is a principle of Natural Justice that a person is disqualified to act as a judge if he is a party to the dispute.

Enquiry: At the appointed time on the appointed date and place the enquiry will commence by the enquiry officer in the presence of charge-sheeted workman. At the commencement of the enquiry, the enquiry officer should explain the charge-sheet to the worker. If the charge-sheeted workman pleads not guilty, the enquiry should be proceeded. If he pleads guilty in writing, the enquiry need not be proceeded.

Fact-findings: On completion of the enquiry, the enquiry officer is required to submit his findings to the authority authorised to take disciplinary action. He should state in his report, the Proforma of Charge-sheet, charges as well as the explanation given to them. The enquiry officer should not recommend any punishment in his findings.

Decision: The higher management, such as works manager or director, for taking disciplinary action shall consider the findings and if he accepts the findings of guilt, he should inflict appropriate punishment in accordance with the standing orders.

Service of the Order: Any order of punishment should be served on the charge-sheeted workman and this completes the procedure for domestic enquiry.

CONTAINERS AND CLOSURES LIMITED
(Name of the Company)

CHARGE SHEET

Employee's Name.. Department...............................

Occupation............. Token No.........................

Joined The Company... Permanent Or Temporary

<table>
<tr><td>Description of the Charge(s)

Date of Occurrence.........

Time..........

You are charged with the above offence which is treated as misconduct under rule................ of the Certified Standing Order.

You are hereby required to explain in writing the said circumstances alleged against you within 24 hours of the receipt of this charge sheet. Pending further enquiry you are suspended forthwith.

Signature..

Designation..

Date .... Time...............</td><td>Employee's Explanation to Charges

Date.........

Time...........

Signature or L.T.I.
of the employee</td></tr>
<tr><td>The charge was explained to the employee in Hindi/Bengali/Marathi who signed or placed his left thumb impression in acknowledgement of receipt.

Signature or

L.T.I. of the employee</td><td>Witnesses</td></tr>
</table>

HOW TO FRAME A PROPER CHARGE SHEET

In a disciplinary action the charge-sheet is of great importance. The domestic enquiry commences as soon as a charge-sheet is issued to a delinquent employee. In many cases the action of the employer was declared void by the third party forum like a High Court because the faulty charge-sheet was issued by an incompetent person.

The object of charge-sheet is derived from the principle of natural justice that a person charged with an offence should know his guilt so that he may state his view in reply to the charges. It thus provides an opportunity to a person to give explanation for his conduct and to defend himself.

The ordinary law is that any person having the power of appointment has also the power to terminate the service and obviously such person can ask his employee to show cause. Therefore, the established practice is that the appointing authority has the right to issue a charge-sheet. The Supreme Court has accepted the principle that the power to terminate is a necessary adjunct of the power of appointment.

It may happen that an employee was appointed by a person in a department and subsequently he was transferred to other department where it has become necessary to issue him a charge-sheet. But consequent upon his departmental transfer the appointing authority has been changed. The court opined that in such a situation the head of the latter organisation and not the earlier one may initiate a disciplinary action.

Appointing authority is the disciplinary authority. A charge-sheet should be signed and issued by the appointing authority. A mere delegation of power does not make anybody a disciplinary authority. In the absence of any statutory provision permitting delegation of disciplinary authority, any authority other than disciplinary authority has no power to initiate action.

The disciplinary authority must itself frame charges and hold enquiry into them or direct another to hold the enquiry on those charges. An authority other than the disciplinary authority has no power to frame, on its own initiative charges and hold enquiry.

The *second* important matter is that the charges of misconduct should not be vague. The charge-sheet must be very specific and particular. A charge-sheet will be vague if it does not give any indication of charges against any employee. The charges which a person is called upon to meet must be clear, precise and accurate. To avoid vagueness, the charges should be specifically mentioned. There are some misconduct which have been termed under specific names, such as theft, disobedience, negligence of duty, misappropriation, go-slow, strike, violence in the work-place under the service rules or standing order; while drafting a charge-sheet, if the misconduct falls within those specifications, it should be mentioned clearly.

A charge-sheet is not expected to be a record of evidence when it gives the necessary particulars of the misconduct alleged and it cannot be characterised as imprecise.

The *third* important consideration is that the time and date of incident should be mentioned in the charge-sheet. If the charge does not contain particulars of time and place, the charge-sheeted person cannot put up proper defence.

It is always advisable that while mentioning the time of the incident, it should accompany the word, 'about.' It may be that in an enquiry it is found that the incident was committed not exactly at the time but 5 minutes before or after. Although such inaccuracies do not vitiate the charges, it makes the charge-sheet technically defective.

If the charge is of using abusive language towards anybody, then it should be specific as to the language used. Similarly, without giving the particulars of the language, the charge of behaving rudely is also vague. As far as possible, the charge-sheet should not be verbiage. The abbreviations 'etc.' or "any other document" should not be used. Reference should be to a specific person or thing. Nothing should be left implied.

It is always desirable that the charge-sheet is given in a language which can be easily understood by the workman concerned. Considering the low level of educational attainment of workers in our country, it is advisable that when a charge-sheet has been written in English, it should also enclose a translation in the language of the workman concerned. Unless it is done, it will be denial of an opportunity to the employee to defend himself. The Court held that the above demand was very reasonable. The management issues charge-sheets to the workers in English which they cannot understand. In order that workers must know correctly the charges levelled against them, it is necessary that charge-sheet should be given to them in a language which the worker understands.

The *fourth* important consideration is the manner of writing the charge-sheet. It should not show that the employee is guilty of a misconduct. The charge-sheet is merely a description of misconduct alleged against the employee which requires further proof by evidence. So it must not show that the management has already reached a conclusion. If it is so, the whole process becomes an empty formality.

It is also not necessary to mention penalty in the charge-sheet. As the charge-sheet is the beginning of the process and the punishment is the end of the process, it is naturally uncalled for that the end should be mentioned at the beginning.

The delinquent himself would know that punishment would follow if the enquiry went against him. From the frame of the charge itself no prejudice can be inferred. Further, in departmental enquiries the enquiry officer is different from the punishing authority and the enquiry officer only records the evidence at the enquiry.

The *fifth* important consideration is time for rendering explanation to the charge. Reasonable time should be given to the delinquent worker for giving explanation to the charge. What is reasonable or not is a question of fact. While allowing sufficient time to reply to the charges, the explanation should be called in writing, if possible, in the handwriting of the delinquent workman.

Last important point about a charge-sheet is that there is no particular form of a charge-sheet. The law has not prescribed any form so far.

The service of charge-sheet is no less important than the drafting. It is essential that sufficient document should be placed before the enquiry officer to show the *bona fide* of service of the charge-sheet to the delinquent workman.

The practice followed normally is either to get the signature of the workman concerned on the office copy of the charge-sheet or get his signature in the peon book. The service of the charge-sheet should also be directly to the alleged person and not to anybody else. When a peon was sent to the charge-sheeted employee and in his absence, a minor child of his received the same, the Court held it does not prove conclusively the identity of the communication.

If the workman is not available to serve the charge-sheet directly, generally, the standing order provides the procedure to be followed. The first step is to send the charge-sheet by registered post. The refusal to accept a charge-sheet is misconduct. In the Tractor India case, when orders were sent to workers in English they refused to receive the same.

The industrial tribunal held that this amounted to insubordination and gross misconduct. But the labour appellate tribunal held that employees could not be held guilty of refusal to accept the office orders without knowing the contents thereof. The Supreme Court held that the refusal to receive the office orders was deliberate since the workers had been receiving charge-sheets and therefore it constituted a misconduct.

A charge-sheet is sent by registered post and it is returned with the endorsement "not found" or 'left.' When the letter is returned with such remarks, it is wise, as advised by the Supreme Court in the Bata Shoe Company Case, a notice should be published in the name of the workman concerned in the regional language newspaper with wide circulation. But this principle will not apply if the letter comes back with the remark 'refused.' To put up the charge-sheet on the company notice board in case he has refused to take it will not be an excuse. The only remedy available is through publication of the same in the local newspaper.

Grievance Settlement

Employee grievances are situations in which the employees are dissatisfied with the company. The subject of grievance should be discussed under the following headings- *(i)* Basic Considerations of grievance handling. *(ii)* Steps in handling grievances and *(iii)* Principles of handling grievances.

Basic Considerations

Grievance refers to any discontent or dissatisfaction, whether expressed or not and whether valid or not, arising out of anything connected with the company that an employee thinks, believes or even feels, is unfair, unjust or inequitable.

Grievances have considerable significance as harbingers of industrial disputes. Unresolved grievances can become industrial disputes that is why grievances are considered to be tips of the iceberg on industrial conflict. Grievances can be described as 'embryonic' disputes which need to be resolved at the earliest opportunity.

The three cardinal principles of grievance settlement are — settlement at the lowest level, settlement as quickly as possible and settlement to the satisfaction of the aggrieved.

In the *first* place, in handling grievances, stress must be laid either on the causes of trouble or upon the resulting trouble. If an employee is disgruntled because he was not given a due promotion, some may call the unreceived promotion the grievance whereas others may call the disgruntled attitude the grievance. *Secondly*, a grievance arises out of something connected with the company. Something in the company, either its activity or supervision or policy may be the source of a grievance. *Thirdly*, discontent and dissatisfaction may be expressed or implied. However, most companies recognise as grievances only those that are expressed in writing.

Channels of handling grievances should be carefully developed and its information should be disseminated amongst the employees. It is necessary that employees know the channels through which they ventilate grievances. There are two procedures for the settlement of grievances-open door policy and step-ladder procedure. Some companies have an informal and open-door policy for grievance handling and employees are free to go up the top level executives with their grievances for redressal. In large companies open door policy is not suitable. Consequently, most companies have introduced a step-ladder procedure for the settlement of grievances. Under this procedure, an aggrieved employee will first present his grievance to the first-line supervisor. In other words, a grievance should be dealt with in the first instance at the lowest level. If it is settled there to the satisfaction of the aggrieved employee, the matter will end there. In case he is not satisfied with the decision of the supervisor, the employee with grievances will go to the next higher authority — the departmental head. Even if the grievance of the employee is not settled at this stage, provision must be there for a third step in handling grievances. At the third stage, a joint grievance committee reviews the grievance. Employees failing to get satisfaction even at this stage should have ready access to the chief executive of the company. The top executive of the company is established as a final court of appeal. In most of the procedures, the personnel officer does not form a step but his assistance is available for handling grievances. In handling grievances management should avoid, as far as possible, the legalistic approach because constant reference to standing orders might complicate the case.

STEPS IN HANDLING GRIEVANCES

In handling grievances, the following steps are in order: *(a)* Define or describe the nature of the grievance as clearly and as fully as possible; *(b)* Collect all the facts that help to explain how, when, where, why and to whom the grievance occurred; *(c)* Establish tentative solutions to the grievances; *(d)* Collect additional information to check the validity of the tentative solution; *(e)* Apply the solution, and *(f)* Follow-up the case to make sure that it has been handled satisfactorily and the grievance eliminated.

Defining or describing a grievance implies that it has been expressed. Having defined the grievance as clearly as possible, the next step is to gather all pertinent facts connected with the case. The executive handling the grievance must know when the alleged grievance was first experienced, whether it has been repeated or not, how and where it took place and the circumstances under which it transpired. This due process will go a long way to gain the confidence of the employees. Employees should be fully convinced that management is perfectly sincere in seeing that justice is done. After getting a clear picture of the grievance, the next step involves the establishment of tentative solutions. On the basis of the tentative solutions facts are gathered. The executive establishes a tentative solution and then observe critically whether his hypothesis is right or wrong. If he thinks it wrong, then he sets up another tentative solution and proceeds this way until he finds the right answer.

In the next step tentative solutions have to be verified. It is now necessary to take each bit of available information and to match it against the possible solution. If sufficient information has not already been gathered, an effort will be made for more information. The executive may hold further conference with aggrieved employee and question other employees. Having reached a final decision, it should be applied without delay. *Lastly*, the executive should not conclude that the grievance has been settled until a check is made to determine whether the employee's attitude has been favourably changed.

There are several checking methods. The most commonly used method is casual observation — take note of how that employee is taking the decision, whether favourably or unfavourably. The *second* method is more direct to ask the employee whether he is satisfied with the decision. The *third* method is to hold a general discussion with the employee with a view to deducing his attitude indirectly. The *fourth* method is to ask other employees about the aggrieved employee's reactions.

Principles of Handling Grievances

In handling grievances, a number of principles has been discovered by trial and error, which, if strictly followed, is likely to lead to desirable results.

Grievance procedure should be demonstrably fair. The attitude of supervisor is very important. He should accept the employee's right to appeal as long as no by-passing is involved. In a unionised company, supervisors should also recognise the employees' right to be represented by a union official, if they so desire.

The provision of a grievance procedure should be definite and clear. No grievance procedure can work satisfactorily unless there are definite provisions, consistently adhered to determining what is to be done, when and by whom. Every employee should know: *(i)* to whom grievances are to be filed and *(ii)* in what form — written or oral.

The grievance procedure should be simple. The grievance procedure should be simple enough so that it can be easily understood even by the employees who have had little formal education.

It should function promptly and speedily. Prompt action is not only desirable from the complaint's point of view, but also from the management's point of view. Since delay causes frustration and tempers may rise, it is necessary that grievances should be dealt with speedily. It is a common saying that justice delayed is justice denied and this is equally true in the industrial world. Moreover, any unnecessary delay constitutes another grievance. Settlement of grievances "in the shortest possible time and at the lowest level possible" is the ideal.

In the grievance procedure, the supervisor should develop an attitude towards his employees that will result in gaining their confidence. To gain confidence, the supervisor must show the right attitude towards the aggrieved employees. He should display a sincere interest in the problems of the employee and a willingness to be of help. Although the supervisor is mainly the representative of management to the employees, he is also a representative of employees to management.

In handling grievances, supervisors must have confidence in themselves, be fully aware of their responsibilities and be ready to carry them. An executive who has no self-confidence soon finds that his employees are aware of this and tend to be wary of him. Employees do not like to come to such a supervisor with their grievances and will go over his head. As a result the prestige of the executive suffers.

Total effects of decision should be considered. In handling grievances, thoughts must be given not only to the short-run effects of a decision but also to its long-run implications. A decision reached today has an immediate effect and also likely to have an influence upon the future relationship between employees and management. Consequently, grievances should be handled in terms of their total effect on the company and not merely in terms of their individual or immediate effect.

In handling grievances the executive should remember that it takes a long time to gain the confidence of employees but it can be lost over-night by a foolish decision or inapt handling of a single grievance. Every grievance must be considered important however insignificant it appears. Eternal vigilance is not only the price of liberty but also of good industrial relations.

Lastly, labour and management should solve their difficulties through the process of bargaining and negotiation. Actually, this does not always happen. Hence, it is necessary to provide for the services of third person — the arbitrator — to help in solving grievances.

❑ ❑ ❑

13

EMPLOYER-EMPLOYEE COMMUNICATION: MANAGER AS COMMUNICATOR

Introduction

Communication is the lifeline for animals, plants, humans and anything one can think of in this universe. The need for communication is as strong as any other biological needs of humans. Communication is central to everything that we do. The ability to communicate determines the success or failure of one's activities and goal. For every organisation, communication is an indispensable activity. The organisation is held together by communication. It is through communication that different persons, groups and departments in an organisation are linked together to attain a common goal. Communication is a managerial skill which is essential for planning, execution of plans, directing people and controlling the activities of the organisation.

Communication has become an essential instrument in all walks of human life. A sensory communication with physical and biological surroundings to find food, protection and to reproduce the species can be traced to man's evolution itself. Sensory communication was not enough for mankind for survival. Hence was the need to discover the symbolic communication called 'language'.

DEFINITION AND NATURE

The term 'communication' is derived from the Latin *Communis*, meaning common, and thus when we communicate we are trying to establish a 'commonness' of ideas with someone. Communication may be defined as the sharing of meaning, it is the process by which an individual transmits stimuli to modify the behaviour of other individuals. It is therefore an influence process. It may also be viewed as a process of meaningful interaction among human beings.

Knowledge alone is not adequate for managerial success; it requires knowledge plus ability to communicate accurately. The popular saying 'knowledge is power' should be modified to "applied knowledge is power". And to apply it requires effective communication.

It is through effective communication that an executive ultimately gets work done by others. Therefore a successful executive must know the art of communication. Moreover, communication is a means whereby the employees can be properly motivated to execute company plans enthusiastically. It is the means by which behaviour is modified, change is effected and goals are achieved.

By communication we mean the broad field of human interchange of facts and opinions and not the workings of the telephone, telegraph, radio and the like. Communication is the process of transferring information from an information source to a destination. Because of its pervasive nature, communication is referred to as the network that binds together all the members and activities within an organisation. Administrative communication can be best regarded as a form of social communication in which there are five elements :

A COMMUNICATOR (Sender or speaker) who
TRANSMITS
MESSAGE to a
COMMUNICATE to influence the behaviour
of the communicatee as seen in his
RESPONSE.

In Lasswell's popular paradigm, it is a question of "who says what in which channel to whom with what effect"?

Stated differently, in all cases of communication there will found to be a communicator, the person communicated to, the message, the communication channel and the purpose of the communication.

Chester Barnard envisages communication as the means by which people are linked together in an organisation in order to achieve a central purpose. Group activity is impossible without information transfer because,

The Hawthorne studies revealed the communications problem of modern industry and stress was laid upon channels of communication, semantic problems and frames of reference. The inference drawn from the studies was that if individuals could understand one another this would remove the major cause of industrial discontent. Most of the problems relating to industrial relations are due to lack of communication.

Effective Communication

Effective communication can be defined as the simultaneous, identical understanding of the content and intent of a message by the sender and the receiver :

Sender		Message		Receiver		Message
A	→	B	→	C	→	**B**

In the above diagram, both sender A and receiver C have the same message, B. But communication is not effective where sender A sends message B, but receiver C receives message D.

Sender		Message		Receiver		Message
A	→	B	→	C	→	**D**

Effective communication is an absolutely vital tool for effective leadership of any kind. To be a leader a man must speak up. He must have something to say. He must persuade his listeners. One management expert has rightly put it : Top management may generate the most brilliant policies and strategies and may be motivated by the soundest philosophy. But if these are not transmitted all down the line accurately and effectively, top management may be left operating in a vacuum.

The first executive function is to develop and maintain a system of effective communication — the tool for understanding. It is commonly said that what nerves are to human organism, communications are to an industrial system. Since management has been described as getting works done by people, it is necessary to communicate what the management wishes to accomplish by the various tasks which the organisation has undertaken. Communication is also an intra management problem. It is the force that binds the people of an organisation together. Through communication they can attain a common view-point and understanding and cooperate to accomplish organisational objectives. Good communication presupposes a two way flow of information from the top down and from the bottom up. It can be compared to a mighty river on the banks of which business life is built. Everything that happens affects it, imposes stresses and strains upon it, changing its flow and causing whirls and eddies within the main current.

Dams have been built to impede it and bridges to span it. Some are able to use its power to their own ends but for others its dark waters are treacherous.

The art of communication is old but its rise to prominence in personnel administration is comparatively recent. Communication is a mutual exchange of facts, thoughts, information or emotions. It requires presentation and reception, resulting in common understanding among all parties. To communicate is to inform, to tell, to show or to spread information. Furthermore, it has two major objectives to inform and to influence.

There is a lot of difference between merely communicating and communicating with a well-defined purpose, and only through planned, positive communication can management project true leadership. Only through conscious, strong communication can a leader extend the force of his character and his ideas. Communication is the pattern of contract out of which attitudes are created. Since favourable attitudes have been found to be the basis for job satisfaction and increased productivity, good communication is the foundation for sound management.

McGregor sees communication as a major factor in influencing others, All social interaction involves communication. In industry communication is a two-way traffic whereby objectives, orders and policies are transmitted downward and desires and dissatisfactions are transmitted upward. From the managerial point of view, communication is the means by which management gets the work done. It can affect both morale and commitment and efficiency of the employees. A successful executive should have the ability to receive, analyse and transmit information in motivating his subordinates in the right direction. Thus, effective communication is a skill of management.

Dictionary meaning of communication is news, or the act of making oneself understood or means of sending information from one place to another. Communication is the link between knowledge and information. Possession of knowledge is of no use until it is converted into information. In industry communication transmits orders for work, aids in doing the work, buying raw materials and in advertising and selling the product. It is the means used for hire, fire, promote, praise, urge, censure, persuade and so on. Communication plays a major role in dealing with employer-employee relations problems, employee productivity, in short, with all human relations matters. Both experiment and experience indicate that bad communication is often the root cause of many problems.

Secrecy breeds rumours and hush-hush attitude breeds harmful rumours. As far as possible, management should supply all relevant information to employees. The employees of an organisation have great curiosity to know what the company is going to do with, say, computers or puja-bonus or D.A.'s. If the management does not provide information the employees will concoct information through grape-vine rumours which may have damaging results for the company. In order to avoid such problems it is the duty of the management to supply all the relevant information through appropriate media at the right time.

Communication is not confined solely to employees. Management must communicate with its customers, owners, the community as well as its prospective and present employees. But our discussion is restricted to employer-employee communication or administrative communication which is essentially internal to the organisation and applies to persons who are members of the same organisation.

At one time communication was a one-way process of giving orders to subordinates. Both experiment and experience show that one-way communication is much less effective than two-way exchange and has gradually given way to a two-way process.

Communication Process

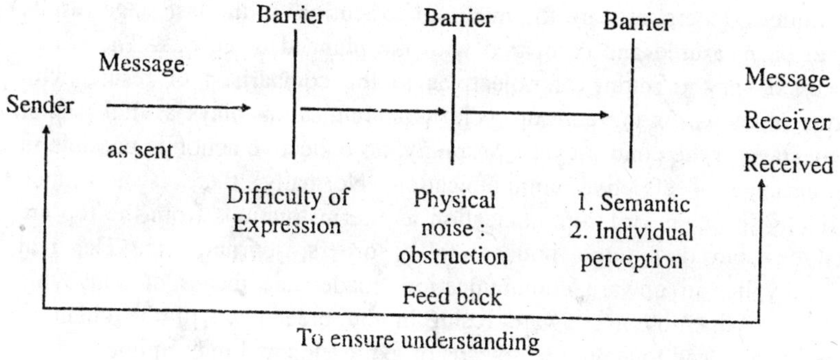

IMPORTANCE OF COMMUNICATION

The aim of setting up an effective communication system is to exchange facts and information in a manner which is acceptable to all concerned and which will lead to willing and cooperative action. A good communication system helps to establish rapport that is complete and effective in promoting productive efficiency, industrial peace, prosperity and growth. It will lead to better productivity through well informed employees, greater degree of consultation and the working environment will be more tolerable as the workers and managers will be working in an atmosphere of mutual trust and confidence. All hurdles in the way of adequate communication must be removed. Through effective communication management becomes aware of the nature and potentialities of the work-force. What course of action are available in making decisions and how the organisation may be profitably directed. Since favourable attitudes have been found to be the basis for job satisfaction and increased productivity, good communication is a foundation for sound management. If the communication system is carefully planned and applied, it will reduce workers' resistance to the acceptance of new ideas and changes.

Most of the conflicts in the industry are not basic but are caused by misunderstood motives and ignorance of facts. Proper communications between interested parties reduce the points of friction and minimize those that inevitably arise. Three-way communication can also help to minimize corporate politics. Just as bacteria multiply abundantly in dark places, so does the germ of corporate politics. Shedding light through good communication on the various facets of business operations tends to eliminate the breeding ground.

The importance of communication cannot be overemphasised. Every industrial organisation has certain economic and social objectives for which it has come into existence and continues to exist. Planning aims at fulfilling those objectives. To formulate the plan the planners have to depend on mutual discussions, conferences, reports, meetings, published statements of company policies, etc. Planning involves execution. Orders, discussions, committees, letters, etc. are the media of execution. In the last stage results are to be measured and compared with the planned objectives. The whole process from the setting of objectives to the comparison of results with norms is known as the control cycle. Communication plays a vital part at every stage of the control cycle. *Secondly*, no collective action is possible in the absence of effective communication. Normally, there is not much difficulty in downward communication as the instructions from the top are easily conveyed through notices, talks, orders, journals etc. The real difficulty lies in upward communication. Inadequate means of conveying thoughts and emotions upward result in the breakdown of the chain of response and lead to aggressive means of expression and indiscipline.

An organisation is composed of leaders and the led. In a small one-to-one, Robinson Crusoe type of enterprise the face-to-face communication prevails which makes the problems a simple one. The larger the enterprise becomes, the system of communication becomes more and more complex. As an organisation grows and becomes more and more complex, its workers are separated from its top management both physically and socially. As the gap between them widens, emotional tensions develop in individuals at all levels which tend to prevent mutual understanding. Management looks to effective communication as a key to these human relations problems.

Information to be communicated has been broadly divided into two categories — that which management desires its employees to have and that which its employees want. Really speaking there is no conflict as between what employees want to know and what management wants to tell them. What an employee wants to know may be determined by survey techniques.

Numerous studies indicate that the employee is interested mainly in matters which affect his job, his earnings and his chances for advancement. *First,* he seeks information on matters of security. *Secondly,* he is interested in promotional opportunities — how he can get ahead. *Thirdly,* he wants to know opportunities for participation. The supervisor too is interested in these matters but in addition, he wants to know lines of authority and management's willingness to stand behind him.

Communication within industry encompasses intra-management communication as well. Supervisors should be thoroughly informed about company policy and informed first. Through their day-to-day personal contacts, supervisors are well-informed of employee thinking and feeling. Middle management should keep the top management informed of employee desires, thinking, suggestions and reactions. The principal means of intra-management communication are day-to-day personal contact between supervisors, foremen, conferences, bulletins and news-letters, counselling, etc. By improving intra-management communication, a company goes a long way towards welding together its management groups.

Types of Communication

To be effective communication must be a three-directional affair : *(i)* vertical and downward-from top management downwards : *(ii)* vertical and upward - from the workers upwards and *(iii)* horizontal or lateral in both directions. The passing of information to persons lower in the organisational structure is vertical and downward communication. When the top management is conscious of the need for conveying information down the line, this job is fairly well done in the normal relationship. Personal contacts and operations procedures provide the most commonly used and most efficient means of communicating between top management and the divisional heads below the level of top management. An answer coming back through the established channels is vertical and upward. Workers are given chances to communicate with the management mainly through grievance procedures, suggestion schemes and joint committees. Horizontal communication is more of an informal nature. Communication between different departments is known as horizontal or lateral. If a departmental head needs some information from another departmental head he might telephone him directly.

MEDIA AND METHODS OF COMMUNICATION

Media of communication range from talking to silence. In between the two, there are many such as notices, orders, telephone, letters etc. Methods of communication can be grouped into four classes — oral, written, gestural, and visual or pictorial. Oral methods include talks between employee and supervisors, meetings, collective bargaining, grievance procedure, joint committees, etc. Important written methods are newsletters, company magazines, annual reports, letters and advertisements in the press. Visual or pictorial methods include charts, graphs, posters, cartoons, symbols, filmstrips etc. In view of the illiteracy and multiplicity of languages amongst the workers, pictorial posters, symbols or film-strips are very effective. Communication experts suggest that more than 50% of what is communicated between individuals occurs non-verbally, in other words through body language, gesture, facial expressions, eyegaze and posture. Certain methods are useful for one-way transmission of information from management to employees. These include posters, bulletin- boards, company magazines, newsletters, internal broadcasting, etc. Two-way channels of communication include collective bargaining, grievance procedure, joint committees or job-training courses, etc.

We discuss below some important media of communications in detail.

House Magazine and Wall Newspaper

The internal house magazine is an important channel of communication through which the management can tell the story of industry to the employee. It is a platform from where management can write direct to the employees and if tactfully used, can be an important method of creating team spirit. It can explain the policies of the management; it can disseminate right information in the right time and in the right manner; it can remind the workers of their responsibilities from time to time; it can explain the advantages of the various welfare schemes that are in operation; it can create amongst the workers a sense of belonging. There are two types of house magazines - the news-bulletin and magazine proper. In the news- bulletin only news of topical interest are published, but in a full-fledged magazine, news, articles, short-stories, poems are all published. The news-bulletins are less costly but a magazine proper is preferable because it provides an informal means through which management policy and programmes can be explained to the workers and at the same time it gives the employees an opportunity to express their thinking, feeling and desires. Management must use it as a propaganda machine.

In this country editorial functions are performed either by the public relations department or by the personnel department. The editor should have an advisory committee to help him. In the context of multiplicity of languages amongst the workers, the magazine should be in the language of the majority of the employees or if possible, bi-lingual.

In our country small and medium sized companies cannot afford to run a magazine proper as it is costly.

Experience has shown that company periodicals very often suffer from management's failure to co-operate with the editor. Management does not take a positive interest in the publication and it does not allow the editor sufficient freedom of action. High degree of illiteracy amongst the workers severely restricts the effectiveness of the media.

A wall newspaper is an important means of disseminating information for it provides current news. Compared to a printed house magazine it is extremely cheap. But the disadvantages are that a number of employees cannot read it at the same time and that an employee cannot take it home and read at his convenient time.

Notice Boards and Posters: Every factory has notice boards on which notices are pasted. In putting a notice board the following rules should be kept in mind : *(i)* notice board should be placed where all employees can see them well; *(ii)* they should be attractive, well-lighted and protected from weather; *(iii)* boards should not be cluttered up; *(iv)* current and important notices should be displayed.

Posters are used to publicise a matter. But it is not proper to disfigure the walls of the work-room with a large number of posters. But this criticism is not applicable in case of important posters such as safety poster, important announcement, accident rate and so on.

Films: Films are used in industry particularly as aids in training, morale building and for public relations work. In our country the use of films in industry as a method of communication is not extensive because of high cost. An objection to the use of films is that they are one-way channels of communication — the audience's role is passive.

Collective Bargaining: Collective bargaining, if carried on in an atmosphere of friendly co-operation and mutual understanding, can be utilized successfully as a communication method itself. Unfortunately, it is often carried on in an atmosphere of strife and tension, thus preventing the full utilization of its communication potential. Many management and union people come to the bargaining table with their minds made up and not in a mood to consider the view points of the other party. Despite this, there is a board field of mutual understanding between unions and managements and collective bargaining as a means of communication is making headway.

Grievance Procedure: A formal grievance procedure is an important means of upward communication. Union officials aid in the communicating process by expediting settlement of grievance. A grievance, if properly handled, should not go beyond the initial stages. Even a small grievance, if not promptly settled, may develop into a major trouble. It is for this reason that an adequate grievance procedure is essential to good communication.

Annual Report to Employees: In USA and UK, many companies mail annual reports to employees directly at their homes. Annual Report is an excellent vehicle for publishing management's philosophy. Annual Reports devote most of its space to the financial results of the year's operations. But, of late, they are also giving attention to accomplishments in terms of difficulties overcome, products manufactured markets served and expansion achieved.

Suggestion and Speak up Schemes: Employee suggestion scheme is a great morale builder because it helps an employee to identify himself with the enterprise. Employees are invited to submit their ideas and proposals. Suggestions are a valuable source of information on employee thinking and provide an opportunity for personal contact between employee and management. Suggestion systems, if properly administered, promote good employer-employee relations. A good monetary reward should be given for accepted suggestions. Many employees think that instead of cash reward, the suggesters should be rewarded through promotion or salary increases. Many public sector companies in India have set up suggestion scheme. For example, Sindri Fertilizers have introduced such scheme in 1969 under the supervision of the personnel manager. All the employees irrespective of rank are eligible to participate in the suggestion scheme.

THE GRAPE-VINE

The Grape-Vine communication may be either formal or informal. Formal communication is the vehicle for enforcing the relationships between positions. Thus, when a manager asks the foreman to do or not to do something by virtue of his position, it is formal communication. Informal communication is based on the informal relationships that grow up in an organisation. It develops as a result of inadequate formal structures.

The grape-vine is the network of informal communication. Through these informal channels flow information, advice and even orders. The grape-vine exists in all offices and factories. It thrives on lack of information. It is a powerful communicator, it is rapid but unpredictable. It fills the gap where formal channels have been ineffective. The prevalence of rumours in a plant often indicates a breakdown in the formal communication system. Clerks, workers and professionals have their own particular system of communication. In all organisations changes are always taking place. Let a change occur and at once through the medium of the grape-vine, rumours will spread everywhere like a wild fire. In an hour, many stories are repeated, exaggerated and believed. Prompt publication of facts, both good and bad, is the best defence. Some organisations have established rumour clinics to provide instant answers to objectionable rumours. The grape-vine by itself is not bad. It may be used for transmitting valuable information. It is not the information but its distortion which is harmful. Unless it is properly guided, it may beget disastrous results.

Communication Failure — Barriers to Communication

The three main barriers to communication are delay, distortion and dilution. Delay is caused by the faulty working of the distribution system.

Distortion of information or message is caused by personal idiosyncrasies of the intermediate communicators, by impatient or faulty listening of the communicatee, inadequate vocabulary, badly chosen and empty words, by psychological barriers caused by prejudice, preconceived notion, distrust of the communicator, misinterpretation of his intention and so on. Status consciousness among managerial personnel may cause distortion and dilution in communication. Sharing information with subordinates is interpreted as loss of status, as status is equated with the possession of greater knowledge, Dilution of communication is caused by an 'yes man' telling the boss what he wants to hear rather than giving him a correct feedback. Let us explain communication of failures in greater detail.

Firstly, major barrier to communication is the egocentric tendency of all human beings to view every activity from a highly personal point of view. Communication is not the simple speaking and hearing of words and sentences. Each man creates for himself a set of filters which affect the transmission of communication from one individual to another. The sender's filter causes him to project ideas which are related to his personal frame of reference and the receiver receives the message from his point of view.

Communication is complete only when it has entered the recipient's minds. There is no use is speaking if no one listens. Listening is more difficult than speaking. It is said that one hears with the ears but listens with the mind. Empathic listening is what is required. This involves the skill to listen for feelings and not merely for words. This is an art.

Secondly, major barrier to communication is the tendency to evaluate and judge others. This can be a fault of both sender and receiver, although it is more commonly the receiver who evaluates and judges the sender. The evaluation is made not only of the communication but also of the sender himself, his dress, speech habits and physical appearance. Instead of listening to the actual communication, the receiver analyses other irrelevant facts and often rejects the message on such grounds.

Thirdly, hierarchy and status can be barriers to communication. Effective communication exists where anyone in the organisation is allowed to contact anybody who can help him solve his problems. But organisational hierarchy restricts channels through which communication should move officially. Members have to contact others through formal channels only which may cause hardships. In the organisational hierarchy, a certain status is attached to a position, which boosts the ego of the incumbent. Subordinates become aware of the existence of such status in their relationships with their superiors. This may distort the upward communication process. Subordinates do not report their problems and short-comings, because of status, they cannot be frank with their boss.

Fourthly, communication can be thwarted if the potential content of the message threatens the psychological or economic well-being of the recipient. People hear only what they want to hear, but if the message has a bad content, the receiver pretends of not hearing it. This gap can be eliminated by removing fear and distrust. Many companies used AVOs (Avoid Verbal Orders) to stress the importance of using written rather than oral communication in order to prevent this type of problems. As mentioned by Koontz and O'Donnell, in oral communication something in the order of 30 per cent of the information is lost in each transmission. Therefore, in large scale enterprise, it is impossible to rely on oral communication from one level to another.

Lastly, semantics blocks widen communication gap. Words and concepts have different meanings for different persons. Even the most careful use of a dictionary cannot eliminate misunderstanding. As far as possible, use words which the receiver can understand. Words having more than one meaning should be avoided in order to remove misunderstanding.

Evaluation of Communication Media

It is necessary to investigate the reasons why in the same organisation, some conferences produce results while others produce nothing, why some talks succeed and others do not.

It is very difficult to measure the effectiveness of communication media because it involves intangible human relations factors such as improved attitudes and morales, job satisfaction, mutual understanding, etc. Some companies frankly admit that they do not try to evaluate the effectiveness of their programme pointing out that it is impossible to set a value on such intangible factors. But with the development of communicating techniques have come methods of evaluating them such as employee attitude surveys, or opinion polls, rate of turnover, discussion with key individuals, exit interviews and suggestion systems.

❑ ❑ ❑

14

LABOUR POLICY

Labour policy in India has been evolving in response to specific needs of the situation to suit requirements of planned economic development and social justice and has two fold objectives – maintaining industrial peace and promoting the welfare of labour.

In free India, labour policy of the Government has been influenced from time to time by the impact of changing circumstances but some constituents of the policy have remained more or less unchanged. In a developing economy where labour organisations were relatively weak, there was a profound distrust of the employer as a profit seeking exploiter and of labour organisation as communist in outlook; so the government had to play a major role in delineating certain parameters of industrial relations. This evolution could not be left largely to bipartite negotiations and confrontations between labour and management over the years, as has been the process of evolution in developed economies. Again, after independence a concern for rapid economic growth, helped by industrial productivity also urged the Government to assume the leadership role in this area. Loss of production caused by industrial warfare was to be prevented.

There were also commitments made to labour by the Congress Party while fighting for independence. The Karachi Resolution (1931) of the Indian National Congress on industrial workers stated that the state was to safeguard the interests of industrial workers, ensuring that suitable legislation should secure them a living wage, healthy conditions, limited hours of labour and protection from the economic consequences of old age, sickness and unemployment. Women and children were also to be protected in various ways and accorded special benefits. It was appreciated that labour's aspirations for a better state of things would be intensified after independence.

The term labour policy involves a number of overlapping concepts. The universe of labour policy is so wide that no camera can take a full picture. Labour policy covers so wide spectrum of objectives and one is at liberty to select the subject of labour policy of one's preference. The literature on the subject is a mixture of light and shade.

Labour policy usually refers to the laws and measures applicable to labour employed in organised industries. In the narrower sense, it covers such subjects as attitude to labour, industrial relations, wages, social security trade union, etc. In India a labour policy has been evolving through the institutional framework built up for its formulation.

The study of labour policy may be spread over three periods : *(i)* from the middle of the 19th century to the end of the World War I, *(ii)* from 1919 to 1947, and *(iii)* from 1947 to the present day.

During the *first* period, the policy of the Government was to protect the social system from workers rather than to protect workers from the social system. The government was mainly interested in enforcing penalties for breach of contract and in regulating the conditions of work with a view to minimise the competitive advantage of the indigenous employers against the British employers. The Workmen's Breach of Contract Act of 1859 and the Employees' & Workmen's Breach of Contract Act of 1860 are examples of the first objective and the Factories, Plantations and Mines Acts are examples of the second objective. Apart from realising these objectives, these early labour laws secured for the employees protection against exploitation by employers. In this period there was legislation but no clear-cut labour policy.

During the *second* period (1919-'47), labour policy received a new significance due to the following developments : *(i)* emergence of the International Labour Organisation, *(ii)* formation of the All India Trade Union Congress in 1920, *(iii)* constitutional developments in India under which popular ministries were formed in the Provinces and *(iv)* the passing of the Trade Unions Act in 1926. The Royal Commission on Labour in India reported in 1931. Its recommendations influenced the labour policy of the Government till the beginning of the next period. Labour policy during this period consisted of improving working conditions at work places and providing certain social benefits like compensation for employment injuries and occupational diseases and maternity benefits. Another development was the passing of the Trade Unions Act which provides for the registration of trade unions and protection of trade unionists and trade union officials from civil and criminal liability for conducting *bona fide* trade union activities.

During the period, the groundwork of labour policy was prepared but the superstructure was yet to be built on this groundwork. In other words, there was labour legislation without a comprehensive labour policy.

The *third* period starts with the attainment of independence in 1947 and continues up to the present day. The attainment of independence led to the growth of a national labour policy. The main postulates of labour policy operating in the country since the beginning of this period could be summed up as follows :

(i) Recognition of the State, the custodian of the interests of the community, as the catalyst of change and welfare programmes.

(ii) Recognition of the right of workers to peaceful direct action if justice is denied to them.

(iii) Encouragement to mutual settlement, collective bargaining and voluntary arbitration.

(iv) Intervention by the State in favour of the weaker party to endure fair treatment to all concerned.

(v) Primacy to maintenance of industrial peace.

(vi) Evolving partnership between the employer and employees in a constructive endeavour to promote the satisfaction of the economic needs of the community in the best possible manner.

(vii) Ensuring fair wage standards and provisions of social security.

(viii) Co-operation for augmenting production and increasing productivity.

(ix) Adequate enforcement of legislation.

(x) Enhancing the status of the worker in industry, and

(xi) Tripartite consultation.

The industrial worker of today has acquired a dignity not known to his predecessor. He is no longer the unskilled coolie of the days gone by, engaged in an unending struggle to eke out his existence, neglected by society except for his labour and with very limited aspirations. He has now a personality of his own. He shares the benefits, albeit meagre, which a welfare state with a vast population and inadequate resources can offer and some more. He enjoys a measure of social security, he is secure in his employment once he enters it; he cannot be dismissed unjustly and has been given statutory protection against retrenchment and lay off. Since independence, there has been a continuous rise in his money incomes. Several new amenities are a part of his working life both because of legislation and because of conditions of the new industries require the provision of these of facilities.

Labour policy in a dynamic society should be directed to the well-being of the working class on the one hand and the realisation of labour's vital contribution to the progress of the economy, on the other hand.

Labour policy in an expanding economy should have the following objectives : *(i)* protection against exploitation of labour by the employer through the enactment of the Minimum Wages Act, *(ii)* recognition of workers' role in production, *(iii)* a fair deal to labour, *(iv)* provision against contingencies to which labours are exposed through the development of social security measures and *(v)* the development of industrial democracy by setting up of Works Committees, and Joint Management Councils.

While the groundwork of labour policy was prepared during the 40s, the 50s of the century built the impressive superstructure on this groundwork. The Constitution of India and the Planning Commission are mainly responsible for raising the superstructure.

The Constitution of India clearly indicates the lines along which labour policy should be directed. Articles 39, 41, 42 and 43 indicate the directions of labour policy. The provisions are as follows :

Article 39 lays down that the state shall, in particular, direct its policy towards securing :

(i) that the citizens, men and women equally have the right to an adequate means of livelihood;

(ii) that the ownership and control of the material resources of the community are so distributed as best to subserve the common good;

(iii) that the operation of the economic system does not result in the concentration of wealth and means of production to the common detriment;

(iv) that the strength and health of workers, men and women, and the tender age of children are not abused and that citizens are not forced by economic necessity to enter avocations unsuited to their age or strength;

(v) that there is equal pay for equal work for both men and women;

(vi) that childhood and youth are protected against exploitation and against moral and material abandonment.

Then Article 41 provides: The State shall, within the limits of its economic capacity and development, make effective provision for securing the right to work, to education and to public assistance in case of unemployment, old age, sickness, disablement and other cases of undeserved want.

Article 42 provides: The State shall make provision for securing just and humane conditions of work and for maternity relief.

Article 43 provides: The State shall endeavour to secure, by suitable legislation or economic organisation or in any other way, to all workers, agricultural, industrial or otherwise, work, a living wage, conditions of work ensuring a decent standard of life and full employment.

The Planning Commission is responsible for the formulation of national labour policy. The Four Five Year Plans state the underlying principles of the national labour policy. The essence of the policy is to build a structure of industrial democracy consistent with the objectives of a socialist pattern of society.

1. Attitude to Labour

The First Five Year Plan says, 'our approach to labour problems rests on considerations which are related on the one hand to the requirements of the well-being of the working class and on the other to its vital contribution to the economic stability and progress of the country. The worker is the principal instrument in the fulfillment of the targets of the Plan and in the achievement of the economic progress generally. His co-operation will be an essential factor in creating an economic organisation in the country which will best subserve the needs of social justice'.

Thus, we find that the Planning Commission has a very encouraging attitude to labour and its role in the socio-economic development of the country. The Commission points out that all the necessary steps should be taken to improve the working and living conditions of the working class; but there should also be a keen realisation on the part of labour of the fact that in an underdeveloped economy, it cannot build for itself a better life except on the strong foundations of a higher level of productivity to which it has itself to make a vital contribution.

The First Plan was drawn up in the context of a growing consciousness of the importance of industrial labour in the national economy. Certain assurances were given to labour in recognition of its rights which had long been neglected. An attempt was made in the First Plan to give concrete shape to these assurances and to give labour a fair deal consistent with the requirements of other sectors of the economy.

Regarding the policy towards labour in the public sector, the Planning Commission laid down the following principles: *(i)* Wages in public undertakings should not be less favourable than those prevailing in the neighbouring private concerns. These working conditions and welfare arrangements should in fact serve as models; *(ii)* The Board of Directors of public undertakings should have on it a few persons who can understand labour problems, the labour point of view and who have sympathy with the aspirations of labour; *(iii)* The benefits of all labour laws which are applicable to similar private concerns should also be made available to the workers of public concerns and as a rule exemption from such legislation should not be granted; *(iv)* There should be progressive participation of labour in the running of many matters of the undertaking with a view to making the workers feel that in practice as well as in theory, they are partners in the undertaking; *(v)* The growth of healthy trade unions in these undertakings should be encouraged. There should not be any restrictions on industrial and commercial employees of Government concerns exercising their trade union rights like any other employees; *(vi)* Collective bargaining embracing both economic and non-economic demands between workers and management should be encouraged; and *(vii)* Agreements between the management and the representatives of workers should be entered into for increasing output and reducing costs, combating absenteeism and checking offences against discipline.

Much of what has been said in regard to labour policy in the First Plan holds good as a basis for the future. However, in the light of the socialist pattern of society, within which setting the Second Plan has been framed, necessary changes in the labour policy has to be made. A socialist society is built up not solely on monetary incentives but on ideas of service to society and willingness on the part of the latter to recognise such service. It is necessary in the context that the worker should be made to feel that in his own way he is helping to build a progressive State. The creation of industrial democracy is, therefore, a pre-requisite for the establishment of a socialist society.

The Third Plan states that the fruits of progress should be shared in an equitable manner and that in a socialist society the working class has an important role and a great responsibility and these will grow with the rising tempo of industrialization.

As a result of this attitude to labour, certain measures have been laid down as conditions for the realisation of the desired goal. It has been rightly emphasised in the First Plan that adequate provisions have to be made for the basic needs of the workers in respect of food, clothing and shelter so as to enable them to remain in a state of health and efficiency. Besides the satisfaction of these basic needs they should have their due share in social and economic progress in the shape of improved health services, wider provision of social security, better educational opportunities and increased recreational facilities.

2. Social Security

An important aspect of labour policy is provision for social security measures. The need for social security has been conceded by the Planning Commission when it says that lack of social security impedes increased production, leads to larger labour turnover, and prevents building up of a stable and efficient labour force. The First Five Year Plan was content with saying that the Employees' State Insurance Act and the Provident Fund Acts should be properly implemented before any new steps can be taken because of the novelty, administrative and other difficulties and financial implications of the scheme. The Second Plan has suggested the extension of the schemes to cover industries and commercial establishments having

10,000 workers or more in the country as a whole and the integration of both the provident fund and sickness insurance scheme under one administration.

The social security approach has so far extended mainly to wage earners in organised industry. There are some groups whose condition calls for closer attention on the part of the community. The Third Plan has suggested to extend the social security measures to cover the physically handicapped, old persons unable to work, women and children, where they are altogether lacking in the means of livelihood and support. With a view to enabling voluntary and charitable organisation, municipal bodies, panchayats and panchayat samities to develop their activities with the help of local communities and giving a little support, a proposal to constitute a small relief and assistance fund has been made.

One important requirement of a social security scheme is that it should be oriented to secure full employment or reduce the evils of unemployment among the educated persons. Prof. Adarkar recommended that a scheme of unemployment insurance should be enforced in the country. But as yet no provision has been made for this aspect of social security in our social security scheme.

3. Industrial Relations

One of the most important ingredients of labour policy relates to industrial relations. The First Plan embodies the Indian ideology to industrial relations. The Plan emphasises the harmonious relations between labour and capital. The employer-employee relationship is, in fact, a kind of partnership for promoting the community's economic needs. Industrial relations should be so developed as to enable the worker to take a greater share in the working of the industry. Accordingly, there should be the closest collaboration at all levels between employers and employees for increased production, improvement of quality, reduction of costs and elimination of waste.

The workers' right to association, organisation, and collective bargaining should also be accepted as fundamental to the mutual relations of labour and capital. Trade unions should be welcomed and helped as part and parcel of the industrial system. When differences arise, they should be settled in a spirit of reasonable adjustment, keeping the good of industry and the welfare of the community in view. As a last measure, differences should be settled by impartial investigation and arbitration.

The Second Plan laid greater emphasis on avoidance of disputes at all levels, including the last stage of mutual negotiations, namely, conciliation. If disputes could not be avoided, recourse should be had to mutual negotiations and voluntary arbitration. The Second Plan made an advance over the First when it recognised the desirability of an increasing measure of association of employees in the management of the industry.

The Third Plan based its approach on moral rather than legal sanctions. The development of industrial relations in the Third Plan rests on the foundations created by the working of the Code of Discipline which has stood the strain of the test during the last three years. It is also expected that the procedures laid down in the Code of Discipline for the recognition of union would pave the way for the growth of strong and healthy trade unionism in the country. The Fourth Plan reiterated that labour relations continued to be regulated by the protective legislative measures introduced in earlier Plan periods and the tripartite agreements.

One disquieting feature of industrial relations policy is the too much insistence on the use of government machinery to settle the industrial disputes ever since the country became free. The main feature of this machinery has been the too frequent use of the adjudication process. The Government machinery of compulsory arbitration is set in motion without giving adequate chance to the parties to exhaust the other means to settle their differences. This has a very demoralising effect on the trade unions as well as employers' organisation. Dr. R. K. Mukherjee has rightly remarked; 'Compulsory arbitration is virtually a denial of the workers' right to strike from which flows their right to collective bargaining and is no where in existence except in Australia and in the totalitarian countries'.

4. Wage and Social Security

It is to be noted that there is no formal wage policy in India. However, this does not imply that we have to deal with a state of vacuum. Actually, evidence of a wage policy like framework is available in various *ad hoc* policy statements made by the Government, some of which have also been incorporated in the labour policy.

The chief objectives of a wage policy in underdeveloped countries are five fold: *(i)* minimum wage, *(ii)* ceiling on wage incomes, *(iii)* wage structure, *(iv)* price stability and *(v)* export promotion.

(a) Minimum Wage: There is need for a floor income for workers in 'sweated' trades. Left uncontrolled, the wage levels would be extremely low. There is therefore a need to fix some minimum wages to prevent exploitation of labour. According to H.A. Turner, the protection of workers against exploitation or unduly low wages remains wage policy's major pre-occupation for the underdeveloped areas.

(b) Wage Ceiling: The question of wage ceiling is important because of the damaging inflationary consequences that follow from an uncontrolled upward movement of wages.

Productivity-based wage increases should form the upper limit. This does not, however, imply that all labour productivity increases should be pocketed by the workers. In the interest of promoting a faster economic growth, a higher proportion of increased resources should be ploughed back into industry, with consumption levels rising only slowly as a consequence.

(c) Wage Structure: Wage structure refers to a set of relationships between rates of pay for different jobs. Proper wage relationship between jobs facilitates the acquisition of skills, provides an incentive to higher productivity and encourages the allocation of labour towards expanding sectors of the economy in which demand for labour is increasing. Rational wage differentials should reflect skill, responsibility, experience and hazards.Those jobs which carry a higher degree of these factors should pay more than those having lower requirements. Labour will be motivated to acquire skill, training and experience since these would bring them higher remuneration.

The recommendation of the Second Five Year Plan to set up wage boards for the settlement of wage disputes was extended to many other industries in the Third Plan, as in the Iron and Steel Industry. On the question of the payment of bonus, it was decided to appoint a commission to study the problems connected with bonus.

In the Fourth Plan (1969-74) in the sphere of Industrial Relations continued emphasis was laid on measures adopted in the earlier plans. Another important development during this period was that the minimum wages were fixed for agriculture, labour and trades.

The Fifth Plan suggested that there was a need to improve labour welfare amenities already existing by integrating them into more comprehensive social security package and expand the coverage of the employees state insurance scheme and the family pension scheme.

The Sixth Plan (1980-85) besides stressing the need to strengthen and revitalise scheme of workers' participation suggested, the expansion of two major social security measures – The Employees' Provident Fund Scheme should be extended to employees in smaller establishments and those in rural areas. The second was the need to extend the ESI schemes to newer areas.

During the Eighth Plan period Employees' Pension Scheme (1995) for industrial workers was introduced. Under the scheme, pension at the rate of 50% is payable to the employees on retirement/super annuation on completion of 33 years' contributory service. A minimum 10 years' service is required for entitlement to pension.

(d) Price Stability: Containing inflationary pressures should be an element of wage policy. Hyper galloping inflation damages the economic health of a nation, fosters social discontent and erodes workers' real wage resulting in constant endeavours to grant money wage increases to protect it. Such wage increases add further pressure to price rise and perpetuates the price-wage cycle. Moreover, runaway inflation hurts the low-paid workers more than others since the purchasing power of their real income is reduced.

This obviously conflicts with the objective of raising their standards of living.

(e) Export Promotion: A developing country is badly in need of technical know-how, machinery and industrial raw materials from foreign countries. To pay for these things, foreign exchange is required which is mainly earned through export promotion.; Increased productivity and price stability are necessary to boost up exports. A rational wage policy is one which accelerate nation's development process and faster economic growth.

An important ingredient of labour policy is the setting up of an appropriate wage structure. The Five Year Plans have realised the importance of a suitable wage policy. Owing to post-war inflationary conditions and the fear of inflation consequent on wage rise, the First Plan was more anxious to restrict wages simultaneously with restrictions on profits. The Plan states that any upward movement at this juncture, will further jeopardise the economic stability of the country if it is reflected in costs of production and consequently raises the price of the product. For workers too, such gains will prove illusory because in all likelihood they will soon be cancelled by a rise in the general price level and in the long run, the volume of employment may be adversely affected. Such an increase in wages should, therefore, be avoided. Any steps to restrict wage increases should be preceded by similar restrictions on the distribution of profits. Subject to this, wage increases should be granted under the following circumstances : *(i)* to remove anomalies or where the existing rates are abnormally low; *(ii)* to restore the pre-war real wage as a first step towards the living wage, through increased productivity resulting from rationalisation and the renewal or modernisation of plant.

The Second Five Year Plan has suggested a wage policy which aims at a structure with rising real wage. The Plan has recognised the workers' right to a fair wage, but it could not implement it on account of the absence of relevant data. It believes that improvement in wages can result mainly from increased productivity. The introduction of payment by results should be extended to areas where at present this principle does not apply. Earnings beyond the minimum wage should be necessarily related to results. Workers should be consulted before a system of payment by results is introduced in an establishment. An important feature of wage policy for the Fourth Plan is that future wage increases will have to be linked with higher productivity with a view to holding down the price-line.

The main aim of wage policy as envisaged, points out the National Commission on Labour, is to bring wages in conformity with the expectations of the working class and in the process seek to maximise wage employment.

Second Plan emphasised the need to maintain existing wage differentials. The Fourth Plan, however, reversed the earlier stand on wage differentials and favoured their narrowing. No steps have yet been taken to rationalise wage differentials.

For better implementation of the Minimum Wages Act, the machinery for inspection has been strengthened during the Third Plan period.

The socialist pattern of society proposed requires that a worker's claims to improve his social and economic status should be recognised. In their turn, workers, too have to realise their responsibilities. Hard and efficient work on the one hand and avoidance of indiscipline on the other, will be needed for achieving the goal which the economy desires to reach.

'Labour Policy in India has been evolving in response to specific needs of the situation in relation to industry and the working class and has to suit the requirements of a planned economy.'

In 1966, the Government of India had set up a National Commission on Labour to make recommendations on various aspects of labour policy. The Commission submitted its Report in 1969. The Report is under consideration of the Union Government in consultation with the State Governments and the employers' and workers' organisations. The recommendations of the Commission will influence and provide the guideline of the present and future labour policy of the Government.

A Critical Review of the Labour Policy

In many countries of the world the labour policy of the Government goes through recurring cycles consisting of the following three stages : (1) Repression (2) Toleration and (3) Encouragement. We have gone through the whole cycle – we have to begin a new one. It has to be a no-nonsense labour policy, more realistic with heavy stress on the promotion of collective bargaining, social discipline and hard work. The policy has to be more result-oriented and less soft towards the demands of labour that are not linked with an increase in their productivity. Economically it is very unsound – and it eventually leads to national bankruptcy – to impose wage scales and social security measures for which the industries can ill afford to pay. The new policy should be based on a sound principle that 'good work should be rewarded and bad work should be punished.'

Although the Third Plan claims that Labour Policy in India has been evolving in response to specific needs of the situation in relation to industry and the working class and has to suit the requirements of a planned economy, nevertheless it is criticised as more idealistic and imitative than pragmatic, largely unrelated to the needs of the situation in India. Thus John Marsh, a foreign expert, observes : 'You have introduced labour legislation which is far in advance of many older industrial countries and I should say that some parts of your legislation subscribe to theory rather than proved and established practice'. Thus, one serious blunder on the part of our Government has been to run away from the facts of life and to seek refuge in ivory tower of their own. They have a mania of bringing forth new pieces of legislative measure year after year without getting worried about their implementation and proper execution. They get despaired of them very soon and hit upon new fantastic idea of ineffective codes and conventions based upon moral force at a time when there is such a serious moral erosion of values and crisis of character.

Secondly, "while our labour policy is general and idealistic, labour administration is unintegrated and inadequate. There is an undoubted appreciation of the need for specialised administrative machinery for the formulation and execution of policy and legislation".

Thirdly, the Indian National Trade Union Congress in its Memorandum on Labour Policy in the Third Plan draws attention to one important aspect of labour policy by saying that failure to evolve satisfactory industrial relations is due to the scant attention given by the Government in implementing the various policies regarding labour. The Memorandum emphasised that Government should be more alive to the implementation aspect.

Fourthly, the labour policy is not conducive to increased production which is the primary pre-condition of economic growth. There are different aspects of the policy which impede the more basic process of institutional development and reduce the freedom of employers in the name of safeguarding the interests of labour, e.g. if a factory is closed down due to financial difficulties the entrepreneur has to pay retrenchment compensation.

Moreover it is contended that present labour policy encourages indiscipline among workers. There is too much pampering, too much experimentation and lack of forethought. The overall result is that, today, in industries there is a certain spirit of indiscipline.

Fifthly, we have no list of priorities; we have built a very ambitious labour programme in the air without any sound base. We have done nothing to solve trade union rivalries, we have not even given them a representative status. The unorganised labour in the urban areas and in the villages in agricultures, has no patron. The government has supplanted collective bargaining by compulsory arbitration rather than supplementing it. The government has hardly been the ideal employer whereas it has imposed hosts of responsibilities upon the private sector. 'Public sector and the Government of India have carefully avoided whatever policies the UK and other advanced countries have adopted with regard to their employees, but very high flown humanitarian approaches are suggested for the private employer towards their employees'. The government have thought of compulsory insurance, bonus, leave etc. without even evolving a coherent wage policy. We try to run without even knowing how to walk. We have taken a vow to create a socialist order of society but have been nowhere near it even after almost two decades of our independence.

Sixthly, we are nowhere near the position in which the State itself becomes the guardian of the interests of the workers and protects and promotes them with all its resources and strength. But there have been distinct gains. As Mr. S.A. Dange, the well-known communist labour leader has observed : 'Those who have seen, worked and lived in 1939 and see things to-day, definitely see a change, an advance in the life and demeanour of the working class in India.' Further Mr. Dange enumerates the following seven 'vital counts' on which the workers since the end of the war, have made advance : (1) Substitution of 8 hour for 9 hour day; (2) Bonus, gratuity and provident fund have become common, (3) Contributory health insurance for industrial workers has been introduced, (4) Holidays with pay have become a right, (5) Laws and conventions govern service conditions, (6) Right of the worker to demand neutralization of rise in the cost of living has been conceded and (7) The case of standard rates for the job, gradations and minima have been conceded even though standardization of wages and their differentials has yet to be achieved.

Lastly, some disinterested experts have expressed the opinion that the labour policy has been prejudicial to the larger interests of the community as a whole. A major factor impeding private investment today is the enormous change that has occurred in regard to conditions under which labour may be employed in factories covered by various legislative measures. Apart from the effect of these measures on the costs of labour to industry, they have greatly reduced the freedom of employers to adjust the labour complement or to enforce disciplinary measures or to rationalise in order to step up production. These have had an adverse effect on the incentive to invest.

Thus, our labour policy is rather an embodiment of philosophy of economics than an economics of philosophy.

❑ ❑ ❑

15

BONUS — LEGAL PROVISIONS

Introduction

During First World War practice of paying bonus started. Bonuses paid during 1919-22 were profit bonuses. In 1923 millowners were unable to pay bonus due to bad trade. During second war demand for bonus revived for two reasons (1) Industries earning large profit and (2) Price rise — Judges declared bonus as a matter of right. Under Payment of Bonus Act, Payment of minimum bonus of 4% is obligatory.

BONUS — LEGAL PROVISIONS

The Beginnings of Bonus in India

It was during the First World War that the practice of paying "war bonus" started for the first time in the cotton textile industry in Bombay and in Ahmedabad. In July 1917 an increase of 10 per cent in wages was granted to textile workers in Bombay to enable them to meet the rise in prices. A circular issued by the Bombay Millowners' Association in January, 1918 announced that war bonus of 10 percent would be raised to 15 per cent with effect from January 1, 1918. At the end of 1918 a strike was called at the Century Mill, which soon spread throughout the industry. The dispute was eventually settled, the employers agreeing to raise the war bonus from 15 per cent to 35 per cent. The amount was then termed a "Special allowance" on account of the high price of foodstuffs.

It may be noticed that these payments were, in fact, not bonus at all in the sense in which it is understood today but what is now called dearness allowance to compensate workers for the rise in the cost of living.

On December 1, 1919, the employers sanctioned payment of a "Bonus" to all operatives who were on the muster roll on December 31, 1919 at rates varying according to the length of service. However a strike was called on January 2, 1920, in support of certain demands, one of which said that while the mill-hands were grateful to the employers for the bonus promised, they would request that for certain workers more liberal terms might be granted. The Bombay Labour Settlement Committee, a committee of the millowners, replied to the demand thus : "The Committee can make no definite announcements as regards the "annual bonuses". The question is one of profits and goodwill and no undertaking can be given". Nevertheless, on October 20, 1920, the Committee of the Millowners decided to recommend payment of a bonus of one month's pay on the same scale as in the previous years. Bonus on similar terms was recommended in November 1921 and again in November 1922.

The bonuses declared in the four years 1919-1922, were presumably profit bonuses as the millowners had indicated in their notices of January 24, 1920, that the question was "one of profits and goodwill". But the position was at best vague as the millowners had indicated in their reply of January 27, 1921 that in fact an annual bonus or one month's pay had been paid whether the mill did well or not".

The millowners announced on July 23, 1923, that owing to bad trade they would be unable to pay bonus for 1923. This led to a general strike towards the end of January 1924. On February 22, 1924 the Government of Bombay appointed the Bonus Disputes Committees presided over by Sir Norman McLeod, Chief Justice of Bombay. The Committee was asked (1) to consider the nature and basis of bonus which had been granted to the employees in the cotton textile mills of Bombay since 1919 and to declare whether the employees had established any enforceable claim, customary, legal or equitable ; and (2) to inquire into the profits made in each year since 1917 with a view to comparing these profits with the profits made in the year 1923 and to report on the contention of the millowners that the grant of bonus similar to that paid in previous years was not justified by the profit of the mill industry as a whole in 1923.

The workers' case before the Committee was that as the increase in wages allowed from the year 1917 owing to war conditions had been called "war bonus" and as annual bonuses had been paid for five consecutive years, the mill workers had come to look upon the annual bonus as part of their wages and that, therefore, they had just claim against the millowners.

The Committee, however, came to the conclusion that the mill workers had not established any enforceable claim, customary, legal or equitable, to the payment annually of a bonus and that such a claim would not be upheld in a court of law. The Committee also found that the total profits before allowing depreciation amounted to Rs. 53 lakhs or Rs. 119 lakhs if the income tax on the profits for the year 1923 only was debited, that the amount required for depreciation amounted to Rs. 170 lakhs, and that the result of the working of the cotton textile industry as a whole showed that there was justification for the contention of the millowners that the profits did not admit of payment of bonus.

The Committee's first conclusion naturally tended to support the dictionary meaning of bonus, namely, that it was "a boon or gift over and above what is nominally due as remuneration to the receiver" (New English Dictionary), or a "gratuity to workmen beyond their wages" (Concise Oxford Dictionary) or again "payments made of grace and as of right" (Earl of Brikenhead in Sutton V. Attorney-General). The Second conclusion suggested that such as *ex gratia* payment could not be expected except when there were surplus profits remaining after meeting prior charges.

The Committee, nevertheless, threw out a hint as to the manner of meeting such claims — a method which was eventually to take bonus out of the category of *ex gratia* payment. It said : ".....it is question of bargaining between the workers and the employers in which consideration might be given to principles of equity. It is not a question of determining what is the contract between the parties".

In 1921, a dispute about bonus arose in the cotton textile industry in Ahmedabad. Pandit Madan Mohan Malaviya, who mediated in it, observed : 'When a mill has made handsome profits, the workers who have by their faithful co-operation enabled the mill to earn such profits should, as an ordinary rule, be given at the end of each year a bonus equal to one month's salary. When the profits have been extraordinarily handsome, millowners might very properly and wisely give a larger bonus to the workmen.

The late twenties and the early thirties were years of depression and consequently there were no major bonus disputes during that period. Even so, bonuses continued to be given on an *ad hoc* basis in a few industrial undertakings.

Bonus During and Immediately After the Second World War

Two developments which arose in the early stages of the Second World War served as the justification for the renewed spate of bonus demands made by workers practically in every industry. The *first* was the accrual of large profits to industries as a result of the war-time demand. The *second*, and chronologically later, development was the steady and substantial rise in the prices of essential consumer goods. As industrial disputes increased in number and threatened to affect the regular working of factories, the Government of India introduced the system of compulsory adjudication of disputes under Rule 81-A of the Defence of India Rules.

Workers in the cotton textile industry in Bombay have often taken the lead in extracting concessions from employers. In March 1940 there was a general strike in the textile mills in Bombay on the question of dearness allowance. The Government of Bombay, watching the progress of the dispute, felt that one of the causes of industrial unrest was the desire of workers to share in the profits. At the instance of the Government, the Bombay Millowners' Association decided that its member mills should grant their workers a cash bonus for the calendar year 1941 equivalent to 12½ per cent of their actual earnings exclusive of dearness allowance. Similarly for 1942 a bonus equivalent to one-sixth of the total earnings exclusive of dearness allowance was granted. Such annual payments continued till 1945.

Various other bonus disputes had necessarily to be referred to tribunals or courts for adjudication. Adjudicators, grouping for enlightenment without precedent or principles and lacking guidance from appellate or revisional courts, formulated their own ideas of social, legal or normal justice for granting or denying bonus claims.

Several adjudicators of the early period held that in the absence of a contract, express or implied, workers were not entitled to claim bonus as a matter of right and that in the absence of proof of excessive profits, it was not possible to allow bonus as an *ex gratia* payment.

But there were others who were by no means certain of bonus being only an exgratial payment. This was a period of wavering and indecision — of doubt whether bonus was only a gift or whether it could amount to a right.

Some adjudications, not wishing to go quite so far as to decide that bonus could be claimed as a matter of 'right', met workers' claims half way by granting a limited amount of bonus on board principles of equity, justice, and good conscience. In one of the earlier cases, the adjudicator said that it was expedient from the point of view of the employers themselves that the workers in industries essential for the due prosecution of the war should be kept contented and happy and that if some concerns like that Standard Vacum Oil Company and Caltex (India) Limited were making large profits, "it seems but fair to me that an infinitesimal fraction of these profits may well be given by way of bonus to the workers in these companies, without whose labour and co-operation these unusually large profits could not have been made available to these companies." On these considerations he awarded one month's wage as bonus.

In United Provinces Sugar Co., and their employees, it was held that bonus as a share of profits could not be claimed as a matter of right every year but that if a concern had an unusually profitable year, some part of the extra profits should be distributed "as an award and encouragement to workers".

On this basis several adjudicators awarded one-twelfth or one-eighth of the total annual earnings as bonus.

Bonus as a Matter of Right

Judicial decision was, however, not slow to come upto workers' expectations, probably because wages were still very low in those days and profits invariably very high. As early as 1942 Justice Chagla, adjudicating on a dispute between the General Motors (India) Limited and its workmen, said : "It is almost a universally accepted principle now that the profits are made possible by the contribution that both capital and labour make in any particular industry and I think it is also conceded that labour has a right to share in the increased profits that are made in any particular period. But the distribution of increased profits amongst workers is better achieved by the giving of an annual bonus than by a further increase in wages. Wages must be fixed on the basis of normal conditions". The adjudicator was obviously anticipating future trends, and perhaps influencing them, when he observed that it was also "conceded" that labour had a 'right' to share in the increased profits.

These observations, which pleaded powerfully for recognition of labour's right to profit sharing, were quoted with approval in a large number of adjudications of that period.

By the end of the Second World War the view that labour was entitled to a share in profits as a matter of right seems to have got more or less well established. Adjudicators were only searching for the right words to uphold labour's right to bonus.

In a dispute between the Textile Labour Association, Ahmedabad, and the Ahmedabad Mill Owners Association, the Industrial Court, Bombay, said that although bonus was an *ex gratia* payment and could not be legally demanded, bonus was in the nature of a reward. It was a reward "for work already done by them, which has resulted in such high profits". The Court went on to say: "Such additional payment is not a pure gift because a gift may have no relation to any work done or to be done by the donee, but it is a reward inasmuch as it is asked for as an extra payment for work actually done." Though such a claim could not be enforced in a court of law, it could become the subject matter of an industrial dispute. Here the Court was trying to justify bonus more as an extra remuneration or wage payment than as profit-sharing.

In the Lahore Electric Supply Company's case, the adjudicator had no difficulty in justifying bonus as profit-sharing. Though bonus was not a legal right which could be enforced in a court of law, "the advancement of economic thought and industrial relations had led to a state of affairs where the workers claim for a share in the profit of industry may be legitimate and may have a certain normal and economic right".

In Indian Hume Pipe Co. Ltd., V.E. M. Nanavutty, the Bombay High Court ruled that payment of bonus could be demanded by workmen "as of right, that is to say as a payment which should be made by the employer as extra remuneration for work done by the employees under a contract, express or implied".

In a dispute between 36 cotton mills in West Bengal and their employees, the Industrial Tribunal said that when bonus was demanded for work done out of which the employers had made high profits "the demand is not for any payment gratis but the price of labour". It added; "....... the demand of bonus though not based on legal right raising out of contract, expressed or implied, has to be decided on broad principles of equity and justice".

It will be seen from the cases mentioned above that adjudicators of this period-war and early post war — were wavering between treating bonus as extra remuneration for work done and viewing it as sharing in the profits jointly created by labour and management. But all agreed on one point, namely, that a claim to bonus, while not enforceable in a civil court, could be adjudicated upon as a matter of right.

It was the Industrial Court, Bombay, which in a series of cases, shaped the concept of bonus as we understand it today. In a dispute decided in 1947 between the Rashtriya Mill Mazdoor Sangh and the Millowners' Association, Bombay, the Court observed : 'The justification for such demands as 'industrial matter' arises especially when wages fall short of the living wage standard and the industry makes huge profits part of which are due to the contribution which the workers made in increasing production. The demand for a bonus is, therefore an industrial claim when either or both these conditions are satisfied'.

In a dispute between the same parties relating to 1948 and decided in 1949, the Industrial Court, Bombay, reiterated the view it had expressed in 1947. As this case and the one relating to the bonus demand in the next year were the cases from which the Labour Appellate Tribunal evolved the 'Full Bench Formula' later on, we might notice the Court's observations at some length. The Court said : "Such a demand (for bonus) derives its strength, where the living wage standard has not been reached, from a feeling of deficiency in the means to attain the necessary standard of living. Therefore, bonus in such circumstances no doubt serves as a temporary satisfaction, wholly or in part, of his need. Theoretically, adequate wages and dearness allowance should be the first charge on an industry..... Labour as well as the working capital employed in the industry both contribute to the profit made and both are, therefore, entitled to claim a legitimate return out of the profit; and such legitimate return so far as labour is concerned, must be based on the living wage standard. It is however, to be remembered that a claim to bonus might be admissible even if the living wage standard were completely attained. It may, therefore, be stated that so long as the living wage standard has not been attained, the bonus partakes primarily of the character of the satisfaction, often partial and temporary, of the deficiency in the legitimate income of the average worker in an industry, and that once such income has been attained it would also partake of the character of profit-sharing. Owing to this dual character of bonus, it would be a mistake to regard a demand for bonus as a demand for profit-sharing pure and simple. Even if it be held, as the Committee on profit-sharing have held that profit-sharing on a fifty-fifty basis would be equitable, it would be proper in our opinion, when the living wage standard has not been reached for labour to demand even a greater share after the gross profits have been reduced by depreciation, reasonable reserves, dividend and suitable provision for taxation".

Payment of Bonus

This profit-sharing concept also resulted in a bonus being paid at the end of the year to the employees. Good companies began to pay upto three months pay as bonus to their employees even in years which did not justify such a high bonus payment. This led to a belief in the mind of the worker that the employers were holding back a part of their wage and paying it at the end of the year under title "bonus" as a "deferred wage". This concept unfortunately was practically legalised by the Payment of Bonus Act, 1965.

The Payment of Bonus Act, 1965

This Act came into operation on May 29, 1965, replacing an ordinance, which came into force on September 25, 1965. It provides for payment by the employer to every employee in an accounting year of a minimum bonus of 4% (later increased to 8½ per cent (or Rs. 80 whichever is higher) for the accounting year commencing in 1971 by the Payment of Bonus (Amendment) Act, 1972 of the salary or wages earned by the employee during the accounting year or forty rupees (Rs. 25 in case of employees under 15 years of age) whichever is higher, irrespective of whether there are profits in the accounting year or not (S. 10). Thus, this provision is a deviation from the well recognised principle that bonus is payable only out of the profits.

The Act provides for calculation of available surplus as the gross profits after deducting certain sums such as depreciation and development rebate or allowance admissible under the Income-tax Act and other items (Sections 5 and 6 and Schedules). Where such surplus exceeds the minimum bonus payable, the employer is required to pay such surplus, in lieu of such minimum bonus, in proportion to the salary or wages of the employee subject to a minimum of 20 per cent of such salary or wage (S. II). In case of an employee whose salary or wage exceeds Rs. 750 per month, the bonus is to be calculated as if his salary or wages were Rs. 750 per month (S. 12). The excess of allocable surplus not distributed is to be carried forward for being set on upto the fourth succeeding accounting year (S.15).

This Act applies to (a) every factory as defined in the Factories Act, 1948 and (b) every other establishment in which 20 or more persons are employed on any day during an accounting year. Subsequent reduction to less than 20 employees will not make the Act inapplicable (S.1). The word 'establishment" is a far wider term than factory.

The 'Bonus Commission's Report' explains the concept of bonus as "sharing by the workers in the prosperity of the concern in which they are employed". They further contended that "in the case of low paid workers such sharing in prosperity augments their earnings and so helps to bridge the gap between the actual wage and the need-based wage". A properly conceived bonus system linked to profit does provide a measure of desirable flexibility to the wage structure.

The Act however does not apply to certain classes of employees, e.g. employees of the Life Insurance Corporation of India, insurer carrying on general insurance business, seamen under the Merchant Shipping Act. 1958, the Indian Red Cross Society, universities and other educational institutions as well as institutions not established for the purpose of profit (S. 32).

❑ ❑ ❑

16

INDIA AND THE ILO

The International Labour Organisation is a permanent inter-governmental agency which was established in 1919. India has been a member of this international institution since its inception in 1919.

It was Robert Owen who rose from the position of an ill-paid apprentice to that of a wealthy textile manufacturer in Scotland, pleaded for the international action to improve the conditions of labour. Thirty years later Daniel Legrand, an Alsatian manufacturer sent memorials to the French, British and Prussian Governments to enact an international law to protect the working classes against excessive labour which is the principal cause of their physical deterioration, their social degradation and their being deprived of the blessings of family life. A resolution in favour of international legislation was adopted by the first Congress of the Workers' International in Geneva in 1866. But all these attempts were not very effective for the establishment of International Labour Organisation. Nevertheless, trade unionists, social reformers and philanthropists continued to agitate for international action in order to improve the conditions of industrial life of labour. This movement culminated in the formation of International Association of Labour Legislation in 1897. Later this association founded an International Labour Office in Basle and drafted the first International Labour Convention prohibiting the night work of women and the use of phosphorous in the manufacture of matches. The provisions of this convention could not be implemented on an international scale due to lack of interest on the part of major government. With the end of the First War, there was a general feeling that any attempt to create a better world should include some systematic effort to improve labour conditions. The Allied Powers duly took note of this feelings and appointed a Commission on Labour Legislation which recommended the creation of a permanent agency for regulating the conditions of employment from the international aspect. As a result, of the recommendations the International Labour Organisation became into being in 1919.

AIMS OF THE ILO

The main aims of the ILO are as follows :

- To remove injustice, hardship and privation of large masses of toiling people all over the world.
- To improve their living and working conditions and thus establish universal lasting peace based upon social justice.
- The regulation of hours of work, laying down the maximum workload for day and week.
- To give suggestions and recommendations for the prevention of unemployment.
- To take steps and give special attention for the protection of children, young persons and women.
- To take suitable steps for the protection of interests of those workers who have been employed in countries other than their own.
- To take steps for the recognition and implementation of the principle of freedom of association.
- To take steps for the recognition and implementation of the principle of equal remuneration of work of equal value.
- To make provision for vocational and technical education.

Structure

The ILO is a tripartite organisation consisting of representatives of Government, employers and workers of the member countries. There is a parity of representation as between government and non-government groups and also between employers and workers groups.

Declaration of Philadelphia

The Declaration of Philadelphia which is also a part of the ILO's constitution, was adopted at the twenty sixth session of the International Labour Conference held in Philadelphia.

The Declaration reaffirmed the fundamental principles on which the ILO is based; namely :

- Labour is not a commodity;

- Freedom of expression and of association are essential to sustain progress;
- Poverty anywhere constitutes a danger to prosperity everywhere.

The war against want requires to be carried on with unrelenting vigour within each nation and by continuous and concerted international effort in which the representatives of employers and workers, enjoying equal status with those of governments join with them in free discussion and democratic decision with a view to promotion of the common welfare.

The Declaration asserted that the central aim of national and international policy must be the attainment of conditions in which all human beings have the right to pursue their material well-being and their spiritual development in conditions of freedom and dignity of economic security and equal opportunity. It enjoins on the ILO to examine and consider all international economic policies and measures in the light of the objective.

PRINCIPAL ORGANS OF THE ILO

The principal organs of the ILO are :

- International Labour Conference;
- Governing Body; and
- International Labour Office.

International Labour Conference

International Labour Conference is held once a year. It is the supreme policy making body for the whole organisation. Every country is represented by four delegates, two representing the government, one representing employers and one representing workers. All delegates have the right to vote independently. The main object of the Conference is to draft international minimum social and labour standards. These can take the form of Conventions or Recommendations. A convention is an international treaty which has to be approved by two-thirds of the delegates of the conference before it is adopted.

Governing Body

The Governing Body is the chief executive body of the Organisation. As such, it meets more often, normally four times a year. This body is also tripartite in character with a membership of 40-20 for governments, 10 each representing employers and workers. Out of the 20 Government members, 10 represent countries of chief industrial importance which thus have a seat without having to stand for election. India is one of these 10.

International Labour Office

The International Labour Office is responsible for day-to-day organisation and activities. The office employs at the Headquarters in

Geneva about 1,000 officials from more than 60 different countries whose knowledge, experience and advice are available to all member States. The Office has a Liaison Office with the United Nations in New York, 5 regional field offices, branch offices in 12 countries including India and correspondents in 37 countries.

PRINCIPAL ACTIVITIES

The work of the ILO may be divided into three parts — legislative, operational, educational and general.

The International Labour Code

The legislative work of the ILO consists of the conventions and recommendations adopted by the International Labour Conference since 1919. This goes under the name of the International Labour Code.

Technical Assistance

Although the ILO has been rendering technical assistance ever since it was established, the operational activities on a systematic basis started only in 1950 with the ILO's participation in the Expanded Programme of Technical Assistance of the United Nations and the Specialized Agencies. The main fields in which the ILO has been rendering technical assistance are manpower organisation, productivity and management development, cooperation, social security and labour conditions. The technical assistance provided by the ILO takes these forms : providing technical assistance experts to countries asking for them, organising regional seminars, awarding fellowships, study grants and supplying equipment.

Educational Programme

Increasing importance has been attached by the ILO in recent years to activities designed to strengthen the institutions through which labour policies are formulated and applied. The ILO's work in this field comprises :

A growing programme of training for labour administrative staff, particularly labour inspectors, employment service officers and junior officials;

Workers' education programme to assist workers to take part effectively in workers' movements and fulfil their trade union and related functions;

Extension of the activities in the field of management development;

A promotional circulation to the ILO's work in the field of labour management relations, designed to encourage the growth of cooperative relations between organised labour and employers and the establishment in 1960, of the International Institute for Labour Studies.

India's Relationship with the ILO

India's relationship with the ILO dates back to the day of its birth in 1919. India has been benefitted by the ILO in the following fields.

Upto 1919 there was no important labour legislation in India. All major labour laws in India date from that year. The constitution of the ILO provided that the Conventions and Recommendations passed by the International Labour Conference should be brought before the national parliament within 18 months of their adoption.

India has ratified so far 30 conventions, a list of which has been given at the end.

The ILO has been providing technical assistance and guidance for the implementation of social security programmes, programmes of vocational training, training within industry and employment services and workers' education for improving economic and social life of the workers. ILO is assisting for improving the productivity of industry and workers.

A branch office of the ILO was established in 1928 in New Delhi and has continued its existence ever since. Besides action as a major link in the worldwide network of the ILO the Branch office acts as a clearing house of information and is responsible for maintaining relations with Government authorities and employers' and workers' organisations. The Branch office issued in 1957 a publication entitled Labour Legislation in India which traces the history of labour legislations in India from the beginning to the present time.

Evaluation

In the 50 years of its existence, the ILO has worked consistently for the achievement of universal and lasting peace which can be established only if it is based upon social justice. Thus, the principal function of the ILO in this quest for social justice has been to safeguard the rights and promote the well-being of working people all over the world. The struggle for social justice means struggle for elimination of all forms of discrimination.

In all its activities the ILO has advocated conciliation and compromise among its three constituents — governments, employers and workers. It is the principle of tripartite cooperation that has provided strength to the ILO. The principle presupposes that social justice can be achieved without class struggle or class conflict. We in India have been considerably influenced by the principle of 'tripartism' in the labour field.

The National Commission on Labour has observed that India's participation in the ILO over the years has been meaningful. Our country has offered assistance to the international community.

The commission recommended that the government should seek to ratify the convention which have been held up because of technical and administrative difficulties. The Commission further said that source of the conventions dealing with fundamental human rights have not yet been ratified by our country.

The Commission recommended that International obligations which devolve on India as a result of our long association with the ILO have to be discharged in several directions :

By adopting the aims and objects of the ILO for national actions.

By cooperating at the international and regional levels in the programmes of the ILO and

By progressive implementation of the standards set up by the ILO.

IMPORTANT ILO CONVENTIONS RATIFIED BY INDIA

Title of Conventions

No. 1 Hours of Work (Industry) Convention, 1919.

No. 2 Unemployment Convention, 1919.

No. 3 Night Work (Women) Convention, 1919.

No. 4 Minimum Age (Industry) Convention, 1919.

No. 5 Night Work of Young Persons (Industry) Convention, 1919.

No. 6 Right of Association (Agriculture) Convention, 1921.

No. 7 Weekly Rest (Industry) Convention, 1924.

No. 8 Minimum Age (Trimmers and Stokers) Convention, 1921.

No. 9 Medical Examination of Young Persons (Sea) Convention, 1921.

No. 10 Workmen's Compensation (Occupational Diseases) Convention, 1925.

No. 11 Equality of Treatment (Accident Compensation) Convention, 1925.

No. 12 Inspection of Emigrants Convention, 1926.

No. 13 Seamen's Articles of Agreement Convention, 1928.

No. 14 Minimum Wage Fixing Machinery Convention, 1928.

No. 15 Marking of Weight (Packages Transported by Vessels) Convention, 1929.

No. 16 Forced Labour Convention, 1930.

No. 17 Protection against Accidents (Dockers) Convention, (Revised), 1932.

No. 18 Night Work (Women) Convention (Revised), 1934.

No. 19 Underground Work (Women) Convention, 1935.

No. 20 Final Articles Revision Convention, 1946.

No. 21 Labour Inspection Convention, 1947.

No. 22 Employment Service Convention (Revised), 1948.

No. 23 Night Work (Women) Convention (Revised), 1948.

No. 24 Night Work Young Persons (Industry) Convention (Revised), 1948.

No. 25 Equal Remuneration Convention, 1951.

No. 26 Discrimination (Employment & Occupations) Convention, 1948.

❑ ❑ ❑

17

LABOUR LEGISLATION

I

Labour legislation is a most dynamic institution in modern society. From a simple restraint on child labour in Great Britain in 1881, labour legislation has become an important agency of the State for the regulation of working and living conditions of men and women throughout the world. The rapid development of labour legislation is due to the fact that it is an integral part of modern social organisation. Like slave labour in ancient times, serf labour in medieval times and indentured labour in transitional periods, the relics of all of which are still to be found in many backward countries; Free labour is the direct result of growing industrialism and democracy and the labour legislation is the institution through which the State protects the interests and ameliorates the moral and material conditions of the working classes.

There is a fundamental difference between the law regulating labour under slavery, serfdom and indenture and that regulating labour under free contract. While the main object of the former was to safeguard the interests of the employers, modern labour legislation aims at safeguarding the interests of the worker in modern industry. With the growth of democracy, the forces of attention has been transferred from the employer, who was usually a powerful person, to employee who is usually a weak man.

Modern labour legislation has two distinguishing features. The *first* feature is its continuity. As the society is dynamic, labour legislation which is an institution of society, must also be growing. What is more important is not mere growth but progress, which depends upon its ability to bring continuously within the reach of the working classes various social achievements in the form of better health, greater safety, shorter hours and a higher standard of living, thus offering them more facilities for moral and spiritual development. Labour legislation can realise this object only through continued evaluation of its principles in the light of progress in art, science and philosophy.

The *second* feature of labour legislation is universality. It is due to the fact that it is the direct result of modern industrialism. It is the growth of industrialism in most countries which has brought about similar labour conditions and led to the enactment of more or less similar labour measures. But, in spite of its universality, local conditions should be taken into consideration in the enactment of labour legislation in each country.

FUNDAMENTAL PRINCIPLES OF LABOUR LEGISLATION

Although the protection of labour in industry is the motive force behind labour legislation, there are other forces which influence the course of its development and determine its nature. The most important factor is the abolition of servitude and the establishment of free contract and development of physical and mental resources of the working classes which form an increasingly large proportion of the population, with a view to securing the welfare of the society as a whole. *Thirdly*, the betterment of working and living conditions of the labour population in order to increase industrial efficiency and assure the increase of national productivity and *finally*, amelioration of national labour conditions through international labour agreements. All these underlying forces of labour legislation may be classified under four categories, namely, (1) social justice, (2) social welfare, (3) national economy and (4) international solidarity.

1. Social Justice

An outstanding force in social evolution is social justice which means the establishment of equality in social relationship. The first step in establishing social justice is to protect those who cannot protect themselves. Modern industrialism involving the use of power, machinery and large-scale production and giving rise to industrial towns, has brought about complete changes in the working and living conditions, some of which are detrimental to the moral, material and intellectual welfare of workers. Since workers, especially women and children, are often unable to protect themselves, the State, the supreme authority and the guardian of the people, has undertaken legislative measures on their behalf.

The guiding principles of labour legislation is the establishment of social justice is an equitable relationship between employers and workers. In spite of political equality, there exists a great divergence between employers and workers in the economic status which often deprives the latter of their political rights. The lack of economic security makes the actual position of workers much inferior to that of their employers. But the existence of a democratic society depends upon administration of social justice to all classes of people. It is on the principle of social justice that the State undertakes to equalise the status of workers with that of employers, to grant them freedom of association and the power of collective bargaining and to mediate or arbitrate in the case of industrial conflict.

The most important condition for equalizing industrial relationship between employers and workers is the abolition of servitude. Labour has passed through the following four stages in the process of social evolution — (1) slavery, (2) serfdom, (3) indenture and (4) free contract. Under slavery labour was regarded not as a human being but as a personal property of his master and which could be brought and sold in the market. Under serfdom labour achieved a certain amount of freedom, he has free part of the time and was obliged to serve his lord only when called upon but still the lord wielded great power over the life of labour and the latter could achieve his freedom only by cash payment or flight. Under the indenture system the labourer acquired a still large amount of freedom; he had to serve only for a fixed period of time and often at the stipulated rate of wages, though desertion, idleness or neglect of work still made him liable to criminal punishment. It is only under free contract that the labourer has acquired full freedom and the right to bargain with his employer on an equal footing.

2. Social Welfare

Social welfare is another important principle underlying labour legislation. There exists an immense potentiality of human resources which can be developed for the advancement of social welfare. The main object of all rational activities is social progress. The most important means for the achievement of social progress is social welfare. The principle of social welfare differs from that of social justice as the latter preconceives of some standard of equity which must be extended to working classes through labour legislation, whereas the former does not necessarily recognise such a standard but only conceives of an ideal of evolutionary society in which humanity may find its increasing perfection and which working classes may realise through progressive labour legislation. Social justice may be said to look backward in search of a standard and to conceive of a rather static society while social welfare looks definitely forward and contemplates of a dynamic society. As an ideal social welfare is rather vague but in its very vagueness lies its real strength. It is the ideal of 'better manhood' and 'better society' which has drawn many visionaries and philanthropists to the movement for labour legislation in most countries.

Measures which look forward to the betterment of society should be classified under this principle. Since the future of society depends upon the physical and mental development of the child, child labour legislation together with protection of women falls under this category. To this must be added all measures for the moral and material welfare of workers who form by far the majority of the population in all industrial countries.

Protection of children was the first motive force for the regulation of industrial labour in India as well as in most other countries. It was, in fact, the historical origin of labour legislation in England. Since the child is the future member of society, social welfare depends upon the fullest and richest growth of childhood. The development of physical and mental capabilities of the child has become the prime concern of society and the most important principle of child labour legislation in modern times. The admission of children to industrial occupation has been made conditional upon a three-fold requirement — *(i)* minimum age, *(ii)* physical fitness and *(iii)* elementary education. What is more important is the fact that the present tendency in child labour legislation is to liberate the child from all premature labour which may interfere with its full development.

Closely connected with the development of childhood is the question of the conservation of womanhood, on which depends not only the welfare of women themselves, but also of society in general and of children in particular. For a long time woman had been considered a 'minor' in a legal sense of the word and the State had no difficulty in extending its protective power to women in the new industrial organisation and to pass laws on their behalf. These early legislative measures have been supplemented by a series of measures which may fall under three headings —

A woman may be conceived of in a three-fold capacity — (1) worker, (2) wife and (3) mother.

Firstly, as a worker, woman has always been in charge of the household and has often assisted man in agricultural and handicraft. With the transfer of her work from the household to the factory, she has become an industrial worker. The state has passed laws for her protection against excessive hours, insanitary conditions, dangerous work and underground employment in mines.

Secondly, woman is also wife and the builder of the home and the pivot of the family life upon which has been built up the present social framework. Her presence is therefore needed at night when all members of the household are at home. Moreover, night work outside the household and in the company of strangers may not always be morally good. The State has therefore, prohibited the night work of women except under some special conditions.

Lastly, woman is also mother and as such she is the bearer and rearer of the future generation. The physical and moral development of the child is dependent upon the health and welfare of the mother. The realisation of this fact has led to another series of legislative measures such as maternity benefit, and the provision for creches.

Another important method of achieving social welfare is the improvement of environment which can be best achieved by welfare work. Welfare work seeks to create better physical and social environments and to offer greater facilities for the moral and material advancement of the workers. The scope of welfare work is varied depending upon the stage of industrial development of the country concerned but may be roughly divided into four categories — (1) housing (2) health, (3) recreation and (4) culture.

3. National Economy

National economy is another guiding principle of labour legislation. The first and foremost object of national economy is the increase of national wealth. As far as labour legislation is concerned, national economy has a four-fold concern. *First,* the ensuring of the normal growth of industry for benefit of the nation as a whole, especially in India where national productivity is far behind and per capita income is the lowest among the advanced nations; *secondly,* the provision for better working and living conditions which is lower than that of any other industrially advanced country; *thirdly,* the adjustment of the wage system with a view to increasing the purchasing power of workers and creating a stable home market on which depends continued production and finally the development of social insurance with a view to check misery and privation through the loss of income arising from accident, sickness, invalidity, old age, premature death and involuntary unemployment.

4. International Solidarity

International solidarity is another important principle of labour legislation. It means the improvement of national labour conditions through international labour conventions. This solidarity is achieved by the ratification or adoption of conventions and recommendations of the International Labour Conference and the application of their principles to National Labour Legislation.

Though attempts were made as early as 1881 by the Swiss Government to come to an understanding with different Governments on the question of International Labour Legislation, it was not until after the First World War that all the nations fully realised the need of international co-operation for labour legislation. The International Labour Organisation, an organ of the League of Nations, was created in 1919 for improving labour conditions throughout the world and for establishing a better relationship between employers and employees as well as among different nations through common-understanding, in which the representatives not only of governments but also of employers and employees could take an active part. Since 1922, India has been a permanent member of the ILO. The active participation by India in the rise and growth of the ILO has not only helped in the development of international solidarity but has also profoundly influenced her own national labour legislation. Although labour legislation was undertaken by the Government of India towards the end of the 19th century, but the progress was very slow. It was only after the inauguration of the ILO in 1919 and the adoption by the International Labour Conference of various draft conventions and recommendations since then that labour legislation in India has received a new impetus.

EVOLUTION OF LABOUR LEGISLATION

In India labour legislation was undertaken in advance of the emergence of labour organisations. The incentive to labour legislation was furnished not by the humanitarian considerations of enlightened manufactures but by the discovery of ceratin Manchester Cotton manufacturers in 1870 that a cotton textile industry was developing in Bombay. At that time industrialists in India could use their labour in any manner they liked as there was no factory laws. The result was the exploitation of labour, especially of children and women labour by employers. Thus industrialists in India had the advantage of cheap labour in comparison with the British industrialists where labour laws existed and the Manchester Cotton manufacturers became jealous of the Indian Cotton mill and wanted to curb its development. The Manchester Chamber of Commerce sent in 1874 a deputation to the Secretary of State for India to apply the same factory laws to the Indian mills as were applicable to the British factories so as to neutralise the unfair advantages which the Indian manufacturers were enjoying due to long hours of work and large scale employment of child and women labour. A Factory Commission was appointed in 1875, to investigate the need of the required legislation. The Commission revealed the fact that the mills worked from sun-set to sun-rise, there was no fixed weekly holiday and even children of 7 were engaged in the factory. The Bombay Government shelved the Commission's report as the majority did not favour the idea of regulating working hours in the factories, through legal measures. But the Manchester interests, however, continued to carry on their agitation for factory legislation.

It was in 1875 when some social workers of Bombay under the leadership of Mr. Sorabjee Shaporjee Bengalee started an agitation to draw the attention of the Government to the miserable conditions of the workers and to the need for some factory legislation. As a result of the agitation the first Factories Act was passed in 1881.

In the early days the policy of the Government was to protect the social system from workers rather than to protect workers from the social system. Moreover, whatever labour legislation was undertaken, was also with reference to specific industries and not for the general class of industrial workers.

Defects

The defects of labour legislation in India have been due to the lack of proper development of a national labour policy. Prior to World War II, there was practically no social attitude or public opinion on the labour question and no demand was made for an adequate solution of any outstanding labour problem. Most of the measures were, therefore, forced upon Government by extraneous circumstances. Plantation legislation was, for instance, enacted for granting planters a security over their labourers; factory legislation owes its origin to the rivalry of Manchester interests and even in the recent past labour legislation was undertaken for the fulfillment of international obligation, which, however important in itself, cannot take the place of a national labour policy.

It has been rightly criticised that many of the labour laws are 'half-baked and hastily devised'. Close at the heels of an Act come amendments and then more amendments to amend the amendments.

Employers complain, not without reason, that government's labour legislation programme is quite unrelated to the needs of the present situation in India. They contend that the obligations imposed on employers under various labour laws contribute to raise the cost of production and weaken India's competitive position in the world market.

II

Labour legislation roughly fall into the following categories. (1) Factory and Establishment Legislation; (2) Plantation Legislation; (3) Mining and Mineral Legislation; (4) Transport Legislation; (5) Wage Legislation; (6) Social Security Legislation; (7) Industrial Relations Legislation and (8) Miscellaneous Legislation.

1. Factory and Establishment Legislation

The most important labour legislation in India relates to the factories. The need for regulation of hours of work and conditions of employment of industrial workers was recognized in India from the middle of the 19th century. The *first* comprehensive legislation for regulating labour in factories was passed in 1881. Indian Factories Act, 1881 applied to all factories other than seasonal factories which used power and employed 100 or more persons. The Act prohibited the employment of children below 7 years of age, limited to 9 hours the work of children between the ages of 7 and 12, provided for a mid-day interval of rest for one hour and a weekly holiday for children only.

But this legislation was widely evaded by the mills. As a result the Indian Factories Act, 1991 was passed. This Act was an improvement of the previous Act. This Act applied to all factories employing 50 persons and using power. It raised the minimum age of employment to 9 years, prohibited the employment of children and women at night and limited the work of women to 11 hours per day, provided for an interval of 1½ hours for rest in between the work and one day's rest for all workers including men.

It was more effective than the previous Act, but it also failed to improve the condition of labour as ginning mills and seasonal factories were outside its purview and the enforcement machinery was exceedingly weak. As a result of much agitation the Factories Act of 1911 was passed. This Act regulated for the first time, the hours of work of adult male industrial workers and covered seasonal factories which work for less than 4 months in a year. The Act limited the hours of work of adult male workers to 12 a day and of children to 6 a day in textile factories, with a rest interval of half an hour. The Act contained extensive provisions regarding health and safety and effective inspection of the administration of factories. The condition of factory labour in India undoubtedly improved as a result of this legislation but the condition was not quite satisfactory even now.

Partly as a result of the International Labour Organisation in 1920 and the Washington Conventions and partly as a result of growing social consciousness of the people, the Factories Act was amended in 1922 making some important changes in the provisions. This Amending Act was extended to include all industrial undertakings using mechanical power and employing 20 or more persons. It raised the age of employment to 12 years, laid down that children between the ages of 12 and 15 would not be employed for more than 6 hours a day, restricted the working hours of all adults to 11 hours per day and 60 hours per week with a rest interval of one hour after every 6 hours of work and a weekly holiday.

The Royal Commission on Labour submitted its report in 1931 and made several important recommendations for the amendment of Factories Act of 1911. As a result, the Factories Act of 1934 was passed. This Act applies to all manufacturing establishments employing 20 or more persons and using power. Factories were divided into seasonal and perennial factories, the former working for less than 180 days in a year, while perennial factories included all those establishments which worked for more than 180 days in a year. The maximum hours of work for adult in perennial factories were fixed at 10 per day and 54 per week while for seasonal factories the limit was fixed at 11 per day and 60 per week. The hours of works for children were reduced to 5 per day. The principle of spread-over was introduced for the first time and the number of consecutive hours of work was fixed at 13 for adults and 6½ for children. Overtime was required to be paid of the rate of 1½ times of the ordinary wages. There were also provisions for health, safety and welfare.

The Indian Factories Act of 1948 replaced the Factories Act of 1934, removed a number of defects and has filled some gaps in the previous legislation. The 1948 Act applies to all industrial establishments employing 10 or more workers where power is used and to those employing 20 or more workers whether power is used or not. The main provisions of the Act are as follows : *(i)* Daily working hours shall not be more than 9 hours and weekly not more than 48 hours in a week of 6 days; *(ii)* one days' rest in a week shall have to be given to a worker; *(iii)* at least 1/2 hour's rest shall have to be given after 5 hours' work; *(iv)* workers with 240 days' work in a year are entitled to 1 day's leave with wages for every 20 days' work; *(v)* no overtime work is permitted without prior sanction of the inspector; *(vi)* for more than 9 hours' work in a day or 48 hours' work in a week the workers shall be paid twice their normal rate of wages; *(vii)* not more than 50 hours of overtime are allowed in a quarter of year; *(viii)* factories employing more than 250 workers must have canteen for workers on no profit basis and *(ix)* factories employing more than 500 workers must employ qualified welfare officers.

2. Plantation Legislation

Plantation was the first organised industry in India in which workers came under legislative control. Plantation legislation began to develop in India in connection with the tea industry in Assam. Owing to scarcity of labour in the province, workers had to be imported from other provinces and the character of these workers was thus migratory. The early legislative measures were more protective of the planters than of their workers. The Tea District Emigrant Labour Act of 1932 deals mainly with the regulation of recruitment of workers for tea gardens in Assam so as to prevent recruitment by enticement and false representation and to ensure proper arrangements for journey to Assam. The Act empowered the State Government subject to the control of the Central Government, to declare any area to be controlled emigration area and an assisted emigrant may be forwarded to Assam by a licensed forwarding agent acting on behalf of an employer. Such assisted recruits can be sent only by prescribed routes where feeding and accommodation arrangements have been made by the agents. Every emigrant labourer is entitled to repatriation to his own place at the expense of the employer after completing 3 year's service or even earlier under certain circumstances. Children under 16 must not migrate unless accompanied by partners and married woman without the consent of her husband. The Act does not contain any provision regulating accommodation, sanitation, water supply, medical treatment wages, hours of work, rest, recreation and other welfare arrangements for workers employed in tea estate. This Act is not actually a labour legislation as it does not regulate working conditions in tea plantation, but it is really an emigration legislation.

The reports of the Labour Investigation Committee point out that in plantations (1) wages are inadequate, (2) housing conditions are unsatisfactory and (3) medical services require substantial improvement and expansion. The Committee suggested the enactment of a separate Plantation Labour Act for the whole of India as the conditions of life and employment on plantations are quite different from those in other industries. As a result, the Plantation Labour Act was passed in 1951. The main provisions of the Act are as follows : (1) Employers are required to arrange for the supply of wholesome drinking water for all workers and for providing sufficient number of latrines and urinals separately for men and women. (2) Every planter employing 150 or more workers must maintain canteen. (3) Planters are required to provide for recreational and educational facilities for the workers and their children. (4) Every planter employing 50 or more women must-provide for creches. (5) Planters employing 300 or more workers must appoint Welfare Officers. (6) Sickness and maternity allowances are to be provided subject to rules framed by State Governments. (7) Planter must provide for every worker and his family necessary housing accommodation.

The Act fixes the weekly working hours for adults at 54 and for children and adolescents (persons between 15 and 18 years) at 40. The Act does not fix the daily working hours but lays down that no workers is to work for more than 5 hours without a rest interval of half an hour. The spread-over has been fixed at 12 hours a day.

The Act prohibits the employment of children under 12 years of age and night work between 7 p.m. and 6 a.m. is prohibited for women and children. Every worker shall be allowed leave with wages at the rate of *(i)* if an adult, one day for every 20 days of work, and *(ii)* if a young person, one day for every 15 days of work. Leave can be accumulated to a maximum period of 30 days.

3. Mining Legislation

Modern mining was introduced in India early in the 19th century but the necessity of regulating employment of labour was not realised by government until the nineties. The First Act concerning the mine was passed in 1901 on the basis of the Report of the Mining Committee appointed in 1895. The main object of the Indian Mines Act, 1901 was to solve the problems of health and safety of the miners. It empowers the Chief Inspector of Mines to prohibit employment of children under 12 and of women in mines which were dangerous to their health and safety. The defect of this Act was the absence of any statutory limitation to working hours.

In 1923, a new Indian Mines Act was passed to carry out the recommendations of the Washington Conferences. The main provisions of the Act were as follows; *(i)* limitation of weekly hours of work to 54 underground and 60 above ground, *(ii)* limitation of the working days to 6 in a week and *(iii)* prohibition of the employment of children under 13 years of age in mines. One of the fundamental defect of this Act was the absence of any statutory limitation of daily hours of work. A new Amending Act was passed in 1928, making unlawful the employment of any person for more than 12 hours in any one day. After the adoption of Underground Work (Women) Convention by the International Labour Conference in 1935, the Government of India prohibited the underground employment of women in mines in 1937.

On the basis of the recommendations of the Royal Commission on Labour a new Amending Act was passed in 1935. This Act regulated the hours of work above ground to 54 a week and 10 days with at least one hour's rest for six hours' work and for work underground to 54 in a week and 9 a day. It prohibited the employment of children under 13 in mines and included provisions relating to safety in mines.

The Indian Mines Act of 1923 was amended again in 1936, 1937, 1940 and 1946.

After the passing of the new Factories Act of 1948, the Central Government was thinking of revising the legislation relating to mine workers and to bring it in line with the legislation concerning factory workers. Indian Mines Act of 1923 placed greater emphasis on the safety of mine workers than on the measures relating to their welfare. The Central Government introduced the new Mines Bill in the Parliament in 1949 to revise the legislation concerning mine workers. The Bill was passed and the Mines Act came into force in 1952. Provisions relating to *(i)* health, *(ii)* safety and *(iii)* welfare are elaborate in this Act of 1952.

The main provisions of the Act are as follows: (1) In every mine both above and below ground arrangements shall be made to provide and maintain wholesome drinking water. (2) Sufficient number of latrines and urinals should be provided separately for males and females. (3) Provision has been made for the maintenance of first-aid boxes equipped with prescribed contents. (4) Provision has been made for maintenance of ambulances and stretchers and ambulance room containing the prescribed equipment in charge of medical and nursing staff in every mine employing over 500 workers. (5) The Act limits the hours of work of adult workers at 9 per day and 48 per week if employed above ground and 8 per day and 48 per week if employed below ground. No person shall be allowed to work in a mine for more than 6 days in a week. After 5 hours' continuous work, the worker must be given rest for half an hour. (6) All mine workers are entitled to overtime payment if the working hours exceed 48 hours. The rate for the underground worker shall be twice his ordinary rate of wage for the overtime worked and for surface workers 1½ times of that rate. (7) The Act fixed the minimum age for employment in mines at 15 and prohibits the employment of children underground. The minimum age for employment below ground has been raised from 17 to 18. (8) No woman shall be employed at any time of the day or night underground and no woman shall be employed in any mine. (9) It provides that every person employed in a mine shall be entitled to leave with wages after 12 months' continuous service — 14 days, if he is a monthly paid employee and 7 days, if he is a weekly paid employee.

The Indian Mines Act, 1952 was amended in 1960. This Amending Act provides for the payment of overtime at a uniform rate of twice the ordinary rate of wages for persons employed both above and below ground.

4. Transport Legislation

Transport is a general term applicable to several classes of industries which have no basis of unity except that of serving the same common function of communication. There is therefore no body of law which may be properly called transport legislation. The series of legislation which have been developed for transport are those which relate to *(i)* railways, *(ii)* shipping, *(iii)* docks and ports and *(iv)* road transport. The Central Government has, of late, undertaken legislative measures for air transport workers and regulations regarding their service conditions have been framed in 1955.

The most important transport legislation is that for railway workers. So far as railway workshops are concerned, they come under the Factories Act but other railway workers received no protection till 1930. It was in 1930 that the Indian Railways Act of 1890 was amended and a new chapter was added which deals with hours of work and periods of rest of all railway employees except those covered under the Factories Act, Mines Act and the Merchant Shipping Act. On the basis of the Justice Rajadhyaksha Award, the Act was again amended in 1956. The Amending Act deals with hours of works and period of rest. All railway servants have to be given a rest of not less than 24 consecutive hours in a week. Overtime is to be paid at not less than 1½ times the ordinary rates of pay.

Another series of transport legislation is that relating to shipping for the regulation to which a consolidating Act amending the Indian Merchant and Shipping Act was passed in 1923. The Act was amended on several occasions and has now been repealed by the Merchant Shipping Act of 1958.

Another class of transport workers requiring legislative protection are the labour employed in ports of docks. As a result of the 1929 ILO Convention and the recommendations of the Royal Commission on Labour, Indian Dock Labourers Act, 1934 was passed. This Act was not put into effect till February, 1948. It empowers the Government to make regulations for the safety of the dock-workers employed in loading and unloading of ships and the Government framed regulations in 1948 which provide safeguards to the dock workers against the dangers to which they may be exposed.

With a view to eliminate the hardship caused to dock workers on account of the casual nature of their work, the Government in 1948 passed the Dock Workers' (Regulation of Employment) Act, following the general principles of U.K. Dock Workers (Regulation of Employment) Act of 1946. The Act authorises the Central Government in case of major ports and State Governments in respect of other ports, to frame a scheme for registration of dock workers with a view to secure great regularity of employment for them and to regulate the employment and conditions of work of all dock workers, registered or not, in ports. The object of the schemes are to ensure greater regularity of employment for dock workers and to regulate their conditions of work.

The Motor Transport Workers Act of 1961 provides for the welfare of motor transport workers and to regulate the conditions of their work. It seeks to regulate matters like hours of work, spread-over, overtime, leave with wages, welfare facilities etc. in motor transport undertaking, employing 5 or more workers.

5. Wages Legislation

Largely as a result of their recommendations of the Royal Commission on Labour, the Payment of Wages Act was passed in 1936. The objective of the Act was to ensure regular and prompt payment of wages and to prevent the exploitation of wage earners by arbitrary deductions and fines.

One important class of wage legislation relates to minimum wages. The need for fixing minimum wages for industrial labour has everywhere been recognised in modern states, especially in sweated industries and in industries where workers are not organised and where their position is exploited by the employers. In England legislation was passed in 1909 for fixing minimum wages in a certain groups of industries. The first minimum wages legislation was undertaken in 1912 in USA and in 1915 in France.

The Minimum Wages Act was passed in India in 1948. The aim of the Act is to fix minimum wages in certain employments wherein sweated labour is most prevalent or where there is a big chance of exploitation of labour. The Act empowers the Central or State Governments as the case may be, to fix minimum rates of wages in respect of scheduled employments. The Act provides for fixation of different minimum rate of wages for time work, piece work, overtime work for different scheduled employments, for different class of works in the same employment for adults, adolescents, children, apprentices and for different localities. The minimum rate fixed or revised may consist of *(i)* a basic rate of wages and a cost of living allowance, *(ii)* a basic rate of wages with or without the cost of living allowance and cash value of concessions for supply of essential commodities, or *(iii)* an all-inclusive rate.

6. Social Security Legislation

Workmen's Compensation Act of 1923 is the *first* important social security legislation in India. The Act as amended in 1962, applies to workers earning upto Rs. 500 p.m. and protects them against accidents involving incapacity, permanent disability and death.

One class of social security legislation relates to maternity benefits. The first Maternity Benefit Act was passed by the Bombay Government. As a result of the recommendations of the Royal Commission, Maternity Benefit Acts were passed in many Provinces. At percent, Maternity Benefit Acts exist in all States. The Maternity Benefit Act of 1961, applies to all mines, plantations and factories except those covered by the ESI scheme. The main provisions of the Act are as follows : *(i)* the payment of maternity benefit to women workers, after they have put in 160 days' service during 12 months preceding the date of expected delivery, *(ii)* period of benefit will be 12 weeks, *(iii)* rate of benefit will be the average daily wage, *(iv)* payment of medical bonus of Rs. 25 is provided for pre-natal confinement and postnatal care has not been provided free of charge, *(v)* six weeks' leave with wages is granted at the rate of maternity benefit in case of miscarriage, and *(vi)* mothers are to be allowed two nursing breaks for nursing the child until the child attains the age of 15 months.

The Employees' State Insurance Act of 1948 is the most important piece of social security legislation. The benefits provided under the Act are *(i)* sickness benefit, *(ii)* maternity benefit, *(iii)* disablement benefit, *(iv)* dependant's benefit and *(v)* medical benefit.

Another important piece of social security legislation relates to Provident Fund. The Employees Provident Funds Act of 1952 applied in the first instance to factories employing 50 or more persons, in six major industries. The Central Government has been authorised to extend the Act to other industries and to those factories also which employ less than 50 persons and to any factory whose employer and a majority of employees agree to come under the Act. Undertakings owned by the Central or State Governments or by a local authority were placed outside the scheme, but by an amendment in 1958, the Act now applies to such establishments also. The Act was amended in 1960, extending its scope to establishments employing 20 or more persons. The Act was again amended in 1962 which empowered the Central Government to enhance the rate of provident fund contribution from 6¼% to 8% in an establishment covered under the Act.

The Scheme originally covered employees whose basic wages did not exceed Rs. 300 p.m. but from 1952, as a result of amendments of the schemes, employees getting pay upto Rs. 1,000, have been covered under the scheme.

7. Industrial Relations Legislation

Industrial Relations Legislation fall under three categories: *(i)* Trade Union Legislation, *(ii)* Industrial Employment Standing Order Legislation and *(iii)* Industrial Dispute Legislation.

The Indian Trade Union Act of 1926 and its amendment govern the trade union movement in our country. The main object of the Act is to give registered trade unions a legal and corporate status and their executives and members immunity from civil and criminal liability in respect of strikes.

The Industrial Employment (Standing Orders) Act of 1946 requires employers in industrial establishes to define with sufficient precision the conditions of employment under them and to make the said conditions known to all men employed by them.

Legislation for setting labour strikes was introduced by the Trade Disputes Act of 1929. Under the Act, the Government was empowered to appoint a Court of Enquiry or a Board of Conciliation. The Court or Board tried to bring about a settlement, but the decision was not legally binding on the parties concerned. Strikes and lock-outs in public utility service, without proper notice were made illegal. The emergency war-time legislative measures convinced the Government of their utility and led it to incorporate them in the permanent labour code of the country. The Industrial Disputes Act was accordingly passed to replace the Trade Disputes Act of 1929.

The Industrial Disputes Act was passed in 1947 with a view to improve the existing industrial relations between employers and the employees and for avoiding strikes and lock-outs specially in public utility services and essential undertakings and for providing machinery for peaceful settlement of industrial disputes and constituting joint works committees for enquiring into and settling individual grievances and day to day difficulties. The Industrial Disputes Act introduced the principles of compulsory arbitration and prohibited strikes without notice in respect of public utility services.

8. Miscellaneous Legislation

In addition to different classes of law mentioned above, there are also legislative measures relating to workers in the respective fields, namely, Shops and Establishments Act, the Working Journalists'(Conditions of Service) and Miscellaneous Provision Act, 1955, the Apprentices Act of 1961, etc.

India, by 1980 had a spate of labour legislations not to be found in any country at India's level of economic development. The standards laid down by the ILO have been accepted and measures are undertaken to come into closer conformity with the provisions of the International Labour Code. Although satisfactory progress has been achieved in the directions of labour legislation, nevertheless we have yet to travel a long way on the road to social justice.

❑ ❑ ❑

18

FINDINGS AND RECOMMENDATIONS OF THE NATIONAL LABOUR COMMISSION, 1969

The Royal Commission on Labour was appointed as far back as 1931. The Labour Investigation Committee (Rege) reported in 1946. Since independence industrial landscape has undergone a thorough change. Necessity was felt for a fresh and comprehensive review of the labour situation in the country. Consequently, the National Commission on Labour, headed by Dr. Gajendra Gadkar, was appointed in December, 1966. The Commission submitted its report in August, 1969. The terms of reference of this Commission were: *(i)* to review the change in the conditions of labour since independence and to report on existing conditions of labour, *(ii)* to review the existing legislative and other provisions intended to protect the interests of labour, to assess their working and to advise how far these provisions serve to implement the Directive Principles of State Policy in the Constitution on labour matters and the national objectives of establishing a socialist society and achieving planned economic development, *(iii)* to study and report in particular on : *(a)* the levels of workers' earnings, the provisions relating to wages, the need for fixation of minimum wages including a national minimum wage, the means of increasing productivity, including the provision of incentives to workers; *(b)* the standard of living and the health, efficiency, safety, welfare, housing, training and education of workers and the existing arrangements for administration of labour welfare — both at the Centre and in the States; *(c)* the existing arrangement for social security; *(d)* the state of relations between employers and workers and the role of trade unions and employers' organisations in promoting healthy industrial relations and the interests of the nation; *(e)* the labour laws and voluntary arrangements like the Code of Discipline, Joint Management Councils, Voluntary Arbitration and Wage Boards and the machinery at the Centre and in the States for their enforcement; *(f)* measures of improving conditions of rural labour and other categories of unorganised labour and *(g)* existing arrangements for labour intelligence and research and *(h)* to make recommendations on the above matters.

MAIN FINDINGS AND RECOMMENDATIONS OF THE COMMISSION

Indian Worker — Adaptation to Change

Over the last 20 years, the trend towards stabilisation of industrial labour has strengthened. A worker today is far more urban in taste and outlook than his predecessor. He has acquired a dignity not known to his predecessor. He has now developed a personality of his own. With the changing industrial landscape, growth of new industrial townships and dispersal of activity, a process of industrial 'culturisation' of working class has set in.

A worker is now conscious that education is essential for improved earnings. He is keen about self-education at adult literacy centres. He is even more keen about the education of his children and their future. The role of political parties and trade unions in making workers aware about their surroundings has been significant. The handling of labour-management relations is getting increasingly professionalised.

Over the years, the profile of agricultural labour has perceptibly changed. He is politically conscious. His aspirations are higher than before; he is responsive to the opportunities for change and development. Attachment to land and to the rural way of life, so common with the village elders, do not hold the same fascination for the village youth.

Recruitment Agencies and Practices

On the whole, impersonal methods of recruitment are gradually gaining ground in the organised sector. Recruitment through contractors still operates, though on a reduced scale, in mines and plantations. The exploitative character of such agencies of supply is on the decline due to the spread of awareness among job-seekers.

Over the last 20 years, the National Employment Service has played a useful role in bringing together employers and workers. NES should be extended to all towns with a labour force of 10 thousand and more, so that rural workers may take increasing advantage of this service. NES has to be a free and voluntary organisation and to be strengthened to help efficient utilisation of manpower and particularly critical skills required for planned economic growth. Provision of gainful employment to physically handicapped persons should form part of an enlightened social policy.

Training, Induction and Promotion

The Training and Employment Organisations in the State should be under the State Labour Department. The main burden of training of workers should necessarily fall upon industry. The States should supplement rather than supplant the activities of employers in this matter. It should step in only in such areas where employers cannot undertake training programmes.

As a general rule, seniority should be the basis for promotion especially among the operative and clerical categories in the lower rank. In respect of middle management, technical and administrative personnel, seniority-cum-merit should be the criterion. For higher managerial, technical and administrative personnel, merit alone should be the guiding factor.

Working Conditions

(1) Safety: A safety officer should be appointed in all factories employing 1,000 or more workers. Safety committees should be set up in every factory employing 100 or more workers. States which have not yet formed safety councils or introduced safety awards should do so. Safety Councils should be set up for all major industries and for those involving hazardous occupations.

(2) Hours of Works: The current requirements of the economy do not permit immediate reduction in working hours. As conditions improve working hours should be brought down to 40 a week but in two stages; in the first they should be brought down to 45. Working hours during the night shift should be reduced. A credit of 10 minutes should be given for each hour of work in the night shift. Six hours' work should thus entitle a worker to extra payment for one hour. The Plantations Labour Act, 1951, should be amended to reduce the prescribed hours of work from 54 to 48.

(3) Holidays: Uniformity in the number of paid national and festival holidays is desirable. Every employee should be allowed in a calendar year, 3 national and 5 festival holidays.

SOCIAL SECURITY

Workmen's Compensation

All workers including supervisors employed in the occupations covered under the Workmen's Compensation Act, 1923 should be eligible for compensation for work.

A scheme of Central Fund for Workmen's Compensation should be evolved. All the employers who are subject to the Workmen's Compensation Act, should pay to this fund a certain percentage of total wage as monthly contributions to cover the cost of the benefit and of administration. The fund should be controlled by the ESI Corporation. Periodic cash payments may be made to injured workers and their dependents by the Corporation. A similar scheme in respect of mines may be made by the Welfare Commissioners who control various welfare funds for coal, mica and iron ore mines.

A worker should be entitled to higher compensation for disablement resulting from industrial accidents. It should be in the form of subsistence allowance in cases where the worker remains unemployed because of the disablement.

A scheme of Central Fund may be evolved for maternity benefit on the lines suggested for workmen's compensation. Pending the creation of this Fund, the Maternity Benefit Act, 1961, should be adopted in all States as early as possible.

Full-fledged medical colleges should be started at places where there are large and well-equipped ESI hospitals.

The wage limit for exemption from payment of employees contribution should be raised to Rs. 4 per day.

A scheme of 'no-claim bonus' for insured persons who do not claim any benefit during a year should be evolved.

The Provident Funds Act at present does not apply to establishment employing between 10-20 persons. It should be extended to those establishments and the minimum rate of contribution therein fixed to 6¼ per cent. Wherever the present rate of contribution is 6¼ per cent, it should be raised to 8 per cent and where the current rate is 8 p.c., it should be raised to 10 p.c. Conversion of a part of provident fund into retirement-cum-family pension is desirable. In cases where the rate of contribution is raised to 10 p.c. from employers and employees, a portion of the contribution should be converted into pension.

Lay-off and Retrenchment Compensation

A long-term solution for the contingency of unemployment lies in adopting a scheme of unemployment insurance for all employed persons. The present provisions for retrenchment and lay-off compensation should continue during the transition period.

Integrated Social Security

The aim should be to work gradually towards a comprehensive social security plan by pooling all the social security collections into a single fund from which different agencies can draw upon for disbursing benefits according to needs. It should be possible over the next few years to evolve an integrated social security scheme which will, with some marginal addition to the current rate of contribution, take care of certain risks not covered at present. This will be limited to the benefits of *(i)* provident fund and retirement/family pension and *(ii)* unemployment insurance.

Wage Policy

Wage differentials, so far as they reflect differences in productivity, should be tolerated. A certain amount of disparity between industrial and agricultural wages is necessary and must continue for the general health of the economy. Wage policy should aim at a progressive increase in real wages. At the same time, any substantial improvement in real wages cannot be brought about without increasing productivity. The main aim of wage policy as envisaged is to bring wages in conformity with the expectations of the working class and in the process seek to maximise wage employment.

Minimum Wage

The Commission has drawn a line between a minimum wage and a need-based minimum wage. Once the minimum rates of wages are fixed, it is the obligation of employers to pay the said wages irrespective of the capacity to pay. The appropriate government revise wages prescribed under the provision of the Minimum Wages Act at least once in every three years. The Schedules to the Minimum Wages Act should be periodically revised so that employments which cease to employ sweated labour are deleted and such employments as employ sweated labour are added to the Schedule. The employment limit for enabling a State Government to fix up minimum wage for a particular employment included in the Schedule to the Act should be reduced from 1,000 to 500 in the whole State.

A national minimum wage in the sense of a uniform monetary rate of remuneration for the economy as a whole is neither feasible nor desirable, but a regional minimum can be attempted under the present circumstances. The need-based minimum wage and the wages at the higher levels of a fair wage, may be introduced by convenient phasing, keeping in mind the extent of the capacity of the employer to pay the same.

There should be periodic adjustment of wages taking into account changes in the cost of living. It would be best to leave it to the wage fixing authorities to choose the index (local or all India) they consider suitable for the purpose of linking dearness allowances. The capacity to pay is not a relevant consideration for dearness allowances at the minimum level.

It would be more practical to merge D.A with the basic wage at the base year of the revised series of working class consumer price indices which will be constructed on the basis of family living surveys. The aim of such merger should be to rationalise the existing wage structure and make basic wages more realistic than at present. For Government employees, the Commission has recommended the setting up of a pay commission immediately.

Incentives and Bonus

The application of incentive schemes has generally to be selective and limited to industries and occupations in which it is possible to measure the output of workers or a group of workers concerned and in which it is possible to maintain a fair degree of control over the quality of production. Incentive schemes should cover as many employees of an undertaking as possible and need not be confined only to operatives. The inclusion of supervisory personnel as beneficiaries of incentives can have a vital role in improving efficiency. Incentive schemes should be simple so that workers are able to understand its full implications.

The system of annual bonus has come to stay and may continue in future. Some establishments which used to pay bonus before the passing of the Payment of Bonus Act, 1965, has stopped paying bonus because the Act does not apply to them. 'Government' should make a suitable amendment to the Act to cover such establishments under the Act.

Rationalisation and Automation

Rationalization and Automation have an important role to play in the developing countries. They are expected to stimulate economic development; mass production will create more demand for raw materials and components and in the process help generate employment in the long run. In the short run, however, employment declines with automation. If the general rate of growth of the economy is high, re-employment of the unemployed will be possible. A phased introduction of more advanced technological and labour saving techniques and devices has to be initiated guaranteeing simultaneously that employment opportunities do not suffer. Any scheme of automation should satisfy the following conditions :

(i) It accommodates labour that may be rendered surplus,

(ii) It results in higher productivity and efficiency,

(iii) It improves the level of earnings of workers by ensuring to them equitable share in the gains due to automation and

(iv) It leads to reduction in cost and benefits the country/community.

The process of automation and rationalization should be introduced in consultation with the workers representatives and carried out in suitable stages.

Machinery for Wage Fixation

The Committee Method of fixation of minimum wages under the Minimum Wages Act, which gives satisfaction to the parties because of their having a part in deciding what to pay or what to accept should be followed in preference to the method by which wages are notified by authorities.

Wage Boards have done some useful work and they should continue and that where there are differences, the chairman's verdict should be considered to be an award. Where the recommendations are unanimous, they should be made statutorily binding.

The operation of the Payment of Wages Act has benefitted the working class. Non-payment of Wages or unauthorised deductions are now not as common as before. Malpractices, however, prevail but mostly in the unorganised and small scale industries. Government should have necessary powers to raise the present limit of Rs. 400 per month below which the Payment of Wages Act, 1936, is applicable.

WORKERS ORGANISATIONS

The basis on which a trade union should be organised is a matter to be determined by workers themselves in the light of their own needs and experience. Formation of craft/occupation unions should be discouraged. Formation of centre-cum-industry and national industrial federations should be encouraged.

Apart from paying attention to the basic responsibilities towards their members, unions should also undertake social responsibilities such as promotion of national integration, instilling in their members a sense of responsibility towards industry and the community, etc.

There should be no ban on non-employees holding positions in the executive of the unions. Steps should be taken to promote internal leadership and to hasten the process, the permissible limit of outsiders in the executives of the unions should be reduced.

The minimum number required for starting a new union should be raised to 10 p.c. of regular employees of a plant or 100 whichever is lower. The minimum membership fee of a union should be raised from the present level of 25 paise per month to Re. 1 per month.

One important recommendation made by the Commission is the obligation imposed upon all employers to recognize a representative union and to deal with the said union as the sole bargaining agent on behalf of his employees. Once such a union is recognised by the employers, the process of negotiation and settlement by collective bargaining will be facilitated. This is the best way in a democratic set-up to settle disputes peacefully and respectably.

EMPLOYER'S ORGANISATIONS

Public sector undertakings should be encouraged to join their respective industrial associations. Registration of employers organisations should be made compulsory. Employers organisations should encourage collective bargaining. From the point of view of labour-management relations, employers associations should *(i)* undertake promotion of collective bargaining at various levels; *(ii)* encourage observance and implementation by their members of bipartite and tripartite agreements in real spirit and form; *(iii)* expedite implementation of wage awards by members; *(iv)* work towards elimination of unfair labour practices by employers; *(v)* encourage adoption by members of personnel policies conducive to productivity and industrial peace; *(vi)* promote rationalisation of management to improve productivity; *(vii)* arrange employers education in the concept of labour partnership in industry for ensuring identity of interests of labour and management and for promoting harmony in the goals of industry and the community; and *(viii)* work towards the collective welfare of its members through training, research and communication, in the field of labour-management relations.

Industrial Relations

Conditions have to be created for promotion of collective bargaining. The most important condition is statutory recognition of a representative union as the sole bargaining agent.

Collective bargaining cannot exist without the right to strike or lock-out. But other forms of labour protests such as 'go-slow', and 'work-to-rule' may be treated as unfair labour practices under the Standing Orders.

For the first time, a 30 day limit is proposed to be placed on any legitimate strike in non-essential industries, while for 'essential' industries, the Commission has provided a self-contained Code and machinery which, it claims, will make strike wholly unnecessary.

The Commission feels that the Government cannot be final authority to decide whether an issue should go for arbitration or not, and has suggested modification of the present system of joint consultative machinery for Central Government employees. It has, however, stated that prohibition of strikes would be justified if an effective alternative for settlement of unresolved disputes is provided.

While recognizing the validity and relevance of strikes and lock outs in certain situations the NLS has suggested the imposition of some restrictions including a limit on the duration. In essential industries, the right to strikes or lock-outs should be made redundant by requiring the IRCs to adjudicate when mutual negotiations fail and parties do not agree to arbitration. A compulsory strike notice and a strike ballot open to all members of the union have also been recommended by the NLC.

Having recognised the legitimacy of strikes and lock-outs, in certain given situations, the NLC has left it to the IRC to terminate the strike/lock-out even before the prescribed period after considering the motion in that behalf from the appropriate Government. The penalties which have been provided for unjustified strikes, or lock-outs, would, in the

Commission's opinion, ultimately avoid strikes and lock-outs and in due course, persuade the parties to settle their differences by negotiations.

Conciliation can be more effective if it is freed from outside influence and the conciliation machinery is adequately staffed. The conciliation machinery should be a part of the proposed Industrial Relations Commission. With the growth of collective bargaining and the general acceptance of recognition of representative unions and improvement in attitudes, the grounds will be cleared for wider acceptance of voluntary arbitration.

The Commission is of the view that *'gheraos'*, apart from their adverse effects on industry and the economy of the country, strike at the very root of trade unionism. It depreciates resort to *'gheraos'* which invariably tend to inflict physical duress on persons affected and endanger not only industrial harmony but also create problems of law and order. If such means are to be adopted by labour for realisation of its claims, trade unions may come into disrepute. It is the duty of all union leaders therefore to condemn this form of labour protest as harmful to the interests of the working class itself.

'Gherao' cannot be treated as a form of labour protest since it involves physical coercion rather than economic pressure. It is harmful to the working class and in the long run may effect national interest.

In certain essential industries where cessation of work may cause harm to the community, the right to strike may be curtailed but with the simultaneous provision of an effective alternative to settle the disputes. Every strike or lock-out should be preceded by a notice.

The present arrangement for appointing *ad hoc* industrial tribunals should be discontinued. An Industrial Relations Commission on a permanent basis should be set up at the Centre and one in each State for settling 'interest' dispute.

The Commission, in making its most important recommendation regarding the setting up of IRCs at the State as well as at the National level, has been motivated by the desire for insulating the settlement machinery against political pressure.

The National Industrial Relations Commission should be appointed by the Central Government for industries for which that Government is the appropriate authority. Each State should have an Industrial Relations Commission for settlement of disputes for which the State Government is the appropriate authority. The proposed IRCs will be high powered bodies independent of the executive. The main functions of the National and State Industrial Relations Commissions will be *(i)* adjudication in industrial disputes, *(ii)* conciliation and *(iii)* certification of unions as representative unions.

The IRCs will have both judicial and non-judicial members. The judicial members including presidents of the National/ States IRCs, are to be appointed from among people eligible for appointment as Judges of High Courts.

The Conciliation Wing of the Commissions will consist of conciliation officers with the prescribed qualifications and status. There will be people with or without judicial qualifications in the cadre of conciliators. The functions relating to certification of unions will vest in a separate wing of the National State IRC.

Standing Labour Courts should be constituted in each State. Members of the Labour Court will be appointed by Government on the recommendations of the High Court. Labour Courts will deal with disputes relating to rights and obligations, interpretation and implementation of awards and claims arising out of rights and obligations under the relevant provisions of law or agreements as well as disputes in regard to unfair labour practices and the like.

Works Committees may be set up only in units which have a recognised union. The Union should be given the right to nominate the worker-members of the Works Committee.

When managements and unions are willing to extend cooperation in matters they consider to be of mutual advantage, they set up a Joint Management Council.

Grievance Procedure should be simple and have a provision for at least one appeal. The procedure should ensure that it gives a sense of *(i)* satisfaction to the individual worker, *(ii)* reasonable exercise of authority to the manager, and *(iii)* participation to unions. A formal grievance procedure should be introduced in units employing 100 or more workers. A grievance procedure should normally provide three steps : *(a)* submission of a grievance by the aggrieved worker to his immediate superior, *(b)* appeal to the departmental head, and *(c)* appeal to a bipartite grievance committee representing the management and the recognised union.

LABOUR IN PUBLIC SECTOR

Suitability of the candidate and his availability for at least 5 years should be the criteria for selection for a senior position in a public undertaking. At the supervisory level, recruitment has to be on an all India basis since the quality of personnel is a crucial factor. The claim for preferential treatment to 'sons of the soil' in appointments in regional establishments has been described as 'plainly inconsistent with the philosophy of one citizenship'.

'We thought', the Chairman qualified 'that it would be unwise to shut our eyes to the hard facts and realities of life'. In his view the Commission has formulated recommendations that may be reasonable and fairly worked out within limits. For example, in certain unskilled categories of employees, it would be convenient to the employer for several reasons to employ local labour. Where there is a choice between two persons who are equally qualified, the local person will get the preference.

Government (Industrial) Employees

In case of Government industrial employees engaged in essential services, the prohibition of strike would be justified. Such prohibition of strike, however, have to be accompanied by the provision of an effective alternative for settlement of unresolved disputes. This will lead to settlement of disputes by negotiations and agreements. All the same, there will be need for a statutory arbitration machinery.

There should be a wider scope for discussion in the Joint Consultative Machinery on all matters which can be brought within its purview. The limited scope provided in a Joint Consultative Machinery for arbitration is a deficiency which should be removed if the industrial employees of Government are to be treated on the same footing as other industrial employees. A Pay Commission should be appointed immediately to review the wages and other conditions of service of industrial employees of Government.

Unorganised Labour-Contract Labour

A stricter regulation of contract work than at present is called for. The general direction of policy should be towards abolition of contract labour in due course.

Construction Workers

The possibility of introducing a decasualisation scheme should be explored to ensure greater security of employment for construction workers. Mobile dwellings should be provided for construction workers at work sites.

Casual Labour

There should be a better regulation of conditions of casual labour. If employment is discontinued for a short period and the worker is re-employed, this short period should not be treated as a break in services. After a casual worker completes a stipulated period of service he should be allowed the same benefits which a regular worker enjoys.

Workers in Shops and Commercial Establishments

Working conditions in shops and commercial establishments are at present governed by State enactments. The Central Government should enact a comprehensive legislation for the purpose. It should be applicable to units which have a stipulated minimum number of workers or have an annual turnover above a stipulated limit.

A better understanding of the problems of different categories of unorganised labour is essential to the formulation of suitable ameliorative measures. Detailed surveys about the conditions of work in these employments should be undertaken.

The Commission's Report was placed on the table of both Houses of Parliament by the Minister of State for Labour, Employment and Rehabilitation, Mr. Bhagwat Jha Azad. While submitting the Report to the Union Labour Minister, the Chairman of the Commission described the recommendations as 'crucial' and expressed the hope that the report would furnish rational guidelines for the country's industrial development and growth for the next 25 years.

The recommendations of the Commission in regard to a sound industrial relations system have been under discussion with the representatives of employers and workers' organisations. In pursuance of a suggestion made by the Union Minister of Labour and Rehabilitation at a Conference of Trade Union Organisations, held in May, 1971, the INTUC, the AITUC and the HMS have been having mutual discussions amongst themselves to evolve an agreed consensus on the question of recognition of unions and the dispute settlement machinery. At the 27th Session of the Indian Labour Conference held in October, 1971, they asked for and were given, six months time to conclude their discussions. Meanwhile, however, following the declaration of emergency, the representatives of employers' and workers' organisations met on December 5, 1971 and adopted a declaration pledging their support to the maintenance of uninterrupted production in an atmosphere of industrial peace. At a subsequent meeting of the representatives of the employers' and workers' organisations, a Working Party of Employers and Workers was constituted to formulate concrete measures to (1) give effect to the declaration of the workers' and employers' representatives at the meeting held on December 5, 1971 and (2) suggest the outlines of a suitable machinery which would ensure speedy settlement of industrial disputes.

The Working Party was informed by the workers' representatives that they had already covered considerable ground in their discussions and had come to a tentative agreement in respect of the basic questions of trade union recognition and the mechanism of dispute settlement. The participating trade union organisations –INTUC, AITUC and HMS- have also agreed to set up a National Trade Union Council to eliminate inter-union rivalry and promote healthy trade unionism.

❑ ❑ ❑

19

INDUSTRIAL RELATIONS IN THE CONTEXT OF GLOBALISATION

The period following liberalisation witnessed the arm of state shifting in favour of the employers as against the employees in the earlier period. Consequently, the workers were on the defensive and this led to a sharp decline in mandays lost due to strikes by 36.9 percent during 1992-97 as against 1986-91. Since workers remained subdued in the liberalisation period, the employers did not need to declare lockouts either as a retaliatory measure or as a normal weapon to subdue workers. This is corroborated by the fact that mandays lost due to lockouts declined by a relatively smaller percentage i.e., 25.7 per cent in the post liberalisation period as against the pre-liberalisation period.

In the wake of the so called New Industrial Policy (NIP) there was widespread expectation in certain quarters that the time had come for labour policies to be dovetailed with industrial policies so that both moved in a unified direction than in opposite directions. There was much talk about the so called 'exit policy'. Till December 6, 1992, the Congress Government had the tacit support of the Bharatiya Janata Party whereby the former could show a decisive shift towards the right. But the Ayodhya crisis snapped Congress's support base in the BJP. Congress had to anchor itself to the left for support. Then came the most important speech of the Prime Minister Davos conference where he said something to this effect;'People did not elect me to deprive them of their livelihood.' The pendulum stopped thereafter due to the compulsions of successive coalition governments which increased political uncertainty following three general elections during 1996 and 1999. In October 1999, the Government constituted the Second National Commission on Labour on the recommendations of the Indian Labour Conference.

The social and labour effects of the new policies have been a major source of concern. New investments are taking place not where job losses are the most but where job losses are, relatively the least. As a result, job creation, if at all, is not occurring where it is needed most. Productive employment creation and maintaining the social order being the responsibility of the state, state governments would have to strive hard to preserve the employments and create a conducive environment for further job creation. It then becomes imperative for them to review their industrial and labour policies to woo investment and facilitate the growth of industry and business for further job creation. Whether and how state governments can make a difference in adopting and practising competitive labour policies is, then, a moot question.

The Government of India would articulate and implement social and labour issues till the 1960s when the same party used to rule at the centre and in most states. But since 1969, non-Congress and regional parties came to power in the states and four times at the centre. State Goverments began to ask for greater provincial autonomy including in matters relating to labour, which has been on the 'concurrent list' since the British days. Both trade unions and employers' organisations submitted memoranda reflecting their views on labour issues to the Sarkaria Commission set up in the 1980s to renew Centre-State relations. The problem is compounded by the definition of "appropriate government" particularly in the case of Central Government undertakings with plants or operations extending to more than one State. While the administrative machinery in the Central Government is responsible for the overall performance of the enterprise, labour-management relations in plants came, in several cases, under the jurisdiction of the Government of the State where the enterprise was located. Political differences among parties in power caused problems for individual enterprises. Also when major policy issues were discussed at labour ministers' conference, Government representatives would take a stand on the lines of ideology of the ruling party at the Centre and or the States. Given the diversity of the context, the seriousness of the political ferment and pendulum-like swinging of Government policies over the years, one wonders whether India will ever have a unified labour policy.

State Governments are business too. According to a report of the Comptroller and Auditor General of India, the number of State Government companies increased significantly from 168 in 1969-70 to 840 in 1986-87 and to over 1,000 in 1990s. In every State, the state electricity boards and state road transport corporations were the biggest with a total investment of over Rs.137 crore in 1986-87. The electricity boards had a negative return of 13 percent on average. The cumulative losses of 514 State Government enterprises were over Rs. 20 billion.

Some State Governments are endeavouring to make adjustments and improve their image so that they can attract investment and save/create jobs. While the Central Government did not resort to even a single privatisation overtly till the end of 1999, many states were ahead with privatisation openly. Raipuria refers to the privatisation and restructuring of electricity boards (Meghalaya, Orissa, Andhra, Haryana and U.P.), profit-sharing with employees (Rajasthan Roadways), a renewal fund on the lines of the National Renewal Fund (Rajasthan) for employees of sick units which were closed, issue of project-specific bonds (Gujarat and Rajasthan) and promotion of tourism through the private sector (Sikkim). Andhra Pradesh, Orissa, Karnataka and many other states also resorted to open privatisation. Several State Governments have a variety of welfare programmes as well. Some political parties continue to oppose privatisation of central public sector undertakings in their own states, regardless whether they are in opposition or a part of the ruling coalition at the Centre even though in their own states as a ruling party, they pursue privatisation, often vigorously.

The industrial relations scenario in different states in India present glaring contradictions. In West Bengal, politically affiliated trade unions, particularly those subscribing to the leftist ideology, are widespread. In Maharashtra-which is the hub of economic activity and widely acclaimed as the commercial capital of the country-enterprise-level unions, which are independent and unaffiliated to any Central federation or political party, have a major presence. In Karnataka, particularly Bangalore, which has been christened the Silicon Valley of India, many firms in the new, non-traditional, high-technology industries are 'union-free.'

In some parts of Gujarat, "footpath unionism" is growing. Some briefless lawyers, among others, mobilise signatures of seven disgruntled employees, register a union and pursue their individual grievances on the lines of contingent litigation; the leaders of such unions will have a sizeable share in the compensation that such workers might get. In Maharashtra, the growing sickness in textile mills and opportunities to reap a bonanza through real estate business in sick and closed mills, opened new vistas for a formidable link between the real estate underworld mafia and trade unions. In some of the industrially and socially backward areas of Andhra Pradesh and Bihar, for instance, radical social movements in some cases assumed the role of trade unions also and began to pursue the cause of workers through militant means, undermining the role of traditional trade unions and making a mockery of the authority of the employer, the district administration and the local police.

Unions may be declining in some parts of the country but not in Orissa, where union leadership is focussing on organising in small and medium-scale industries.

Changing Face of Trade Unions in a Liberalised Economy

Trade Unionism in India is passing through a critical phase and facing unprecedented challenges in a liberalised, privatised global economy. Labour is being pushed from the organised sector to the unorganised sector leading to an increase in causal and contract labour. Downsizing, organisational restructuring, labour laws, political instability, the apathetic attitude of Government and gap in knowledge and skill base are the major factors responsible for this state of affairs. Thus, trade unions have to rethink their position and adopt such strategies which would help them to act as responsible partners in the organisation.

Trade unions are losing their members hip and their influence is declining as labour has shifted to the unorganised sector. These workers are not protected by unions and no sincere efforts have been made to organise them. Plant-based independent unions have increased without affiliating themselves to any central-level federations and have concentrated on plant-level issues such as productivity-based wage settlements. This has weakened the power of unions. Many sick public sector units, unable to compete in an open market system, have compelled trade unions to adopt "concession bargaining" for their existence and survival. The lack of mature leadership and inter-union rivalry continue to be the pertinent issues. Employers are bypassing unions as they find them obstructing the production process. They have started sub-contracting, outsourcing and signing individual contracts. The Government has not been able to provide a method for union recognition and choosing the sole bargaining agent. The law has so far been able to take the unorganised sector in its stride. At this crucial juncture, trade unions' role and functions need to be reviewed and redefined so that they can cope with the restructuring process.

Issues Related to Trade Unions

Trade unions are responsible for maintaining a better industrial relations climate in the organisation. A number of studies have been conducted to explore various issues related to trade unionism.

These studies can be broadly classified into three categories: (1) Macro-level studies on trade unionism; (2) Studies on trade union growth, structure and activities; (3) Behavioural studies.

(1) Macro-Level Studies: Macro-level studies have focused on economic, social, technical and legal issues and their effect on union functions as well as union-management relationships. Early studies on unions pleaded for legal protection, and the promotion of professional trade unionism through the provision for union recognition, for better interaction between the state and unions (Ghosh, 1960; Johri, 1967). Some studies have discussed the role of unions in economic development, their problems, the attitudes of the government, the emerging trends in trade unionism, and causes of union-management conflict (Padmanabhan, 1980; Nigam, 1984). Monappa (1985) studied the formation of white-collar unions, blue-collar unions, crafts unions, and several other types of unions working in various sectors. Tulpule (1990) emphasised that unions, should pay attention to broader issues like respect for human rights, civil liberties and public policy. Studies also report that unions are organisationally, financially and numerically weak as the industrial working class is docile and economically poor (Ramaswamy & Ramaswamy, 1981; Masilamani and Haribabu, 1986; Sheth, 1993). Recent studies have reported that industrial restructuring led to retrenchment, employment loss, casualisation of employment and contract employment. This has resulted in a decline of the union membership and weakening of the union power (Mahalingam, 1992; Mathur, 1992; Neogi, 1992; Venkataratnam, 1992; Sheth, 1993).

(2) ***Trade Union Growth, Structure and Functions :*** Many studies have focussed their attention on micro-level issues faced by unions in a particular industry or geographical area. Textile industry has been studied by many author's at different places (Murphy, 1981; Ramaswamy, 1977; Gaur, 1986; Bhangoo, 1989; Gani, 1988). It has been found that the employers try to repress militant trade unionism and force trade union leaders to accept employers' terms for recognition (Mamkootam, 1977; Sherlock, 1989). Chatterji (1980) examined the emergence of unions, their organisational characteristics, interactions with political parties and public policy in the states of West Bengal, Karnataka and Rajasthan, and found that national bodies set the organisational goals for unions in the states. Bograte (1970), in his study of Indian ports, found that political affiliation has contributed to the growth and development of trade unions, but Singh (1990) found that it was also responsible for damaging the image of unions among workers. Modi (1995), in his study of the Punjab Road Transport Corporation, mentioned that workers expect trade unions to facilitate the redressal of workers'; grievances, secure higher economic benefits, educate workers, and protect against victimisation and exploitation by the management. The management feels that trade unions adopt numerous unfair labour practices and workers blindly follow the unions. In a similar study, Parmar (1997) found that unions have an extra responsibility in building industrial peace in the organisation as perceived by workers. Workers also believe that multiplicity of trade unions have led to inter-union rivalries.

(3) ***Behavioural Studies :*** Many studies have emphasized the role of psychological, social and economic factors. Economic and security motives

are among the important factors for workers to join unions. (Ramaswamy 1977; Gani, 1988; Bhangoo, 1989; Cheema, 1990). Several studies have found that low identification with the union, poor leadership, fear of victimisation, illiteracy, multiplicity of unions and sheer apathy are the major causes for lack of workers' participation in union activities (Das, 1985; Monga, 1978; Dayal and Sharma, 1970). Singh (1971) found that workers with low job-satisfaction join unions, but Monga and Magga (1981) found that satisfied workers actively participate in union activities. The employee's perception of union-member relationship is also a determinant of satisfaction (Jarley, Kuruvilla and Casteel, 1990). It was observed that unions influence the labour-management relationship and also effect the human resource policies and practices (Gallagher, 1983; Ng and Maki, 1994). Many studies have also found that unionised firms have a formal grievance procedure, merit-seniority system for promotion, compared to non-unionised firms (Kaufman and Kaufman, 1987). It was found that top-level management hold an anti-union attitude towards unions (Das and Manimala, 1997), but Dayal (1997) found that middle and junior-level managers have anti-union attitudes. Subramanian and Rao (1997) found that unions now are reorienting themselves to play the role of a progressive partner and co-operating with the management for achieving economic goals. Studies on union leadership found that outside leaders are indispensable in trade unions because of their education, income and inclination towards leftist ideology (Mathur, 1965). Many studies have focussed on the domination of a leader's personality (Mathur, 1965), the conflict between loyalty to the trade union and to their kith and kin (Das, 1967), the political character of outside leaders influencing their role in unions, internal conflict between leader and their union role (Sheth and Jain, 1968). Singh (1980) observed that the perception of workers and managers about the goals pursued by the union leaders is different from the goals professed by the managers. Monga(1979) found that trade union leaders in India are well versed in union affairs. Masihi (1985) observed that fast, strike, gherao and dharna, are used more by outside leaders than by inside leaders.

Sood (1984) found that 16 per cent of the leaders are paid union officials and have political affiliations. Leaders are fairly militant and a majority of them are not only victimised by the management but also harassed by the police. Leaders are usually satisfied with workers' attitude and their participation in union activities. Rao (1986) concluded that some union leaders are democratic in their functioning, and they do not involve themselves to a great extent in politics. It can be said that unions want affiliation with political parties for a better leadership and bargaining power, but it is also responsible for inter-union rivalries and retarded development of internal leadership (Reddy, 1972; Ashraf, 1974; Aziz, 1974; Ramaswamy, 1977; Chatterji, 1980).

Thus, it can be said that economic and security motives still continue to be the major cause for unionisation. Unions have negatively affected the industrial economy and slowed down industrial growth. Restructuring experiences of many firms such as ITC, Dunlop, Asian Paints, Bata and Eicher have shown that unions as institutions have invariably weakened, putting a question mark on their representative status. Some of the major controversial issues such as political affiliation, members' participation in union activities and attitudes of actors are being discussed below.

(i) Political affiliation of unions : India trade unions are influenced by political parties, which provide ideological support for their sustainability. Political affiliation contributed to the growth of unionism in the early stages but proved detrimental later on. Trade union leaders support the idea of political affiliation but workers and managerial personnel do not favour an active role of political parties in trade union activities in the changing economic scenario.

(ii) Union participation of members : Low job satisfaction was found to be related with favourable attitude towards union, but it has also been found that satisfied workers participate more actively in union activities. The economic motive is countered by safe-gaurds against victimisation as the primary motive behind joining unions.

(iii) Attitude of actors : Resistance to unionism was found to be higher as one goes up in the managerial hierarchy as trade union leaders oppose the strategic decisions taken by top-level managers. It was also found that middle and junior-level managers have more of an anti-union attitude because of their direct interaction. Union leaders are willing to assume equal responsibility along with the management to maintain a good relationship, to educate workers on accident-free and safe work methods, and maintain discipline for the growth and development of the organisation. They exploit workers and underestimate the significance of internal communication but have played major role in non-work-related issues.

TOWARDS A CONCEPTUAL MODEL

After an overview of the literature related with the various aspects of trade unionism, it is important to examine the functions of trade unions in the market economy by identifying those factors which have influenced union participation and the changes in attitude and strategies of union leaders towards management.

In order to explain the role of trade unions and its impact upon individual and organisational growth and development, a tentative conceptual model has been developed. This model (Figure 1) shows:

(a) the external environment factors affecting the functions of trade unions;

(b) internal factors related to the organisation, such as power dynamics, economic restructuring efforts like the voluntary retirement scheme (VRS), downsizing, subcontracting and outsourcing; and

(c) the impact on individual and organisational-level outcomes such as IR climate, productivity and growth, labour-management relations, wage and salary matters, workers' participation in management, and industrial disputes like strikes and lockouts.

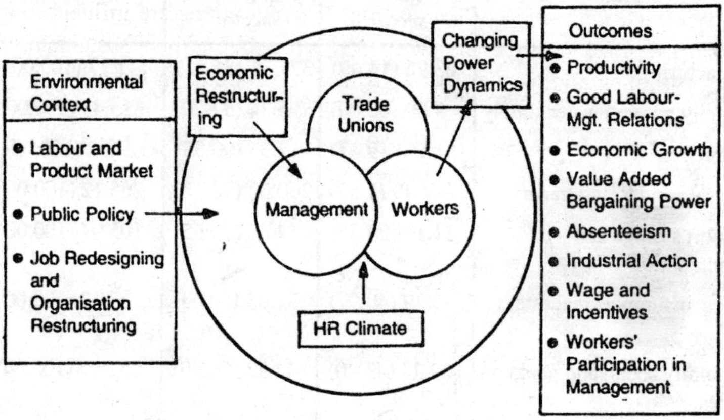

Fig. 1
A tentative conceptual model showing the affects of external and internal factors on trade union relations with workers and management and its impact on an organisation.

1. External Environment

(i) Labour and Product Market : There has been a *major shift of employment from the organised sector to the unorganised sector due to various factors.* The *agricultural sector,* the largest employer of the work force (62.60 percent), is also shrinking day by day. All these have led to the growth of self-employed, causal and contract labour. The share of agricultural employment in the country has declined from 70.70 per cent in 1977-78 to 62.60 per cent in 1993-94, while the share of the *non-agricultural sector* has increased from 29.30 per cent in 1977-78 to 37.40 per cent 1993-94. The organised manufacturing sector had a negative growth-rate in employment between 1983 and 1987 and a low growth-rate (0.04 per cent) during 1988-94 leading to jobless growth (Gill,1999). The *unorganised sector* in all non-agricultural activities is more than 80 per cent and the *organised sector* accounts for less than 20 per cent of the labour.

TABLE –1

Share in Employment of Organised and Unorganised Sector in Non-Agricultural Activities in India (1993-94).

[Accounted for 91.89 percent of total employment in the country whereas the share of the organised sector was barely 8.19 percent in 1993-94. The share of the unorganised sector.]

(in lakh persons)

Sector	*Organised sector*	*Unorganised sector*	*Total*
Manufacturing	63.96 (14.49)	377.31 (85.51)	441.27 (100.00),
Electricity gas and water supply	9.69 (62.80)	5.74 (37.20)	15.43 (100.00)
Construction	12.27 (9.47)	117.35 (90.53)	129.62 (100.00),
Wholesale and Retail trade	4.49 (1.69)	260.63 (98.31)	265.12 (100.00)
Transport storage and communication	31.10 (29.35)	74.87 (70.65)	105.97 (100.00)
Finance, insurance, real estate etc.	15.29 (40.97)	22.03 (59.03)	37.32 (100.00)
Community social and personal services	109.27 (43.40)	142.52 (56.60)	251.79 (100.00)
Total	246.07 (19.74)	100.45 (80.26)	1246.52 (100.00)

Note : Data pertain to the year 1993 in the case of the organised sector and to the year 1993-94 in the case of the unorganised sector. (Figures in brackets show percentage share).

Source : Kulshreshtha and Singh (1999).

The share of causal wage employment in the total employment in the country has increased from 18.4 per cent in 1977-78 to 33.5 per cent in 1993-94. Increased casualisation of employment and its concentration in the unorganised sector has posed a challenge for unions to organise them. Employment in the organised manufacturing sector is declining and there is no expansion of employment in the public sector on the cards. It is now clear that a majority of people who will join the workforce in the near future have to find work as self-employed or casual workers (Visaria and Minhas, 1991). Organisations are taking advantage of the favourable labour market and have changed their nomenclature from manufacturing to marketing companies, and subcontracting product manufacturing to ancillary companies (such as Aristocrate Luggage, which is a marketing company, while manufacturing is undertaken in the Satara-based Universal Luggage Company's name). As the marketing company is flat and lean, the profit is bigger and it is not sent back to the production unit so that the employees of the manufacturing organisation have no opportunity to share it or ask for an increase in wages.

(ii) Public Policy : Labour Policies : Which focus mainly on the organised sector, *have not been able to fully protect the interest of labour in the unorganised sector.* Political instability is also responsible for this state of affairs. **The Second National Commission on Labour has been set up by the government which may recommend an umbrella legislation ensuring a minimum protection for unorganised-sector workers.** The Government has also proposed several changes in the Industrial Disputes Act, 1947 and Trade Union Act, 1926, in order to make it relevant in the changing economic scenario. The proposed changes in the Industrial Disputes Act would restrict strike options and dilute the need for permission for a lockout, while the changes in the Trade Union Act would check the multiplicity of trade unions, streamline their functions, and restrict the interference of outsiders (The Financial Express, March 8, 2000).

(iii) Job Redesigning and Organisational Restructuring : Technological changes and automation have resulted in job-loss, change in work-design and skill-gap among workers. Workers resist technological changes and automation as they think these factors are responsible for their current status. People with enriched jobs are also reluctant to join unions. Restructuring leading to a thinner and flatter organisational structure, has changed the roles and relationships of the people. As the elasticity of the high skilled workers is very little, they bargain with the employers at their own terms without the help of the unions. Since rigid job-design and inflexible work-structure is the stuff of union power, any attempt of job-redesigning is being opposed by union leaders (Ramaswamy, 1999). It is causing fear among the workers, and they think that they will loose their jobs and unions will also loose control over the workers.

2. Internal Environmental Factors

(i) Downsizing and Subcontracting : Many public and private sector organisations have offered VRS to their employees to restructure the organisation in the name of rightsizing with the ultimate objective to reduce labour cost and enhance organisational competitiveness (Lam and Reshaf, 1999). The list of companies offering VRS to their employees and the number of employees so far displaced (Table 2) provides a clear picture of the present scenario.

TABLE – 2
Enterprise-wise Statistics of Employees Granted VR

Unit	*No. of persons employed*			*No. of persons granted VR so far*
	1990-91	1991-92	1992-93	
SAIL	1,90,609	1,89,193	1,88,352	16,928
DTC	40,684	40,193	39,478	3,799
MMTC	3,836	3,648	3,246	715
FCI	68,502	67,788	66,631	18
MFI	2,685	2,584	2,543	75
EIL	3,373	3,426	3,541	54
NTC(TN)	11,990	12,015	11,702	2,137
HI	2,748	2,722	2,722	117
HMT	28,508	27,771	27,015	1,588
MFE	1,473	1,566	1,579	89
BCPL	1,668	1,467	1,369	311
ECIL	7,892	7,874	7,653	192
MECON	3,817	3,794	3,748	37
CIL	6,72,866	7,61,550	6,63,349	13,328
NFDC	282	277	248	40
BPT	30,185	29,903	26,614	1,481

Source : Guha (1996).

Hindustan Ciba-Geigy purportedly closed down its Bhandup unit in Maharashtra as all the 1,000, employees accepted VRS, and the management was of the opinion that trade unions are not cooperating in the modernisation process. But it was actually done to wind up the sick unit and start production in a backward area with fewer workers and at a cheaper labour cost. As per the estimates of the industry, the public sector got rid of more than two lakh employees and paid Rs. 2,373 crores as compensation (**The Economic Times, December 4, 1997**). Rapid advances in information technology have reduced the need for a large layer of middle managers to process and interpret information, and feed the data to top management. As a result, organisations became flat and thin, bringing workers closer to the management and reducing the need of unions. The production process is also being subcontracted to ancillary units whereas assembling and marketing is done by the main unit. A number of companies have subcontracted production outside the main unit. A list is being presented here (Table 3).

TABLE – 3
Percentage of Production Transferred to Outside Main Unit.

Name of company	*1980*	*1993*
Pfizer	8	38.61
Cadbury	7	30,00
Hindustan Lever (soap)	0	15.00
Hindustan Lever (detergent)	5	50.00
Rallifan	10	50.00
Murphy	15	100.00
Bush	10	(approx) 100.00

Source : Shrouti and Nandkumar (1994).

(ii) HR Policy : HR policies are not favourable to unions as employees establish a direct link with employers (Saini, 1997). Unions feel uncomfortable with HR practices and consider employers' direct links with workers as anti-union. Emerging HR policies, team work, reduced hierarchies and flat structures, continuous improvement (Kaizen), decentralisation of decision-making, reward systems, training, performance reviews and counselling, quality circles, Quality of Work Life (QWL), and employee welfare have created a better labour-management relationship and, in the process, bypassed unions.

(iii) Changing Power Dynamics : The external as well as the internal environment has affected the power dynamics between the union and the management. The management is said to possess control power (Masilamani, 1992), or ownership power (Finkelstein, 1992). Trade unions can check the power of the management over individual employees in an organised manner. Hence, unions are said to possess collective power (Masilamani, 1987). Technological upgradation, modernisation, product sophistication, and change of manufacturing companies to marketing companies have enhanced the power of the management. Ancilliarisation of bulk production, casualisation of employment, and retrenchment along with the entry of knowledge workers, the lack of internal leadership and the political affiliation of unions have weakened the power of trade unions. Earlier unions used to check the unilateral power of the management leading to a more or less balanced power structure. Now, management has become comparatively stronger and unions have lost their power. Thus, unions have lost their countervailing power in a liberalised economy (Sheth, 1993).

3. Individual and Organisational Outcomes

The external environment, organisational restructuring process and HR climate have led to an unbalanced power structure and adversely affected the individual, and organisational-level effectiveness. Trade unions can lower labour productivity by adopting restricting work practices and frequent industrial action (Metcalf, 1990). Maki and Meredity (1986) were of the opinion that unions have an overall negative effect on productivity. Leigh (1986) observed that unionised workers tend to be less satisfied than non-unionised workers with their jobs. Many studies have found that higher unionisation rates have been associated with decreased profitability, slower growth, decreased investment in plant, equipment, research and development (Bronars and Deere, 1990; Bronars, Deere and Tracy, 1994). Abowd (1985), and Connolly, Hirsch and Hirschey (1986) were of the view that union-organising activity may result in the fall of share prices of the firm involved. Trade unions can also boost production by creating a satisfied workforce if there is a balanced wage-structure and favourable working conditions. The presence of a strong union not only stops the exploitation but also makes managers less lethargic. Unions may play an important role in enhancing the productivity if better labour-management relations prevail in the organisation. Lack of trust and co-operation among the parties adversely affects production and deteriorates industrial relations. So management should share the information through the participative management process and treat the unions as equal partners in business for better labour-management relations. In turn, trade unions can work to maintain industrial safety and reduce absenteeism by helping the workers and solving their problems. Unions can go for a fair contract with the management and co-operate for the overall economic growth of the organisation.

Trade union militancy has resulted in a los of man-hours leading to low productivity. As in Andhra Pradesh, the PWG-sponsored trade union 'SIKASA' in the coal industry is involved in settling labour disputes with management. Similarly, in Kerala and West Bengal also, labour and trade union militancy is one of the major causes for low industrial development. There has been a decrease in the number of strikes but the number of lockouts is increasing, indicating a decline in union power. According to the ILO report, India loses more man-hours as a result of strikes and lockouts than almost any other country but the number of workers involved in strikes and lockouts is considerably lower than Brazil, Italy or Spain. This indicates that the basic premise of industrial pluralism and the regulation of conflict have not been achieved. There is a growth of small, independent and industry-level unions which are not affiliated to any central federation. The number of strikes and lockouts called by unions and management is considerable. Table 4 shows the gravity of the situation and calls for consideration by unions and management.

TABLE – 4
Number of Disputes

Year	*Strikes*	*Lock-outs*	*Total*
1991	1278	532	1810
1992	1011	703	1714
1993	914	479	1393
1994	808	393	1201
1995	732	334	1066
1996	—	—	1166
1997	—	—	1305

Source : Bhattacherjee (1999).

Young, educated and career-driven workers are keen to support internal unions focusing on local/enterprise issues rather than national issues. There has been no serious attempt to organise unorganised-sector workers by trade unions as they are controlled by powerful political leaders having vested interest. Adversarialism is so deeply rooted in Indian trade unions that they cannot imagine themselves making common cause with capital or even recognise that they may have shared interests. Some of the bitterly fought industrial relations disputes by companies like Bata, Philips and Hindustan Lever have been over the management's demand for flexible work practices. Trade unions have done little to address the changing reality of the new work environment except expressing helplessness when losing union membership. Trade unions are also perceived as institutions protecting the unproductive workforce who have no social responsibility. They have lost the support of the public by going for frequent strikes in public utility services like telecom, transport etc. and building a bad image. Trade unions have not changed their agenda beyond wage-bargaining. Technological upgradation, retraining, skill-upgradation and professional growth have not yet become an important issue. Trade union leaders have not contributed significantly to the economic development of the country as they are guided by vested self-interest and political motives.

LABOUR FLEXIBILITY AND INDUSTRIAL RELATIONS

The rapid growth of industrialisation in many parts of the world over the past quarter of a century have been contributed largely by lower labour costs and more flexible labour supply. This reflects the relative lack of protective regulations, weak system of collective bargaining, lack of working class traditions and expectations and reduced role of unions. Market as an institution now has overpowered the old 'protective' institution and society is tending to more from 'status' to 'contract' and in the sphere of labour-management relations is giving primacy to managerial prerogatives and rationality.

The structure of industrial relations in the post-war period was drawn from the spirit of Welfare State. Hence labour market was based on the vast majority of men being in secure full-time wage employment with women being in jobs as 'secondary workers'. Within employment and the labour market, the growing forms of labour control were bureaucratic and paternalistic in nature. Even as early as 1929, Slichter saw the danger of this approach and its effect on industrial relations. Under Welfare Capitalism much of the paternalistic approach was taken over by the State itself. The unions and the State played the roles of protectors of labour interest. Industrial relations now were governed by statutory pro-collective regulations backed by voice regulations through unions and employee associations, mainly through tripartism. Not only was centralised or sectoral collective bargaining favoured and trade union confederations and employers' organisations regarded as legitimate part of governance, but statutory regulations promoted collective institutions and procedures.

In the wake of growing impact of globalisation, State and firms both claim that they need to reduce fiscal and labour costs. Hence there is a trade-off between flexibility and security. Employers are pursuing different kinds of flexibility leading to various types of insecurity on the part of the workers in traditional sense. In the new framework of industrialisation, the unions and State find themselves to play 'a soft' role and make balance between flexibility and security. There have been various examples of countries practising balance between flexibility and security. There have been various examples of job security on the one hand and growth in a conducive industrial relations situations on the other.

The present structure of Indian Industrial Relations draws its spirit from the concept of Welfare State. At the time of independence, several labour laws were enacted to protect the labour from exploitation. Labour policy was directed initially in maintaining harmony for ensuring the realisation of the objectives of economic planning. To deal with industrial conflict four types of institutions were created.

(i) Intervention to labour laws;
(ii) Industrial democracy;
(iii) Code of conduct; and
(iv) Consultation machinery.

Among all these, state intervention has played the dominant role. Whenever conflict arose between employer and employee State came in between to sort out the problems. In the process, State introduced an array of regulations, particularly in favour of workers which continuously added to market rigidities. This also added to the higher adjustment cost to the employers and consequently low demand for labour in Indian industries. Hence the laws of job protection itself impeded the job creation. Moreover, on several occasions industrial conflicts took violent form resulting in gheraos, lock-outs and even deaths. Given the intensity of industrial unrest and resultant violence, it is doubtful whether India has a unified industrial relations system.

In the wake of New Economic Policy, Government is deregulating Indian industries in order to compete with multinationals. There was a gradual retreat of State from the arena of industrial relations. On the collective bargaining point, there is ascendancy in managerial rights and new technologies, structural and other adjustments seem to have made unions' position much more vulnerable today than anytime in the past. The growing flexibility in Indian industries has left the unions with little memberships and little things to do. Accordingly, workers are resorting to more covert form of protest instead of calling strikes with the help of union (Go-slow, work to rule, non-cooperation etc. are covert forms of protest). This has been true even in the States where ruling political parties are guided by left ideology and are understood to be more committed to the cause of workers' welfare. Virmani noted that collective bargaining has failed us therefore we must give collective bargaining. Farms are restructuring without unions' involvement by adopting various strategies.

The growth of flexibility world has not left the Indian industries untouched. The firms are restructuring the entire labour structure in favour of non-permanent and non-regular workers. The growth of flexibility has altered the entire scenario of industrial relations. The growing spate of flexibility has reduced the numerical strength of unions and their presence at the firm levels is scanty. The prospective growth of flexibility is a further threat to the active roles of unions and hence reduces the role of tripartism of collective bargaining in conflict resolutions between employers and the employees.

Since the traditional IRS in India has been based on the concept of vast majority of the men being in secure full-time wage employment it loses its significance with growing proportion of non-regular employment on account of growing flexibility in Indian industries. Hence the old institution of IRS are no longer capable of dealing with conflict resolutions between employers and employees.

The traditional framework recognises three principal sectors in industrial relations :

(i) Unions;

(ii) Employers; and

(iii) State.

In Indian industrial relations unions have been characterized as militant, employers legalistic and Government soft and tender minded. However, in recent times, with the weakening of unions, on account of their decreasing memberships, employers have become more militant. On the other hand, unions are becoming legalistic and the State is gradually withdrawing from the IR scene. Union militancy is reflected in the form of strikes and employers' militancy is reflected in the increasing number of lockouts.

❑ ❑ ❑

For this Chapter I have heavily drawn upon the papers by Venkata Ratnam, and Manarayajan Dhal & Srivastava presented at the Annual Conference of Indian Labour Economics in December, 2000 at Jabbalpur.

APPENDIX

THE INDUSTRIAL DISPUTES ACT, 1947

An Act to make provision for the investigation and settlement of industrial disputes,and for certain other purposes.

WHEREAS it is expedient to make provisions for the investigation and settlement of industrial disputes, and for certain other purposes hereinafter appearing;

It is hereby enacted as follows:

CHAPTER I
PRELIMINARY

S. 1. Short title, extent and commencement — (1) This Act may be called the Industrial Disputes Act, 1947.

(2) It extends to the whole of India.

(3) It shall come into force on the first day of April, 1947.

NOTES

Object and purpose of the Act — The object of the Industrial Disputes Act, 1947 as its preamble indicates, is to make provision for the investigation and settlement of industrial disputes, which means adjudication of such disputes also. The Act envisages collective bargaining, contracts between union representing the workmen and the management, a matter which is outside realm of the common law or the Indian law of contract-*Premier Automobiles Ltd. vs. Kamlekar Shantaram Wadke of Bombay,* (1976)1 SCC 496: AIR 1975 SC 2238; (1975)11 LLJ 445.

The Calcutta High Court had also occasion to consider the objects, and purposes of the Act in the case of — *The Statesman Ltd. vs. The Second Industrial Tribunal of West Bengal,* 95 CWN 861: (1991) CHN 80. One of the main objects and purposes of the said Act of 1947 is not only to arrange for speedy resolution of industrial adjudication for the purpose of bringing peace and amity in the industry but also to ameleorate the conditions of the workmen, who were, previously to such enactment, exposed to the vagaries of their employers. This Act confers various rights on the workmen to agitate their grievances against their employer before the industrial forum as contemplated under the Act. This is one of the most important piece of social legislation and any interpretation of its provisions is required to be made keeping in mind the welfare of the workmen.

Provision of the Act should be liberally interpreted — Industrial Disputes Act is a legislation intended to bring about peace and harmony between labour and management in an industry and for that purpose, it makes provision for the investigation and settlement of industrial disputes. It is, therefore, necessary to interpret the definitions of "industry", 'workman', 'industrial dispute', etc. so as to advance the object of the Act. Disputes between the force of labour and management are not be excluded from the operation of the Act by giving narrow and restricted meaning to expressions in the Act. A pragmatic and not a pedantic approach must be adopted — *S.K. Verma vs. Mahesh Chandra,* AIR 1984 SC 1462; (1983)2 LLJ 429: 1983 Lab IC 1483.

S. 2. Definitions — In this Act, unless there is anything repugnant in the subject or context,-

(a) "appropriate Government" means-

(i) in relation to any industrial dispute concerning any industry carried on by or under the authority of the Central Government or by a railway company or concerning any such controlled industry as may be specified in this behalf by the Central Government or in relation to an industrial dispute concerning [a Dock Labour Board established under Section 5A of the Dock Workers (Regulation of Employment) Act, 1948, or [the Industrial Finance Corporation of India Limited formed and registered under the Companies Act, 1956] or the Employees' State Insurance Act, 1948 or the Board of Trustees constituted under Section 3A of the Coal Mines Provident fund and Miscellaneous Provisions Act, 1948, or the Central Board of Trustees and the State Board of Trustees constituted under Section 5A and Section 5B, respectively, of the Employees' Provident Fund and Miscellaneous Provisions Act, 1952, 5b[***] or the Life Insurance Corporation of India established under Section 3 of the Life Insurance Corporation Act, 1956, or [the Oil and Natural Gas Corporation Limited registered under the Companies Act, 1956] or the Deposit Insurance and Credit Guarantee Corporation established under Section 3 of the Deposit Insurance and Credit Guarantee Corporation Act, 1961, or the Central Warehousing Corporation established under Section 3 of the Warehousing Corporations Act, 1962, or the Unit Trust of India established under Section 3 of the Unit Trust of India Act, 1963, or the Food Corporation of India established under Section 3, or a Board of Management established for two or more contiguous States under Section 16 of the Food Corporation Act, 1964, or [the Airports Authority of India constituted under Section 3 of the Airports Authority of

India Act, 1994] or a Regional Rural Bank established under Section 3 of the Regional Rural Banks Act, 1976, or the Export Credit and Guarantee Corporation Limited or the Industrial Reconstruction Corporation of India Limited], or [the National Housing Bank established under Section 3 of the National Housing Bank Act, 1987] or [the Banking Service Commission established under Section 3 of the Banking Service Commission Act, 1975, or] [an air transport service, or a banking or an insurance company], a mine, an oil field, a Cantonment Board or a major port, the Central Government, and]

(ii) in relation to any other industrial disputes, the State Government;

[(aa) "arbitrator" includes a umpire;]

(aaa)] "average pay" means the average of the wages payable to a workman —

(i) in the case of monthly paid workman, in the three complete calendar months,

(ii) in the case of weekly paid workman, in the four complete weeks,

(iii) in the case of daily paid workman, in the twelve full working days,

proceed in the date on which the average pay becomes payable if the workman had worked for three complete calendar months or four complete weeks or twelve full working days,as the case may be, and where such calculation cannot be made,the average pay shall be calculated as the average of the wages payable to a workman during the period he actually worked;]

[(b) "award" means an interim or a final determination of any industrial dispute or of any question relating thereto by any Labour Court, Industrial Tribunal or National Industrial Tribunal and includes an arbitration award made under Section 10A;]

[(bb) "banking company' means a banking company as defined in Section 5 of the Banking Companies Act, 1949 (10 of 1949), having branches or other establishments in more than one state, and includes [the Export-Import Bank of India] [the Industrial Development Bank of India,] the Reserve Bank of India, the State Bank of India, [a corresponding new bank constituted under Section 3 of the Banking Companies (Acquisition and Transfer of Under -taking) Act, 1970 (5 of 1970)], [a corresponding new bank constituted under Section 3 of the Banking Companies (Acquisition and Transfer of Undertakings) Act, 1980, and any

subsidiary bank] as defined in the State Bank of India Subsidiary Banks) Act, 1959 (38 of 1959);]

(c) "Board means a Board of Conciliation constitute under this Act;

[*(cc)* "closure" means the permanent closing down of a place of employment or part thereof;]

(d) "conciliation officer" means a conciliation officer appointed under this Act;

(e) "conciliation proceeding" means any proceeding held by a conciliation officer or Board under this Act;

[*(ee)* "controlled industry" means any industry the control of which by the Union has been declared by any Central Act to be expedient in the public interest;]

(f) "Court" means a court of Inquiry constituted under this Act;

(g) "employer" means —

(i) in relation to an industry carried on by or under the authority of any department of [the Central Government or State Government], the authority prescribed in this behalf, or where no authority is prescribed the head of the department;

(ii) in relation to an industry carried on by or on behalf of a local authority, the chief executive officer of that authority;

(gg) "executive" in relation to a trade union, means the body, by whatever name called, to which the management of the affairs of the trade union is entrusted;]

(i) a person shall be deemed to be "independent' for the purpose of his appointment as the chairman or other member of a Board, Court or Tribunal if he is unconnected with industrial dispute referred to such Board, Court or Tribunal or with any industry directly affected by such dispute:

[**Provided** that no person shall cease to be independent by reason only of the fact that he is a shareholder of an incorporated company which is connected with, or likely to be affected by, such industrial dispute; but in such a case, he shall disclose to the appropriate Government the nature and extent of the shares held by him in such company;]

[*(j)* "industry" means any systematic activities carried on by co-operation between an employer and his workmen (whether such workmen are employed by such employer directly or by or through any agency, including a contractor) for the production, supply or distribution of goods or services with a view to satisfy human wants or wishes (not being wants or wishes which are merely spiritual or religious in nature), whether or not. —

(i) any capital has been invested for the purpose of carrying on such activity; or

(ii) such activity is carried on with a motive to make any gain on profit, and includes —

(a) any activity of the Dock Labour Board established under Section 5A of the Dock Workers (Regulation of Employment) Act, 1948;

(b) any activity relating to the promotion of sales or business or both carried on by an establishment,

but does not include —

(1) any agricultural operation except where such agricultural operation is carried on in an integrated manner with any other activity (being any such activity as is referred to in the foregoing provisions of this clause) and such other activity is the predominant one.

Explanation — For the purpose of this sub-clause agricultural operation" does not include any activity carried on in a plantation as defined in clause *(f)* of Section 2 of the Plantation Labour Act, 1951 (69 of 1951); or

(2) hospital or dispensaries; or

(3) educational, scientific, research or training institutions; or

(4) institutions owned or managed by organisations wholly or substantially engaged in any charitable, social or philanthropic service; or

(5) khadi or village industries; or

(6) any activity of the Government relatable to the sovereign functions of the Government including all the activities carried on by the departments of the Central Government dealing with defence research, atomic energy and space; or

(7) any domestic service; or

(8) any activity, being a profession practised by an individual or body of individuals, if the number of persons employed by the individual or body of individuals in relation to such profession is less than ten; or

(9) any activity, being an activity carried on by a co-operative society or a club or any other like body of individuals, if the number of persons employed by the co-operative society, club or other like body of individuals in relation to such activity is less than ten;]

(k) "industrial dispute" means any dispute or difference between employers and employers on between employers and workmen, or between workmen and workmen, which is connected with the employment or non-employment or the terms of employment or with the conditions of labour, of any person;

[*(ka)* "industrial establishment of undertaking" means an establishment or undertaking in which any industry is carried on:

Provided that where several activities are carried on in an establishment or undertaking and only one or some of such activities is or are in an industry or industries, then —

(a) if any unit of such establishment or undertaking carrying on any activity being an industry, is severable from the other unit or

units of such establishment or undertaking, such unit shall be deemed to be a separate industrial establishment or undertaking;

(*b*) if the predominant activity or each of the predominant activities carried on in such establishment or undertaking or any unit thereof is an industry and the other activity or each of the other activities carried on in such establishment or undertaking or unit thereof is not severable from and is, for the purpose of carrying on, or aiding the carrying on of, such predominant activity or activities, the entire establishment or undertaking or, as the case may be, unit thereof shall be deemed to be an industrial establishment or undertaking;]

[*(kk)* "insurance company" means an insurance company as defined in Section 2 of the Insurance Act, 1938 (4 of 1938), having branches or other establishments in more than one State;]

[*(kka)* "khadi" has the meaning assigned to it in clause (d) of Section 2 of the Khadi and Village Industries Commission Act, 1956 (61 of 1956;]

[*(kkb)*" Labour Court" means a Labour Court constituted under Section 7;]

[*(kkk)* "lay-off" (with its grammatical variations and cognate expressions) means the failure, refusal or inability of an employer on account of shortage of coal, power or raw materials or the accumulation of stocks or the break-down of machinery [or natural calamity or for any other connected reason] to give employment to a workman whose name is borne on the muster rolls of his industrial establishment and who has not been retrenched;

Explanation — Every workman whose name is borne on the muster rolls of the industrial establishment and who presents himself for work at the establishment at the time appointed for the purpose during normal working hours on any day and is not given employment by the employer within two hours of his so presenting himself shall be deemed to have been laid-off for that day within the meaning of this clause:

Provided that if the workman, instead of being given employment at the commencement of any shift for any day is asked to present himself for the purpose during the second half of the stift for the day and is given employment then, he shall be deemed to have been laid-off only for one-half of that day of;

Provided further that if he is not given any such employment even after so presenting himself; he shall not be deemed to have been laid-off for the second half of the shift for the day and shall be entitled to full basic wages and dearness allowance for that part of the day;]

(l) ' lock-out means the [temporary closing of a place of employment], or the suspension of work, or the refusal by an employer to continue to employ any number of persons employed by him;

[(la) "major port" means a major port as defined in clause (8) of Section 3 of the Indian Ports Act, 1908 (15 of 1908);

(lb) "mine" means a mine as defied in clause (j) of sub-section (l) of Section 2 of the Mines Act, 1952 (35 of 1952);]

[(ll) "National Tribunal"means a National Industrial Tribunal constituted under Section 7B;]

[(lll) "office bearer", in relation to a trade union, includes any member of the executive thereof, but does not include an auditor;]

(m) "prescribed" means prescribed by rule made under this Act;

(n) "public utility service" means —

(i) any railway service [or any transport service for the carriage of passengers or goods by air];

[(ia) any service in, or in connection with the working of, any major port or dock;]

(ii) any section of an industrial establishment, on the working of which the safety of the establishment or the workmen employed therein depends;

(iii) any postal, telegraph or telephone service;

(iv) any industrial which supplies power, light or water to the public;

(v) any system of public conservancy or sanitation;

(vi) any industry specified in the [First Schedule] which the appropriate Government may, if satisfied that public emergency or public interest so requires, by notification in the *Official Gazette*, declare to be a public utility service for the purpose of this Act, for such period as may be specified in the notification:

Provided that the period so specified shall not, in the first instance, exceed six months but may, by a like notification, be extended from time to time,by any period not exceeding six months, at any one time, if in the opinion of the appropriate Government, public emergency or public interest requires such extension;

(o) "railway company" means a railway company as defined in Section 3 of the Indian Railways Act, 1890 (9 of 1890);

[(oo) "retrenchment" means the termination by the employer of the service of a workman for any reason whatsoever, otherwise than as a punishment inflicted by way of disciplinary action, but does not include —

(a) voluntary retirement of the workman; or

(*b*) retirement of the workman on reaching the age of superannuation if the contract of employment between the employer and the workman concerned contains a stipulation in that behalf; or

[(*bb*) termination of the service of the workman as a result of the non-renewal of the contract of employment between the employer and the workman concerned on its expiry or of such contract being terminated under a stipulation in that behalf contained therein; or]

(*c*) termination of the service of workman on the ground of continued ill-health;]

[(*p*) "settlement" means a settlement arrived at in the course of conciliation proceeding and includes a written agreement between the employer and workmen arrived at otherwise than in the course of conciliation proceeding where such agreement has been signed by the parties thereto in such manner as may be prescribed and a copy thereof has been sent to [an officer authorised in this behalf by] the appropriate Government and the conciliation officer;]

(*q*) "strike" means a cessation of work by a body of persons employed in any industry acting in combination, or a concerned refusal, or a refusal under a common understanding, of any number of persons who are or have been so employed to continue to work or to accept employment;

[(*qq*) "trade union" means a trade union registered under the Trade Unions Act, 1926 (16 of 1926);]

[(*r*) "Tribunal" means an Industrial Tribunal constituted under Section 7A and includes an Industrial Tribunal constituted before the 10th day of March, 1957, under this Act;]

[(*ra*) "unfair labour practice" means any of the practices specified in the Fifth Schedule;

(*rb*) "village industries" has the meaning assigned to it in clause(*h*) of Section 2 of the Khadi and Village Industries Commission Act, 1956 (61 of 1956);]

[(*rr*) "wages" means all remuneration capable of being expressed in terms of money, which would, if the terms of employment, express or implied, were fulfilled, be payable to a workman in respect of his employment, or of work done in such employment, and includes —

(*i*) such allowance (including dearness allowance) as the workman is for the time being entitled to;

(*ii*) the value of any house accommodation or of supply of light, water, medical attendance or other amenity or of any service or of any concessional supply of foodgrains or other articles;

(*iii*) any travelling concession;

(iv) any commission payable on the promotion of sales or business or both;]

but does not include-

(a) any bonus;

(b) any contribution paid or payable by the employer to any pension fund or provident fund or for the benefit of the workman under any law for the time being in force;

(c) any gratuity payable on the termination of his service;]

(s) "workman" means any person (including an apprentice) employed in any industry to do any manual, unskilled, skilled, technical operational, clerical or supervisory work for hire or reward, whether the terms of employment be express or implied, and for the purpose of any proceeding under this Act in relation to an industrial dispute, includes any such person who has been dismissed, discharged or retrenched in connection with, or as a consequence of, that dispute, or whose dismissal, discharge or retrenchment has led to that dispute, but does not include any such person —

(i) who is subject to the Air Force Act 1950 (45 or 1950), or the Army Act,1950 (46 of 1950), or the Navy Act, 1957 (62 of 1957); or

(ii) who is employed in the police service or as an officer or other employee of a prison; or

(iii) who is employed mainly in managerial or administrative capacity; or

(iv) who, being employed in a supervisory capacity, draws wages exceeding one thousand six hundred rupees *per mensem* or exercises, either by the nature of the duties attached to the office or by reason of the powers vested in him, functions mainly of a managerial nature.]

NOTES

Appropriate Government determination of [Section 2 (a)] – In deciding the appropriate Government in respect of an industrial dispute the proper question to consider is "where did the dispute arise". Ordinarily if workers are working in a separate establishment, the dispute would arise at that place. There should be some nexus between the dispute and the territory of the State and not between the industry and the territory of the State. In case of transfer the dispute arises not at the Head Office where the order of transfer was passed, but at the place where the workman who was transferred was working-*Workmen vs. Shri Ranga Vilas Motors (Pvt.) Ltd.*, (1967) II SCR 528: AIR 1967 SC 1040: (1967) II LLJ 12.

Where the undertaking is run by an incorporated company and not directly by the Central Government or any of its Department, then the company cannot be said to be carrying on the business under the authority of the Central Government. In effect the company is separate from its shareholders and the mere fact that the entire share capital was contributed by the Government, and the shares are held by the President and some officers of the Government, does not make it an agent of the President or the Central Government. The fact that the Ministers can appoint the Directors and can give them instruction is immaterial- *Heavy Engineering Mazdoor Union vs. State of Bihar,* (1969) I SCC 765; (1969) III SCR 995: AIR 1970 SC 82; (1969) II LLJ 549.

Hindustan Aeronautics Ltd., a company wholly owned and controlled by the Central Government has two units-one at Barrackpore in West Bengal and another at Bangalore. The question arose whether the State of West Bengal was competent to refer the dispute between the management of Barrackpore unit and employees employed by the unit for adjudication. Held that the reference by the State of West Bengal of the dispute was valid- *Hindustan Aeronautics Ltd. vs. Workman,* AIR 1975 SC 1737: (1975) II LLJ 336.

The business of the Provident Fund Organisation is governmental in character and does not pertain to any industry to which the Employees Provident Fund and M.P. Act applies. The Central Government and not the State Government is the appropriate Government in the matter of industrial disputes arising between the management and workmen of the Regional Fund Organisation—*R.P.F. Commissioner vs. Workmen,* AIR 1984 SC 1897. (1984) II LLJ 503 : 1984 Lab IC 1682.

Award definition of [Section 2(b)] — The definition of the word "award" shows that it can be either an interim or final determination either of the whole of the dispute referred to the Tribunal or of any question relating thereto. Thus, it is open to the Tribunal to give an award about the entire dispute at the end of all proceedings. This will be final determination of the industrial dispute referred to it. It is also open to the Tribunal to make an award about some of the matters referred to it whilst some others still remain to be decided. This will be an interim determination of any question relating thereto. In either case it will have to be published as required by Section 17. Such awards are however not in the nature of interim relief. Interim relief on the other hand, is granted under the power conferred on the tribunal under Section 10(4) with respect to matters incidental to the points of dispute for adjudication — *Management of Hotel Imperial, New Delhi vs. Hotel Workers' Union,* (1960) I SCR 476: AIR 1959 SC 1342 : (1959) II LLJ 544.

Industry, meaning and scope of [Section 2 (j)] — Where there is (i) systematic activity, (ii) organised by co-operation between employer and employee (the direct and substantial element is chimerical) and (iii) for the production and/or distribution of goods and services calculated to satisfy human wants and wishes (not spiritual or religious but inclusive of material things or services geared to celestial bliss), *prima facie,* there is an industry in the enterprise.

Absence of profit motive or gainful objective is irrelevant, be the venture in the public, joint, private or other sector.

The true focus is functional and the decisive test is the nature of the activity with special emphasis on the employer-employee relations.

If the organisation is a trade or business it does not cease to be one because of philanthropy animating the undertaking.

Although the sub-section uses the words of the widest amplitude in its two limbs, their meaning cannot be magnified to overreach itself – *Bangalore Water Supply vs. A. Rajappa,* (1978) I LLJ 349 SC: 1978 Lab IC 467.

Sovereign functions of the State, if falls within the definition of 'industry' —

Sovereign functions of the State cannot be included in industry, but if there are industrial units severable from the essential functions and possess an entry of their own it may be plausible to hold that the employees of those units are workmen and those undertakings are industries — *Bangalore Water & Sewerage Board vs. A. Rajappa,* (1978) I LLJ 349 SC : 1978 Lab IC 467.

Hospital, if fall within the definition of 'industry' – The character of the activity involved in running a hospital brings the institution of the hospital within s. 2(j). It makes no difference that the hospital is run by the Government. It is the character of the activity which decides the question as to whether the activity in question attracts the provision of s 2(j)- *State of Bombay vs. Hospital Mazdoor Sabha,* AIR 1960 SC 610: (1960) I LLJ 251.

Public Works Department of the Government of Tamil Nadu if an industry — Held that the Public Works Department of the Government of Tamil Nadu is not an industry in respect of its activities relating to construction of government buildings such as hospitals, colleges, schools, and court buildings, so the work-charged employees of the department are not workmen under the provision of the Industrial Disputes Act — *D. Padmanawan vs. State Tamil Nadu,* (1976) II LLJ 83 Mad.

University, if falls within the definition of 'industry' – Education in its true aspect is more a mission and a vacation rather than a profession or trade or business, however wide may be the denotation of the two latter words under Act. That is why it would be unreasonable to hod that educational institutions are employers within the meaning of s.2(g) or that work of teaching carried on by them is an industry – *University of Delhi vs. Ram Nath,* (1964) II SCR 703: AIR 1963 SC 1873: (1963) II LLJ 335.

Office of professionals, if falls within the definition of 'industry'— In the case of liberal professions, the contribution of the usual type of employees employed by the professionals to the value of the end-product (viz. advice and services rendered to the client) is so marginal that the end-product cannot be regarded as the fruit of the co-operation between the professional and his employees – *Bangalore Water Supply and Sewerage Board vs. A. Rajappa,* (1978) II SCC 213: 1978 SCC (L & S) 215.

Co-operatives if falls within the definition of 'industry' – Co-operative Societies are also industries. Even if the society is worked by members only, unless of course they are few and self-serving, the society would be an "industry" because, the member-workers are paid wages and there can be disputes about rates and scales of wages among the categories, that is, workers and workers or between workers and employer — *Bangalore Water Supply and Sewerage Board vs. A. Rajappa,* (1978) II SSC 213: 1978 SCC (L & S) 215.

Company owing flats, if industry — A company owning several flats which have been let out to tenants provides various facilities to its tenants in those flats, i.e., free supply of electricity, washing and cleaning of floors and laboratories, lift service, electrical repairs and replacing, sanitary repairs and replacing, etc. and for that purpose the company engaged some employees like sweepers, plumbers, lift man, darwans, pump-man, electric and other labourers, bill collector and bearers etc. in connection with these properties. A dispute arose between the company and its employees with regard to wages, scales of pay and dearness allowance and gratuity. The matter was referred for adjudication to the Tribunal. The question arose as to whether the company is an "industry" under section 2(j) of the Act. The Supreme Court affirmed the is of the Calcutta High Court in the case of —*Karnani Properties Ltd, vs. State of West Bengal* AIR 1990 SC 2047: (1990)4 SSC 472: 61 FLR 592: 1990 BBCJ 108 by holding that the activity carried on by the company falls within the ambit of the expression "industry:" as defined in the Act as was construed also by the Supreme Court in the case of —*Bangalore Water Supply & Sewerage Board,* AIR 1978 SC 548.

Irrigation Department of the State Government, if industry — The Supreme Court in the case of – *Des Raj vs. State of Punjab,* AIR 1988 SC 1182: (1988) II JT 145: (1988) II SCC 537 finds it difficult to hold that the activities of the State Government by organising its Survey and Investigation Division in the Irrigation Department through which the State Government rendered services in the matter of supplying water by constructing canals and dams does not come within the ambit of the sovereign or legal function of the State Government. Such services to the people at large, falls within the ambit of the expression "industry" as defined in Section 2(j) of the Act.

Industrial dispute meaning and scope of [Section 2(k)] — The adjective "industrial" in the expression "industrial dispute" stipulates that the definition does not take it its ambit disputes and difference of all sorts. The definition covers only those disputes which bears upon the relationship of employers and workmen of industry and the terms of employment and conditions of labour. The Act equally contemplates disputes between employers and employers or employers and workmen or workmen and workmen. Certain disputes can never be considered under the Act such as disputes between Government and an industrial establishment or between workmen and non-workmen or management and non-workmen — *Madras Gymkhana Club Employee's Union vs. Madras Gymkhana Club,* 1968 Lab IC 547: AIR 1968 SC 554.

Industrial dispute, if written demand is necessary to be brought into existence [Section 2(k)] — Act nowhere contemplates that the dispute would come into existence in any particular, specific or prescribed manner. For coming into existence of an industrial dispute a written demand is not a *sine qua non.* The term "industrial dispute" connotes a real and substantial difference having some element of persistency and continuity till resolved and likely if not adjusted to endanger the industrial peace of the undertaking or the community. When parties are at variance and the dispute or difference is connected with the employed, or non-employment or the terms of employment or with the conditions of labour there comes into existence an industrial dispute—*Shambhu Nath Gayal vs. Bank of Baroda,* (1978)11 LLJ 660.

Industrial dispute covers dispute raised by workmen not in employment — The definition of the expression "industrial dispute" is wide enough to cover a dispute raised by the employer's workmen in regard to the non-employment of others who may not be his workmen at the material time-*Kays Constructions Co. (P) Ltd. vs. Workmen,* AIR 1959 SC 208: (1958) II LLJ 660.

Dispute espoused by minority union, if industrial dispute — It cannot be said that there was no industrial dispute or this was only an individual dispute. The espousal of a dispute can be made even by a minority union having a membership of substantial number of workmen – *Pradip Lamp Works, Patna vs. Workmen,* (1969)19 FLR 385: (1970) I LLJ 507.

Dispute raised by unregistered and unorganised union, if industrial dispute – It would be an erroneous view if it were said that for a dispute to constitute an industrial dispute it is a requisite condition that it should be sponsored by a recognised union or that all the workmen of an industrial establishment should be parties to it. A dispute becomes an industrial dispute even where it is sponsored by a union which is not registered or where the dispute raised is by only some of the workmen— *State of Bihar vs. Kripa Shankar Jaiswal*, (1962) II SCR 1: AIR 1961 SC 304: (1961) I LLJ 334.

Factum of Resignation — The question whether dispute relating to the factum of resignation comes within the meaning of the industrial dispute as defined in Section 2(k) of the said Act was discussed in the case of —

Manabendra Kumar Choudhury vs. The First Labour Court, 94 CWN 743 wherein it was held that resignation implies a cessation of the relationship of employer and employee and inextricably connected with non-employment of a person.

"Lay-off", meaning and scope of the expression [Section 2(kkk)]. – Lay-off may be due to the reasons which are mentioned in the definition itself. Although reasons include 'any other reason', but the other reasons should be allied or analogous to the reasons already specified. If there is strike or slow down of production in one part of the establishment then subsequently lay-off in other parts would be similar to the reasons specified in the definition–*Koirbetta Estate vs. Rajamanikam,* AIR 1960 SC 893 : (1960) II LLJ 275.

"Lay-off" for reasons beyond control of the employer – Mere letter from bank expressing its reluctance to afford financial facilities is not sufficient to show that the company acting through their managing agents completely failed to raise the necessary finance. The letter written two months after the declaration of lay-off cannot be considered. The fat that the company was incurring losses did not show that the financial position was beyond their control–*Workmen vs. Dewan Tea Estate,* (1964)5 SCR 548 : AIR 1964 SC 1458 : (1964)I LLJ 358 : (1964)8 FLR 167.

Lock-out, when justified [Section 2(I)] – Just as strike is a weapon available to the employees for enforcing their industrial demands, lock-out is a weapon available to the employers to persuade the workers by coercive process to agree to their point of view. The liability of the employer in case of lock-out would depend upon whether the lock-out was justified and legal or not. Where the Manager was violently attacked and other members of staff were threatened, the lock-out was fully justified—*Koirbetta Estate vs. Rajamanickam,* (1960)3 SCR 371 : AIR 1960 SC 983 : (1960-61)18 FJR 241 : (1960)I FLR 107.

Retrenchment, when justified [Section 2(00)] — Once it is conceded that there was an occasion for effecting economy, the conclusion is inescapable that the conduct of the appellant in closing the department and dividing its work amongst its other employees cannot be reasonably characterized as improper or as amounting to an unfair labour practice—*Hotel Ambassador vs. Workmen,* (1936) FLR 140 : (1963)II LLJ 87.

Retrenchment on the ground of ill-health — The expression "ill-health" used in sub-clause (c) of aforesaid Section 2(00) has been construed relatively and in its context and must have a bearing on the normal discharge of duties. In considering this phrase the Supreme Court in the case of—*Anand Bihari vs. Rajasthan State Road Transport Corporation, Jaipur,* AIR 1991 SC 1003 held that if on account of a workman's disease or incapacity or debility in functioning, the resultant product or the services is likely to be affected in any way or to become a risk to the health, life or property of the consumer the disease or incapacity as to be categorised as ill-health for the purpose of the said sub-clause. Otherwise, the purpose, of production for which the service of the workman are engaged will be frustrated and worst still in cases such as they will endanger their lives and property of the consumer. Hence, the Supreme Court has put a realistic not a technical or pedantic meaning on the said phrase. The aforesaid construction would suddenly cover cases of drivers who have developed a defective or subnormal vision or eye-sight which is bound to interfere with their normal working as drivers. It was held that the termination of the services of the workers who were found unfit for driving the buses clearly falls within the sub-clause (c) of Section 2(00) and as such termination would not amount to retrenchment within the meaning of the said Section of the Act. Hence, the termination *par se* is not illegal because the provisions of Section 25F had not been followed while effecting it. However, the Supreme Court felt the need of providing compensatory relief such as alternative employment to those persons as service condition of such workmen.

Termination and retrenchment, distinction — Whatever the reason, every termination spells retrenchment. A termination takes place where a term expires either by the active step of the master or the running out of the stipulated term. To protect the weak against the strong this policy of comprehensive definition has been effectuated. Termination embraces not merely the act of termination by the employer, but fact of termination howsoever produced. to write into the order of appointment the date of termination confers no immunity from Section 25F(b) read with proviso to Section 25F(a)—State *Bank of India vs. N. Sundara money,* (1976)I SCC 822 : 1976 SCC (L&S) 136 : AIR 1976 SC 1111 : (1976)I LLJ 478.

Termination of probationer for unsuitability, if amounts to retrenchment — Retrenchment as definition s. 2(00) of the Act covers every case of termination of service except those which have been embodied in the definition. Hence, discharge from employment or termination of service of a probationer would also amount to retrenchment—*Karnataka S.R.T. Corpn. vs. Baraiah,* (1984)I LLJ 110 : (1984)64 FJR 52 : AIR 1983 SC 1320.

Settlement, binding nature of [Section 2(p)]—A settlement arrived at otherwise than in the course of limitation proceedings shall bind only the parties thereto and not all the workmen. As such the union which is not a party to the settlement can raise dispute over issues covered by the settlement and the Government would be free to refer it if it is otherwise deemed expedient—*Tata Chemicals Ltd. vs. Workmen,* (1978) III LLJ 22 : 1978(36) FLR 339 : (1978) II SCC 42.

A tripartite settlement, arrived at in course of conciliation proceedings in terms of Section 18(3) of the Act binds not only the parties to the dispute which the conciliation officer has settled but also all the workmen of the establishment, present or future—*Jobanputra vs. Kalelkar,* (1965) I LLJ 543 Bom.

Strike, what is and what is not [Section 2(q)]—Refusal under a common understating to continue work is a strike and if in pursuance of a common understanding the employees entered the premises of the bank and refused to take their pens in their hands, that would no doubt be a strike—*Punjab National Bank vs. All India Punjab National Bank Employees' Federation,* AIR 1960 SC 160 : (1959) II LLJ 666.

When the pen down strike led to rowdy demonstrations and violence thus shaking the credit of the bank, the contention of strikers that they were peaceful and did nothing more than occupying the seats would not warrant reinstatement—*Punjab National Bank vs. All India Punjab National Bank Employees' Union,* AIR 1960 SC 160 : (1959) II LLJ 666.

When the management substituted a weekly day of rest without giving the notice of change, then refusal to work on the day which was their weekly day of rest would not amount to strike—*Tata Iron & Steel Company Ltd. vs. Their workmen,* AIR 1960 SC 879 : (1960) I LLJ 580.

While it is an accepted principle that workmen can resort to strike in order to press their demands, it is an equally settled law that the management have the right to employ other workmen during a period of strike to keep the industry functioning—*Oriental Textile Finishing Mills vs. Labour Court,* AIR 1972 SC 277 : 1972 Lab IC 157.

Strike and Lock-out, difference of—Strike means cessation of work in combination of refusal of workmen of an industry to continue to work in pursuance of a common understanding. Lock-out means refusal of the employer to allow a number of his workmen to attend their duties without terminating their services. Lock-out is the counter part of strike. In either case the relationship or employer and employee subsists. Lock-out, like strike implies a collective dispute which must be either antecedent to or simultaneous (but no subsequent) with the refusal to employ or to work. Refusal to work in obedience of an unjustified or illegal order does not amount to strike. But if upon refusal of workmen to carry out a legal and justified order the work is stopped, this cannot be treated as lock-out. Retrenchment of a number of workmen on ground of rationalisation does not amount to lock-out. Termination of service is one thing the and lock-out is another—*Laxmi Devi Sugar Mills Ltd. vs. Labour Tribunal,* (1953)2 LLJ 224; *National Coal Co. Ltd. vs. L.P. Dave,* (1958) I LLJ 84 Pat.

Workman, tests to determine [Section 2(s)— Where an employee has multifarious duties and a question is raised whether he is a workman or someone other than a workman, the test that court must employ in order to determine the question is what was the primary, basic or dominant nature of duties for which the person whose status is under enquiry was employed. If he is incidentally asked to do some other work which may not necessarily be in tune with the basic duties, these additional duties cannot change the character and status of the person concerned—*Aykal Govind Raj Rao vs. Ciba Geigy of India Ltd.*, AIR 1985 SC 985 : 1985 Lab IC 1008 : (1985) II LLJ 401.

'Workmen' within the meaning of the I.D. Act — The work of preparing bank reconciliation statements cannot be said to be work of supervisory nature. Similarly direction given by a clerk to other clerks to take note from certain documents and submit reports to him cannot be treated as managerial or supervisory function. Difference in salary is not the decisive factor for considering an employee to be non-workman. Lastly by the mere use of the expression "covenanted contractual cadre", clerks and assistants cannot be elevated to the rank of officers. Such hig-sounding nomenclatures are, apart from being misleading, contrary to India's constitution culture—*Arkal Govind Raj Rao vs. Ciba Geigy of India Ltd.*, AIR 1985 SC 985 : 1985 Lab IC 1008.

The person in charge of security of the factory who was designated as chargeman security had to look after the security of the factory and its property and depute the security guards to be on duty at different places and make the visitors sign the Register maintained for their purpose. He had no power to appoint or dismiss any security guard. Hence duties and functions of the employee were neither managerial nor supervisory in nature-*Ved Prakash Gupta vs. Delton Cable India Pvt. Ltd.*, 1984 Lab IC 658 : (1984) I LLJ 546 : AIR 1984 SC 914.

A Development Officer of the Life Insurance Corporation has no authority to bind the Corporation in any way. He cannot appoint agents or take disciplinary actions against them. He has only to inspire them to work efficiently. He has no administrative control on them. The agents are not his subordinates. He has in fact no subordinate under him. The appellation "Development Officer" is not very significant in deciding whether or not such officer is a workman. The Development Officer cannot be said to be engaged in any administrative or managerial work – *S.K. Verma vs. Mahesh Chandra*, AIR 1984 SC 1462 : (1963) II LLJ 429.

Persons employed for the maintenance of apartment owners – A company owns certain apartments which are specifically declared under Apartment Ownership Act. The said company engaged certain employees for rendering services to the maintenance of the said apartments. The question came up for consideration in the case of —*Hanshree Apartment Owner's Association vs. Hanshree Apartment Owner's Employee's Union,* 95 CWN 1004: (1991)I CHN 287 as to whether the services rendered by the members employed in the apartments would amount to an activity within the meaning of industry under Section 2(j) of the Act. The court relied upon decision of

—*Karnani Properties Ltd.* (supra) and held that the services rendered by the countless menials would undoubtedly come within the scope of the definition of industry under Section 2(j) of the said Act. And, the services so rendered by the same servant to the succeeding owners who are larger in numerical strength would not change the nature and character of the services rendered and as such activity or services would still continue to be an industry so long as it continues to be a systematic activity with or without any profit motive. Even plurality of either employers or employees may be a factor in determining the nature of services rendered in a given circumstance. The court further held that services rendered by the members of the employees association, particularly the employees concerned make them "workmen" within the meaning of Section 2(s) of the said Act. Even the court held that some common spaces which are let on hire on specific occasion to the apartment owners on payment of charges constitute an activity which will come within the purview of the definition of industry within the meaning of Section 2(j) of the said Act. The court further held that the parking spaces are let out to the apartment owners for a consideration, which has no manner of connection with the apartments. These spaces are also serviced by the employees employed by the Board of Management and as such the domesticity of such servant at least vanishes at this point.

Appraiser of Gold, if workman—A person who has been engaged as an appraiser by a bank is required to perform the services of weighing and testing the gold ornaments offered to be pledged to the bank to secure loans. For this purpose, he was allotted commission/wages. Being terminated by the bank, he successfully sought a reference from the Government to the Labour Court which ultimately set aside the said order of termination. The short question as to whether he was a "workman" as defined in the Act was answered in the negative in the case of —*Management of M/s Puri Urban Cooperative Bank vs. Madhusudan Sahu,* AIR 1992 SC 1452. In dealing with the question, the Supreme Court found absence of any jural relationship of master and servant between he appraiser and the bank and as such it refused to term him as a workman for the purpose of the Act. The appraiser was required to weigh the ornaments and to appraise their quality, purity and value. The work so required to be done was left to him exclusively, as it depended on his skill, technique and experience. Besides under the terms of engagement he was required to, and he did, execute a bond indemnifying and holding himself responsible to the bank for all his acts and commissions as an appraiser and be accountable for the loss sustained by the bank on account of under-valuation of the gold pledged with it. Thus, the nature of work which he is required to do does not go to establish a master-servant relationship. The Supreme Court, upon evaluation of different particulars and totality, of circumstances, came to the conclusion that no master and servant relationship stand established in the engagement of such an appraiser of ornaments the order of re-instatement by the Tribunal and the High Court were set aside.

Section Salesman, if workman— The question whether a person serving as a Section Salesman come within the definition of "workman" was discussed in the case of – *T.P. Srivastava vs. National Tobacco Co.*, AIR 1991 SC 2294. He was employed to do canvassing and promoting sales for the company. The duties involve the suggesting of ways and means to improve the sales, a study of the type or status of the public to whom the product has to reach and a study of the market condition. He was also required to suggest about the public in market and meals, advertisement including the need for posters, holders and cinema slides. These duties require the imaginative and corrective mind which cannot be termed as either manual, skilled, unskilled or clerical in nature. The supervising work of the other local salesman was part of his work considered by the Tribunal as only incidental to his main work of canvassing and promotion in the area of his operation. The Supreme Court refused to term such a person as a workman after following the ratio of the decision of the Supreme Court in—*Burmah Shell Oil Storage and Distribution Co. vs. Burmah Shell Management and Staff,* AIR 1971 SC 922, *D.S. Nagraj vs. Labour Office, Karnal,* (1972)42 FJR 440 (AP), *J.J. Dechane Distributor vs. State of Kerala,* (1974) 2 Lab LJ 9 : 1974 Lab IC 379 (Kerala). The Supreme Court held that the Industrial Disputes Act is not applicable to such person, but as a long period of over sixteen years had elapsed the Supreme Court thought it unjust to leave such person without any remedy at the stage. A direction to the management was issued to pay such compensation as is necessary to meet the ends of justice.

Teachers, whether works — Though an educational institution has been treated to be an 'industry' in the decision of the Supreme Court in the case of —*Bangalore Water Supply & Sewerage Board vs. Rajappa,* AIR 1978 SC 548, yet the teachers employed by the educational institutions where the said institutions are imparting primary, secondary, graduate of post-graduate education cannot be called a 'workmen' within the meaning of Section 2(s) of the Act. Imparting of education is in the nature of a mission or a noble vocation. The clerical work, if any, they may or is only incidental to their principal work of teaching. Thus the Supreme Court in the case of—*A. Sundarambal vs. Government of Goa, Daman & Diu,* AIR 1988 SC 1700 refuted the contention that having regard to the object of the Act, all employees in an industry except those falling under the four exceptions (i) to (iv) in Section 2(s) of the Act should be treated as workmen. An acceptance of such an argument in the opinion of the Supreme Court will render the words "to do any skilled or unskilled, manual, supervisory, technical or clerical work" meaningless. Absence of these words might have justified a liberal construction. The decision in—*May and Baker (India) Ltd. vs. Their Workman,* AIR 1967 SC 678 precludes the court from taking such a view.

The aforesaid along with the case of – *Suresh Chandra vs. State of U.P.,* (1988)1 Lab IC 263 was considered by the Calcutta High Court in the case of – *Satya Narayan Tantia vs. State of West Bengal,* (1991)1 Cal HN 322 : (1991)1 Cal LT (HC) 405 : (1991)1 Cal HN 322, wherein it was held that though Section 2(j) of the said Act gives an exhaustive definition of 'industry' yet excludes educational institutions under clause (3) of the explanation. Section 2(j) has been inserted by the Amendment Act (XXXXVI) of 1982. The Calcutta High Court held that educational institutions never comes under the purview of industry because the West Bengal Board of Secondary Education Act, 1963 and Regulations framed thereunder contain comprehensive provisions for the protecting the interest of the teaching staff. Hence, the Court finds no reason to make the Industrial Disputes Act applicable to decide a dispute relating to a staff of an educational institution. The entire dispute relating to the suspension and dismissal of a person employed as a peon of the school arises in his capacity as an employee of the school and as such his remedy lies before the Appeal Committee according to the said Regulations and as such he is not entitled to seek redress of his grievance under the Industrial Disputes Act. The Court, indeed, observes that if there was any statue covering the entire ambit of disputes in a particular field, the said dispute must be adjudicated by the competent authority under the said statute and not under any other different statue. Any resort to jurisdiction other than that prescribed by the Regulations has been demarcated and interference by the State Government in referring the matter under section 10 read with Section 2(a) of the Industrial Disputes Act to the Tribunal was held to be unjustified and such reference was quashed.

S. [2A. Dismissal etc., of an individual workman to be deemed to be an industrial dispute— Where any employer discharges, dismisses, retrenches or otherwise terminates the services of an individual workman, any dispute or difference between the workman and his employer connected with, or arising out of, such discharge, dismissal retrenchment or termination shall be deemed to be an industrial dispute notwithstanding that no other workman nor any union of workmen is a party to the dispute.]

NOTES

Section 2A of the Act-meaning and scope of— We would therefore be justified in concluding that in enacting Section 2-A, the legislature intended that an individual workman who was discharged, dismissed or retrenched or whose services were otherwise terminated should be given relief without it being necessary of the relationship between the employer and the whole body of employees being attracted to that dispute and the dispute becoming a generalised one between labour on the one hand and the employer on the other— *Chemicals and Fibres India Ltd. vs. D.G. Bhoir & others,* (1975) Supply SCR 415.

Section 20(2) of the Industrial Disputes Act while conferring exclusive right on the recognised union to represent workmen in any proceeding under the Act and simultaneously denying the right to a workman to be represented by any individual workman has taken care to retain the exception as enacted subsequently in Section 2A. This legal position is reiterated in Section 20(2)(b) of the Act—*Balmer Lawrie Worker's Union vs. Management,* (1985)2 SCR 492.

Removal of the name of a workman from the rolls would constitute retrenchment and would be an industrial dispute within the meaning of Section 2A of the Industrial Disputes Act, 1947-*H.D. Singh vs. Reserve Bank of India,* AIR 1986 SC 132.

Retrospective effect of Section 2A, when valid—Even though Section 2A came into force with effect from 1st December, 1965, it would be permissible for the aggrieved workman of the instant case to invoke the provision of Section 2A to secure justice though the order of dismissal was passed earlier than 1st December, 1965 because the dispute arising from dismissal etc. of such workman was alive when Section 2A came into force—*Rustom & Hornby Pvt. Ltd. vs. T.B. Tandon,* (1976)1 SCR 119 SC.

Section 2A of the Act was amended to permit individual workman to ask for a reference in the case of individual dispute. This amendment was assented by the President on December 1, 1965. The Rajasthan Shops and Establishments Act, 1958 also received the assent of the President on July 14, 1958. On March 8, 1972 Chapter 6A including Section 28A was inserted in the Rajasthan Act. Therefore, the material provisions of the Rajasthan Act is the subsequent Act. Under Article 254 (2) of the Constitution of India, if there was any law made by the said chapter reserve for assent of the President and has made by the said chapter reserved for assent of the President and has received the assent of the President, the State Law would prevail in the State even if there is an earlier law by the Parliament on a subject in the Concurrent List. Both of these Acts in the opinion of the Supreme Court tread the same field, and if there is any conflict with each other, Section 28A of the Rajasthan Act would apply being later law. Of course, the Supreme Court in the aforesaid case of—*National Engineering Industries Ltd. vs. Shri Kishan,* AIR 1988 SC 329 : (1988) Supp. SCC 80 : 1988 Lab IC 384 did not find any conflict between the said two Acts which tread the same field. Both these Acts deal with the rights of the workman or employee to get redressal and damages in case of dismissal or discharge, but there is no repugnancy because there is no conflict between these two Acts, in pith and substance. There is no inconsistency between these two Acts. These two Acts are held to be supplemental to each other.

CHAPTER II
AUTHORITIES UNDER THIS ACT

S. 3. Works Committee— (1) In the case of any industrial establishment in which one hundred or more workmen are employed or have been employed on any day in the preceding twelve months, the appropriate Government may by general of special order require the employer to constitute in the prescribed manner a Works Committee consisting of representatives of employers and workmen engaged in the establishment so however that the number of representatives of workmen on the Committee shall not be less than the number of representatives of the employer. The representatives of the workmen shall be chosen in the prescribed manner from among the workmen engaged in the establishment and in consultation with their trade union, if any, registered under the Indian Trade Unions Act, 1926.

(2) It shall be the duty of the Works Committee to promote measures for securing and preserving amity and good relations between the employer and workmen and, to that end, to comment upon matters of their common interest or concern and endeavour to compose any material difference of opinion in respect of such matters.

S. 4. Conciliation Officers—(1) The Appropriate Government may, by notification in the *Official Gazette,* appoint such number of persons as it thinks fit, to be conciliation officers, charged with the duty of mediating in and promoting the settlement of Industrial disputes.

(2) A conciliation officer may be appointed for a specified area or for specified industries in a specified area or for one or more specified industries and either permanently or for a limited period.

S. 5. Board of Conciliation—(1) The appropriate Government may as occasion arises, by notification in the *Official Gazette,* constitute a Board of Conciliation for promoting the settlement of an industrial dispute.

(2) A Board shall consist of a chairman and two or four other members, as the appropriate Government thinks fit.

(3) The chairman shall be an independent person and the other members shall be persons appointed in equal number to represent the parties to the dispute and any person appointed to represent a party shall be appointed on the recommendation of that party :

Provided that, if any party fails to make a recommendation as aforesaid within the prescribed time, the appropriate Government shall appoint such person as it thinks fit to represent that party.

(4) A Board, having the prescribed quorum, may act notwithstanding the absence of the chairman or any of its members of any vacancy in its number :

Provided that, if the appropriate Government notifies the Board that the services of the chairman or of any other member have ceased to be available, the Board shall not act until a new chairman or member, as the case may be has been appointed.

S. 6. Courts of Inquiry—(1) the Appropriate Government may as occasion arises by notification in the *Official Gazette* constitute a Court of Inquiry for inquiring into any matter appearing to be connected with or relevant to an industrial dispute.

(2) A court may consist of one independent person or of such number of independent person as the appropriate Government may think fit and where a Court consists of two or more members, one of them shall be appointed as the chairman.

(3) A Court, having the prescribed quorum, may act notwithstanding the absence of the chairman or any of its members or any vacancy in its number :

Provided that, if the appropriate Government notifies the Court that the services of the chairman have ceased to be available, the Court shall not act until a new chairman has been appointed.

S. 7. Labour Courts—(1) The appropriate Government may, by notification in the *Official Gazette,* constitute one or more Labour Courts for the adjudication of industrial disputes relating to any matter specified in the Second Schedule and for performing such other functions as may be assigned to them under this Act.

(2) A Labour Court shall consist of one person only to be appointed by the appropriate Government.

(3) A person shall not be qualified for appointment as the presiding officer of a Labour Court, unless —

(a) he is, or has been, a Judge of a High Court; or

(b) he has, for a period of not less than three years, been a district Judge or an Additional District Judge; or

(c) * * * * *

(d) he has held any judicial office in India for not less than seven years; or

(e) he has been the presiding officer of a Labour Court constituted under any Provincial Act or State Act for not less than five years.

S. 7A. Tribunals—(1) The appropriate Government may, by notification in the *Official Gazette,* constitute on or more Industrial for the adjudication of industrial disputes relating to any matter, whether specified in the Second Schedule or the Third Schedule [and for performing such other functions as may be assigned to them under this Act.

(2) A Tribunal shall consist of one person only to be appointed by the appropriate Government.

(3) A person shall not be qualified for appointment as the presiding office of a Tribunal unless—

(a) He is, or has been, a Judge of a High Court; or

[(aa) he has, for a period of not less than three years, been a District Judge or an Additional District Judge;]

(4) The appropriate Government may, if it so thinks fit, appoint two persons as assessors to advise the Tribunal in the proceeding before it.

S. 7B. National Tribunals—(1) The Central Government may, by notification in the *Official Gazette,* constitute one or more National Industrial Tribunals for the adjudication of industrial disputes which, in the opinion of the Central Government, involve questions of national importance or are of such a nature that industrial establishments situated in more than one State are likely to be interested in, or affected by, such disputes.

(2) A National Tribunal shall consist of one person only to be appointed by the Central Government.

(3) A person shall not be qualified for appointment as the presiding office of a National Tribunal [unless he is, or has been a Judge of a High Court].

(4) The Central Government may, if it so thinks fit, appoint two persons as assessors to advise the National Tribunal in the proceeding before it.

S. 7C. Disqualifications for the Presiding Officer of Labour Courts, Tribunals and National Tribunals— No person shall be appointed to, or continue in, the office of the presiding officer of a Labour Court, Tribunal or National Tribunal, if—

(a) he is not an independent person; or

(b) he has attained the age of sixty-five years.

S. 8. Filling of Vacancies— If, for any reason a vacancy (other than a temporary absence) occurs in the office of the presiding officer of a Labor Court, Tribunal or National Tribunal or in the office of the chairman or any other member of a Board or Court, then, in the case of a National Tribunal the Central Government and in any other case, the appropriate Government, shall appoint another person in accordance with the provisions of this Act to fill the vacancy, and the proceeding may be continued before the Labour Court, Tribunal, National Tribunal, Board or Court, as the case may be, from the stage at which the vacancy is filled.

S. 9. Finality of orders constituting Boards, etc.—(1) No order of the appropriate Government or of the Central Government appointing any person as the chairman or any other member of a Board or Court or as the presiding officer of a Labour Court, Tribunal or National Tribunal, shall be called in question in any manner; and no act or proceeding before any Board or Court shall be called in question in any manner on the ground merely of the existence of any vacancy in, or defect in the constitution of, such Board or Court.

(2) No settlement arrived at in the course of a conciliation proceeding shall be invalid by reason only of the fact that such settlement was arrived at after the expiry of the period referred to in sub-section (6) of Section 12 or sub-section (5) of Section 13, as the case may be.

(3) Where the report of any settlement arrived at in the course of conciliation proceeding before a Board is signed by the chairman and all the other members of the Board, no such settlement shall be invalid by reason only of the causal or unforeseen absence of any of the members (including the chairman) of the Board during any stage of the proceeding.

CHAPTER IIA

NOTICE OF CHANGE

S. 9A. Notice of change—No employer, who proposes to effect any change in the conditions of service applicable to any workman in respect of any matter specified in the Fourth Schedule, shall effect such changes,

(a) without giving to the workmen likely to be affected by such change a notice in the prescribed manner of the nature of the change proposed to be effected; or

(b) within twenty-one days of giving such notice:

Provided that no notice shall be required for effecting any such change:

(a) where the change is effected in pursuance of any [settlement or award]; or

(b) where the workmen likely to be affected by the change are persons to whom the Fundamental and Supplementary Rules, Civil Services (Classification, Control and Appeal) Rules, Civil Services (Temporary Service) Rules, Revised Leave Rules, Civil Service Regulations, Civilians in Defence Services (Classification, Control and Appeal) Rules or the Indian Railway Establishment Code or any other rules or regulations that may be notified in this behalf by the appropriate Government in the *Official Gazette,* apply.

NOTES

Notice of change—The requirement of the notice would arise if the workmen are likely to be affected prejudicially. A change in the condition of service should be understood in that sense. The object of the section is to prevent a unilateral action by the employer changing the conditions of service of workmen to their prejudice. Section 9A is not applicable when workmen are given option to accept the change or continue on the existing terms—*Tamil Nadu Electric Workers Federation vs. M.S. Electricity Board,* (1962) II LLJ 136 Mad.

S. 9B. Power of Government to exempt— Where the appropriate Government is of opinion that the application of the provisions of Section 9A to any class of industrial establishments or to any class of workmen employed in any industrial establishment affect the employers in relation thereto so prejudicially that such application may cause serious repercussion on the industry concerned and that public interest so requires, the appropriate Government may, by notification in the *Official Gazette,* direct that the provisions of the said section shall not apply, or shall apply subject to such conditions as may be specified in the notification, to that class of industrial establishments or to that class of workmen employed in any industrial establishment.]

CHAPTER IIB
REFERENCE OF CERTAIN INDIVIDUAL DISPUTES TO GRIEVANCE SETTLEMENT AUTHORITIES

S. 9C. Setting up of Grievance Settlement Authorities and reference of certain individual disputes to such authorities—(1) The employer in relation to every industrial establishment in which fifty or more workmen are employed or have been employed on any day in the preceding twelve months, shall provide for, in accordance with the rules made in that behalf under this Act, a Grievance Settlement Authority for the settlement of industrial disputes connected with an individual workman employed in the establishment.

(2) Where an industrial dispute connected with an individual workman arises in an establishment referred to in sub-section (1), a workman or any trade union of workmen of which such workman is a member, refer, in such manner as may be prescribed, such dispute to the Grievance Settlement Authority provided for, by the employer under that sub-section for settlement.

(3) The Grievance Settlement Authority referred to in sub-section (1) shall follow such procedure and complete its proceedings within such period as may be prescribed.

(4) No reference shall be made under Chapter III with respect to any dispute referred to in this Section unless such dispute has been referred to the Grievance Settlement Authority concerned and the decision of the Grievance Settlement Authority is not acceptable to any of the parties to the dispute.]

CHAPTER III
REFERENCE OF DISPUTES TO BOARDS, COURTS OR TRIBUNALS

S. 10. Reference of Disputes to Boards, Courts or Tribunals—(1) [Where the appropriate Government is of opinion that any industrial dispute exists or is apprehended, it may at any time,] by order in writing,—

(*a*) refer the dispute to a Board for promoting a settlement thereof; or

(*b*) refer any matter appearing to be connected with, or relevant to, the dispute to a Court for inquiry; or

(*c*) refer the dispute or any matter appearing to be connected with or relevant to, the dispute, if it relates to any matter specified in the Second Schedule, to a Labour Court for adjudication; or

(*d*) refer the dispute or any matter appearing to be connected with, or relevant to, the dispute, whether it relates to any matter specified in the Second Schedule or the Third Schedule, to a Tribunal for adjudication :

Provided that where the dispute relates to any matter specified in the Third Schedule and is not likely to affect more than one hundred workmen, the appropriate Government may, if it so thinks fit, make the reference to a Labour Court under clause (c):]

[**Provided further** that] where the dispute relates to a public utility service and a notice under section 22 has been given, the appropriate Government shall, unless it considers that the notice has been frivolously or vexatiously given or that it would be inexpedient so to do, make a reference under this sub-section notwithstanding that any their proceedings under this Act in respect of the dispute may have commenced :

[**Provided also** that where the dispute in relation to which the Central Government is the appropriate Government, it shall be competent for that Government to refer the dispute to a Labour Court or an Industrial Tribunal as the case may be constituted by the State Government.]

[(1A) Where the Central Government is of opinion that any industrial dispute exists or is apprehended and the dispute involves any question of national importance or is of such a nature that industrial establishments situated in more than one State are likely to be interested in, or affected by, such dispute and that the dispute should be adjudicated by a National Tribunal, then, the Central Government may, whether or not it is the appropriate Government in relation to that dispute, at any time, by order in writing, refer the dispute or any matter appearing to be connected with, or relevant to, the dispute, whether it relates to any matter specified in the Second Schedule or the Third Schedule, to a National Tribunal of adjudication.]

(2) Where the parties to an industrial dispute apply in the prescribed manner, whether jointly or separately, for a reference of the dispute to a Board, Court, [Labour Court, Tribunal or National Tribunal], the appropriate Government, if satisfied that the persons applying represent the majority of each part, shall make the reference accordingly.

(2A) An order referring an industrial dispute to a Labour Court, Tribunal or National Tribunal under this Section shall specify the period within which such Labour Court, Tribunal or National Tribunal shall submit its award on such dispute to the appropriate Government :

Provided that where such industrial dispute is connected with an individual workman, no such period shall exceed three months :

Provided further that where the parties to an industrial dispute apply in the prescribed manner, whether jointly or separately, to the Labour Court, Tribunal or National Tribunal for extension of such period or for any other reason, and the presiding officer of such Labour Court, Tribunal or National Tribunal considers it necessary or expedient to extend such period, he may for reasons to be recorded in writing, extend such period by such further period as he may think fit :

Provided also that in computing any period specified in the sub-section, the period, if any, for which the proceedings before the Labour Court, Tribunal or National Tribunal had been stayed by any injunction or order of a Civil Court shall be excluded :

Provided also that no proceedings before a Labour Court, Tribunal or National Tribunal shall lapse merely on the ground that any period specified under this sub-section had expired without such proceedings being completed.]

(3) Where an industrial dispute has been referred to a Board [Labour Court, Tribunal or National Tribunal] under this Section, the appropriate Government may by order prohibit the continuance of any strike or lock-out in connection with such dispute which may be in existence on the date of the reference.

(4) Where in an order referring an industrial dispute to [a Labour Court, Tribunal or National Tribunal] under this Section or in a subsequent order, the appropriate Government has specified the points of dispute for adjudication, [the Labour Court or the Tribunal or the National Tribunal, as the case may be], shall confine its adjudication to those points and matter incidental thereto.

(5) Where a dispute concerning any establishment or establishments have been, or are to be, referred to a [Labour Court, Tribunal or National Tribunal] under this Section and the appropriate Government is of opinion, whether on an application made to it in this behalf or otherwise, that the dispute is of such a nature that any other establishment, group or class or

establishments of a similar nature is likely to be interested in or affected by, such dispute, the appropriate Government may, at the time of making the reference or at any time thereafter but before the submission of the award, include in that reference such establishment, group, or class of establishments, whether or not at the time of such inclusion any dispute exists or is apprehended in that establishment, group or class of establishments.

(6) Where any reference has been made under sub-section (1A) to a National Tribunal, then notwithstanding anything contained in this Act, no Labour Court or Tribunal shall have jurisdiction to adjudicate upon any matter which is under adjudication before the National Tribunal, and accordingly,—

(a) if the matter under adjudication before the National Tribunal is pending in a proceeding before a Labour Court or Tribunal, the proceeding before the Labour Court or the Tribunal, as the case may be in so far as it relates to such matter, shall be deemed to have been quashed on such reference to the National Tribunal; and

(b) it shall not be lawful for the appropriate Government to refer the matter under adjudication before the National Tribunal to any Labor Court or tribunal for adjudication during the pendency of the proceeding in relation to such matter before the National Tribunal.

[*Explanation*—In this sub-section, "Labour Court" of "Tribunal" includes any Court or Tribunal or other authority constituted under any law relating to investigation and settlement of industrial disputes in force in any State.]

(7) Where any industrial dispute, in relation to which the Central Government is not the appropriate Government, is referred to a National Tribunal, then, notwithstanding anything contained in this Act, any reference in Sections 15, 17, 19, 33A, 33B and 36A to the appropriate Government in relation to such dispute shall be construed as a reference to the Central Government but, save as aforesaid and as otherwise expressly provided in this Act, any reference in any other provisions of this Act to the appropriate Government in relation to that dispute shall mean a reference to the State Government.]

(8) No proceedings pending before a Labour Court, Tribunal or National Tribunal in relation to an industrial dispute shall lapse merely by reason of the death of any of the parties to the dispute being a workman, and such Labour Court, Tribunal or National Tribunal shall complete such proceedings and submit its award to the appropriate Government.]

NOTES

Reference of disputes by appropriate Government—Appropriate Government has to determine whether *prima facie* an industrial dispute exists or is apprehended or the claim is frivolous or bogus in view of extraneous or irrelevant reasons and not for industrial peace and harmony. If this administrative power is not exercised on grounds germane or relevant to the exercise of the power, it is liable to be subject to judicial review – *Ram Avtar Sharma vs. State of Haryana,* AIR 1985 SC 915 : (1985)II LLJ 187.

An order of reference hastily drawn often gives rise to unnecessary disputes thus prolonging the life of the industrial adjudication. So the courts must attempt to construe the reference not too technically or in a pedantic manner but fairly and reasonably—*Express News Papers (P) Ltd. vs. Workmen,* AIR 1963 SC 569 : (1962)II 227 : (1962)5 FLR 205.

If the workman points out the defect in the domestic enquiry in this written claim statement before the Labour Court or the Tribunal, the management has the opportunity to not the defect and make request to the adjudicating forum to lead evidence to prove the charges in its written statement. If it does not choose to do so at that stage, it cannot be allowed to do so at any later stage of the proceeding by filing application for the purpose. If the employer makes a request for adducing evidence at later stage, before conclusion of the proceedings, he has to explain the delay as well as the reason for not making the request at the initial stage. If the reasons are unconvincing, the Tribunal would be justified in rejecting the request—*Sambhunath Goyal vs. Bank of Baroda,* AIR 1984 SC 289 : 1983 Lab IC 1697.

Order of reference is bad-in-law if it does not reflect contentions of respective parties — The reference proceeded on the basis that there was termination of service inspite of the contention of the management that for long unauthorised absence of the workman from duty, the workman was considered to have abandoned the job. In the circumstances, the only question left open for adjudication was whether the termination was legal or not. The Government having failed to consider the entire set of circumstances brought about by the management, the order of reference was bad in law—*Sitaram Vishnu Shirodkar vs. Administrator, Government of Goa & Others,* (1985)I LLJ 481.

Public Sector Corporations must not question maintainability of reference on technical grounds — When the Central Government in all solemnity, refers an industrial dispute of adjudication, a public sector corporation which is an instrumentally of the State should welcome decision by the Tribunal on merits so as to absolve itself of any charge of being a bad employer or of victimisation etc., and should not attempt to evade decision on merits by raising preliminary objections on rigid technical grounds and drag the women from Court to Court wasting public time and money – *S.K. Verma vs. Mahesh Chandra,* AIR 1984 SC 1462 : 1983 Lab IC 1983 : (1983)II LLJ 429.

Employers should not adopt technical and hyper technical pleas to tire out employees of the proceedings — It has been our sad experience to find employers trying to stifle the efforts of employees in their legitimate claims for benefits permissible under the law by tiring them out in the adjudication proceedings by raising technical and hyper technical pleas and dragging the proceeding on for years together on such peals. Employers should meet the case of employees squarely on merits and get them adjudicated quickly. This would help industrial peace – *H.D. Singh vs. Reserve Bank of India,* AIR 1986 SC 132.

Reference made without application of mind, if valid – Even though as to the factual existence of the industrial dispute and of the expediency to refer the dispute for adjudication, the government is the sole judge, yet any reference to the scheme of the Act leaves no manner of doubt that government must consider the relevant materials in forming its opinion on germane consideration. However, when the satisfaction is based on non-consideration of the relevant materials or considerations not germane to the issue, then the opinion requires to be interfered under Articles 226 or 227 of the Constitution of India — *Orient Paper Mills Sramik Congress vs. State of Orissa,* (1988)II LLJ 75.

When a company had taken a lenient and instead of termination of services, decide to demote a workman, the State Government had no material before it to consider the same as termination of services of the workmen before making any reference to Tribunal. Absence of such a material to arrive at the necessary satisfaction that there was an order of termination of services from the post of Principal Correspondent and a new appointment to the post of Staff Reporter indicates non-application of mind on the part of the State Government which warrants interference by the court exercising power under Article 226 of the Constitution of India — *M/s. Aaj Kaal Publishers Ltd. vs. State of West Bengal,* (1992)1 CHN 21 : (1991) 1 Cal LT 446.

S. 10A. Voluntary reference of disputes to disputes to arbitration – (1) Where any industrial dispute exists or is apprehended and the employer and the workman agree to refer the dispute to arbitration, they may, at any time before the dispute has been referred under Section 10 to a Labour Court or Tribunal or National Tribunal, by a written agreement, refer the dispute to arbitration and the reference shall be to such person or persons (including the presiding officer of a Labour Court or Tribunal or National Tribunal) as an arbitrator or arbitrators as may be specified in the arbitration agreement.

(1A) Where an arbitration agreement provides for a reference of the dispute to an even number or arbitrators, the agreement shall provide for the appointment of another person as umpire who shall enter upon the reference, if the arbitrators are equally divided in their opinion, and the award of the umpire shall prevail and shall be deemed to be the arbitration award for the purposes of this Act.

(2) An arbitration agreement referred to in sub-section (1) shall be in such form and shall be signed by the parties thereto in such manner as may be prescribed.

(3) A copy of the arbitration agreement shall be forwarded to the appropriate Government and the condition officer and the appropriate Government shall, within [one months] from the date of the receipt of such copy, publish the same in the *Official Gazette*.

(3A) Where an industrial dispute has been referred to arbitration and the appropriate Government is satisfied that the persons making the reference represent the majority of each party, the appropriate Government may, within the time referred to in sub-section (3), issue a notification in such manner as may be prescribed; and when any such notification is issued, the employers and workmen who are not parties to the arbitration agreement but are concerned in the dispute, shall be given an opportunity of presenting their case before the arbitrator or arbitrators.

(4) The arbitrator or arbitrators shall investigate the dispute and submit to the appropriate Government the arbitration award signed by the arbitrator or all the arbitrators, as the case may be.

[(4A) Where an industrial dispute has been referred to arbitration and a notification has been issued under sub-section (3A), the appropriate Government may, by order, prohibit the continuance of any strike or lockout in connection with such dispute which may be in existence on the date of the reference.]

(5) Nothing in the Arbitration Act, 1940 (10 of 1940), shall apply to arbitration this Section.

NOTES

Publication of arbitration agreement, if mandatory—The question whether the arbitration agreement is to be published in the *Official Gazette* as required under Section 10A (3) of the Act came up for consideration in the case of— *Karnal Leather Karamchari Sanghatan vs. Liberty Footwear Co.*, AIR 1990 SC 247 : (1989)II LLJ 550 : (1989) 4 SCC 448 : (1989) 59 FLR 547. In determining the question the Supreme Court does not find the reason although it has discussed a number of judgement of different High Courts in the State cases. The Supreme Court came to the conclusion that in the context in which the word "shall" has been used, there is little doubt about obligation to publish the agreement in the *Official Gazette*. See also

Kathyee Cotton Mills Ltd. vs. District Labour Officer, (1989)1 Lab LJ 417 and *Workmen of Woodlands Hotel vs. K. Srinivasa Rao,* (1972)42 FJR 223.

Time for publication—The voluntary arbitration is a part of infrastructure of dispensation of justice in the industrial adjudication. The Act seeks to achieve social justice on the basis of collective bargaining which is a technique by which dispute as to conditions of the employment is resolved amicably by agreement rather than coercion. The dispute is settled peacefully and voluntarily although reluctantly between labour and management. The arbitrator thus falls within the purview of statutory tribunals. When a dispute is referred to arbitration, it is therefore necessary that the workers must be made aware of the dispute as well as the arbitrator whose award ultimately would bind them. They must know what is referred to arbitration, who is their arbitrator and what is in store for them. They must have an opportunity to share their views with each other and if necessary to place the same before the arbitrator. This is the need for collective bargaining and there cannot be collective bargaining without involving the workers. The Union only helps the workers in resolving their disputes with management but ultimately it would be for the workers to take decisions and suggest remedies. Thus, the Supreme Court held that the arbitration agreement must be published before the arbitrator considers the merits of the dispute. Non-compliance with this requirement would be fatal to the arbitral award. *Karnal Leather Karmachari Sanghatam vs. Liberty Footwear Co.* AIR 1990 SC 247 : (1989) II LLJ 550 : (1989)4 SCC 448 : (1989)59 FLR 547.

Voluntary arbitration and Tribunal arbitration — If alternative remedies— The Supreme Court in the aforesaid case of *Karnal Leather Karmachari Sanghatan* (supra) held that Sections 10 and 10A of the Act are the alternative remedies to settle an industrial dispute. An industrial dispute can either be referred to an Industrial Tribunal for adjudication under Section 10, or the parties can enter into a arbitration agreement and refer it to an arbitrator under Section 10A. But once the parities have chosen their remedies under Section 10A, the Government cannot refer the dispute for adjudication under Section 10. The Supreme Court in the aforesaid case refused to sustain a reference made by the government under Section 10(1) when there is an arbitration agreement under Section 10 of the Act.

CHAPTER IV
PROCEDURE, POWERS AND DUTIES OF AUTHORITIES

S. 11. Procedure and powers of conciliation officers, Boards, Courts and Tribunals —(1) Subject to any rules that may be made in this behalf, an arbitrator, a Board, Court, Labour Court, Tribunal or National

Tribunal shall follow such procedures as the arbitrator or other authority concerned may think fit.]

(2) A conciliation officer or a member of a Board, [or Court or the presiding officer of a Labour Court, Tribunal or National Tribunal] may for the purpose of inquiry into any existing or apprehended industrial dispute, after giving reasonable notice, enter the premises occupied by any establishment to which the dispute relates.

(3) Every Board, Court, [Labour Court, Tribunal and National Tribunal] shall have the same powers as are vested in a Civil Court under the Code of Civil Procedure, 1908 (5 of 1908), when trying a suit, in respect of the following matters, namely :

(a) enforcing the attendance of any person and examine him on oath;

(b) compelling the production of documents which are material objects;

(c) issuing commissions for the examination of witnesses;

(d) in respect of such other matters as may be prescribed;

and every inquiry or investigation by a Board, Court, [Labour Court, Tribunal or National Tribunal], shall be deemed to be a judicial proceeding within the meaning of Sections 193 and 228 of the Indian Penal Code.

(4) A conciliation officer [may enforce the attendance of any person for the purpose of examination of such person or call for] and inspect any document which he has ground for considering to be relevant to the industrial dispute [or to be necessary for the purpose of verifying the implementation of any award or carrying out any other duty imposed on him under this Act, and for the aforesaid purposes, the conciliation officer shall have the same powers as are vested in a Civil Court under the Code of Civil Procedure, 1908 (5 of 1908) [in respect of enforcing the attendance of any person and examining him or of compelling the production of documents.

(5) A Court, Labour Court, Tribunal or National Tribunal may, if it so thinks fit, appoint one or more person having special knowledge of the matter under consideration as assessor or assessors to advise it in the proceeding before it.

(6) All conciliation officers, members of a Board or Court and the presiding officers of a Labour Court, Tribunal or National Tribunal shall be deemed to be public servants within meaning of Section 21 of the Indian Penal Code (45 of 1860).

(7) Subject to any rules made under this Act, the costs of, and incidental to, any proceeding before a Labour Court, Tribunal or National Tribunal shall be in the discretion of that Labour Court, Tribunal or National Tribunal and the Labour Court, Tribunal or National Tribunal, as the case may be, shall have full power to determine by and to whom and to what extent and subject to what conditions, if any, such costs are to be paid, and

to give all necessary directions for the purposes aforesaid and such costs may, on application made to the appropriate Government by the person entitled, by recovered by that Government in the same manner as an arrear of land revenue.]

[(8) Every [Labour Court. Tribunal or National Tribunal,] Shall be deemed to be Civil Court for the purposes of [Sections 345, 346 and 348 of the Code of Criminal Procedure, 1973 (2 of 1974).]

NOTES

Procedure of adjudication in Labour Courts etc.—Tribunals exercising quasi-judicial function are not courts. They are not bound to follow the procedure prescribed for trials in courts; nor are they bound by strict rules of evidence. They can obtain material informations through all channels without being fettered by rules & procedures governing proceedings in courts. The only obligation which the law casts on them is that such informations received must not be relied upon unless those are put to the party against whom it is to be use and the party is given opportunity to explain them — *State of M.P. vs. C.S. Waishampayan*, AIR 1961 SC 1623.

Jurisdiction of Civil Court to entertain labour disputes – The Civil Court shall have no jurisdiction if the dispute is an industrial and relates to the enforcement of a right or an obligation created under the Industrial Disputes Act. If, however, the dispute is industrial arising out of a right or liability created under the general common law and not under the Industrial Disputes Act, the jurisdiction of the civil court is in alternative leaving it to the election of the suitor to choose, the forum — *Premier Automobiles Ltd. vs. Kamlekar Shantaram Wadke*, 1976 SCC (L & S) 70.

Jurisdiction of Civil Court relating to relief to reinstatement and back wages – The Industrial Disputes Act not only confers the right on a worker for reinstatement and back wages if the order of termination or dismissal is not in accordance with the Standing Orders but also provides a detailed procedure and machinery for getting this relief. Therefore, an adequate remedy is available to the workmen under the scheme of the Act itself which provides for relief of reinstatement and back wages. Where the said relief was sought before the Civil Court by filing the suit, the scheme of the Act clearly excludes the jurisdiction of the Civil Court by implication in respect of remedies which are available under this Act. In these circumstances, the Supreme Court in the case of *Jitendra Nath vs. Empire of India and Ceylone Tea Co.*, AIR 1990 SC 255 : (1989) 3 SCC 582 : 1989 SCC (L & S) 552 : (1989) 4 SLR 214 held that civil court had no jurisdiction to entertain such a suit as there is an apparent implied exclusion of its jurisdiction — *Dhulabhai vs. State of M.P.*, AIR 1969 SC 78 followed.

Award of compensation for loss of future employment – Keeping in view the expressed desire of the workmen the court have awarded monetary compensation to the workmen taking into account, wages and benefits like bonus, ex-gratia, payment for loss of employment for fifty-two months, gratuity, leave salary and compensation for loss of future employment. The total amount of monetary compensation that has been awarded to each of the workmen is in the range of one lac. The Supreme Court in the case of *Workmen of Bharat Fritz Werner vs. B.F. Werner,* AIR 1990 SC 1054 : (1990) 3 SCC 565 did not find any infirmity in the determination that has been made by the High Court with regard to the aforesaid amount and rejected the contention that monetary compensation was inadequate.

S. [11A. Powers of Labour Courts, Tribunals and National Tribunal to give appropriate relief in case of discharge or dismissal of workmen — Where an industrial dispute relating to the discharge or dismissal of a workman has been referred to a Labour Court, Tribunal or National Tribunal for adjudication and, in the course of the adjudication proceedings, the Labour Court, Tribunal or National Tribunal, as the case may be, is satisfied that the order of discharge or dismissal was not justified, it may, by its award, set aside the order of discharge or dismissal and direct reinstatement of the workman on such terms and conditions, if any, as it thinks fit, or give such other relief to the workman including the award of any lesser punishment in lieu of discharge or dismissal as the circumstances of the case may require :

Provided that in any Proceeding under this Section the Labour Court, Tribunal on National Tribunal, as the case may be, shall rely only on the materials on record and shall not take any fresh evidence in relation to the matter.]

NOTES

Purpose and import of Section – Section 11A was inserted in the industrial Dispute Act by the Amendment Act of XXXXV of 1971. In interpretating the provisions of the said section the Calcutta High Court in the case of—*Mihir Kumar Hazra Chowdhury vs. Union of India,* 93 CWN 572 : 1983 Lab IC (NOC) 45 (Cal) held that in discharging the statutory obligation of considering the question of reference the Government should not have assessed the merits of the order. Since the dismissal from service is an industrial dispute under Section 2A of the Act, a reference of such dispute is necessary because it may ensure to benefit the concerned workman because a tribunal even after coming to the finding that the order of dismissal was not otherwise vitiated, may held the case does not warrant the extreme punishment of dismissal from service and as such order of dismissal did not justify in the facts and circumstances of the case.

The repugnancy between this Act and the Shops and Establishment Act — The Supreme Court in the case of — *National Engineering Industries Limited vs. Shri Kishan*, AIR 1988 SC 329 : 1988 Supp 80 : 1988 Lab IC 384 : 56 FLR 148 held that where a person has been working as an internal auditor on a monthly salary whose main duties were mainly reporting and checking up on behalf of the management. The said person would be a "workman" within the meaning of Section 2(s) of the Act and not supervisor after indicating the nature of duties performed by him. The Court did not find him doing any kind of supervisory work as a report of a checking clerk is not a supervisory. He was undoubtedly checking up on behalf of the employer but he had no independent right or authority to take the decision and his decision did not bind the company.

Adjudication of dispute by stages on preliminary point and merit discouraged by Supreme Court — There was a time when it was thought that preliminary issues should be decided first. But the time has arrived for reversal of that policy where delay may lead to misery or jeopardise industrial peace, Tribunals should decide all issues in dispute at the same time. Tribunals and Courts called upon to decide preliminary question must consider whether part adjudication is really necessary and whether it will not lead to other woeful consequence – *D.P. Maheshwari vs. Delhi Administration,* (1983)II LLJ 426 SC.

The aforesaid case was also considered by the Calcutta High Court in the case of — *Indian Cable vs. Fifth Industrial Tribunal,* 93 CWN 486 : (1989) 1 Cal HN 204. Upon consideration of the aforesaid judgement of the Supreme Court and different High Courts the Calcutta High Court followed the decision of the Supreme Court and held that threshold part adjudication of the matter should be made. In other words, the preliminary point whether the person is a workman or not shall be heard along with merits. The judgement has also emphasized upon woeful consequences which a person thrown out of employment is bound to face and the Courts adopted such a tribunal would suddenly cause prejudice to the parties. The High Court has followed the reasoning of the Supreme Court that decision on jurisdictional fact would hamper the expeditious disposal of the matter affecting a workman. The procedure has to evolve because the advantage was being taken by the employer in holding up the proceeding for number of years.

However, the judgement of the Supreme Court in — *D. P. Maheshwari* (supra) has been distinguished in the case of – *Hooghly Dock & Port Engineers Ltd. vs. Third Industrial Tribunal, West Bengal,* (1992)2 CHN 161 where the Calcutta High Court directed to dispose of the preliminary issue as the fact of reference is dependent on determination of preliminary issue. In that case the question arose whether the workmen concerned were entitled to any increase in their wages under the valid tripartite settlement. While distinguishing the judgement of the Supreme Court, the Court held that the judgement in the case of — *D.P. Maheswari* (supra) is a case of industrial dispute concerning dismissal or imposition of major penalties. Therefore, the proposition laid down by the Supreme Court in the above case does not apply to the facts of the case under consideration, inasmuch as this is not a case where if the preliminary issue is decided first it will bring misery to the workmen. It was further held that the practice of deciding preliminary issue alongwith the merits of the case will not be followed in all cases.

Power of Labour Courts etc. to give appropriate relief to discharged or dismissed workman — Not doubt it has been emphasised by the Supreme Court in its various decision that an employer is expected to hold a proper enquiry before dismissing or discharging the workman. If that requirement is satisfied an employer will by and large escape the attack that he has acted arbitrarily or *mala fide* or by way of victimisation. If there has been no enquiry held by the employer or if the enquiry is held to be defective, it is open to the employer to adduce evidence for the first time before the Tribunal to justify the order of discharge or dismissal – *Workmen vs. Firestone Tyre and Rubber Co. of India (P) Ltd.*, (1973)I LLJ 278 : 1973 Lab IC 851 SC.

If a proper enquiry is conducted by the employer and a correct finding is arrived at regarding the misconduct, even though the Tribunal may differ from those conclusions, it has to give very cogent reasons for rejecting the view of the employer. Further, the Tribunal is now at liberty to hold that the punishment is not justified because the misconduct alleged and proved is such that it does not warrant dismissal or discharge. To come to a conclusion either way the Tribunal will have to reappraise the evidence for itself – *Workmen vs. Firestone Tyre and Rubber Co. of India (P) Ltd.*, (1973)I LLJ 278 : 1973 Lab IC 851 SC.

If the question of reinstatement and or compensation is referred to the Tribunal for adjudication, the question of granting interim relief till the decision would be a matter incidental thereto under Section 10(4) and need not be specifically referred to it – *Hotel Imperial, New Delhi vs. Hotel Workers Union*, AIR 1959 SC 1342 : (1959-60) 17 FJR 39 : (1960)1 SCR 476.

The proviso to the Section IIA emphasises that the Tribunal, in adjudicating on the misconduct, the punishment and the relief to be granted to the workman must arrive at his conclusion on the basis of the "materials on record" before it. What are those materials on record have been mentioned in Section 11A. The Tribunal cannot itself call for further or fresh evidence which an appellate authority is competent to do – *Workmen vs. Fire Stone Tyre and Rubber Co. of India (P) Ltd.*, AIR 1973 SC 1227 : (1973)I LLJ 278.

In the instant case, the Supreme Court observed that the punishment awarded to the appellant was shocking disproportionate to the charge framed against the workman. Victimisation or unfair labour practice could well be inferred from the conduct of the management in awarding the punishment of dismissal to the workman for simply abusing some workers and officers. The Supreme Court ordered reinstatement of the workman with full back wages and other benefits including continuity in service. – *Ved Prakash Gupta vs. Delton Cable India (P) Ltd.*, AIR 1984 SC 914 : (1984)I LLJ 546.

When the Tribunal can deviate from the normal rule of reinstatement — The Tribunal can deviate from the normal rule of reinstatement upon a careful consideration of important factors such as fair play towards the employee and the interest of the employer including consideration of discipline in the establishment. The conduct of the workman which led to his dismissal, the nature of his duties, the nature of the establishment and the grounds for which the order of dismissal was quashed are other factors, to be considered in exercising the discretion – *Panitole Tea Estate vs. Workmen,* AIR 1971 SC 217 : (1971)I LLJ 233.

Powers of the Labour Court etc. to grant interim relief – When the matters in respect of the industrial dispute are wrongful dismissal of the workmen, their reinstatement and in the event of an order of reinstatement, payment of arrear wages from the date of dismissal to the date of reinstatement, it cannot be said that the tribunal has no jurisdiction to consider the question of grant of interim pay and allowance – AIR 1952 Punj 134.

The Tribunal while adjudicating upon the question of reinstatement or compensation in respect of discharged or dismissed workman can grant interim relief to the workman if it is admissible, as a matter incidental to the main question in terms of Section 10 (4) of the Industrial Disputes Act, 1974 – *Hotel Imperial, New Delhi vs. Hotel Workers Union,* AIR 1959 SC 1342.

Direction of the High Court – Section 11A of the Act empowers the Industrial Tribunal to go into the question whether the order of discharge or dismissal passed against a workman is justified or not and permits the Tribunal to set aside such order as the circumstances of the case may require. Therefore, it was also open to the High Court to consider that should be the adequate punishment for the misconduct found to have been committed by the workman and take the view that the acts of misconduct found proved against the workman were not such as to warrant dismissal and denial of one half of the back wages for the period of about six years was adequate punishment. The aforesaid direction were given by the High Court while exercising the powers which are to be exercised by the Industrial Tribunal – *Workman of Bharat Fritz Werner (P) Ltd. vs. Bharat Fritz Werner (P) Ltd.,* AIR 1990 SC 1054; (1990) 3 SSC 565 : (1990) 60 FLR 482.

S. 12. Duties of Conciliation Officers — (1) Where any industrial dispute exists or is apprehended, the conciliation officer may, or where the dispute relates to a public utility service and a notice under Section 22 has been given, shall hold conciliation proceedings in the prescribed manner.

(2) The conciliation officer shall, for the purpose of bringing about a settlement of the dispute, without delay investigate the dispute and all matters affecting the merits and the right settlement thereof and may do all such things as he thinks fit for the purpose of including the parties to come to a fair and amicable settlement of the dispute.

(3) If a settlement of the dispute or of any of the matters in dispute is arrived at in the course of the conciliation proceedings the conciliation officer shall send a report thereof to the appropriate Government [or an officer authorised in this behalf by the appropriate Government] together with a memorandum of the settlement signed by the parties to the dispute.

(4) If no such settlement is arrived at, the conciliation officer shall, as soon as practicable after the close of the investigation, send to the appropriate Government a full report setting forth the steps taken by him for ascertaining the facts and circumstances relating to the dispute and for bringing about a settlement thereof, together with a full statement of such facts and circumstances, and the reasons on account of which, in his opinion, a settlement couldnot be arrived at.

(5) If, on a consideration of the report referred to in sub-section (4), the appropriate Government is satisfied that there is a case for reference to a Board, [Labour Court, Tribunal or National Tribunal], it may make such reference. Where the appropriate Government does not make such a reference it shall record and communicate to the parties concerned its reasons thereof.

(6) A report under this Section shall be submitted within fourteen days of the commencement of the conciliation proceedings or within such shorter period as may be fixed by the appropriate Government :

[Provided that, [subject to the approval of the conciliation officer], the time for the submission of the report may be extended by such period as may be agreed upon in writing by all the parties to the dispute].

NOTES

Government's power to make or refuse reference — The Government is competent to decline to make a reference. But the order must be supported by reasons and such reasons must not be irrelevant or extraneous to the decision. Further such reasons must not result in adjudication of the dispute. When the order does not suffer from these defects, it is outside the scope of judicial scrutiny — *C. Munichow-dappa vs. State of Karnataka*, (1985) LLJ 364.

State Government has jurisdiction to reconsider earlier order by which it had refused to refer an industrial dispute for adjudication – *Ramlal vs. Labour Court, Patiala & Others,* (1986)11 LLJ 235.

Duty of Conciliation Officer of giving opportunity of hearing to management — The reference under Section 10 of the Act was held by the Tribunal to be incompetent as the cause of dismissed employee was not espoused by substantial number of workmen. The conciliation officer having submitted a failure report under Section 12(4) of the Act, the Government after applying its mind referred the dispute for adjudication to the Tribunal. Since the first reference was found to be an incompetent on technical ground, it was necessary for the dismissed workman to go before the conciliation officer once again for referring the existing dispute. Therefore, the Government was justified in proceeding on the basis of the failure report submitted to it and no further opportunity was required to be given by the conciliation officer to the management before submitting the report to the Government to make reference. The appropriate Government is to consider the report and decide whether a case for reference has been made out. If it is satisfied that there is a case for reference then only it will make a reference under Section 10 of the Act. The satisfaction of the Government that it is a fit case for reference has been arrived at when the earlier reference was made. When the Government after applying its mind referred the dispute for adjudication and when there was no new fact to be agitated before the conciliation officer in the second round, the dispute does not come to an end after the first reference was held to be incompetent. The nature and character of the dispute did not change. The Government acted erroneously in not referring to the provision of Section 2A of the Act in making the first reference. That was corrected and thereafter the second reference was made under Section 10 read with Section 2A of the Act. The conciliation officer in his second failure report has referred to the reasons why the first reference was held to be incompetent. The Tribunal did not enter into the merits of the case. When the first reference was held to be incompetent or not maintainable there was no reference at all. The Government is therefore justified on the basis of the second failure report submitted to it to make the reference to the existing industrial dispute between the workmen and the management. There being no fresh fact at the time of second reference, no further opportunity was required to be given by the conciliation officer to the management before he submitted report under Section 12(4) for the Second time in the light of what was happened after the first reference has been made. An order of reference under Section 10 of the Act is essentially an administrative act and the expediency of making reference is a matter lying entirely with the jurisdiction or the Act. In such view of the matter the Court in the case of - *Howrah Stores vs. Eighth Industrial Tribunal,* 93 CWN 240 held that reference made by the Government for the second time could not be held to be without jurisdiction solely on the ground that the management was not heard before the failure report was made by the conciliation officer.

S. 13. Duties of Board — (1) Where a dispute has been referred to a Board under this Act, it shall be the duty of the Board to endeavour to bring about a settlement of the same and for this purpose the Board shall, in such manner as it thinks fit and without delay, investigate the dispute and all matters affecting the merits and the right settlement thereof and may do all such things as it thinks fit for the purpose of inducing the parties to come to a fair and amicable settlement of the dispute.

(2) If a settlement of the dispute or of any of the matters in dispute is arrived at in the course of the conciliation proceedings, the Board shall send a report thereof to the appropriate Government together with a memorandum of the settlement signed by the parties to the dispute.

(3) If no such settlement is arrived at, the Board shall,as soon as practicable after the close of the investigation, send to the appropriate Government a full report setting forth the proceedings and steps taken by the Board for ascertaining the facts and circumstances relating to the dispute and for bringing about a settlement thereof, together with a full statement of such facts and circumstances, its findings thereon, the reasons on account of which, in its opinion, a settlement could not be arrived at and its recommendations for the determination of the dispute.

(4) If, on the receipt of a report under sub-section (3) in respect of a dispute relating to a public utility service, the appropriate Government does not make a reference to a [Labour Court, Tribunal or National Tribunal] under Section 10, it shall record and communicate to the parties concerned its reasons therefor.

(5) The Board shall submit its report under this Section within two months of the date, [on which the dispute was referred to it] or within such shorter period as may be fixed by the appropriate Government :

Provided that the appropriate Government may from time to time extend the time for the submission of the report by such further periods not exceeding two months in the aggregate :

Provided further that the time for the submission of the report may be extended by such period as may be agreed on in writing by all the parties to the dispute.

S. 14. Duties of Courts — A Court shall inquire into the matters referred to it and report thereon to the appropriate Government ordinarily within a period of six months from the commencement of its inquiry.

S. 15. Duties of Labour Courts, Tribunals and National Tribunals— Where an industrial dispute has been referred to a Labour Court, Tribunal or National Tribunal for adjudication, it shall hold its proceedings expeditiously and shall, [within the period specified in the order referring such industrial dispute or the further period extended under the second proviso to sub-section (2A) of Section 10], submit its award to the appropriate Government.

NOTES

Object behind the amendment by the Central and State Act — The object behind the amendment as introduced by the Section 10 of I.D. (Amendment) Act, 1982 is to shorten the agony, the object behind the State amendment is to provide sustenance and nourishment to enable the workman to back up his cause before the industrial forum. The Calcutta High Court in the aforesaid case. *The Statesmen Ltd. vs. Second Industrial Tribunal,* 95 CWN 861 : (1991)1 CHN 80 (supra), held that the two provisions cannot be said to occupy the same field. In view of the aforesaid reason the Court held that Section 15(2)(b) of the 1947 Act as inserted by the West Bengal State Legislature by the Amendment Act of 1980 is not rendered inoperative by the subsequent amendment made by the Central Legislature in Section 10(2A) of the Act as inserted by Section 8 of the Act XXXXVI of 1982 and Section 17 of the Parent Act.

Employee in gainful employment during the interregnum between the date of dismissal and date of impugned order, if entitled to benefit— The Court in the aforesaid case of *The Statesman Ltd.* (supra) refused to deprive the workman of the benefits conferred upon him otherwise under the provisions of Section 15(2)(b) although the workman had been in gainful employment during the interregnum between the date of dismissal and date of impugned order.

West Bengal (Amendment) Act, 1980 — Section 15(2)(b) as introduced by the West Bengal Industrial Disputes (Second Amendment) Act, 1980 unmistakably casts an obligation upon the Tribunal to determine the interim relief admissible to the workmen with utmost despatch but it remains silent as to the date or event from which the interim relief would be admissible. The Calcutta High Court in the case of *General Electric Company of India Ltd. vs. Fifth Industrial Tribunal,* (1990)1 CHN 453 : 92 CWN 464 : (1987) 2 Cal LJ 305 (DB) interpreted this Section keeping in view the colour, content and context of the statute as well as bearing in mind that it is a piece of labour and welfare legislation. This Section has been enacted with a view to ameliorate the sufferings of an indigent workman, who has not only lost the source of his income but also the right to fight his cause against his employer. As this Section is required to respond to such urgent social and economic demand, it is the bounden duty of the Court to give a liberal and beneficial interpretation, subject to the limitation of its own language. Following the principle enunciated by the Supreme Court in the case of *Jindal Ltd. vs. Appellate Authority,* AIR 1984 SC 1842 the Court has legitimately reached the conclusion that the interim relief can be granted to a workman from the date of his dismissal.

Writ Court – if justified to interest with the finding of fact by the Tribunal — The writ Court not being a Court of Appeal should not try to upset a finding of fact arrived at, on an appreciation of evidence, by the appropriate forum by substituting its own wisdom in the place and stead of the wisdom of the trying authority by reappreciating the evidence. This is simply not permissible. There being no apparent error of law or any finding or any palpable perversity by learned Tribunal, writ Court should not attempt to sit in appeal over the finding of the tribunal — *The Statesman Ltd. vs. The Second Industrial Tribunal of West Bengal,* 95 CWN 861 : (1991)1 CHN 80.

Reference – award passed by the Tribunal, interference of hyper-technical grounds not permissible — The object of enacting the Act and of making provision therein to refer dispute to Tribunals for settlement is to bring about industrial peace. Whenever a reference was made by a Government to an Industrial Tribunal it has to be presumed ordinarily that there is a genuine industrial dispute between the parties which requires to be resolved by adjudication. In all such cases an attempt should be made by Courts exercising powers of judicial review to sustain as far as possible the awards made by Tribunal instead of picking holes here and therein the awards on trivial points and ultimately frustrating the entire adjudication process before the Tribunals by striking down awards on hyper-technical grounds – *Calcutta Port Shramik Union vs. The Calcutta River Transport Association,* AIR 1988 SC 2168.

S. 16. Form of report or award — (1) The report of a Board of Court shall be in writing and shall be signed by all the members of the Board or Court, as the case may be :

Provided that nothing in this Section shall be deemed to prevent any member of the Board of Court from recording any minute of dissent from a report or from any recommendation made therein.

(2) The award of Labour Court or Tribunal or National Tribunal shall be in writing and shall be signed by its presiding officer.

S. 17. Publication of reports and awards — (1) Every report of a Board or Court together with any minute of dissent recorded therewith, every arbitration award and every award of a Labour Court, Tribunal or National Tribunal shall, within a period of thirty days from the date of its receipt by the appropriate Government, be published in such manner as the appropriate Government thinks fit.

(2) Subject to the provisions of Section 17A, the award published under sub-section (1) shall be final and shall not be called in question by any Court in any manner whatsoever.

S. 17A. Commencement of the award — (1) An award (including an arbitration award) shall become enforceable on the expiry of thirty days from the date of its publication under Section 17 :

Provided that —

(a) if the appropriate Government is of opinion, in any case where the award has been given by a Labour Court or Tribunal in relation to an industrial dispute to which it is a party; or

(b) if the Central Government is of opinion, in any case where the award has been given by a National Tribunal,

that it will be inexpedient on public grounds affecting national economy or social justice to give effect to the whole or any part of the award; the appropriate Government, or as the case may be, the Central Government may, by notification in the *Official Gazette,* declare that the award shall not become enforceable on the expiry of the said period of thirty days.

(2) Where any declaration has been made in relation to an award under the proviso to sub-section (1), the appropriate Government or the Central Government may, within ninety days from the date of publication of the award under Section 17, make an order rejecting or modifying the award, and shall, on the first available opportunity, lay the award together with a copy of the order before the legislature of the State, if the order has been made by a State Government, or before Parliament, if the order has been made by the Central Government.

(3) Where any award as rejected or modified by an order made under sub-section (2) is laid before the Legislature of a State or before Parliament, such award shall become enforceable on the expiry of fifteen days from the date on which it is so laid; and where no order under sub-section (2) is made in pursuance of a declaration under the proviso to sub-section (1), the award shall become enforceable on the expiry of the period of ninety days referred to in sub-section (2).

(4) Subject to the provisions of sub-section (1) and sub-section (3) regarding the enforceability of an award, the awards shall come into operation with effect from such date as may be specified therein, but where no date is so specified, it shall come into operation on the date when the award becomes enforceable under sub-section (1), or sub-section (3), as the case may be.

NOTES

Award - fixation of date, matter of discretion of Tribunal - interference when justified — Under Section. 17A(4) of Act it is a matter of discretion for the Tribunal to decide having regard to the circumstances of each case from which date award should come into operation and general rule can be laid down to the date from which the Tribunal should bring its award into force and Court shall not interfere with the order of the Tribunal in that behalf unless substantial ground is made out showing unreasonable exercises on its part. In the absence of any material placed before the Tribunal by either party as to whether profits earned by the company for the relevant years had been disbursed or were still available with the company at the time of making the award and a statement showing decreasing trend in the financial position of the company, which is a relevant factor on the question of granting retrospectivity to the award, the discretion exercised by the Tribunal in not giving any retrospective effect to the revision in wages scales and dearness allowances cannot be said to be an unreasonable exercise of the power by the Tribunal — *The Workmen of Metro Theatre Ltd., Bombay vs. M/s. Metro Theatre Ltd., Bombay,* AIR 1981 SC 1685 : (1981)3 SCC 596 : 1981 Lab JC 1230.

S. [17B. Payment of all full wages to workman pending proceedings in higher courts – Where in any case, a Labour Court, Tribunal or National Tribunal by its award directs reinstatement of any workman and the employer prefers any proceedings against such award in a High Court or the Supreme Court, the employer shall be liable to pay such workman, during the period of pendency of such proceedings in the High Court or the Supreme Court, full wages last drawn by him, inclusive of any maintenance allowance admissible to him under any rule if the workman had not been employed in any establishment during such period and an affidavit by such workman had been filed to that effect in such Court :

Provided that where it is proved to the satisfaction of the High Court or the Supreme Court that such workman had been employed and had been receiving adequate remuneration during any such period or part thereof, the Court shall order that no wages shall be payable under this Section for such period or part, as the case may be].

NOTES

Where the Tribunal has ordered reinstatement of the workman with full back wages and the employer has moved the High Court or the Supreme Court challenging the award, the benefit of the award of reinstatement should not be deferred and the workman should be permitted to utilise the benefit of the award. Section 17B does not at all support the view that the benefit of the Section is applicable only when the challenge to the award is rejected *Indian Explosives Ltd. vs. 4th Industrial Tribunal, W.B.,* 1987 Lab IC 525.

Criteria to be fulfilled for making application — While dealing with an application under the said Section the Calcutta High Court in the case of — *Bata India Limited vs. Seventh Industrial Tribunal,* 94 CWN 1015 : (1991)1 Cal LT (HC) 169 indicated the three criteria to be fulfilled before entertaining such an application by the Court. First there must be an award, secondly award must be one of reinstatement and thirdly, workmen must satisfy the Court that he was not otherwise gainfully employed in another establishment during the material period. The application does not contain any averment of not being gainfully employed elsewhere. In matters under Section 33(2)(b) of the Act there is neither any award nor any order of reinstatement. The order of dismissal does not take effect until approval is accorded to it by the Tribunal. If there is no dismissal the question of reinstatement does not arise. Therefore application under Section 17B is not maintainable.

As introduced by Amendment Act XXXXVI of 1982 – S. 17B confers a new jurisdiction as it is a codification in statutory form of a right available to the workmen to get back wages when certain given conditions are satisfied. There are no words in the Section to compel the Court to hold that it cannot operate retrospectively. Before the said Section was introduced there was no bar for the Court for awarding wages. Of course the workmen had no right to claim. This Section recognise such a right to construe it in a manner detrimental to workmen would be to defeat its object. The Supreme Court in the case of – *Bharat Singh vs. Management of New Delhi Tuberculosis Centre,* AIR 1986 SC 842 held that this Section applies even to awards passed on August 21, 1984, if they have not become final.

S. 18. Persons on whom settlements and awards are binding – [(1) A settlement arrived at by agreement between the employer and workman otherwise than in the course of conciliation proceeding shall be binding on the parties to the agreement.]

(2) [Subject to the provisions of sub-section (3), an arbitration award] which has become enforceable shall be binding on the parties to the agreement who referred to dispute to arbitration.]

[(3)] A settlement arrived at in the course of conciliation proceedings under this Act [or an arbitration award in a case where a notification has been issued under sub-section (3A) of Section 10A] or [an award of a Labour Court, Tribunal or National Tribunal] which has become enforceable] shall be binding on –

(*a*) all parties to the industrial dispute;

(*b*) all other parties summoned to appear in the proceedings as parties to the dispute, unless the Board, [arbitrator], [Labour Court, Tribunal or National Tribunal'] as the case may be, records the opinion that they were so summoned without proper cause;

(*c*) where a party referred to in clause (*a*) or clause (*b*) is an employer, his heirs, successors or assigns in respect of the establishment to which the dispute relates;

(*d*) where a party referred to in clause *(a)* or clause *(b)* is composed of workmen, all persons who were employed in the establishment or part of the establishment, as the case may be, to which the dispute relates on the date of the dispute and all persons who subsequently become employed in that establishment or part.

NOTES

Settlement effected through conciliation proceedings, if binds members of dissenting union – If one faction of workmen in the dispute refuses to concur with the terms of the settlement accepted by the other faction, what the conciliation officer has to do is to make a report to the Government under Section 12(4) of the I.D. Act. If he does not do so and make a memorandum of settlement signed by the employer and representatives of one faction, the document cannot be called a settlement as envisaged by Section 12 of the Act and it cannot bind the members of the dissenting faction – *V.M. Nair vs. Hindustan Latex Ltd.,* 1987 Lab IC 950.

If the settlement has been arrived at by a vast majority of the concerned workers with their eyes open and was also accepted by them in its totality, it must be presumed to be just and fair and not liable to be ignored while deciding the reference merely because a small number of workers were not parties to it or refused to accept it or because the Tribunal was of the opinion that the workers deserved a marginal higher emoluments for them, this has thought they did. A settlement cannot be weighted in any golden scales and the question whether it is just and fair has to be answered on the basis of principals duty from those which come into play would industrial dispute is under adjudication. Following the observation laid down in the case of *Herbertsons Ltd. vs. Workmen of Herbertsons Ltd.,* (1977)2 SCR 15: AIR 1977 SC 322. The Supreme Court held that settlement as a whole was just and fair – *M/s. Tata Engineering & Locomotive Co. Ltd. vs. Their Workmen,* AIR 1981 SC 2163 : (1981)4 SCC 627 : (1981) 43 Fac LR 354.

Power implied for addition of parties – The Tribunal cannot exercise the power implied in Section 18(3)(b) so as to widen materially the scope of the reference itself, because basically the Tribunal gets the jurisdiction to deal with an industrial dispute solely from the order of reference under Section 10 of the Act. Such power can be exercised if it appears to the Tribunal that the party to the industrial dispute mentioned in the order of reference cannot completely or adequately represent the interest either on the side of the employer or on the side of the employees. Where the employer named in a reference does not make any representation of the interest of the employer as such, the other person interested in the undertaking of the employer may be added. It is also open to the Tribunal to join such other interest as it deem may necessary if the unions mentioned in the reference fails to represent all the employees of the undertaking. The Supreme Court in the case of – *Hochtief Gammon vs. Industrial Tribunal,* (1964)9 FLR 101 : (1964)II LLJ 460 : (1950-67)4 SCLJ 2374 has laid down the test for exercise of such power and held that though the said sub-section postulates existence of such an implied power in the Tribunal such power is required to be exercised after paying due regard to the limited nature of the said implied power AIR 1954 Mad 369 and AIR 1961 Cal 60.

S. 19. Period of operation of settlements and awards – (1) A settlement [9]* * * shall come into operation on such date as is agreed upon by the parties to the dispute, and if no date is agreed upon, on the date on which the memorandum of the settlement is signed by the parties to the dispute.

(2) Such settlement shall be binding for such period as is agreed upon by the parties, and if no such period is agreed upon, for a period of six months [from the date on which the memorandum of settlement is signed by the partes of the dispute], and shall continue to be binding on the parties after the expiry of the period aforesaid, until the expiry of two months from the date on which a notice in writing of an intention to terminate the settlement is given by one of the parties to the other party or parties of the settlement.

(3) An award shall, subject to the provisions of this Section, remain in operation for a period of one year [from the date on which the award becomes enforceable under Section 17A] :

Provided that the appropriate Government may reduce the said period and fix such period as it thinks fit :

Provided further that the appropriate Government may, before the expiry of the said period, extend the period of operation by any period not exceeding one year at a time as it thinks fit so, however, that the total period of operation of any award does not exceed three years from the date on which it came into operation.

(4) Where the appropriate Government, whether of its own motion or on the application of any party bound by the award, considers that since the award was made, there has been a material change in the circumstances on which it was based, the appropriate Government may refer the award or a part of it [to a Labour Court, if the award was that of a Labour Court or to a Tribunal, if the award was that of a Tribunal or of a National Tribunal] for decision whether the period of operation should not, by reason of such change, be shortened and the decision of [Labour Court or the Tribunal, as the case may be], on such reference shall [15]* * * be final.

(5) Nothing contained in sub-section (3), shall apply to any award which by its nature, terms or other circumstances does not impose, after it

has been given effect to, any continuing obligation on the parties bound by the award.

(6) Notwithstanding the expiry of the period of operation under sub-section (3), the award shall continue to be binding on the parties until a period of two months has elapsed from the date on which notice is given by any party bound by the award to the other party or parties intimating its intention to terminate the award.

[(7) No notice given under sub-section (2) or sub-section (6), shall have effect, unless it is given by a party representing the majority of persons bound by the settlement or award, as the case may be.]

NOTES

Termination of settlement, no formal notice necessary – No form is prescribed for terminating a settlement under Section 19(2) of the Industrial Disputes Act. No formal notice is necessary. Such notice can be inferred from the correspondence between the parties. Though a notice can be inferred from the correspondence there must be a certainty regarding the date of the notice because a settlement shall continue to operate for a period of two months from that date – *India Link Chain Mfg. Ltd. vs. Workmen,* AIR 1972 SC 343 : 1972 Lab IC 200.

In the absence of any form prescribed for terminating the settlement, the charter of demand was held to be substantial compliance with provisions of Section 19(2) – *Cochin State Power & Light Corporation Ltd. vs. Workmen,* (1964)I LLJ 100.

Notice of termination of award should mention a specific date – Though there is no particular form prescribed for termination of award, the notice must state intention to terminate the award with reference to a particular date. When the Union claims that the previous award has been terminated, it must establish the point of time of termination. Mere going on strike or submitting a charter of demand will not fulfil the requirements of Section 19(6) – *Thungabhadra Industries Ltd. vs. Workmen,* AIR 1973 SC 2272 : 1973 Lab IC 1227.

S. 20. Commencement and conclusion of proceedings – (1) A conciliation proceeding shall be deemed to have commenced on the date on which a notice of strike or lock-out under Section 22 is received by the conciliation officer or on the date of the order referring the dispute to a Board, as the case may be.

(2) A conciliation proceeding shall be deemed to have concluded –

(a) where a settlement is arrived at, when a memorandum of the settlement is signed by the parties to the dispute;

(b) where no settlement is arrived at, when the report of the conciliation officer is received by the appropriate Government or

when the report of the Board is published under Section 17, as the case may be; or

(c) when a reference is made to a court, [Labour Court, Tribunal or National Tribunal] under Section 10 during the pendency of conciliation proceedings.

(3) Proceedings [before an arbitrator under Section 10A or before a Labour Court, Tribunal or National Tribunal] shall be deemed to have commenced on the date of the [reference of the dispute for arbitration or adjudication, as the case may be] and such proceedings shall be deemed to have concluded [on the date on which the award becomes enforceable under Section 17A].

S. 21. Certain matters to be kept confidential – There shall not be included in any report or award under this Act any information obtained by a conciliation officer, Board, Court, [Labour Court, Tribunal, National Tribunal or an arbitrator] in the course of any investigation or inquiry as to a trade union or inquiry as to any individuals business (whether carried on by a person, firm or company) which is not available otherwise than through the evidence given before such officer, Board, Court, [Labour Court, Tribunal, National Tribunal or arbitrator], if the trade union, person, firm or company in question has made a request in writing to the conciliation officer, Board, Court, [Labour Court, Tribunal, National Tribunal or arbitrator], as the case may be, that such information shall be treated as confidential; nor shall such conciliation officer or any individual member of the Board [or Court or the presiding officer of the Labour Court, Tribunal or National Tribunal or the arbitrator] or any person present at or concerned in the proceedings disclose any such information without the consent in writing of the secretary of the trade union or the person, firm or company in question, as the case may be :

Provided that nothing contained in this Section shall apply to a disclosure of any such information for the purposes of a prosecution under Section 193 of the Indian Penal Code (45 of 1860).

CHAPTER V

STRIKES AND LOCK-OUTS

S. 22. Prohibition of strikes and lock-outs – (1) No persons employed in a Public utility service shall go on strike in breach of contract –

(a) without giving to the employer notice of strike, as hereinafter provided, within six weeks before striking; or

(b) within fourteen days of giving such notice; or

(c) before the expiry of the date of strike specified in any such notice as aforesaid; or

(*d*) during the pendency of any conciliation proceedings before a conciliation officer and seven days after the conclusion of such proceedings.

(2) No employer carrying on any public utility service shall lock-out any of his workmen —

(*a*) without giving them notice of lock-out as hereinafter provided, within six weeks before locking-out; or

(*b*) within fourteen days of giving such notice; or

(*c*) before the expiry of the date of lock-out specified in any such notice as aforesaid; or

(*d*) during the pendency of any conciliation proceedings before a conciliation officer and seven days after conclusion of such proceedings.

(3) The notice of lock-out or strike under this Section shall not be necessary where there is already in existence a strike or, as the case may be, lock out in the public utility service, but the employer shall send intimation of such lock-out or strike on the day on which it is declared, to such authority as may be specified by the appropriate Government either generally or for a particular area or for a particular class of public utility services.

(4) The notice of strike referred to in sub-section (1) shall be given by such number of persons to such person or persons and in such manner as may be prescribed.

(5) The notice of lock-out referred to in sub-section (2) shall be given in such manner as may be prescribed.

(6) If on any day an employer receives, from any person employed by him any such notices as are referred to in sub-section (1) or gives to any person employed by him any such notices as are referred to in sub-section (2), he shall within five days thereof report to the appropriate Government or to such authority as that Government may prescribe, the number of such notices received or given on that day.

NOTES

Legal lock-out does not give liberty to the employer to act unreasonably –The management cannot behave unreasonably because the lock-out is born lawfully. If by subsequent conduct the Union shows readiness to resume work, management's refusal to restart the industry forfeits the legitimacy of the lock-out – *The Statesman Ltd. vs. Workmen*, AIR 1976 SC 758 : (1976)I LLJ 484.

Where immediately after the workers went on token strike for three days, the management declared lock-out without giving any intimation to the Union prior to starting of the strike, the lock-out was held to be unjustified and workers were allowed 50 per cent of the wages for the Lock-out period

– *Northern Dooars Tea Co. vs. Workmen of Dim Dima Tea Estate*, (1964) I LLJ 436 : (1963)7 FLR 469.

S. 23. General prohibition of strikes and lock-outs – No workman who is employed in any industrial establishment shall go on strike in breach of contract and no employer of any such workman shall declare a lock-out –

(a) during the pendency of conciliation proceedings before a Board and seven days after the conclusion of such proceedings;

(b) during the pendency of proceedings before a [Labour Court, Tribunal or National Tribunal] and two months after the conclusion of such proceedings;

(bb) during the pendency of arbitration proceedings before an arbitrator and two months after the conclusion of such proceedings, where a notification has been issued under sub-section (3A) of Section 10A;

(c) during any period in which a settlement or award is in operation, in respect of any of the matters covered by the settlement or award.

NOTES

Breach of promise to Labour Commissioner not to resort to strike, effect of — In the instant case, the workmen assured the Regional Labour Commissioner that in future they would resort to constitutional means to resolve their disputes with the management and would not stage strike to enforce acceptance of their demands. The workmen did not keep their promise and resorted to strike. Held, such promise to the Labour Commissioner did not amount to a settlement and breach of such promise would not attract clause (c) of Section 23 — *Ballarpur Collieries Co. vs. Presiding Officer*, AIR 1972 SC 1216 : (1972)II LLJ 90.

Employers withdrawal from proceedings before Labour Tribunal, effect of—

In this case, the workmen withdrew from the proceedings instituted on reference under the I.D. Act before the Tribunal after making a petition to the effect that the proceedings did not concern the establishment, held, the proceedings before the Tribunal for contravention of Section 23(b) is not purely between two private parties but involve larger public interest. The workmen by withdrawing from the proceeding cannot avoid the legal consequences flowing from Section 23 *(b)* — *Ballarpur Collieries & Co. vs. Presiding Officer*, AIR 1972 SC 1216 : (1972)II LLJ 90.

Section 23(c) bans strike and lock-out in respect of matters covered by the award. The Section will be applicable till such period as the award remains in operation or binding — *South Indian Bank Ltd. vs. Chacko,* AIR 1964 SC 152 : (1964)I LLJ 19.

S. 24. Illegal strikes and lock-outs-(1) A strike or a lock-out shall be illegal if –

(i) it is commenced or declared in contravention of Section 22 or Section 23; or

(ii) it is continued in contravention of an order made under sub-section (3) of Section 10 [or sub-section (4A) of Section 10A].

(2) Where a strike or lock-out in pursuance of an industrial dispute has already commenced and is in existence at the time of the reference of the dispute to a Board, [an arbitrator, a] [Labour Court, Tribunal or National Tribunal], the continuance of such strike or lock-out shall not be deemed to be illegal, provided that such strike or lock-out was not at its commencement in contravention of the provisions of this Act or the continuance thereof was not prohibited under sub-section (3) of Section 10 [or sub-section (4A) of Section 10A].

(3) A lock-out declared in consequence of an illegal strike or a strike declared in consequence of an illegal lock-out shall not be deemed to be illegal.

NOTES

Illegal Strike cannot be half legitimate — After the conciliatory proceedings failed, the Union without waiting for Government's reference of the dispute for adjudication resorted to strike. Held that the Industrial Tribunal cannot come to the conclusion that the strike was half legitimate. Although strike is a legitimate weapon in the hands of the labour, it is equally important to remember that indiscriminate and hasty use of this weapon without exhausting all avenues for peaceful achievement of the objects should not be encouraged. The award of the Tribunal for 50 pc. wagers was set aside—*Chandramalai Estate vs. Workmen,* AIR 1960 SC 902 : (1960)II LLJ 243.

Strikes and lock-outs when justified and when not—Where the workers started collective bargaining for securing better terms in respect of wages, provident fund, gratuity, leave, etc. and ultimately resorted to strike to induce the employer to accept their demands and reopen negotiations held, the strike was justified—*Swadeshi Industries Ltd. vs. Workmen,* AIR 1960 SC 1258.

When the company changed the weekly off day from Sunday to Saturday consequent upon curtailment of electric power on Saturdays and for that reason the workers resorted to strike, the strike was held unjustified and the lock-out declared in reply of the strike, was justified—*Workmen vs. Sur Iron & Steel Co. Ltd.*, (1971) I LLJ 570.

When the strike was declared illegal, the workers who participated in the strike would, in the absence of proof that they were violent, be entitled to at least 50 percent wages for the period of unemployment—*India General Navigation & Railway Co. vs. Workmen*, AIR 1960 SC 219.

In this case, the employer contended that the representatives of workers did not attend the conciliation proceedings for effecting a settlement and lifting of the lock-out. Held, when the lock-out was found to be not justified, the attitude of the workers towards conciliation was immaterial and workers were entitled to wages — *Itakhoolie Tea Estate vs. Workmen,* AIR 1960 SC 1349.

A lock-out declared at a time when a valid reference on the disputed issues are before the Tribunal, is illegal. But a lock-out during pendency of a void and illegal reference is perfectly legal. The fact that the reference has been subsequently validated by an Act would not render the lock-out illegal—AIR 1950 Mad. 231.

S. 25. Prohibition of financial aid to illegal strike and lock-outs—No person shall knowingly expend or apply any money in direct furtherance of support of any illegal strike or lock-out.

CHAPTER VA

LAY-OFF AND RETRENCHMENT

S. 25A. Application of Sections 25C to 25E — (1) Section 25C to 25E inclusive [shall not apply to industrial establishments to which Chapter VB applies, or] —

(a) to industrial establishment in which less than fifty workmen on an average per working day have been employed in the preceding calendar month; or

(b) to industrial establishments which are of a seasonal character or in which work is performed only intermittently.

(2) If a question arises whether an industrial establishment is of a seasonal character or whether work is performed therein only intermittently, the decision of the appropriate Government thereon shall be final.

[*Explanation.*-In this Section and in Sections 25C, 25D and 25E, "industrial establishment" means —

(i) a factory as defined in clause *(m)* of Section 2 of the Factories Act, 1948 (63 of 1948); or

(ii) a mine as defined in clause *(j)* of Section 2 of the Mines Act, 1952 (35 of 1952); or

(iii) A plantation as defined in clause *(f)* of Section 2 of the Plantations Labour Act, 1951 (69 of 1951)].

NOTES

Section 25A casts an obligation upon the employer who wants to retrench the workmen to give notice. When a workman is retrenched it cannot be said that in its condition of service effected. In order to attract

Section 9A, the employer must be desirous of effecting a change in the condition of service in respect of any matter specified in the fourth schedule. If the change proposed does not cover any matter in the fourth schedule, Section 9A is not attracted and no notice is necessary. It is indisputable position that none of the other preconditions to a valid retrenchment. It is therefore futile to contend that even if termination of service of a workman construed retrenchment it would nevertheless be valid because the notice contemplated by Section 25E would be dispensed with in view of the provisions contained in Section 9A. Therefore, the termination of service amounts to retrenchment, for failure to comply with conditions under Section 25F would render the termination *void ab initio*—L. *Robert D'Souza vs. The Executive Engineer, Southern Railway*, AIR 1982 SC 854 : (1982)1 SCC 645 : (1982)1 SLR 864 : 1982 Lab IC 811.

S. [25B. Definition of continuous service.—For the purposes of this Chapter,—

(1) a workman shall be said to be in continuous service for a period if he is, for that period, in uninterrupted service, including service which may be interrupted on account of sickness or authorised leave or an accident or a strike which is not illegal, or a lock-out or a cessation of work which is not due to any fault on the part of the workman;

(2) where a workman is not in continuous service within the meaning of clause (1) for a period of one year or six months, he shall be deemed to be in continuous service under an employer—

(a) for a period of one year, if the workman, during a period of twelve calendar months preceding the date, with reference to which calculation is to be made, has actually worked under the employer for not less than—

(i) one hundred and ninety days in the case of a workman employed below ground in a mine; and

(ii) two hundred and forty days, in any other case;

(b) for a period of six months, if the workman, during a period of six calendar months preceding the date with reference to which calculation is to be made, has actually worked under the employer for not less than—

(i) ninety-five days, in the case of a workman employed below ground in a mine; and

(ii) one hundred and twenty days, in any other case.

Explanation—For the purpose of clause (2), the number of days on which a workman has actually worked under an employer shall include the days on which —

(i) he has been laid-off under an agreement or as permitted by standing orders made under the Industrial Employment (Standing Orders) Act, 1946 (20 of 1946), or under this Act or under any other law applicable to the industrial establishment;

(ii) he has been on leave with full wages, earned in the previous years;

(iii) he has been absent due to temporary disablement caused by accident arising out of and in the course of his employment; and

(iv) in the case of a female, she has been on maternity leave; so however, that the total period of such maternity leave does not exceed twelve weeks.

NOTES

Continuous service of one year—meaning — Under Section 25B(2) where a workman is not in continuous service within the meaning of clause (1) for a period of one year he shall be deemed to be in continuous service for the same period, if the workman during a period of twelve calendar months preceding the date with reference to which calculation is to be made, has actually worked under the employer for not less than 240 days. The contention that the continuity of service was broken by the two parties of illegal strike and therefore the workmen could not be said to have been in service for not less than one year was negatived in view of the fact that even if the period of illegal strike is excluded the number of days during which the workmen actually worked under the employer would be found to be more than 240 days. That being so the Supreme Court in the case of—*Management of Standard Motor Products of India Ltd. vs. A. Parthasarathy.* AIR 1986 SC 462 : 1986 Lab IC 101 has held that the workmen were in continuous service for a period of one year immediately before the date of closure. The further contention that the number of days on which the workmen actually worked under the employer would be less than 240 days if Sundays and other holidays for which the workmen were paid wages were excluded was also rejected in view of the proposition laid down in the case of—*The Workmen of American Express International Banking Corporation vs. The Management of American Express International Banking Corporation,* 1986 Lab IC 98.

S. 25C. Right of workmen laid-off for compensation — Whenever a workman (other than a *badli* workman or a casual workman) whose name is borne on the muster rolls of an industrial establishment and who has completed not less than one year of continuous service under an employer is laid off, whether continuously or intermittently, he shall be paid by the employer for all days during which he is so laid-off, except for such weekly holidays as may intervene, compensation which shall be equal to fifty per cent of the total of the basic wages and dearness allowance that would have been payable to him had he not been so laid-off :

Provided that if during any period of twelve months, a workman is so laid-off for more than forty-five days, no such compensation shall be payable in respect of any period of the lay-off after the expiry of the first forty-five days, if there is an agreement to that effect between the workman and the employer :

Provided further that it shall be lawful for the employer in any case falling within the foregoing proviso to retrench the workman in accordance with the provisions contained in Section 25F at any time after the expiry of the first forty-five days of the lay-off and when he does so, any compensation paid to the workman for having been laid-off during the preceding twelve months may be set off against the compensation payable for retrenchment.

Explanation.— "Badli workman" means a workman who is employed in an industrial establishment in the place of another workman whose name is borne on the muster rolls of the establishment, but shall cease to be regarded as such for the purposes of this Section, if he has completed one year of continuous service in the establishment.]

NOTES

Lay-off *mala fide*, compensation would not be limited to only what is provided in Section 35C—If the lay-off is *mala fide* in the sense that the employer had deliberately and maliciously created a situation making lay-off inevitable, then it would not be lay-off under Section 2(kkk) and the workman will be entitled to other relief besides what is provided in Section 25C because it will amount to refusal of employment—*Tatanagar Foundry Co. Ltd. vs. Workmen,* AIR 1962 SC 1533.

S. 25D. Duty of an employer to maintain muster rolls of workman—

Notwithstanding that workmen in any industrial establishment have been laid-off, it shall be the duty of every employer to maintain for the purposes of this chapter a muster roll, and to provided for the making of entries therein by workmen who may present themselves for work at the establishment at the appoint time during normal working hours.

S. 25E. Workmen not entitled to compensation in certain cases — No Compensation shall be paid to a workman who has been laid-off –

(i) If he refuses to accept any alternative employment in the same establishment from which he has been laid-off, or in any other establishment belonging to the same employer situate in the same town or village or situate within a radius of five miles from the establishment to which he belongs, if, in the opinion of the employer, such alternative employment does not call for any special skill or previous experience and can be done by the workman, provided that the wages which would normally have been paid to the workman are offered for the alternative employment also;

(ii) If he does not present himself for work at the establishment at the appointed time during normal working hours at least once a day;

(iii) If such laying-off is due to a strike or slowing-down of production on the part of workman in another part of the establishment.

S. 25F. Conditions precedent to retrenchment of workmen. –No workman employed in any industry who has been in continuous service for not less than one year under an employer shall be retrenched by that employer until—

(a) the workman has been given one month's notice in writing indicating the reasons for retrenchment and the period of notice has expired, or the workman has been paid in lieu of such notice, wages for the period of the notice;

(b) the workman has been paid, at the time of retrenchment, compensation which shall be equivalent of fifteen day's average pay [for every completed year of continuous service] or any part thereof in excess of six months; and

(c) notice in the prescribed manner is served on the appropriate Government [or such authority as may be specified by the appropriate Government by notification in the *Official Gazette]*.

NOTES

Retrenchment, nature and extent of employer's rights and obligations— The power of the employer to retrench his workmen is subject to certain limitations. The act must not be actuated by any motive of victimisation or unfair labour practice. The management has the right to decide the strength of its labour force to operate his industry efficiently and if the number of his employees exceeds his reasonable and legitimate needs, he can retrench the surplus staff. Workmen may become surplus on ground of rationalisation or economy but the assessment must be made *bona fide* and on justified grounds of other industrial or trade reasons. When retrenchment is effected for *bona fide* reasons, the Tribunal cannot question the propriety or wisdom of the action of the employer - *Parry and Co. Ltd. vs. Industrial Tribunal,* AIR 1970 SC 1334:(1969)2 SCR 976.

Retrenchment-scope and effect of— The object intended to be achieved by clauses(a) and (b) of Section 25F being different from the object which clause (c) seeks to achieve, it would not be unreasonable to hold that clause (c), unlike clauses (a) and (b) is not condition precedent – *Bombay Union of Journalists vs. State of Bombay,* AIR 1964 SC 1617:(1964)I LLJ 351.

A retrenched employee, to claim retrenchment compensation for service for a number of years, must show that he had worked for not less than 240 days during a period of 12 calendar months in the year immediately preceding the retrenchment and in respect of every year of service – *Ramkrishna Ramnath vs. Labour Court,* 1973 Lab IC 87 SC.

In this case the service of the "Town-in-Charge" of the State Electricity Board was terminated without complying with the condition precedent as envisaged in Section 25F of the I.D. Act. Though the employee was subsequently re-employed as Sub-Station Assistant, the Supreme Court quashed the order of retrenchment and directed that the employee would continue to be in service as town in–charge without interruption with effect from the date of termination and his arrear back wages and other monetary benefits would be paid to him less than what he had received as salary etc. while serving as Sub-Station Assistant on re-employment— *Harimohan Rustogi vs. Labour Court,* (1984) I LLJ 32 SC.

Sending copies of retrenchment notice to authorities under W.B. Industrial Disputes Rules — The object of the proviso to clause (a) was that where it was not possible for the employer to send one month's notice to the two officers as there was decision to retrench the employee with immediate effect, he was legally entitled to send the information immediately after effecting the retrenchment- *Parry & Co.Ltd. vs. Industrial Tribunal,* AIR 1970 SC 1334;(1969) 2 SCR 976.

Termination of service on ground of loss of confidence, if retrenchment—It would be a mistake to hold that termination of service of workman on the ground of loss of confidence could be included in the expression "for any reason whatsoever" in Section 2(oo) of the Industrial Dispute Act — *Kamlesh Kumar Rajnikant Mehta vs. Presiding Officer, Central Government Industrial Tribunal,* 1980 Lab IC 1116:(1980) I LLJ 336 Bom (DB).

Retrenchment compensation payable on retrenchment – A workman can be said to have completed one year's continuous service, if he being in employment for a period of not less than 12 months, had worked not less than 240 days. Therefore a workman who was not at all been employed for a period of 12 calendar months would not be entitled to the compensation payable under Section 25F for the year — *Sur Enamel Stamping Works Ltd. vs. Workmen,* AIR 1963 SC 1914 : (1963) II LLJ 367.

Termination found to be illegal — declaration of continuity in service- Where the termination of service is *ab initio* void and inoperative, there is no question of granting reinstatement because there is no cessation of service and a mere declaration follows that continues to be in service with all consequential benefits. The principle laid down by the Supreme Court in the cases of – *Ruby General Insurance Co.,Ltd. vs. P.P. Chopra,* (1970)1 Lab LJ 63 and *Hindustan Steel Ltd., Rourkela vs. A.K. Roy,* (1970)3 SCR 343 : AIR 1970 SC 1401 was also applied where the termination is illegally established or where there is an ineffective order of retrenchment— *Mohan Lal vs. The Management of M/s. Bharat Electronics Ltd.*, AIR 1981 SC 1253 : (1981)3 SCC 225 : (1981)2 SCJ 233 : 1981 Lab IC 806 : (1981)2 Lab LJ 70.

S. [25FF. Compensation to workmen in case of transfer of undertakings — Where the ownership or management of an undertaking is transferred, whether by agreement or by operation of law, from the employer in relation to that undertaking to a new employer, every workman who has been in continuous service for not less than one year in that undertaking immediately before such transfer shall be entitled to notice and compensation in accordance with the provisions of Section 25F, as if the workman has been retrenched:

Provided that nothing in this Section shall apply to a workman in any case where there has been a change of employers by reason of the transfer, if–

(a) the service of the workman has not been interrupted by such transfer;

(b) the terms and conditions of service applicable to the workman after such transfer are not in any way less favourable to the workman than those applicable to him immediately before the transfer; and

(c) the new employer is, under the terms of such transfer or otherwise, legally liable to pay to the workman, in the event of his retrenchment, compensation on the basis that his service has been continuous and has not been interrupted by the transfer].

S. [25 Q FFA. Sixty day's notice to be given of intention to close down any undertaking— (1) An employer who intends to close down an undertaking shall serve at least sixty days before the date on which the intended closure is to become effective, a notice, in the prescribed manner, on the appropriate Government stating clearly the reasons for the intended closure of the undertaking:

Provided that nothing in this Section shall apply to—

(a) an undertaking in which –

(i) less than fifty workmen are employed, or

(ii) less than fifty workmen were employed on an average per working day in the preceding twelve months,

(b) an undertaking set up for the construction of buildings, bridges, roads, canals, dams or for other construction work or project.

(2) Notwithstanding anything contained in sub-section (1), the appropriate Government may, if it is satisfied that owning to such exceptional circumstances as accident in the undertaking or death of the employer or the like, it is necessary so to do, by order, direct that provisions

of sub-section (1) shall not apply in relation to such undertaking for such period as may be specified in the order].

S. 25FFF. Compensation to workman in case of closing down of undertakings:

(1) Where an undertaking is closed down for any reason whatsoever, every workman who has been in continuous service for not less than one year in that undertaking immediately before such closure shall, subject to the provisions of sub-section.

(2) be entitled to notice and compensation in accordance with the provisions of Section 25F, as if the workman had been retrenched:

Provided that where the undertaking is closed down on account of unavoidable circumstances beyond the control of the employer, the compensation to be paid to the workmen under clause (b) of Section 25F shall not exceed his average pay for three months.

[*Explanation*- An undertaking which is closed down by reason merely of —

(i) financial difficulties (including financial losses); or

(ii) accumulation of undisposed of stocks; or

(iii) the expiry of the period of the lease or license granted to it; or

(iv) in a case where the undertaking is engaged in mining operations, exhaustion of the minerals in the area in which such operations are carried on,

shall not be deemed to have been closed down on account of unavoidable circumstances beyond the control of the employer within the meaning of the proviso to this sub-section.]

(1A) Notwithstanding anything contained in sub-section — (1) where an undertaking engaged in mining operations is closed down by reason merely of exhaustion of the minerals in the area in which such operations are carried on, no workman referred to in that sub-section shall be entitled to any notice or compensation in accordance with the provisions of Section 25F, if—

(a) the employer provides the workman with alternative employment with effect from the date of closure at the same remuneration as he was entitled to receive, and on the same terms and conditions of service as were applicable to him, immediately before the closure;

(b) the service of the workman has not been interrupted by such alternative employment; and

(c) the employer is, under the terms of such alternative employment or otherwise, legally liable to pay to the workman, in the event of his retrenchment, compensation on the basis that his service has

been continuous and has not been interrupted by such alternative employment.

(IB) For the purposes of sub-section (1) and (1A), the expressions "minerals" and "mining operations" shall have the meanings respectively assigned to them in clauses (a) and (b) of Section 3 of the Mines and Minerals (Regulation and Development) Act, 1957 (67 of 1957).

(2) Where any undertaking set-up for the construction of buildings, bridges, roads, canals, dams or other construction work is closed down on account of the completion of the work within two years from the date on which the undertaking had been set-up, no workman employed therein shall be entitled to any compensation under clause (b) of Section 25F, but if the construction work is not so completed within two years, he shall be entitled to notice and compensation under that Section for every [completed year of continuous service] or any part thereof in excess of six months.

NOTES

Closure of the undertaking, if violative of Article 19(1)(g) of the Constitution — It is wrong to say that the employer has no right to close down a business, once he enters it. If he has such a right, as obviously he has, it cannot but be a fundamental right embedded in the right, to carry on any, business guaranteed under Article 10(1)(g) of the Constitution. The owner of a property cannot be asked to part with his property which includes a business undertaking or destroy his property by prohibiting him from closing down the undertaking Section 25-O as a whole (requiring the employer to serve notice of closure to the government) and Section 25-R in so far as it relates to awarding of punishment for infraction of Section 25-O are constitutionally bad for violating Article 19(1)(g)— *Excel Wear and others vs. Union of India,* (1978)11 LLJ 527 : (1984)4 SCC 224: 1978 SCC (L&S) 509.

Closure, matters to be considered by Industrial Tribunal – In case of closure, the Tribunal has only to see if the business has actually been closed or not. In order to constitute closure it is not necessary that the company should be wound up and machinery transferred. Mere notice of closure is not conclusive. The Tribunal has to decide whether there has been closure or not considering all circumstances. There is no principle that closure can be only for financial or similar reasons. The factory may be closed on account of gress by workmen too— *Kalinga Tubes Ltd. vs. Workmen,* AIR 1969 SC 90 : (1969)I LLJ 557.

If an employer threatens closure at a time when the workmen are about to join a Union or transfer allegiance from one Union to another, then that conduct of the employer would constitute unfair labour practice and be covered by item No. 1 — *M.G.K. Union vs. Glass Containers (P) Ltd.,* (1983)I LLJ 331 Bom.

Closure without complying with the requirements of Section 25FFA and 25FFF, effect of—Section 25FFA contemplates 60 day's notice to be given by the employer to the Government of his intention to close down the undertaking. It must state the reason for the closure. Section 30-A of the Act imposes a penalty on the employer who closes down his undertaking without complying with the provisions of Section 25FFA. Mere application made by the employer to the Government in terms of Section 25-O in August, 1977 and May, 1978 cannot be considered compliance of Section 25FFA when these applications were refused by the Government. So the closure was effected without complying with the provisions of Section 25FFA. The employer by not offering closure compensation to the workmen within a reasonable time contravened Section 25FFF too. So the employer is clearly punishable for the omissions under Section 30-A— *M.G.K. Union vs. Glass Containers (P) Ltd.*, (1983)I LLJ 327 Bom.

Rule of res judicata, applicability to proceeding before Industrial Tribunals — That the rule of *res judicata* applies to proceeding before the Industrial Tribunals has been consistently held by the Supreme Court in a number of cases. Although the entire Civil Procedure Code is not made applicable to industrial adjudication the principles of *res judicata* laid down under Section 11 of the Code of the Civil Procedure, however, are applicable, wherever possible, for very good reason. This is so since multiplicity of litigation and agitation or reagitation of the same dispute at issue between the same employer and employees will not be condusive to industrial peace which is the principal object of all labour legislation bearing on industrial adjudication— *Burn & Co., Calcutta vs. Their Employees,* 1956 SCR 781:AIR 1957 SC 38, *The Army & Navy Stores Ltd., Bombay vs. Their Workmen,* (1951)2 Lab LJ 31, *Workmen vs. M/s. Straw Board Manufacturing Co.Ltd.,* (1974)3 SCR 703:AIR 1974 SC 1132. But the Supreme Court refuses to lay down a broad proposition that a question which was once decided can never be agitated. There are certain classes of cases like dispute regarding wage structure, service condition etc. which arise as circumstances change and new situation arise which may not be barred by the rule of *res judicata.* The question whether a person was or was not an employee under a management after a particular date is one which cannot be reagitated in a subsequent case. In the circumstances a particular case if it has already been decided finally by the Tribunal by competent jurisdiction is an earlier case where the said question necessarily arose for decision. Where the one and the only ground on which the claim of the workman for compensation in Section 25FFF of the Act was negatived, was that the workmen had ceased to be employees by reason of notice of discharge and where the validity of the notice of discharge was directly and substantially in issue of the first reference, the second Tribunal was in error in re-examining the issue relating to the validity of the notice of discharge and in expressing a contrary view. The award subsequently passed by the second Tribunal was therefore quashed by the Supreme Court— *M/s. Bharat Barrel & Drum Manufacturing Co.Pvt. Ltd. vs. Bharat Barrel Employees Union,* AIR 1987 SC 1415.

Compensation payable in case of transfer of undertaking — S. 25FFF makes provision for payment of compensation to workmen in cases of closure of an undertaking and consists of two parts. Sub-section (1) contemplates that when an undertaking is closed down for any reason whatsoever the workmen are entitled to notice and payment of compensation in accordance with the said provision, as if the workmen had been retrenched.The proviso to said sub-section (1),however, limits the payment of compensation to average pay for three months, if the undertaking is closed down on account of unavoidable circumstances beyond the control of the employer. The Explanation to the proviso further makes it clear that in the circumstances mentioned therein, including financial difficulties and financial losses, it would not be deemed that the undertaking and been closed down on account of unavoidable circumstances beyond the control of the employer within the meaning of the proviso.Where initially there was no intention on the part of the company to effect closure, but the company was constrained to declare a closure only after repeated notices and warnings and it was forcefully prevented from implementing a scheme of nationalisation, the first part of the said Section applied to other case under consideration and as such the workmen will be entitled to compensation in accordance with the proviso to said Section of the Industrial Disputes Act — *Presidency Jute Mills Co. Ltd. vs. The Fifth Industrial Tribunal,* (1991)2 CLJ 263 : (1992)1 CHN 381.

S. 25G. Procedure for retrenchment— Where any workman in an industrial establishment, who is a citizen of India, is to be retrenched and he belongs to a particular category of workmen in that establishment, in the absence of any agreement between the employer and the workman in this behalf, the employer shall ordinarily retrench the workman who was the last person to be employed in that category, unless for reasons to be recorded the employer retrenches other workman.

NOTES

Departure from normal rule "last come first go" when legal – The rule "first come last go" is intended to secure equitable treatment to the employees when owing to some exigencies it is necessary to retrench some workmen. But in the application of the rule the interests of the business cannot be overlooked. If retention of a clerical employee is regarded as necessary in the interest of the business, that opinion cannot be discarded on the ground that other clerk senior to him was retrenched — *Om Oil & Oil*

Seeds Exchange Ltd., Delhi vs. Workmen, AIR 1966 SC 1657:(1966)II LLJ 324.

S. 25H Re-employment of retrenched workmen — Where any workmen are retrenched, and the employer proposes to take into his employ and persons, be shall, in such manner as may be prescribed, give an opportunity [to the retrenched workmen who are citizens of India, to offer themselves for re-employment, and such retrenched workmen] who offer themselves for re-employment shall have preference over other persons.

S. 25I. *[Recovery of moneys due employers under this Chapter.] Rep.by the Industrial Disputes (Amendment and Miscellaneous Provisions) Act, 1956. (36 of 1956) S. 19 (w.e.f. 10.3.1957).*

S. 25J. Effect of laws inconsistent with this Chapter — (1) The provisions of this Chapter shall have effect notwithstanding anything inconsistent therewith contained in any other law [including standing orders made under the Industrial Employment (Standing Orders) Act, 1946 (20 of 1946):

[**Provided** that where under the provisions of and by other Act or rules, orders or notifications issued thereunder or under any standing orders or under any award, contract of service or otherwise, a workman is entitled to benefits in respect of any matter which are more favourable to him than those to which he would be entitled under this Act, the workman shall continue to be entitled to the more favourable benefits in respect of that matter, notwithstanding that he receives benefits in respect of other matters under this Act.]

(2) for the removal of doubts, it is hereby declared that nothing contained in this Chapter shall be deemed to affect the Provisions of any other law for the time being in force in any State in so far as that law provides for the settlement of industrial disputes, but the rights and liabilities of employers and workmen is so far as they relate to lay-off and retrenchment shall be determined in accordance with the provisions of this Chapter].

NOTES

Provisions contained in this Act—if inconsistent with A.P.Shops and Establishments Act, 1966 — Section 25J of this Act lays down that chapter VA shall have effect notwithstanding any inconsistency therewith contained in any other law. The proviso to the sub-section (1) however saves any higher benefit available to workmen under any law, agreement or settlement or award. Section 25J(2) makes a distinction between any machinery provided by any State law for settlement of industrial disputes and substantive rights and liabilities arising under the said chapter where a lay-off or retrenchment takes place. It provides that while Section 25J would not affect the provision in a State law relating to settlement of industrial disputes, the rights and liabilities of employers and workmen in so far as they relate to lay-off and retrenchment shall be determined in accordance with chapter of the present Act. Section 41(1) and (3) of the A.P. Shops and Establishments Act prescribes alternative authorities to settle a dispute arising out of a retrenchment. Thus authorities may exercise their jurisdiction under the State Act but they have to decide such dispute in accordance with other provisions of this chapter VA. The rights arising out of retrenchment can be enforced by a workman personally by himself filing an appeal under Section 41(1) of the State Act. It is not necessary that reference should be sought under the Central Act by collective action of the workers. Therefore if the employees are "workman" and the management is "industry" as defined in the Central Act and action taken by the management amounts to "retrenchment" then the rights and liabilities of the party are governed by the provisions of chapter VA of the Centrai Act and the said rights and liabilities may be adjudicated upon and enforcing in proceedings before the authorities under Section 41(1) and (3) of the State Act. After considering the provisions of the Central and the State Act the Supreme Court in the case of– *The Krishna Dist. Co-operative Marketing Society Ltd. Vijaywada vs. Purnachandra Rao* AIR 1987 SC 1960 did not find any implied repugnancy between the Central Act and the State Act.

CHAPTER VB
SPECIAL PROVISIONS RELATING TO LAY-OFF, RETRENCHMENT AND CLOSURE IN CERTAIN ESTABLISHMENTS

S. 25K. Application of Chapter VB — (1) The provisions of this Chapter shall apply to an industrial establishment (not being an establishment of a seasonal character or in which work is performed only intermittently) in which not less than one hundred workmen were employed on an average per working day for the preceding twelve months.

(2) If a question arises whether an industrial establishment is of a seasonal character or whether work is performed therein only intermittently, the decision of the appropriate Government thereon shall be final.

S. 25L. Definition — For the purposes of this Chapter, —

(a) "industrial establishment" means —

(i) a factory as defined in clause (j) of Section 2 of the Factories Act, 1948 (63 of 1948);

(ii) a mine as defined in clause (j) of sub-section (1) of Section 2 of the Mines Act, 1952 (35 of 1952); or

(iii) a plantation as defined in clause (f) of Section 2 of the Plantations Labour Act,1951 (69 of 1951);

(*b*) notwithstanding anything contained in sub-clause (ii) of clause (a) of Section 2,—

(i) in relation to any company in which not less than fifty-one per cent of the paid-up share capital is held by the Central Government, or

(ii) in relation to any corporation [not being a corporation referred to in sub-clause (i) of clause (a) of Section 2] established by or under any law made by Parliament,

the Central Government shall be the appropriate Government.

S. 25M. Prohibition of lay-off — (1) No workman (other than a *badli* workman or casual workman) whose name is borne on the muster rolls of an industrial establishment to which this Chapter applies shall be laid-off by his employer except with the prior permission of the appropriate Government or such authority as may be specified by that Government by notification in the *Official Gazette* (hereafter in this Section referred to as the specified authority), obtained on an application made in this behalf, unless such lay-off is due to shortage of power or to natural calamity, and in the case of a mine, such lay-off is due also to fire, flood, excess of inflammable gas or explosion.

(2) An application for permission under sub-section (1) shall be made by the employer in the prescribed manner stating clearly the reasons for the intended lay-off and a copy of such application shall also be served simultaneously on the workmen concerned in the prescribed manner.

(3) Where the workmen (other than *badli* workmen or causal workmen) of an industrial establishment, being a mine, have been laid-off under sub-section (1) for reasons of fire, flood or excess of inflammable gas or explosion, the employer, in relation to such establishment, shall, within a period of thirty days from the date of commencement of such lay-off, apply, in the prescribed manner, to the appropriate Government or the specified authority for permission to continue the lay-off.

(4) Where an application for permission under sub-section (1) or sub-section (3) has been made, the appropriate Government or the specified authority after making such enquiry as it thinks fit and after giving a reasonable opportunity of being heard, to the employer, the workmen concerned and the persons interested in such lay-off, may, having regard to the genuineness and adequacy of the reasons for such lay-off, the interests of the workmen and all relevant factors by order and for reasons to be recorded in writing, grant or refuse to grant such permission and a copy of such order shall be communicated to the employer and the workmen.

(5) Where an application for permission under sub-section (1) or sub-section (3) has been made and the appropriate Government or the specified authority does not communicate the order granting or refusing to

grant permission to the employer within a period of sixty days from the date on which such application is made, the permission applied for shall be deemed to have been granted on the expiration of the said period of sixty days.

(6) An order of the appropriate Government or the specified authority granting or refusing to grant permission shall, subject to the provisions of sub-section (7), be final and binding on all the parties concerned and shall remain in force for one year from the date of such order.

(7) The appropriate Government or the specified authority may, either on its own motion or on the application made by the employer or any workman, review its order granting or refusing to grant permission under sub-section (4) or refer the matter or, as the case may be, cause it to be referred, to a Tribunal for adjudication :

Provided that where a reference has been made to a Tribunal under this sub-section, it shall pass an award within a period of thirty days from the date of such reference.

(8) Where no application for permission under sub-section (1) is made, or where no application for permission under sub-section (1) is made within the period specified therein, or where the permission for any lay-off has been refused, such lay-off shall be deemed to be illegal from the date on which the workmen had been laid-off and the workmen shall be entitled to all the benefits under any law for the time being in force as if they had not been laid-off.

(9) Notwithstanding anything contained in the foregoing provisions of this Section, the appropriate Government may, if it is satisfied that owing to such exceptional circumstances as accident in the establishment or death of the employer or the like, it is necessary so to do, by order, direct that the provisions of sub-section (1), or, as the case may be, sub-section (3) shall not apply in relation to such establishment for such period as may be specified in the order.

(10) The provisions of Sections 25C (other than the second proviso thereto) shall apply to cases of lay-off referred to in this Section.

Explanation.—For the purposes of this Section, a workman shall not be deemed to be laid-off by an employer if such employer offers any alternative employment (which in the opinion of the employer does not call for any special skill or previous experience and can be done by the workman) in the same establishment from which he has been laid-off or in any other establishment belonging to the same employer, situate in the same town or village, or situate within such distance from the establishment to which he belongs, that the transfer will not involve undue hardship to the workman having regard to the facts and circumstances of his case, provided that the wages which would normally have been paid to the workman are offered for the alternative appointment also.

S. [25N. Conditions precedent to retrenchment of workmen — (1) No workman employed in any industrial establishment to which this Chapter applies, who has been in continuous service for not less than one year under an employer shall be retrenched by that employer until,—

(*a*) the workman has been given three months' notice in writing indicating the reasons for retrenchment and the period of notice has expired, or the workman has been paid in lieu of such notice, wages for the period of the notice; and

(*b*) the prior permission of the appropriate Government or such authority as may be specified by that Government by notification in the *Official Gazette* (hereafter in this Section referred to as the specified authority) has been obtained on an application made in this behalf.

(2) An application for permission under sub-section (1) shall be made by the employer in the prescribed manner stating clearly the reasons for the intended retrenchment and a copy of such application shall also be served simultaneously on the workmen concerned in the prescribed manner.

(3) Where an application for permission under sub-section (1) has been made, the appropriate Government or the specified authority, after making such enquiry as it thinks fit and after giving a reasonable opportunity of being heard to the employer, the workmen concerned and the persons interested in such retrenchment, may, having regard to the genuineness and adequacy of the reasons stated by the employer, the interests of the workmen and all other relevant factors, by order and for reasons to be recorded in writing, grant or refuse to grant such permission and a copy of such order shall be communicated to the employer and the workmen.

(4) Where an application for permission has been made under sub-section (1) and the appropriate Government or the specified authority does not communicate the order granting or refusing to grant permission to the employer within a period of sixty days from the date on which such application is made, the permission applied for shall be deemed to have been granted on the expiration of the said period of sixty days.

(5) An order of the appropriate Government or the specified authority granting or refusing to grant permission shall, subject to the provisions of sub-section (6), be final and binding on all the parties concerned and shall remain in force for one year from the date of such order.

(6) The appropriate Government or the specified authority may, either on its own motion or on the application made by the employer or any workman, review its order granting or refusing to grant permission under

sub-section (3) or refer the matter or, as the case may be, cause it to be referred, to a Tribunal for adjudication :

Provided that where a reference has been made to a Tribunal under this sub-section, it shall pass an award within a period of thirty days from the date of such reference.

(7) Where no application for permission under sub-section (1) is made, or where the permission for any retrenchment has been refused, such retrenchment shall be deemed to be illegal from the date on which the notice of retrenchment was given to the workman and the workman shall be entitled to all the benefits under any law for the time being in force as no notice had been given to him.

(8) Notwithstanding anything contained in the foregoing provision of this Section, the appropriate Government may, if it is satisfied that owing to such exceptional circumstances as accident in the establishment or death of the employer or the like, it is necessary so to do, by order, that the provisions of sub-section (1) shall not apply in relation to such establishment for such period as may be specified in the order.

(9) Where permission for retrenchment has been granted under sub-section (3) or where permission for retrenchment is deemed to be granted under sub-section (4), every workman who is employed in that establishment immediately before the date of application for permission under this Section, shall be entitled to receive, at the time of retrenchment, compensation which shall be equivalent to fifteen days' average pay for every completed year of continuous service or any part thereof in excess of six months.]

S. 250. Procedure for closing down an undertaking — (1) An employer who intends to close down an undertaking of an industrial establishment to which this Chapter applies shall, in the prescribed manner, apply, for prior permission at least ninety days before the date on which the intended closure is to become effective, to the appropriate Government, stating clearly the reasons for the intended closure of the undertaking and a copy of such application shall also be served simultaneously on the representatives of the workmen in the prescribed manner :

Provided that nothing in this sub-section shall apply to an undertaking set up for the construction of buildings, bridges, roads, canals, dams or for other construction work.

(2) Where an application for permission has been made under sub-section (1), the appropriate Government, after making such enquiry as it thinks fit and after giving a reasonable opportunity of being heard to the employer, the workmen and the persons interested in such closure may, having regard to the genuineness and adequacy of the reasons stated by the employer, the interest of the general public and all other relevant factors, by

order and for reasons to be recorded in writing, grant or refuse to grant such permission and a copy of such order shall be communicated to the employer and the workmen.

(3) When an application has been made under sub-section (1) and the appropriate Government does not communicate the order granting or refusing to grant permission to the employer within a period of sixty days from the date on which such application is made, the permission applied for, shall be deemed to have been granted on the expiration of the said period of sixty days.

(4) An order of the appropriate Government granting or refusing to grant permission shall, subject to the provisions of sub-section (5), be final and binding on all the parties and shall remain in force for one year from the date of such order.

(5) The appropriate Government may, either on its own motion or on the application made by the employer or any workman, review its order granting or refusing to grant permission under sub-section (2) or refer the matter to Tribunal for adjudication :

Provided that where a reference has been made to a Tribunal under this Sub-section, it shall pass an award within a period of thirty days from the date of such reference.

(6) Where no application for permission under sub-section(1) is made within the period specified therein, or where the permission for closure has been refused, the closure of the undertaking shall be deemed to be illegal from the date of closure and the workmen shall be entitled to all the benefits under any law for the time being in force as if the undertaking had not been closed down.

(7) Notwithstanding anything contained in the foregoing provisions of this Section, the appropriate Government may, if it is satisfied that owing to such exceptional circumstances as accident in the undertaking or death of the employer or the like, it is necessary so to do, by order, direct that the provisions of sub-section (1) shall not apply in relation to such undertaking for such period as may be specified in the order.

(8) Where an undertaking is permitted to be closed down under sub-section (2) or where permission for closure is deemed to be granted under sub-section (3), every workman who is employed in that undertaking immediately before the date of application for permission under this Section, shall be entitled to receive compensation which shall be equivalent to fifteen day's average pay for every completed year of continuous service or any part thereof in excess of six months.

NOTES

Conditions precedent to the consideration of application for closure of business — While dealing with an application for closing down an undertaking a authority concerned should consider the reasons given by the petitioner for the proposed closure. It was incumbent upon the authority concerned to consider what prompted the company to take recourse to such action namely, why the company was gradually reducing the quantum of manufacturing of articles in its own undertaking and instead started purchasing the same from outside. When in passing the impugned order of refusal to grant permission to close down the undertaking the appropriate authority did not indicate in reason therefor, though the workmen were given opportunity of hearing, the opportunity of refuting the contention so urged by the workmen was not, afforded to the company. In such view of the matter the impugned order was held to be invalid and as such was struck down.

S. 25P. Special provision as to restarting of undertakings closed down before commencement of the Industrial Disputes (Amendment) Act, 1976 — If the appropriate Government is of opinion in respect of any undertaking or an industrial establishment to which this Chapter applies and which closed down before the commencement of the Industrial Disputes (Amendment) Act, 1976 (32 of 1976),-.

(a) that such undertaking was closed down otherwise than on account of unavoidable circumstances beyond the control of the employer;

(b) that there are possibility of restarting undertaking;

(c) that it is necessary for the rehabilitation of the workmen employed in such undertaking before its closure or for the maintenance of supplies and services essential to the life of the community to restart the undertaking or both; and

(d) that the restarting of the undertaking will not result in hardship to the employer in relation to the undertaking,

it may, after giving an opportunity to such employer and workmen, direct, by order published in the *Official Gazette,* that the undertaking shall be restarted within such time (not being less than one month from the date of the order) as may be specified in the order.

S. 25Q. Penalty for lay-off and retrenchment without previous permission — Any employer who contravenes the provisions of Section 25M or Section 25N, shall be punishable with imprisonment for a term which may extend to one month, or with fine which may extend to one thousand rupees, or with both.

S. 25R. Penalty for closure — (1) Any employer who closes down an undertaking without complying with the provisions of sub-section (1) of Section 25-O, shall be punishable with imprisonment for a term which may extend to six months, or with fine which may extend to five thousand rupees, or with both.

(2) Any employer, who contravenes an order refusing to grant permission to close down an undertaking under sub-section (2) of Section 25-O or a direction given under Section 25P, shall be punishable with imprisonment for a term which may extend to one year, or with fine which may extend to five thousand rupees, or with both, and where the contravention is a continuing one, with a further fine which may extend to two thousand rupees for every day during which the contravention continues after the conviction.

S. 25S. Certain provisions of Chapter VA to apply to an industrial establishment to which Chapter applies — The provisions of Sections 25B, 25D, 25FF, 25G, 25H and 25J in Chapter VA shall, so far as may be, apply also in relation to an industrial establishment to which the provisions of this Chapter apply.

CHAPTER VC
UNFAIR LABOUR PRACTICES

S. 25T. Prohibition of unfair labour practice — No employer or workman or a trade union, whether registered under the Trade Unions Act, 1926 (16 of 1926), or not, shall commit any unfair labour practice.

NOTES

Unfair labour practice and victimisation, meaning and scope of — Strained relation between the employer and office bearers or active workers of the union would be no conclusive evidence to prove victimisation in the domestic enquiry because in that case Union official may always take the plea against charges of misconduct—*Anandabazar Patrika (P) Ltd. vs. Employees,* AIR 1964 SC 339.

Dismissal may sometimes raise the inference of victimisation but no such inference can arise when the Court is of opinion that the punishment is to some extent harsh—*Tata Oil Mills Ltd. vs. Workmen,* (1963)II LLJ 79.

Withdrawal of recognition of the Union on justified ground cannot be successfully assailed by raising the plea of victimisaiton-*Titagar Paper Mills Co. Ltd. vs. Ram Naresh Kumar*, (1961)I LLJ 511.

The onus of establishing the plea of victimisation and unfair labour practice will be upon the person pleading it mere allegations, and vague suggestions are not enough. The Tribunal shall arrive at its own conclusion after weighing carefully the entire evidence of both sides. Further victimisation must be directly connected with the activities of the concerned employer. A proved misconduct is antithesis of victimisation — *Bharat Iron Works vs. B.B. Patel,* AIR 1976 SC 98 : 1976 Lab IC 4.

S. 25U. Penalty for committing unfair labour practices-Any person who commits any unfair labour practice shall be punishable with imprisonment for a term which may extend to six months or with fine which may extend to one thousand rupees or with both.

CHAPTER VI
PENALTIES

S. 26. Penalty for illegal strikes and lock-outs — (1) Any workman who commences, continues or otherwise acts in furtherance of, a strike which is illegal under his Act, shall be punishable with imprisonment for a term which may extend to one month, or with fine which may extend to fifty rupees, or with both.

(2) Any employer who commences, continues, or otherwise acts in furtherance of a lock-out which is illegal under this Act, shall be punishable with imprisonment for a term which may extend to one month, or with fine which may extend to one thousand rupees, or with both.

S. 27. Penalty for instigation, etc. — Any person who instigates or incites others to take part in, or otherwise acts in furtherance of, strike or lock-out which is illegal under this Act, shall be punishable with imprisonment for a term which may extend to six months, or with fine which may extend to one thousand rupees, or with both.

S. 28. Penalty for giving financial aid to illegal strikes and lock-outs — Any person who knowingly expends or applies any money in direct furtherance or support of any illegal strike or lock-out shall be punishable with imprisonment for a term which may extend to six months, or with fine which may extend to one thousand rupees, or with both.

S. 29. Penalty for breach of settlement or award — Any person who commits a breach of any term of any settlement or award, which is binding on him under this Act, shall be punishable with imprisonment for a term which may extend to six months, or with fine or with both and where the breach is a continuing one, with a further fine which may extend to two hundred rupees for every day during which the breach continues after the conviction for the first, and the Court trying the offence, if it fines the offender, may direct that the whole or any part of the fine realised from him shall be paid, by way of compensation, to any person who, in its opinion, has been injured by such breach.

S. 30. Penalty for disclosing confidential information — Any person who wilfully discloses any such information as is referred to in Section 21 in contravention of the provisions of that section shall, on complaint made by or on behalf of the trade union or individual business affected, be punishable with imprisonment for a term which may extend to six months, or with fine which may extend to one thousand rupees. or with both.

S. 31. Penalty for other offences — (1) Any employer who contravenes the provisions of Section 33 shall be punishable with imprisonment for a term which may extend to six months, or with fine which may extend to one thousand rupees, or with both.

(2) Whoever contravenes any of the provisions of this Act or any rule made thereunder shall, if not other penalty is elsewhere provided by or under this Act for such contravention, be punishable with fine which may extend to one hundred rupees.

NOTES

Penalties at a Glance
Section 26 to Section 31 of the Act

	Description of offence	*Punishment*
Sec.26 (1)	Any workman found guilty of commencing, continuing or otherwise acting in furtherance of a strike which is illegal.	Imprisonment upto 1 month or fine upto Rs. 50/- or with both.
(2)	Any Employer found guilty of commencing, continuing or otherwise acting in furtherance of a lock-out which is illegal.	Imprisonment upto 1 month or fine upto Rs. 1,000/- or with both.
Sec. 27	Any person found guilty of instigating or inciting others to participate or otherwise acting in furtherance of strike or lock-out which is illegal.	Imprisonment upto 6 months or fine upto Rs. 1000/- or with both.
Sec. 28	Any person found guilty of expending or applying any money knowingly in direct furtherance or support of any illegal strike or lock-out.	Imprisonment upto 6 months or fine upto Rs. 1000/- or with both.
Sec. 29	Any person found guilty of breach or any settlement or award which is binding on him, and	Imprisonment upto 6 months or fine, or with both.
	Where the breach is a continuing one.	Further fine which may be upto Rs. 200/- for every day during the period the breach continues after first conviction.
Sec. 30	Any person found guilty of disclosing any such information in contravention of Section 21.	Imprisonment upto 6 months or fine upto Rs. 2000/-, or with both.
Sec. 30A	Any employer found guilty of closure of undertaking in contravention of Section 25FFA.	Imprisonment upto 6 months or fine upto Rs. 5000/-, or with both.

Sec. 31	(1) Any employer found guilty of contravening provisions of Section 33.	Imprisonment upto 6 months or fine upto Rs. 1000/-, or with both.
	(2) Whoever contravenes any provisions of the Act or any Rule thereof (if no other penalty is provided elsewhere in this Act).	Fine upto Rs. 100/-

CHAPTER VII
MISCELLANEOUS

S. 32. Offence by companies, etc.— Where a person committing an offence under this Act is a company, or other body corporate, or an association of persons (whether incorporated or not), every director, manager, secretary, agent) or other officer or person concerned with the management thereof shall, unless be proves that the offence was committed without his knowledge or consent, be deemed to be guilty of such offence.

S. 33. Conditions of service, etc., to remain uncharged under certain circumstance during pendency of proceeding — (1) During the pendency of any conciliation proceeding before a conciliation officer or a Board or of any proceeding before an arbitrator or a Labour Court or Tribunal or National Tribunal in respect of an industrial dispute, no employer shall,—

(*a*) in regard to any matter connected with the dispute, alter, to the prejudice of the workman concerned in such dispute, the conditions of service applicable to them immediately before the commencement of such proceeding; or

(*b*) for any misconduct connected with the dispute, discharge or punish, whether by dismissal or otherwise any workman concerned in such dispute,

save with the express permission in writing of the authority before which the proceeding is pending.

(2) During the pendency of any such proceeding in respect of an industrial dispute, the employer may, in accordance with the standing order applicable to a workman concerned in such dispute or, where there are no such standing orders, in accordance with the terms of the contract, whether express or implied, between him and the workman—

(*a*) alter, in regard to any matter not connected with the dispute, the conditions of service applicable to that workman immediately before the commencement of such proceeding; or

(*b*) for any misconduct not connected with the dispute, discharge or punish, whether by dismissal or otherwise, that workman :

Provided that no such workman shall be discharged or dismissed, unless he has been paid wages for one month and an application has been made by the employer to the authority before which the proceeding is pending for approval of the action taken by the employer.

(3) Notwithstanding anything contained in sub-section (2), no employer shall, during the pendency of any such proceeding in respect of an industrial dispute, take any action against any protected workman concerned in such dispute—

(a) by altering, to the prejudice of such protected workman, the conditions of service applicable to him immediately before the commencement of such proceeding; or

(b) by discharging or punishing, whether by dismissal or otherwise, such protected workman,

save with express permission in writing of the authority before which the proceeding is pending.

Explanation.— For the purposes of this sub-section, a "protected workman", in relation to an establishment, means a workman who, being a member of the executive or other office bearer of a registered trade union connected with the establishment, is recognised as such in accordance with rules made in this behalf.

(4) In every establishment, the number of workmen to be recognised as protected workmen for the purposes of sub-section (3) shall be one per cent of the total number of workmen employed therein subject to a minimum number of five protected workmen and a maximum number of one hundred protected workmen and for the aforesaid purpose, the appropriate Government may make rules providing for the distribution of such protected workmen among varies trade unions, if any, connected with the establishment and the manner in which the workmen may be chosen and recognised as protected workmen.

(5) Where an employer makes an application to a conciliation officer, Board, an arbitrator, a Labour Court, Tribunal or National Tribunal under the proviso to sub-section (2) for approval of the action taken by him, the authority concerned shall, without delay, hear such application and pass, within a period of three months from the date of receipt of such application, such order in relation thereto as it deems fit :

Provided that where any such authority considers it necessary or expedient so to do, it may, for reasons to be recorded in writing, extend such period by such further period as it may think fit :

Provided further that no proceedings before any such authority shall lapse merely on the ground that any period specified in this sub-section had expired without such proceedings being completed.

NOTES

Alteration of service and awarding punishment to workmen prohibited under certain circumstances — The object of the legislature in enacting Section 33 is to protect the workman concerned in the dispute which forms the subject matter of pending conciliation or adjudication proceedings and to ensure that the pending proceeding are concluded in a peaceful manner. The Section recognises that the employer may, on any occasion, be justified in discharging or dismissing an employee and so it allows the employer to take such action subject to the condition that he must either seek prior permission ins writing of the Tribunal before which the proceeding is pending or apply to the Tribunal for approval of the action taken by him — *Punjab Beverages (P) Ltd. vs. Suresh Chand,* (1978)2 SCC 144 : 1978 SCC (L&S) 165.

The expression "workmen concerned in the dispute" includes not only individual workman directly interested in the dispute which forms the subject matter of the pending proceeding but also all workmen who have or could have sponsored the dispute and would be bound by the award – *New India Motors (P) Ltd. vs. K.T.Morris,* AIR 1960 SC 875.

If no unfair labour practice or *mala fide* or victimisation is found, the Tribunal is bound to give the permission asked for, provided a *prima facie* case was made out—*Central India Coal Field vs. Ram Bilas,* AIR 1961 SC 1989 : (1961)I LLJ 546.

The dismissed workman who claims protection of Section 33 has to establish that he is a workman concerned in the dispute which is subject matter of the pending conciliation or adjudicatory proceedings. If he fails to prove this fact, he cannot avail Section 33-A—*Digwadih Colliery vs. Ramjit Singh,* (1964)II LLJ 143; 22 FJR 385.

The ban imposed by Section 33(1) and 33(2) does not prevent the employer from taking action against his workmen for reasons not based on misconduct. If the termination of service is for loss of confidence in the employee for his unsuitability, the termination cannot be reviewed by the Tribunal—*Air India Corporation vs. A. Rebellow,* AIR 1972 SC 1343: 1972 Lab IC 668.

Withdrawal of the application under Section 33(2) for approval of the action of discharge or dismissal, effect of—The withdrawal of application made by the employer to the Tribunal for approval of the action of discharge or dismissal passed by the employer against workman stood on the same footing as if no application u/s 33(2)(b) has been made. In such case the order passed by the employer dismissing the workman remained to be a contravention of Section 33 (2) (b) but such contravention did not have the effect of rendering the order of dismissal void and inoperative. The withdrawal of the application made under Section 33(2)(b) stands on the same footing as if no application under the section has been made. There is no decision on its merits and it cannot be said that approval has been refused by the Tribunal—*Punjab Beverages (P) Ltd. vs. Suresh Chand,* AIR 1978 SC 445 : (1978)II LLJ 1 SC.

S. 33A. Special provision for adjudication as to whether conditions of service, etc., charged during pendency of proceedings — Where an employer contravenes the provisions of Section 33 during the pendency of proceedings before a conciliation officer, board, an arbitrator, a Labour Court, Tribunal or National Tribunal, any employee aggrieved by such contravention, may make a complaint in writing, in the prescribed manner,—

(a) to such conciliation officer of Board, and the conciliation officer or Board shall take such complaint into account in mediating in, and promoting the settlement of, such industrial dispute; and

(b) to such arbitrator, Labour Court, Tribunal or National Tribunal and on receipt of such complaint the arbitrator, Labour Court, Tribunal or National Tribunal, as the case may be, shall adjudicate upon the complaint as it were a dispute referred to or pending before it, in accordance with the provisions of this Act and shall submit his or its award to the appropriate Government and the provisions of this Act shall apply accordingly.

NOTES

Object and scope of — A contravention of Section 33 in the foundation on which a complaint under sec. 33A can be entertained. Only a workman who is concerned in the pending dispute can allege contravention of Section 33-*Syndicate Bank vs. Ramnath,* AIR 1968 SC 231 : 1968 Lab IC 207.

While adjudicating a proceeding in under Section 33A, the Tribunal cannot grant interim relief which the workman is entitled to get only if he finally succeeds---*Deloi Cloth & General Mills vs. Rameswar Dayal,* AIR 1961 SC 689 : (1960)II LLJ 712.

Two important aspects of employment are the nature of duties of the post and the emoluments attached to the post. Because the driver used to do the work of packer when vehicle was not available, he could not be compelled to act as full time packer and such order would amount to illegal change of service conditions---*Hindustan Lever Ltd. vs. Ram Mohan Roy,*-(1973)4 SCC 141.

Before Section 33A was introduced, to seek remedy for illegal change of conditions of service, workmen had to act under Section 10. Since that remedy caused inordinate delay, Section 33A was enacted for adjudication as to whether Section 33 has been contravened and the Tribunal shall adjudicate as if it is a dispute referred to it in accordance with the provisions of the Act—*Punjab Beverage (P) Ltd. vs. Suresh Chand,* (1978)2 SCC 144 : 1978 SCC (L & S) 165.

S. 33B. Power to transfer certain proceedings—(1) The appropriate Government may, by order in writing and for reasons to be stated therein, withdraw any proceeding under this Act pending before a Labour Court, Tribunal or National Tribunal and transfer the same to another Labour Court, Tribunal or National Tribunal, as the case may be, for the disposal of the proceeding and the Labour Court, Tribunal or National Tribunal to which the proceeding is so transferred may, subject to special directions in the order of transfer, proceed either *de novo* or from the stage at which it was so transferred :

Provided that where a proceeding under Section 33 or Section 33A is pending before a Tribunal or National Tribunal, the proceeding may also be transferred to Labour Court.

(2) Without prejudice to the provisions of sub-section (1), any Tribunal or National Tribunal, if so authorised by the appropriate Government, may transfer any proceeding under Section 33 or Section 33A pending before it to any one of the Labour Courts specified for the disposal of such proceedings by the appropriate Government by notification in the *Official Gazette* and the Labour Court to which the proceeding is so transferred shall dispose of the same.

NOTES

Section 33B authorises the appropriate Government to withdraw any proceeding before the Labour Court or Tribunal and transfer it for disposal for another Labour Court or Tribunal. The exercise of such power can be made *suo motu* or on representation of parties. The expression "may" in sub-section (1) confers a discretionary power upon appropriate Government making a decision as to whether the powers have to be exercised or not. But one a decision is reached for transfer of a pending case the requirement of assigning reasons becomes mandatory. Failure to give reasons or indicating reasons not germane would render such decision invalid. Where the State Government has resorted to such power on the representation of the workman without affording any opportunity to management which is a party to the pending proceeding, recourse to such power will invalidate the decision of the Government. Denial of opportunity to the management is itself a fatal flaw to the order of transfer. The Supreme Court found that the Government itself was misled by the representation of the workman as would appear from the reason for such transfer—*Mc Nally Bharat Engineering Company Limited vs. State of Bihar,* (1990)2 SCC 48 : 1990 SCC (L&S) 189 : (1990)II LLJ 211.

S. 33C. Recovery of money due from an employer — (1) Where any money is due to a workman from an employer under a settlement or an award or under the provisions of Chapter VA or Chapter VB, the workman himself or any other person authorised by him in writing in this behalf, or, in the case of the death of the workman, his assignee or heirs may, without prejudice to any other mode of recovery, make an application to the appropriate Government for the recovery of the money due to him and if the appropriate Government is satisfied that any money is so due, it shall issue a certificate for that amount to the Collector who shall proceed to recover the same in the same manner as an arrear of land revenue :

Provided that every such application shall be made within one year from the date on which the money became due to the workman from the employer :

Provided further that any such application may be entertained after the expiry of the said period of one year, if the appropriate Government is satisfied that the applicant had sufficient cause for not making the application within the said period.

(2) Where any workman is entitled to receive from the employer any money or any benefit which is capable of being computed in terms of money and if any question arises as to the amount of money due or as to the amount at which such benefit should be computed, then the question may, subject to any rule that may be made under this Act, be decided by such Labour Court as may be specified in this behalf by the appropriate Government within a period not exceeding three months. :

Provided that where the presiding officer of a Labour Court considers it necessary or expedient so to do, he may, for reasons to be recorded in writing, extend such period by such further period as he my think fit.

(3) For the purpose of computing the money value of a benefit, the Labour Court may, if it so thinks fit, appoint a commissioner who shall, after taking such evidence as may be necessary, submit a report to the Labour Court and the Labour Court shall determine the amount after considering the report of the commissioner and other circumstances of the case.

(4) The decision of the Labour Court shall be forwarded by it to the appropriate Government and any amount found due by the Labour Court may be recovered in the manner provided for in sub-section (1).

(5) Where workmen employed under the same employer are entitled to receive from him any money or any benefit capable of being computed in terms of money, then, subject to such rules as may be made in this behalf, a single application for the recovery of the amount due may be made on behalf of or in respect of any number of such workmen.

Explanation.—In this Section "Labour Court" includes any Court constituted under any law relating to investigation and settlement of industrial disputes in force in any State.

NOTES

Application under Section 33C(2) if barred by limitation — Industrial adjudication should not encourage unduly belated claim. But not limitation is prescribed for an application under Section 33C (2)—*Central Bank of India vs. P.S. Rajagopalan*, AIR 1964 SC 743 : (1963)II LLJ 89.

When the claim is based on award and the Labour Court is intended just for executing the award, the question of delay is irrelevant so far as making of reference by the Government is concerned—*Bombay Gas Co. Ltd. vs. Gopal Bhiba*, (1963)II LLJ 608 : AIR 1964 SC 752.

Scope of Section 33C(2) — Individual workman can avail the benefit of this provision without having recourse to Section 10(1) or depending on the Union to espouse his cause. Cases which fall under Section 10(1) cannot however be brought under Section 33C(2). The Section is of the nature of an executive provision. The Court can interpret the award or settlement on which the right of the employees rest. The Section applies to monetary and non-monetary benefits. In case of monetary benefit it applies where such benefit is due but there is dispute over calculation thereof. The Section applies even to such cases in which their claim to the benefit is disputed by the employer—*Chief Mining Engineer, East India Coal Co. vs. Rameswar*, AIR 1968 SC 218 : 1968 Lab IC 197 : (1968)I LLJ 6.

Jurisdiction of Labour Court exercising powers Under Section 33C(2)— In exercising jurisdiction under Section 33C (2) the Labour Court acts as an execution Court. The foundation of workman's claim thereunder is the pre-existing entitlement of money or any benefit against the employer. Employer's denial would not oust Labour Courts' jurisdiction to determine whether the right in question exists. The Court may determine questions which are incidental or ancillary to the issue but cannot decide matters which lie within the jurisdiction of the Tribunal upon reference under Section 10(1)—*G. M. Ordnance Parachute Factory, Kanpur vs. Labour Court*, 1987 Lab IC 366 All.

Jurisdiction of Labour Court : Rate of wages — Where there was no dispute regarding the rates of wages and minimum rate of wages fixed by the Government under the Act were admitted by the parties and where the workmen demanding the minimum wages so fixed which was denied to the workmen on extraneous grounds the Labour Court under Section 33C(2) of the Act possesses jurisdiction under the Act to decide the same. And remedy under Section 20 of the Minimum Wages Act is not available to the workmen.

Reinstatement by the Tribunal, if permissible — The employer has, on a fair appraisal of the conduct of the employee, *bona fide* arrived at an honest opinion that the employer would not be benefitted any longer by the service of the employee as he had lost confidence in him. Such as opinion of the employer based on an objective satisfaction of the facts and circumstances, but not initiated by any *mala fide* motive can never be said to be arbitrary or whimsical. No employee on whom the employer has lost confidence can be forced upon the employer as the choice is and must be with the employer about the confidence and satisfaction of the service of the employee and same cannot be substituted either by the Tribunal or by the Court. This should not be understood to mean that the Tribunal or the Court has no power or competency to interfere in appropriate case where the employer's opinion is not based on any material or it is perverse or it is *mala fide* or arbitrary. Normally, then the court or the Tribunal would not interfere with the honest and *bona fide* opinion supported by the materials of the employer—*National Insurance Co. Ltd. Hyderabad vs. M. Viswanath,* 1977 Lab IC 242. Where the employer for the conduct of the employee stood exposed to the risk of loosing a valuable client, it is not proper for the Tribunal to reinstate the employee. But the formation of opinion must be *bona fide.* The law on the subject relating to the confidence of the employer and employee and the powers of the employer to terminate the services of the employee on whom the employer looses confidence may very well be noticed in a catena of following decisions rendered by the Supreme Court which governs the field—*Eastern E & T Co. vs. Baldev Lal,* 1975 Lal IC 1435 : AIR 1975 SC 1892 and *M/s. Chembur Co-operative Industrial Estate Ltd. vs. M. M. Chatre,* (1975)31 Fac LR 186 : AIR 1975 SC 1725 and *L. Michael vs. Johnson Pumps Ltd.,* AIR 1975 SC 661 : 1975 Lab IC 399.

Dismissal : Propriety of the order of reinstatement — Ever since the decision of the Federal Court in—*Western India Automobile Association vs. Industrial Tribunal, Bombay,* 1949 FCR 321 : AIR 1949 FC 111 settled the position in law is that the Industrial Tribunal has the jurisdiction to direct reinstatement in appropriate cases. In a case of wrongfully dismissal the normal rule adopted in industrial adjudication is to order reinstatement. There are however, exceptions to this rule and even when it is found that the dismissal was wrongful the workman has ben denied reinstatement for the reason that it would not be expedient to direct instalment. The reinstatement has not been regarded as either desirable or expedient in certain cases where, there exists strained relationship between employer and the employee, when the post occupied by the aggrieved employee has been one of trust and confidence, or when though dismissal or discharge was unsustainable, owing to some infirmity, in the impugned order, the employee was found to have been guilty of an activity subversive or prejudicial to the interest of the industry—*Hindustan Steel Ltd. vs. A.K. Ray,* (1970)3 SCR 343 : AIR 1970 SC 1401. In case where it is felt that it will not be desirable or expedient to direct reinstatement the workman is compensated monetarily by awarding compensation in lieu of reinstatement for loss of future employment. The Supreme Court set aside the direction with regard to the reinstatement of the workman against whom the misconduct has been found established which involves threatening the highest executive with dier consequences, wrongfully confining him in his room and compelling him to withdraw the notice. These acts of misconduct pertain to acts subversive of discipline on the part of the workman concerned of whom three were office bearers of the Union. It could not be said that these workmen had acted at the instigation of somebody. Taking into consideration the fact and circumstances of the aforesaid case and keeping in view the interests of the industry the Supreme Court passed the aforesaid order and in lieu of reinstatement compensation for loss of future employment were directed to be paid by the Supreme court—*Workmen of Bharat Fritz Werner (P) Ltd. vs. Bharat Fritz Werner (P) Ltd.*, AIR 1990 SC 1054 : (1990)3 SCC 565 : (1990)60 FLR 482.

S. 34. Cognizance of offences — (1) No Court shall take cognizance of any offence punishable under this Act or the abetment of any such offence, save on complaint made by or under the authority of the appropriate Government.

(2) No Court inferior to that if a Metropolitan Magistrate or a Judicial Magistrate of the first class shall try any offence punishable under this Act.

S. 35. Protection of persons — (1) No person refusing to take part or to continue to take part in any strike or lock-out which is illegal under this Act shall, by reason of such refusal or by reason of any action taken by him under this Section, be subject to expulsion from any trade union or society, or to any fine or penalty, or to deprivation of any right or benefit to which he or his legal representatives would otherwise be entitled, or be liable to be placed in any respect, either directly or indirectly, under any disability or at any disadvantage as compared with other members of the union or society, anything to the contrary in the rules of a trade union or society notwithstanding.

(2) Nothing in the rules of a trade union or society requiring the settlement of disputes in any manner shall apply to any proceeding for enforcing any right or exemption secured by this Section, and in any such proceeding the Civil Court may, in lieu of ordering a person who has been expelled from membership of a trade union or society to be restored to membership, order that he be paid out of the funds of the trade union or society such sum by way of compensation or damages as that Court thinks just.

S. 36. Representation of parties — (1) A workman who is a party to a dispute shall be entitled to be represented in any proceeding under this Act by:—

(*a*) any member of the executive or other office bearer of a registered trade union of which he is a member;

(*b*) any member of the executive or other office bearer of a federation of trade unions to which the trade union referred to in clause (a) is affiliated;

(*c*) Where the worker is not a member of any trade union, by any member of the executive or other office bearer of any trade union connected with, or by any other workman employed in the industry in which the worker is employed and authorised in such manner as may be prescribed.

(2) An employer who is a party to a dispute shall be entitled to be represented in any proceeding under this Act by—

(*a*) an officer of an association of employers of which he is a member :

(*b*) an officer of a federation of associations of employers to which the association referred to in clause (a) is affiliated;

(*c*) where the employer is not a member of any association of employers, by an officer of any association of employers connected with, or by any other employer engaged in the industry in which the employer is engaged and authorised in such manner as may be prescribed.

(3) No party to a dispute shall be entitled to be represented by a legal practitioner in any conciliation proceedings under this Act or in any proceedings before a Court.

(4) In any proceeding before a Labour Court, Tribunal or National Tribunal, a party to a dispute may be represented by a legal practitioner with the consent of the other parties to the proceeding and with the leave of the Labour Court, Tribunal or National Tribunal, as the case may be.

NOTES

Right of representation of parties by legal practitioners in proceedings under the Act—A lawyer, simpliciter cannot appear before an Industrial Tribunal without the consent of the opposite party and also without leave of the Tribunal. A power of authorney executed by the party would not make the lawyer competent to represent the party. A lawyer can appear before the Tribunal only in the capacity of an office bearer of a registered Trade Union or an officer of an Association of employers and in such case no consent of the other side and leave of the Tribunal would be necessary—*Paradip Port Trust vs. Workmen,* (1972)2 SC 329 : AIR 1977 SC 136 : (1977)1 SCR 537.

In the case of *A.D. Shastri vs. S.D. Patel,* (1975)I LLJ 458 Raj, while the workman objected to the appearance of the Advocate Mr. Rawell as company's representative, the company objected to representation of workman by lawyers Miss Indira Jaising and Mr. Shastri who were respectively the Vice-President and Secretary of the General Labour Union and Caprihans Employees Union. The Tribunal permitted neither Mr. Rawell nor Miss Indira nor Mr. Shastri to act as representative. Disposing the writ petition, the Bombay High Court relied on the judgement of Rajasthan High Court in *Duduwalla & Co. vs. Industrial Tribunal,* AIR Raj 20 and allowed Miss Indira and Mr. Shastri to represent the workmen on the ground that they being office bearers of their respective Trade Unions were competent to represent the workmen before the Tribunal and the fact that they were practising lawyers did not disqualify them from so appearing without the consent of the company.

In the case of *P. Mallesh vs. Industrial Disputes Tribunal (Labour Court), Hyderabad and others,* 1976 (33) FLR 206, the Andhra Pradesh High Court considered the question whether Mr. Srinivasamurty, a legal practitioner was competent to appear for the company in the capacity as Honorary Joint Secretary of the Federation of Andhra Pradesh Chamber of Commerce and Industry. Disposing the writ petition, the learned High Court referred to the judgement of the Rajasthan High Court in *Duduwalla & Co. vs. Industrial Tribunal (supra)* and held that Mr. Srinivasamurty, by virtue of the office he holds under clauses (a) and (b) of Section 36(2) would be entitled to represent the respondent management before the Labour Court. The fact that he is a practising Advocate is absolutely irrelevant and hence Section 36(4) is not attracted.

S. 36A. Power to remove difficulties—(1) If, in the opinion of the appropriate Government any difficulty or doubt arises as to the interpretation of any provision of an award or settlement, it may refer the question to such Labour Court, Tribunal or National Tribunal as it may think fit.

(2) The Labour Court, Tribunal or National Tribunal to which such question is referred shall, after giving the parties an opportunity of being heard, decide such question and its decision shall be final and binding on all such parties.

S. 36B. Power of exempt—Where the appropriate Government is satisfied in relation to any industrial establishment or undertaking or any class of industrial establishments or undertakings carried on by a department of that Government that adequate provisions exist for the investigation and settlement of industrial disputes in respect of workmen employed in such establishment or undertaking or class of establishments or undertakings, it may, by notification in the *Official Gazette,* exempt, conditionally or unconditionally such establishment or undertaking or class of establishments or undertakings from all or any of the provisions of this Act.

S. 37. Protection of action taken under the Act—No suit, prosecution or other legal proceeding shall lie against any person or anything which is in good faith done or intended to be done in pursuance of this Act or any rules made thereunder.

S. 38. Power to make rules — (1) The appropriate Government may subject to the condition of previous publication, make rules for the purpose of giving effect to the provisions of this Act.

(2) In particular and without prejudice to the generality of the foregoing power, such rules may provide for all or any of the following matters, namely :

(a) the powers and procedure of conciliation officer, Boards, Courts, Labour Courts, Tribunals and National Tribunals including rules as to the summoning of witnesses, the production of documents relevant to the subject-matter of an inquiry or investigation, the number of members necessary to form a quorum and the manner of submission of report and awards;

(aa) the form of arbitration agreement, the manner in which or may be signed by the parties, the manner in which a notification may be issued under sub-section (3A) of Section 10A, the power of the arbitrator named in the arbitration agreement and the procedure to be followed by him;

(aaa) the appointment of assessors in proceedings under this Act;

(ab) the constitution of Grievance Settlement Authorities referred to in Section 9C, the manner in which industrial disputes may be referred to such authorities for settlement, the procedure to be followed by such authorities in the proceedings in relation to disputes referred to them and the period within which such proceedings shall be completed;

(b) the constitution and functions of and the filling of vacancies in Works Committees, and the procedure to be followed by such Committee in the discharge of their duties;

(c) the allowance admissible to members of Courts and Boards and presiding officer of Labour Courts, Tribunals and National Tribunals and to assessors and witnesses;

(d) the ministerial establishment which may be allotted to a Court, Board Labour Court, Tribunal or National Tribunal and the salaries and allowances payable to members of such establishments;

(e) the manner in which and the persons by and to whom notice of strike or lock-out may be given and the manner in which such notices shall be communicated;

(f) the conditions subject to which parties may be represented by legal practioners in proceedings under this Act before a Court, Labour Court, Tribunal or National Tribunal;

(g) any other matter which is to be or may be prescribed.

(3) Rules made under this Section may provide that a contravention thereof shall be punishable with fine not exceeding fifty rupees.

(4) All rules made under this Section shall, as soon as possible after they are made, be laid before the State Legislature or, where the appropriate Government is the Central Government, before both Houses of Parliament.

(5) Every rule made by the Central Government under this Section shall be laid as soon as may be after it is made, before each House of Parliament while it is in section for a total period of thirty days which may be comprised in one session or in two or more successive sessions, and if, before the expiry of the session immediately following the session or the successive sessions aforesaid both House agree in making any modification in the rule, or both Houses agree that the rule should not be made, the rule shall thereafter have effect only in such modified form or be no effect, as the case may be; so, however, that any such modification or annulment shall be without prejudice to the validity of anything previously done under that rule.

S. 39. Delegation of powers—The appropriate Government may, by notification in the *Official Gazette,* direct that any power exercisable by it under this Act or rules made thereunder shall, in relation to such matters and subject to such conditions, if any, as may be specified in the direction, be exercisable also—

(*a*) where the appropriate Government is the Central Government, by such officer or authority subordinate to the Central Government or by the State Government, or by such officer or authority subordinate to the State Government, as may be specified in the notification; and

(*b*) where the appropriate Government is a State Government, by such officer or authority subordinate to the State Government, as may be specified in the notification.

S. 40. Power to amend Schedules— (1) The appropriate Government may, if it is of opinion that it is expedient or necessary in the public interest so to do, by notification in the *Official Gazette,* add to the First Schedule any industry, and on any such notification being issued, the First Schedule shall be deemed to be amended accordingly.

(2) The Central Government may, by notification in the *Official Gazette,* add to or alter or amend the Second Schedule or the Third Schedule and on any such notification being issued, the Second Schedule or the Third Schedule, as the case may be, shall be deemed to be amended accordingly.

(3) Every such notification shall, as soon as possible after it is issued, be laid before the Legislature of the State, if the notification has been issued by a State Government, or before Parliament, if the notification has been issued by the Central Government.

THE FIRST SCHEDULE

[See Section 2 (n) (vi)]

Industries which may be declared to be Public Utility Services under sub-clause *(vi)* of clause *(n)* of Section 2

(1) Transport (other than railways) for the carriage of passengers or goods, by land or water

(2) Banking

(3) Cement

(4) Coai

(5) Cotton textiles

(6) Foodstuffs

(7) Iron and Steel

(8) Defence establishments

(9) Service in hospitals and dispensaries

(10) Fire Brigade Service

(11) India Government Mints

(12) India Security Press

(13) Copper Mining

(14) Lead Mining

(15) Zinc Mining

(16) Iron Ore Mining

(17) Service in an oil-field

(18) Service in the Uranium Industry

(19) Pyrites Mining

(20) Security Paper Mill, Hoshangabad

(21) Services in the Bank Note Press, Dewas

(22) Phosphorite Mining

(23) Magnesite Mining

THE SECOND SCHEDULE

(See Section 7)

Matters within the Jurisdiction of Labour Courts

(1) The property or legality of an order passed by an employer under the standing orders;

(2) The application and interpretation of standing orders;

(3) Discharge or dismissal of workmen including reinstatement of, or grant of relief to, workmen wrongfully dismissed;

(4) Withdrawal of any customary concession or privilege;

(5) Illegality or otherwise of a strike or lock-out; and

(6) All matters other than those specified in the Third Schedule.

THE THIRD SCHEDULE

(See Section 7A)

Matters within the Jurisdiction of Industrial Tribunals

(1) Wages, including the period and mode of payment;

(2) Compensatory and other allowances;

(3) Hours of work and rest intervals;

(4) Leave with wages and holidays;

(5) Bonus, profit sharing, provident fund and gratuity;

(6) Shift working otherwise than in accordance with standing orders;

(7) Classification by grades;

(8) Rules of discipline;

(9) Rationalisation;

(10) Retrenchment of workmen and closure of establishment; and

(11) Any other matter that may be prescribed.

THE FOURTH SCHEDULE

(See Section 9A)

Conditions of Service for Change of which Notice is to be given

(1) Wages, including the period and mode of payment;

(2) Contribution paid or payable, by the employer to any provident fund or pension fund or for the benefit of the workmen under any law for the time being in force ;

(3) Compensatory and other allowances;

(4) Hours of work and rest intervals;

(5) Leave with wages and holidays;

(6) Starting alteration or discontinuance of shift working otherwise than in accordance with standing orders;

(7) Classification by grades;

(8) Withdrawal of any customary concession or privilege or change in usage;

(9) Introduction of new rules of discipline, or alteration of existing rules, except in so far as they are provided in standing orders;

(10) Rationalisation, standardisation or improvement of plant or technique which is likely to lend to retrenchment of workmen;

(11) An increase or reduction (other than casual) in the number of persons employed or to be employed in any occupation or process or department or shift, not occasioned by circumstances over which the employer has no control.

THE FIFTH SCHEDULE

[See Section 2 (ra)]

Unfair Labour Practices

I. On the part of employers and trade unions of employees—

(1) To interfere with, restrain from, or coerce, workmen in the exercise of their right to organise, from, join or assist a trade union or to engage in concerted activities for the purposes of collective bargaining or other mutual aid or protection, that is to say—

(a) threatening workmen with discharge or dismissal, if they join a trade union;

(b) threatening a lock-out or closure, if a trade union is organised;

(c) granting wage increase to workmen at crucial periods of trade union organisation, with a view to undermining the efforts of the trade union at organisation.

(2) To dominate, interfere with or contribute support, financial or otherwise, to any trade union, that is to sav—

(a) an employer taking an active interest in organising a trade union of his workmen; and

(b) an employer showing partiality or granting favour to one of several trade unions attempting to organise his workmen or to its members, where such a trade union is not a recognised trade union.

(3) To establish employer sponsored trade unions of workmen.

(4) To encourage or discourage membership in any trade union by discriminating against any workman, that is to say—

(a) discharging or punishing a workman, because he urged other workmen to join or organise a trade union;

(b) discharging or dismissing a workman for taking part in any strike (not being a strike which is deemed to be an illegal strike under this Act);

(c) changing seniority rating of workmen because of trade union activities;

(d) refusing to promote workmen to higher posts on account of their trade union activities;

(e) giving unmerited promotions to certain workmen with a view to creating discord amongst other workmen, or to undermine the strength of their trade union;

(f) discharging office-bearers of active members of the trade union on account of their trade union activities.

(5) To discharge or dismiss workmen—

(a) by way of victimisation;

(*b*) not in good faith, but in the colourable exercise of the employer's right;

(*c*) by falsely implicating a workman in a criminal case on false evidence or on concocted evidence;

(*d*) for patently false reasons;

(*e*) on untrue or trumped up allegations of absence without leave;

(*f*) in utter disregard of the principles of natural justice in the conduct of domestic enquiry or with undue haste;

(*g*) for misconduct of a minor or technical character, without having any regard to the nature of the particular misconduct or the past record or service of the workman, thereby leading to a disproportionate punishment.

(6) To abolish the work of regular nature being done by workmen, and to give such work to contractors as a measure of breaking a strike.

(7) To transfer a workman *mala fide* from one place to another, under the guise of following management policy.

(8) To insist upon individual workmen, who are on a legal strike to sign a good conduct bond, as a pre-condition to allowing them to resume work.

(9) To show favouritism or partiality to one set of workers regardless of merit.

(10) To employ workmen as "badlis", casuals or temporaries and to continue them as such for years, with the object of depriving them of the status and privileges of permanent workmen.

(11) To discharge or discriminate against any workman for filing charges or testifying against an employer in any enquiry or proceeding relating to any industrial dispute.

(12) To recruit workmen during strike which is not an illegal strike.

(13) Failure to implement award, settlement or agreement.

(14) To indulge in acts of force or violence.

(15) To refuse to bargain collectively, in good faith with the recognised trade unions.

(16) Proposing or continuing a lock-out deemed to be illegal under this Act.

II. On the part of Workmen and trade unions of workmen—

(1) To advise or actively support or instigate any strike deemed to be illegal under this Act.

(2) To coerce workmen in the exercise of their right to self-organisation or to join a trade union or refrain from joining any trade union, that is to say—

(*a*) for a trade union or its members to picketing in such a manner that non-striking workmen are physically debarred from entering the work places;

(*b*) to indulge in acts of force or violence or to hold out threats of intimidation in connection with a strike against non-striking workmen or against managerial staff.

(3) For a recognised union to refuse to bargain collectively in good faith with the employer.

(4) To indulge in coercive activities against certification of a bargaining representative.

(5) To stage, encourage or instigate such forms of coercive actions as wilful "go slow" or squatting on the work premisses after working hours or "gherao" of any of the members of the managerial or other staff.

(6) To stage demonstrations at the residences of the employers or the managerial staff members.

(7) To incite or indulge in wilful damage to employer's property connected with the industry.

(8) To indulge in acts of force or violence or to hold out treats of intimidation against any workman with a view to prevent him from attending work.

❑ ❑ ❑